DOCTRINES AND DISCIPLINE

VOLUME 3

UNITED
METHODISM
AND
AMERICAN
CULTURE

DOCTRINES AND DISCIPLINE

Dennis M.
Campbell

William B.
Lawrence

Russell E.
Richey

Editors

Abingdon Press

Nashville

UNITED METHODISM AND AMERICAN CULTURE, VOLUME 3
DOCTRINES AND DISCIPLINE

Copyright © 1999 by Abingdon Press

This book is printed on recycled, acid-free, elemental-chlorine-free paper.

Library of Congress Cataloging-in-Publication Data

Doctrines and discipline / Dennis M. Campbell, William B. Lawrence, Russell E. Richey, editors.
    p.   cm.—(United Methodism and American culture : vol. 3)
    Includes bibliographical references.
    ISBN 0-687-02139-1 (alk. paper)
    1. United Methodist Church (U.S.)—Doctrines.   2. United Methodist Church (U.S.)—Discipline.   3. Methodist Church—United States—Doctrines—History.   4. Methodist Church—United States—Discipline—History.   I. Campbell, Dennis M., 1945- .
II. Lawrence, William Benjamin.   III. Richey, Russell E.
IV. Series.
BX8331.2.D63   1999
287'.6—dc21   99-15044
                                                                                CIP

99 00 01 02 03 04 05 06 07 08—10 9 8 7 6 5 4 3 2 1

MANUFACTURED IN THE UNITED STATES OF AMERICA

Contents

Preface

United Methodism and American Culture

This volume is one of a series of publications deriving from research, consultations, and conferences undertaken under a major grant from the Lilly Endowment, Inc. This five-year study has been based at the Divinity School of Duke University and directed by Dennis M. Campbell and Russell E. Richey, with William B. Lawrence as Project Associate, and with the counsel of an advisory board composed of Jackson W. Carroll, also of Duke and Director of the Ormond Center; Rosemary Skinner Keller, Dean of Union Theological Seminary, New York; Donald G. Mathews, Professor of History, University of North Carolina, Chapel Hill; Cornish R. Rogers, Professor of Pastoral Theology, Claremont; and Judith Smith, then Associate General Secretary, Office of Interpretation, General Board of Higher Education and Ministry, and now Executive Director of Product Development, The United Methodist Publishing House.

The project began under a planning grant that made it possible for the principals to engage in exploratory conversations with a wide array of church members, including board and agency leaders, bishops and district superintendents, clergy and laity, United Methodist faculty, and researchers in other Lilly-sponsored studies. From the counsel received through such exploratory discussions, the project came to pursue three primary objectives:

1. To provide a careful, fresh estimate of the history of Methodism in America, with particular attention to its twentieth-century experience,

2. to attempt a portrait of United Methodism at the dawning of the new century, and

3. to explore policy issues, with a view to the church's effective participation in American society and the world in the future.

We pursued those objectives through sponsored research, through dialogue with the several commissions, committees, and projects studying United Methodism that were launched during the 1992–96 quadrennium, and through a series of conferences and consultations. In the latter process, approximately seventy-five church leaders, scholars, and researchers participated, each working on a specific aspect, theme, or issue from the comprehensive task. From their efforts, we are pleased to now share some of the results in this third volume of essays.

These three studies, organized thematically, touch on all three of our objectives for the "United Methodism and American Culture" project but focus on the first two. A sampling of insights from these studies appeared in the November 1996 issue of *Circuit Rider*. The third objective we addressed in a series of *Leadership Letters*, widely distributed among United Methodists, explicitly raising policy issues for the church. A related, policy-oriented volume (entitled *Questions for the Twenty-First-Century Church*, and published earlier in 1998 by Abingdon Press) addressed questions facing the church at the dawn of the new century. Much of the research undertaken as part of this project could not be accommodated in these few volumes and will appear in *Quarterly Review, Circuit Rider, Methodist History*, and other media.

From the start of this project, Abingdon committed itself to be the "publisher of record" and to make the results appropriately accessible to United Methodism. As part of that commitment and this project, Abingdon has already published *The Methodist Conference in America* (Richey) and will publish a two-volume collaborative effort (involving Richey in addition to Kenneth Rowe and Jean Miller Schmidt), *The Methodist Experience in America*, one volume of which will be narrative, the other a historical soucebook. These two volumes are currently slated to appear also in CD-ROM form.

This project will culminate in three synthetic "statements." One of these, like this volume, will address the church's leadership and be most appropriate for clergy and clergy-to-be. A second will be aimed at the adult laity of the denomination. A third will be in video form and usable in an even wider set of contexts.

Through these "publishing" efforts we seek to open conversations about the future of our church and its role locally and globally in the decades and century ahead.

Introduction

Dennis M. Campbell

In recent years there has been much discussion of a crisis in theology and doctrine in The United Methodist Church. In fact, similar concerns have been voiced in most prominent Christian churches, both Protestant and Catholic. The reasons for this sense of crisis have been variously debated, but our research on the present state and future shape of United Methodism and American culture suggests that throughout The United Methodist Church there is widespread conviction that contemporary Methodism lacks theological identity and conviction. Questions about the particularity of Jesus Christ, about the authority of Christian scripture, about the reasons for evangelization and mission, about ecumenicity and the global church, about the meaning of discipline and holiness, and about the distinctive identity of Methodism are sources not only of debate but of serious divisiveness. This book brings together research and writings dealing with theology and doctrine in Methodism. It demonstrates the complexity of the issues and the diversity of sources and traditions that contribute to serious consideration of theology in the Wesleyan tradition.

The Problematic of Wesleyan Theology

The story of Wesleyan theology begins with John Wesley, the eighteenth-century church leader and theologian who is popularly known as the leader of a revival movement within Anglicanism characterized by attention to experiential religion.[1] Although Methodism gradually developed into a separate church (first in America, and later in England), that certainly was not Wesley's original intention. His efforts were to revive the Church of England by bringing unchurched persons to a personal relationship with Jesus Christ. Wesley's significant organizational skills brought his new converts together into groups, which were connected to one another, and supervised by lay leaders of unusual commitment. The idea of "connection" is one of the original principles of Methodism. It offers an organic vision of multiple groups, and

1

communicates an understanding of the nature of Christian community which affirms that the Christian church is never at its fullness in any one time or place.[2]

From the beginning, therefore, and even within the Anglican context, it is correct to understand Methodism as an institutionalizing movement. Often interpreters have seen Methodism as principally an institutional reality, of interest to the larger Christian community, if at all, because of its extraordinary organizational success. This interpretation is in part due to the fact that Wesley never attempted to be an academic systematic theologian writing for a scholarly audience. His writings were intended to instruct and encourage his followers, and to bring others into the movement. His theological work, however, demonstrates that the Methodist movement, and its institutional manifestations, were grounded in Wesley's interpretation of Christian theology for his own setting. He knew well the Christian tradition and used sophisticated arguments to justify his interpretations and his efforts at change.

Randy Maddox, in his chapter in this book, suggests that one can understand Wesley's theology as primary, or first-order theology in the Anglican tradition. The idea is that Wesley was not a theorist, but a theologian whose work grows out of the practices he lived, advocated, and taught. This is what Maddox means by "practical theology." It represents a different usage from the way the term "practical theology" is usually used today in reference to the practice of Christian ministry by lay or clergy leaders of the church. It is an understanding of the theology of practice that illustrates why theology in the Wesleyan tradition is always grounded in the actual life of the Christian community, and is in service to that community in a direct way.[3]

A priest of the Anglican Church until his death, Wesley consistently argued that he stood firmly in the historic Christian tradition as expressed in Anglicanism. A careful reading of Wesley's writings, however, demonstrates that he deviated from Anglicanism in key places where his understanding of scripture and tradition was such that he thought new interpretations were both acceptable and necessary. A key example of this is in his theology of church and ministry, and particularly his decision to ordain persons for leadership of Methodism in America, even though he had no authority to ordain, since in the Anglican Church only bishops have that prerogative.

On September 1, 1784, in Bristol, Wesley ordained as deacons Richard Whatcoat and Thomas Vasey, two lay leaders in the Methodist movement, and on September 2 he ordained them elders and appointed them to serve in America. He also "ordained" Thomas Coke, already a priest in the Church of England, as "superintendent" and appointed him and Francis Asbury to service as superintendents of the Methodists in America. By taking these steps, Wesley deviated from traditional Anglican theological teaching and practice, but he articulated clear reasons and theological arguments justifying the move. He attended both to Scripture and church tradition to make his case based on experience and reason, arguing that his actions were consistent with his understanding of the Bible, and of Christian antiquity, even if they were inconsistent with his own church. I think it is a mistake to suggest that his actions were merely pragmatic. It is too easy to argue that the needs were there, and therefore he did whatever he needed to do to meet them without regard for theology or church teaching. He knew what he was doing, and he had considered the nature and theology of ordination for many years.[4]

For Wesley, the priority was mission, and mission is a theological reality. This is not just playing with words. Mission involves discerning the work of the Holy Spirit in the world, and responding appropriately with human action and organization. What is demonstrated in this case is two different theological positions, and an understanding of these two positions is essential if one is to understand the "problematic" of Wesleyan theology. The one position gives priority to tradition and church order, the other to responsiveness to current needs as shaped by the immediate experience of the Holy Spirit. Wesley was convinced that evangelical mission must be primary rather than church order, even though he was well aware that church order functions to ensure the integrity of the gospel for mission. His perception was that, in the case of the needs for ordained clergy among the American Methodists, the order of the Church of England was standing in the way of mission. The priority of mission required his extraordinary step of taking ordination into his own hands, and for this he offered careful theological argument and justification.[5]

The teaching of the Anglican Church is that ministry derives from Jesus Christ, and is a gift of God through the Holy Spirit. This ministry takes place through the ecclesiastical structures of the church. Wesley had no trouble with these views. Where he differed was in his conviction that sometimes mission requires going outside of them. The theological integrity of Christian teaching is related to the faithful living of the community of Jesus Christ. The apostolic ministry does not depend on any particular structure or polity, but finds its expression in the essential character of the evangelical mission of the gospel of Jesus Christ. In regard to the theology of ministry, Anglican teaching is that God's mission is advanced through the life of the church, which is ordered through structures given by God. These structures are not altered by individuals, but only by careful process of communal discernment through established structures.

Wesley came to the theological conclusion that the work of the Holy Spirit might occasionally move beyond, and work outside of, the established forms of church order. This resulted in actions which were viewed by his own church as totally wrong. His claim was that as long as they were in conformity with the scriptures, such actions were given by the Holy Spirit for the furthering of the life and work of the church. It was this theological principle which was the basis of his conviction that he could take the extraordinary step of ordaining, even though, in the formal order of the church, he had no authority to do so. He called himself a "*scriptural episcopos*," claiming that the guidance of the Holy Spirit allowed him to act as an *episcopos* in the biblical sense of the term.[6] The priority of the Holy Spirit working directly in church and world is thus an idea at the very heart of Wesleyan theology from its inception. Wesley deviated at a number of places from traditional Anglicanism, and he felt free to bring his own interpretations to the life and work of the church because he was convinced that he could discern the work of the Holy Spirit in the Methodist connection, and in the lives of Methodist leaders and adherents.

The key Methodist theological principles of connection and itinerancy grow directly out of the Wesleyan ecclesiology derived from Wesley's theology of church and ministry. Connection and itinerancy are theological understandings derived from Wesley's experience with the real life settings and experiences of Methodist people in community. Connection goes to the heart of the nature of the church, and itinerancy is a practice that derives from connection and orders the life of leadership and church. Among the conclusions of the study of United Methodism and American Culture is the conviction that the idea of connection as a theological principle has eroded in twentieth-century America and that a recovery of connection is essential to the future of the church.

John Wesley interpreted scripture and tradition in relationship to the realities he faced in eighteenth-century England, believing that the direct presence of the Holy Spirit would guide him in finding a way to be faithful both to tradition and to evangelical mission.[7] In fact he believed that the two would be consistent, but the needs of mission, rather than rules of church order, or of traditional theological interpretation, were most important. Theology in the Wesleyan tradition has tended to emphasize the work of the Holy Spirit as tested by scripture. Wesley, of course, was always working with the overarching context of the Anglican tradition. Once Methodism became separate from Anglicanism, in part because of Wesley's actions in the controversial ordinations, Methodism was a product of, but not bounded by, Anglican teaching. The evangelical priority of mission, perceived as the direct work of the Holy Spirit in both individual and community, became an important theological principle of Wesleyan theology. This approach introduces a dynamic between church tradition and experience that is continually active. In a sense, it is boundless, and this problematic is both the genius and the curse of Wesleyan theology. Although Wesley may not have intended it, this approach to scripture and tradition was later interpreted by his followers, after his death, as an invitation to understand that the Holy Spirit brings about change in the community through the immediate experience of grace that alters convention. This idea, when applied to theology and doctrine, opens the door to varied approaches to theology, and an approach to doctrine that is not fixed but dynamic. This same dynamic approach has usually characterized Methodist thinking about ethics, suggesting that there are multiple norms resulting in diverse approaches to complex problems of the moral life of individuals and of communities. Methodists have no fixed liturgy, no set orders for prayers, no confession of faith to which everyone is required to give assent, and the dominant Methodist understanding of scripture is that its truth derives from interpretation of the meaning of the text rather than from a literal reading of the words of the text.

The American Experience and Methodist Theology

In its North American manifestation, early Methodism emphasized the immediate reality of the Holy Spirit calling persons to experience the forgiving grace of Jesus Christ and to order their lives in conformity with the Christian gospel. The interest of Methodist leadership was conversion, and advocacy of holiness of heart and mind, both personally and in community. From the beginning, Methodists sought to influence the general society in order to infuse it with the principles of what they understood to be the Christian moral life. Emphasis was on the individual's experience of the Spirit's graceful presence, which then had an impact on the larger society. Transformation of the community was a deep concern of the Methodists, but it would come as a result of changing the lives of persons, who were then organized into a connection with influence to change social structures and communal interests.[8]

The experiential tradition that characterized Methodism appealed to American democratic individualism, and shaped the churches in the Methodist tradition accordingly. What early American Methodists took from Wesley was the teaching that it was necessary for men and women to come to an immediate experience of God's saving grace in Jesus Christ, through the gracious work of the Holy Spirit. It was possible for persons to choose to accept this grace, and in turn to choose to participate in their own salvation, by bringing their lifestyle into conformity with Christian principles, as articulated in Methodist teaching. Methodists understood themselves to be called to take the path that led "on to perfection." There was an unusual convergence between the evangelical theology of early American Methodism and the robust confidence of the people who populated the early republic. Methodism proclaimed a Christian gospel of grace and freedom that made sense in the untried, open, and optimistic society of the young nation.[9]

Although Methodism had been present in North America for many years, the Methodist Episcopal Church, a new creation, separate from its British roots, was formally and officially founded in 1784. Following its founding, Methodism in America grew rapidly, especially during the nineteenth century. There are a number of reasons for this growth. The itinerancy, which put preachers into constant direct contact with diverse people everywhere, and the connectional principle, which provided an institutionalizing force to guarantee permanency, were certainly key, but the distinctive message the Methodists delivered was equally important. The message was that God's grace made it possible for persons to shape their lives, and the lives of their communities and nation, in such a way as to conform to Christian principles. It was a message of empowerment, which gave men and women conviction that they had both possibility and responsibility for themselves and for their neighbors. This appealing message fit the circumstances of early America uncommonly well. Methodists reached out to all persons, and did not rest until they had made contact with persons in even the most remote locations. Those at the margin of the dominant society were given attention, as Michael Cartwright's contribution to this book makes clear in reference to the African American community. The African American Methodist tradition developed its own distinctive theological expressions and religious practices.

By every statistical measure, Methodism was an important popular force. Methodism and American culture thus became linked to a degree that made it almost impossible to separate them. Elliott Wright explores this reality in regard to public education in America in his article in this book. To a remarkable degree, between 1784 and 1900, Methodists shaped and controlled public education at the elementary and secondary level. The continuing influence of Methodism in public education into the twentieth century, and up until the latter decades of the century, is equally evident, in part because of the social location of public school leadership. The relationship between Methodism and American culture that developed in the nineteenth century also explains why Fred Herzog, in a striking chapter of this volume, suggests that in their efforts in world missions it was difficult, if not impossible, for Methodists to separate the Christian gospel from the cultural context in which it was embodied. American culture, including its assumptions and institutional realities, was part of the message, even if that was not intended. Similarly, in a trenchant analysis in Volume 4 of this study, Janice Love raises questions about the claims on the part of some that The United Methodist Church is a "world church."[10] The claim that United Methodism is a "world church" can be understood to participate in the kind of Methodist triumphalism that characterized the church exactly one hundred years ago. Careful theological analysis, such as that contained in this book, is necessary to distinguish between the distinct message of Methodism within the world church and the sense of American ambition that makes uncritical claims about the global nature of Methodism.

The message of early American Methodism was easy to communicate and easy to understand. Leaders and adherents were not highly educated persons. The denomination was not a creedal, liturgical, or intellectual movement, although it was shaped by important devotional practices like family and midweek worship, discussed in this volume by Karen Westerfield Tucker. Methodists were not sophisticated theologians, and did not give attention to developing a tradition of scholarly theological reflection. Moreover, they took from Wesley what they had been taught by the early American Methodists, which was not the fullness of his theology, but the evangelical missional emphasis on personal and social conversion. The Anglican context was lost, and along with it the richness, or fullness, of the Christian tradition, as expressed in Anglicanism. Methodists were not well-educated in the writings of Wesley, and eventually they even truncated Wesley's theological position by giving voice only to the evangelical, experiential, and moral dimensions of his life and work.

Methodist theology in the nineteenth century gave primary attention to the dynamics of the Christian life, and particularly to the themes of conversion, salvation, and holiness, especially personal holiness. It benefited from theological encounter with the predecessor bodies of the Evangelical United Brethren Church, which had their own distinctive emphases, as Steven O'Malley makes clear in his contribution to this volume studying the E.U.B. Confession of Faith. Theology was intended to interpret to future Methodist preachers and lay leaders Methodist thinking in regard to grace and freedom, and their implications for the life of the believer. In the latter part of the century, and in the early days of the twentieth century, as Methodists sought to develop a more sophisticated theology in seminaries and universities, they did not look to Wesley, because they knew little of his writings, or to Anglicanism, which did not feature in their experience, but to theology done in the German research universities, which was perceived as the "cutting edge" of theological thinking. There was a subtle, but real shifting of the social location of systematic and constructive theology from the life of the church community to the academic community as Methodist seminaries and universities sought to adopt academic models of teaching, learning, and governance. Professors looked more to the academic community for relationships and rewards and less to the denomination.

The most notable development of Methodist theology in this period was at Boston University, a new Methodist institution which sought to develop a distinctive intellectual tradition. Boston Personalism, which is discussed by Randy Maddox in this book, was the theological invention of Methodist theologians, including Albert C. Knudson, Borden Parker Bowne, and Edgar Sheffield Brightman. The early Personalists got their inspiration from German theologians, and when they set out to address the American context they found the experiential dimension of Wesleyan theology to their liking. Their emphasis on experience, and on the personal, resulted in a theological position that would, in subsequent generations, produce philosophical approaches to theology that sought to expand both the sources and norms of theological authority. Boston Personalism introduced into American Methodist theology a liberal tradition that would be dominant for many years, in part because Boston produced many of the important leaders of the church, bishops, professors, and academic presidents. To a remarkable degree, Boston theologians and ethicists shaped the denomination's educational institutions, through both academic and administrative leadership. The institutional strength of liberalism in Methodism meant that neoorthodox theology, which was influential in America after the First World War, and well into the latter part of the century, was not as strong a force in Methodism as in the denominations of the Reformed tradition. Theologians and church leaders regarded as giants of neoorthodox theology were not primarily based in Methodist schools (though, of course there were exceptions, notably Edwin Lewis at Drew), nor were they shapers of dominant Methodist thinking, except among those Methodists educated at seminaries like Union Theological Seminary in New York (heavily under the influence of Reinhold Niebuhr) or Yale University Divinity School (where Reinhold's brother H. Richard Niebuhr held sway). By the end of the Second World War, Methodism was in need of new thinking in its theological expressions.

Efforts to Recover Roots

In the period after the Second World War there was an effort among some Methodist leaders to rediscover John Wesley and the early sources of Wesleyan theology. The Wesley Works Project, begun by the Methodist-related university-based schools of theology (Boston, Drew, Duke, Emory, SMU), was one of the results of this movement. It was thought that in order to have a recovery of Wesley, it was necessary for there to be a new and authoritative edition of his writings.[11] This effort spawned a gradual flowering of Wesley studies and the development of new initiatives in Wesleyan theology and Methodist studies. It is significant that some of the early leaders of this movement, including Albert Outler, Robert Cushman, and William Cannon, were educated at Yale, where they got a heavy dose of neoorthodox theology in the Reformed tradition. In response, they sought to shape a new approach to theology in Methodism by returning to Wesley himself, and not Wesley as interpreted popularly by American Methodists as simply an evangelical revivalist, nor Wesley as interpreted by the Personalists as advocate of experiential theology.

The recovery of Wesley, of Wesleyan themes in their fullness, and of Wesleyan theological methodology by some theological leaders of the church resulted in efforts to apply these emphases to the official theological life and work of Methodism. In 1968, at the founding of The United Methodist Church, the General Conference appointed a theological commission, chaired by Albert Outler, to work on a new theological statement. In 1972 the General Conference adopted the fruit of their work, and placed it in *The Discipline*. This statement, entitled "Our Theological Task," made the argument that there are four principal sources and norms by which Methodists do theology—Scripture, tradition, experience, and reason. It was argued that these were authentic to Wesley, and represented the way he worked out his theological position in any given case. This statement, which became enormously influential among Methodists, was popularly known as the "Wesleyan quadrilateral." The publishing arm of Methodism picked it up as a defining characteristic of Methodism and produced multiple study books and scholarly volumes devoted to its articulation.

In the turbulent periods of the seventies, as new theological voices in the church, including feminists, African Americans, Native Americans, and Hispanic Americans, sought to set forth theological positions that fit their needs, the idea of the "quadrilateral" was attractive because it implied that the starting point for theology might be any one of the four sources and norms. Experience as a theological starting point was especially attractive for groups who wanted to work out of their own historical and cultural backgrounds. Feminist thought, for instance, argued that the experience of women was a useful base for theological development. The category of reason was attractive to theologians whose interest was to make Christian theology acceptable to the modern mind.

There was a proliferation of theological work challenging traditional approaches to Christian theology and Methodist thinking. These efforts in turn produced attacks on the idea of the quadrilateral as an adequate, or accurate, approach to Wesleyan theology.[12] The objections were mounted from two points of view. One was the result of scholarly study that disputed the claim that there was such a thing as a "Wesleyan quadrilateral."[13] This technical argument was both historical and theological, but it offered support to a second, more popular attack, namely, that the quadrilateral misrepresented Wesley's own approach to theology, which, it was claimed, always started with Scripture.[14] Those who made this argument sought to ground Methodism in an evangeli-

cal tradition in which the Bible functions as the sole (or at least the primary) norm. In 1988, the United Methodist General Conference adopted yet another theological disciplinary statement, which revised significantly the earlier statement "Our Theological Task," and asserted the
priority of Scripture for Methodist theology, while still acknowledging
the role of tradition, experience, and reason.[15] In effect, the new statement was a compromise between those Methodists who continued to
fight for the place of experience and reason as legitimate starting points
for constructive theology and those who insisted that the Bible was the
only starting point for theology that claimed to stand in the Wesleyan
tradition.

Methodism, Contemporary Theology, and the Way Ahead

Controversy about Methodist theology continues at the end of the
twentieth century. Multiple groups within The United Methodist
Church are contending about the sources and norms of theology, the
legitimate limits of theological exploration, the meaning of Christian
identity, and the nature of the Christian moral life. A group called the
Confessing Movement, which met first in 1994, suggested that since
1972, when the General Conference affirmed the disciplinary statement
about the multiple norms of Scripture, tradition, experience, and reason,
The United Methodist Church has been adrift theologically. Dealing
with these controversies, Greg Jones, in this volume, seeks to answer the
question, "What makes United Methodist theology Methodist?"
According to some Methodists, even the revisions of the statement "Our
Theological Task" have not assuaged the problem of relativism. The
codification of these multiple norms under the rubric "quadrilateral"
provided an implicit affirmation of theological exploration starting with
experience and reason, rather than with Scripture and tradition.

In fact, however, the approach to Methodist theology characterized
by the quadrilateral did recognize what had long been the case in the
practice of American Methodist theology. This practice represented one
reading of Wesley's own approach to theological methodology, and
articulated a methodology to explain what I have referred to in this
Introduction as the "problematic of Wesleyan theology." By insisting
that the work of the Holy Spirit, through immediate inspiration inform-
ing the mission of the church, takes priority in theological practice,
Wesley interpreted the biblical witness according to his perception of
experience and reason. This is what happened in the case of the contro-

versial ordinations. If one studies his views of Baptism and Holy Communion, one sees how he interprets these sacraments using the multiple norms of experience, reason, Scripture, and tradition.[16] Wesley did not simply turn to the Bible, or to the tradition of the church. He brought his judgment to bear in light of his immediate experience of the Holy Spirit in the context of the contemporary mission of the church as he understood it. A crucial factor in Wesley's theological methodology, however, was the context of the Anglican Church. Once Methodism was separate from Anglicanism, that context was lost.

The research and study of Methodism and Methodist theology accomplished in our project on United Methodism and American Culture suggests to me that, from its beginnings, Methodism, in its fullness, has sought a balance between continuity and change in theology and doctrine, as well as in the total life of the church. Douglas Strong's contribution to this volume, "Exploring both the Middle and the Margins: Locating Methodism Within American Religious History," is helpful in this analysis. Continuity has been represented by those voices in the church who have sought to articulate the traditional Wesleyan themes of conversion and sanctification in the context of the historic Christian faith. David Lowes Watson, in his article dealing with class leaders and class meetings, is an example of a thinker who believes that continuity with Wesleyan practices holds great promise for today's church. Concerns for holinesss of heart and mind have produced a rich literature of ethics, and strong advocacy for traditional Methodist positions on human sexuality, marriage, family life, use of beverage alcohol, abortion, and gambling. Among these voices have been those working specifically within the evangelical community who advocate a stronger affirmation of the centrality of the Bible for all matters of faith and practice.

Methodism has also been open to exploration in the field of theology in order to be open to change brought by new currents of thought and action. The strain of liberalism represented by Boston Personalism, and its successor developments, including process theology, and the theology characterized by social gospel themes, including liberation theology, are important parts of the story of American Methodism. In contemporary theology, one thinks of John Cobb's work and Ted Jennings' effort to interpret John Wesley as a liberationist.[17] The latter decades of the twentieth century saw the articulation of experience and reason as legitimate starting points for theological exploration, which encouraged experience-based theologies, such as those represented by Feminist,

African American, Womanist, Native American, and Asian communities within Methodism.

The theological story I have briefly recounted here results in an ambiguous situation for Methodist theology, and particularly for the matter of authority in theology at the end of the twentieth century. Although The United Methodist Church affirms the priority of Scripture, and the central place of tradition, reason, and experience in its official statement in *The Discipline,* in fact there is no agreement, and cannot be, as to exactly how these multiple norms actually function for theology. The result is a situation in which various theologians and traditions within Methodist theology have significant followings inside the denomination, but one in which this diversity leads to serious conflict over certain specific issues. Jack Keller's article dealing with the church as a community of moral discourse is an effort to explore a way forward beyond conflict in regard to critical issues of the moral life that divide Methodists, like abortion, homosexuality, the death penalty, and use of military action. Other examples of conflicting theological views in United Methodist theology are the nature and purpose of evangelism, the identity of Jesus Christ, the nature of the Trinity, and the force of doctrine in the church. In fact, persons familiar with the history of Christian theology will recognize that contention over these themes, and others, has been the case throughout two millennia of Christian history. Historical understanding is essential if one is to be a sound theologian.[18]

The problem facing United Methodism at the beginning of the twenty-first century, however, is that some suspect the theological fault line may go deeper.[19] Are there any teachings essential to Christian faith? How is the Trinity to be understood and articulated? Are there any moral teachings prescribed for all Methodists? Is there any teaching authority that could be recognized by those who call themselves Methodists? On these matters The United Methodist Church is deeply divided. Our study of United Methodism and American culture has demonstrated, however, that there have always been divisions on certain matters both theological and ethical. Perhaps the most prominent example is Christian teaching about slavery, a debate that resulted in the actual split of Methodism in the mid nineteenth century. The idea that there was a golden period when there was agreement on matters of theology and doctrine probably has no basis in fact. Thus our theological problems may not be deeper or more acute, and only slightly different, as serious study of the history of doctrine and theological interpretation suggests.

Nevertheless, the problem of authority is complicated for Methodists by the fact that there is no way of resolving theological difference. Diversity is inevitable both because of our history, but also because of our polity. The only way decisions can be made with any force is through the General Conference, the final governing body of the church, and the General Conference is not a body formed in such a way as to be an appropriate arena for serious theological reflection. The General Conference is a delegated political body equipped to deal with the program and structures of the church as institution, but not equipped to work on refining doctrine and theology. As a result, the one place where Methodist discipline seems not to apply is in the arena of theology and doctrine. This is so because it is relatively easy to get General Conference consensus on matters of church structure, and even church program, but not easy, perhaps even impossible, to get consensus on matters of theology and doctrine. I have suggested, and our research shows, that this is so because it is not part of our tradition to seek such binding consensus, and also because it is not part of our tradition to enforce such consensus. Thus an individual preacher has virtually complete freedom about what to teach and preach, and how to structure a service of worship, even if he or she does not have the freedom to decide how to carry out the administrative order of the local church. Methodists tend to be "structural fundamentalists" in regard to polity and open to a wide range of diversity ("live and let live") in regard to theology.[20]

Does United Methodism have a crisis in theology and doctrine at the beginning of the twenty-first century? I think this question is more dramatic than it is helpful. This volume on theology and doctrine suggests that the answer to the question is "no," we do not have such a crisis, because to put it that way is to suggest that our contemporary situation is dramatically different from the situation in theology and doctrine that has characterized Methodism throughout its history. There has never been a time, whether in Wesley's own eighteenth century, the time of dramatic expansion in the nineteenth century, or the period of adjustment to changing status in American society in the twentieth century, when Methodism has had clarity and agreement about theology and doctrine. The theology and practice of Baptism in United Methodism is a particularly good example of this reality. Specific issues come and go, enduring theological themes are played out in varying ways, social and cultural forces shape responses, but throughout its history Methodism has been characterized by dynamic and diverse theological expression.

Perhaps the more important question is, Does it matter that Methodism is in perpetual flux theologically? The answer to this question depends on one's theological point of view. If one is seeking a tradition in which theological expression and doctrinal teachings are neat and clean, then Methodism is not that tradition. I would contend that no such tradition exists, and that to think there is such a tradition is to misread the history of Christian thought and teaching. But specifically in terms of Methodism, at the foundation of the movement is Wesley's insistence that the practice of the Christian life, both individually and collectively, invites and requires an openness to the immediate presence of the Holy Spirit, and the conviction that the inspiration of the Holy Spirit does not cease at any point in history. Accordingly, the Christian mission is propelled forward by change, as well as by continuity with the richness of the tradition. That this was Wesley's practice in theology seems to me clear, as I have suggested with reference both to theological reflection and to the life of the church. If this approach opened the door to creative energy and significant development, it also produced "the problematic of Wesleyan theology." Wesley's approach to theology created a tradition which encourages continuing reinterpretation of doctrine, as well as new understandings of the way in which the Christian faith is manifested through the church in a given time and social location.

The theological challenge for United Methodism in the twenty-first century is to maintain its clear place within the larger Christian tradition, and not to become a dead branch on the trunk of that tradition. Bruce Robbins' article, "Connection and *Koinonia:* Wesleyan and Ecumenical Perspectives on the Church," puts Methodism in the ecumenical and world context, and expresses the hope that Methodism can both learn from, and contribute to, the larger Christian tradition. In the end, God's providential care for the worldwide Christian church will prevail. The truth of the gospel ensures the future of the faith. But those in the Wesleyan tradition will need to make a choice about their participation in God's plan for humankind, and the way in which that plan is announced to the world. The essays in this volume, and research findings published in other volumes in this series, suggest that United Methodism has within it the energy, through the grace of the Holy Spirit, to continue to contribute a distinctive Wesleyan theological emphasis within the worldwide Christian movement.

Randy L. Maddox

In this essay Randy L. Maddox explores the curious reality that American Methodist theologians through most of the nineteenth and twentieth centuries did not use John Wesley, the theologian-founder of Methodism, as a theological mentor. Maddox first explores the nature of Wesley's own theology and finds it to be a primary, or first-order theology in the Anglican tradition. By this he means that Wesley's theology grew directly out of the life of the Christian communities he was establishing and nurturing. Wesley was a sophisticated theologian, but his work was intended to serve the church in an immediate way and was not intended as an exercise in academic theology. As American Methodism became better educated and more wealthy, some of its leaders sought to develop a theological tradition that would rival, or even equal, that of other Christian traditions, especially that represented by Continental theology in its German expression. In doing so, they adopted the dominant modes of theological expression and method, which were foreign to what Maddox sees as the genius of Wesley and Wesleyan Methodism. It was only in the mid to late twentieth century that a recovery of Wesley began to take place. Even so, Maddox argues, American Methodist theology is characterized dominantly by efforts to accommodate prevailing themes and interests of its time in forms appropriate to the academic community rather than to Wesley's conviction that the proper starting point for theology is the dynamic communal life of the church in the world. This is what Maddox calls Wesley's practical theology, and what he thinks constitutes an untapped inheritance.

Is it possible for the theologian to find the kind of resources for first-order theology in the large institutional churches of our time, or is the implication that this kind of theology must grow out of local congregations—and if so, which ones? Can Wesley's methodology be adapted to such a different time and place? Furthermore, the question remains whether the split between theology done in and for the academy, according to its reward structures, and the actual life of the church is so great that it cannot be overcome. Is the kind of practical theology Maddox finds in John Wesley a possibility for United Methodism, or was it unique to Wesley himself?

An Untapped Inheritance:
American Methodism and Wesley's
Practical Theology

Randy L. Maddox

The title of this essay might seem rather eccentric to our larger project. What does a suggested neglect of Wesley's "practical theology" have to do with contemporary United Methodism and its relation to American culture? Let me try to answer that question by sketching the connections that led me to this topic.

I. The Contemporary Need
for Recovering Practical Theology

A recurrent theme in recent analyses of North American culture is the negative impact of pervasive individualism. This individualism is identified as a primary cause of the demise of authentic expressions of community in North American life, and such communal settings are judged essential to forming persons committed to interpersonal responsibility in the public arena.[1] Ironically, this individualism is a progeny of the Enlightenment values of individual rights and religious freedom—values that were central to the construction of cultural alliances and structures in eighteenth-century North America. These values have taken on a shape or power that now serves more to undermine truly communal culture.

Those diagnosing the current malady have often championed religious groups as one of the last hopes for providing microcontexts of true community that can begin to restore in their members a commitment to the good of our larger society.[2] However, individualism has made its way into contemporary religious life as well, fostering understandings of religious identity as simply a matter of individual choices and of religious community as mere associations of like-minded persons. Nowhere is this more evident than in the current splintering of

19

Christian communions into a variety of caucuses.[3] This means that contemporary North American Christian groups (including United
Methodism) are not likely to make the desired contribution to public
culture until they recover more authentic embodiments of character-
forming communal life themselves.[4]

There is growing awareness that any adequate prescription for such a
recovery in Christian groups must include a central theological dimension. This is because character is not a spontaneous achievement.
Rather, the enduring basis of our sense of ourselves in relation to others—hence, of our actions—is a "life narrative" (or, more accurately, its
implicit worldview and affectional dispositions) that we derive from
our communities-of-influence. This narrative may be carefully tran-
scribed into our being or haphazardly imbibed as we go along, it may
have a coherent plot or be a collage of ill-fitting episodes from various
story lines, it may be retained with little editing or be fundamentally
rewritten; whatever the case, its life-orienting influence remains.[5]
Precisely because of this influence, it is incumbent upon Christian communities to evaluate the adequacy of the narratives being instilled in
their members, to shepherd the transcription of their defining narrative,
and to support their members' ongoing personal critique, clarification,
and editing of life narratives. This task is central to what I am calling
"practical theology."

But this primal theological task is precisely where mainline North
American churches, United Methodism included, are broadly judged as
failing at present.[6] Part of this failure may be attributed to the way that
political affirmation of the personal right to choice in matters of religion
has indirectly undermined the ability of religious groups to call their
members to theological or spiritual accountability. However, another
significant factor is that the mainline traditions have acquiesced to a
separation of serious theological activity from the life and practice of
their churches, restricting it to specialized disciplines in the academy.
The notion that theology is fundamentally a "practical" discipline of
shepherding formation of Christian character in the community of faith
has become increasingly foreign to both academy and church. As a
result, pastors and people have turned instead to secular therapists and
managers for the "wisdom" to run their lives and ministries. And this
wisdom has served more to mediate the individualism rampant in culture into the church than to assist the church in forming persons who
can discern and challenge this individualism.

Against this background, it is a sign of hope that there is a growing chorus of voices, both in the academy and beyond, calling for a changed understanding and practice of theology as a practical discipline.[7] One aspect of this call has been the search for prior models to inform the contemporary development of such a theology. I have suggested elsewhere that John Wesley could be one such informative model.[8] This suggestion was rendered problematic from the first by the fact that it has been common for critics to dismiss both Wesley and the movement that he founded as having no serious theological concern. Raising even more suspicion was the broad tendency for Wesley's professional theological descendants to dismiss him as a theologian. At the time, I simply offset both of these dismissals by the recognition that they were measuring Wesley unfavorably in terms of the model of academic theology that was itself now being questioned. It has since seemed to me that, if we are to recover something like Wesley's model of practical theology in our present context, it could be instructive to investigate more closely how and why his earlier American descendants left this inheritance largely untapped. That is the goal of this essay.

II. Wesley's Model of Practical Theology

To appreciate the progressive divergence of American Methodist professional theological activity from the model of Wesley, it is necessary to have a brief sketch of his model in mind. And to understand Wesley's model, it is helpful to set it in historical perspective.[9]

Christian theological activity originated in the pastoral context of shepherding the formation of Christians for their lives in the world. In this preuniversity setting, theology took the primary form of a practical discipline *(scientia practica)*. This form involved a multilayered understanding of the nature of theology. In the most foundational sense, theology was the (usually implicit) basic worldview that framed the disposition and practice of believers' lives. This worldview is not simply bestowed with conversion, it has to be developed. The concern to form and norm this worldview in believers constituted the next major dimension of theology as a practical discipline. This concern took most direct (i.e., first-order) expression in such theological activities as pastoral shepherding and the production of formative materials like catechisms, liturgies, and spiritual discipline manuals. These activities in turn frequently sparked second-order theological reflection on such issues as the grounding for, or interrelationships and consistency of, various theological commitments. But even at this more abstract level early Christian theology retained a practical focus, ultimately basing the most metaphysical reflections about God on the life of faith and drawing from these reflections ethical and soteriological implications. Likewise, while there has been need for apologetic defense of the Christian faith from the beginning, it was initially supplemental to the more formative theological tasks.

Beginning in the twelfth century, the social location of theology in Western Christianity progressively shifted to the emerging universities. In this new location some began to reformulate the nature and task of theology in terms of the Aristotelian model of a theoretical science, which aims at assimilating rationally demonstrated and ordered knowledge *for its own sake.* This model of theology came to dominate the universities, and they came to dominate Western theological debate and pastoral training. In the process, preparation of comprehensive textbooks *(summae)* of doctrinal claims for university education came to be considered the most fundamental form of theological activity. Likewise, the dominant concern of this activity shifted from interacting reciprocally with the life and practice of the Christian community to achieving systematic coherence among the topics included in the textbook. Thus it was that Systematic Theology emerged as the standard of professional theological activity in the West. If it had a close rival, it was Apologetics, which strove to defend the intellectual integrity of Christian faith among the educated. This rivalry was usually overcome by subsuming Apologetics into Systematics. By contrast, "practical theology" was marginalized into an application discipline—reduced to relating the truths previously established by Systematics to the spiritual life, the moral life, or eventually just to the duties of pastors.

Such was the case, that is, with *continental* Western theology. Wesley's Anglican setting differed in some significant ways from these continental developments.[10] This difference was grounded in the Anglican decision not to align with either Protestantism or Roman Catholicism, striving instead to embody a "middle way" *(via media)*. Anglican reformers were convinced that this could best be accomplished by a recovery of the beliefs and practices of the undivided church of the first four centuries. Among the impacts of their resulting intensive study of Early Church writings was renewed influence of the assumptions of theology as a practical discipline. As a prime example of this influence, the official Anglican doctrinal expressions took the form of confessions or creeds (The Thirty-nine Articles), liturgies (*Book of Common Prayer*), and catechetical sermons (The *Homilies*). Influence of the preuniversity model is also reflected in the distrust Anglican theologians of the seventeenth and eighteenth centuries held toward "systems"; they were more concerned to develop the comprehensiveness of the creeds than to concentrate Christian doctrine into a unifying core. And finally, the greater prominence of theology as a practical discipline helped Anglican theology avoid the severity of the Orthodoxy/Pietism split prominent in continental Protestantism (or the Scholastic/Monastic split in Roman Catholicism). As a result, Wesley was trained in an academic setting that was somewhat more successful than its continental counterpart in retaining the interaction of doctrinal reflection and Christian life.

In light of his Anglican training, then, Wesley would not have understood the defining task of theologians to be developing an elaborate system of Christian truth-claims for the academy. This task was, instead, nurturing and shaping the worldview that frames the temperament and practice of believers' lives in the world. Theologians will indeed engage in apologetic dialogues or in reflection on doctrinal consistency, but ideally because—and to the extent that—these are in service to their more central task. In keeping with its defining task, the primary (or first-order) literary forms of theological activity for Wesley would not have been Systematic Theologies or Apologetics, but carefully crafted liturgies, catechisms, hymns, sermons, and the like. And the quintessential practitioner of first-order theology would not be a detached academic theologian, it would be the pastor-theologian actively shepherding a community of faith in the world.

It was precisely this role of pastor-theologian that Wesley adopted as he left the potential isolation of the academy to shepherd the people called Methodists. For the next fifty years he was immersed in the practical-theological task of struggling to discern the wisdom of the Christian tradition in light of the realities and needs of his people's lives, and to nurture their maturation in this wisdom. This work was inevitably contextual and occasional, because of the primacy devoted to the praxis of the Methodist societies (as both the stimulus and the goal of his theological reflection). Yet this focus on praxis was at no expense to the integrity or rigor of the theological task.[11] Indeed, the seriousness with which Wesley pursued this task is evidenced by the numerous practical-theological materials he left behind; besides his well-known sermons, these include conference minutes, letters, controversial essays and tracts, disciplinary guides for Christian life, spiritual biographies, his own journal, and a range of edited creeds, liturgies, prayer books, Bible study aids, hymnals, catechisms, and devotional guides.

In light of his precedent, one might think that Wesley's model of the goal and the primary forms of theological activity would have defined subsequent Methodist practice. As we shall see, this was not the case in professional circles, even if echoes can be discerned at a more popular level. It bears considering at this point whether there was something in Wesley's own practice that helps account for this fact.

One conceivable explanation for why Wesley's model of theological activity found few emulators among his Methodist descendants is that his authorial and editorial work might be assumed to be appropriate only for founders of new theological traditions. But, whatever his descendants may have come to believe, such was surely not Wesley's assumption! He insisted throughout his life that he was not trying to found a new tradition, only to renew Anglicanism. He surely believed that his many practical-theological activities were fitting for any Anglican priest. As he reminded his brother, the work of ordained clergy was much more than simply preaching, it was shepherding the spiritual transformation of those under their care.[12] And he stressed that, to meet this task, every clergyperson must accept and prepare for their role as a "divine" (theologian).[13] While this role may not always require producing *new* liturgies, catechisms, hymns, and so on, it would certainly involve theological discernment in the selection, revision, and use of such materials—along with careful preaching and pastoral care—as pastors seek to nurture authentic Christian character among those in their charge.

While this first explanation is questionable, there were two characteristics of the initial Methodist movement that more likely hindered Wesley's model of practical-theological activity from passing to his descendants. The first of these characteristics was the division of duties that Wesley was forced to make in his movement between priests, preachers, and pastors. Only a handful of ordained parish priests joined the Wesley brothers in their efforts to renew the Anglican church. As a result, John soon began to recruit and appoint traveling lay preachers to spread the Methodist work. While he staunchly defended the right of these unordained itinerants to preach, he conceded their exclusion from the sacramental (and most liturgical and catechetical) aspects of the ministry of the priest. The other limitation of the lay preachers was precisely that they were constantly traveling, which meant they could not provide regular pastoral care and supervision for the Methodist societies. Since the local Anglican priest was seldom sympathetic, Wesley developed an organization of lay "helpers" and class leaders to fulfill major components of this task of pastor. The combination of Wesley's two innovations had the potential of helping to recover the shared role of the entire body of Christ in ministry. But it also had the immediate effect of eliminating almost all candidates for him to mentor in the full range of the ministry of pastor-theologian that he saw as the standard for ordained clergy.

The second relevant characteristic is connected to the first. As laity, the majority of Wesley's preachers lacked formal theological training. This created the danger of theological deviation in the movement. Wesley's immediate response was to prescribe an ambitious course of study for all lay preachers. But he also led the Conference to adopt a rule that no preacher could publish books, hymns, or any other theological works without Conference (i.e., Wesley's) approval.[14] Viewed positively, this rule provided for discernment concerning which practical-theological materials would have formative impact on the Methodist societies. But there are also hints of the more questionable motive of censorship—to keep potential ammunition out of the hands of Methodism's critics. In either case, the effect was to prevent most of Wesley's "apprentices" from emulating his literary forms of theological activity.

In light of these two characteristics, it is significant that one of the few associates that Wesley did encourage to publish (besides his brother Charles) was John Fletcher. Fletcher had taken theological training in Geneva before immigrating from France to England and taking ordination as an Anglican priest.[15] Reflecting the continental model of his training, Fletcher's theological writings were devoted almost entirely to rigorous apologetics for the Wesleyan Methodist positions on cooperant grace and entire sanctification. Wesley valued these apologetics as an important *supplement* to his own practical-theological activity. By contrast, American Methodists would soon make them the *standard* for serious theological activity, and judge Wesley's works as inferior in comparison.

III. American Methodism and Wesley's Practical Theology

This point sets the stage for the central task of this paper—sketching the progressive divergence of dominant American Methodist assumptions about the primary purpose, forms, and social location of theological activity from the model of Wesley, and pondering the causes of this divergence. In keeping with the focus of our larger project, I will concentrate attention on those branches of Methodism leading into the present United Methodist Church. These include most directly The Methodist Episcopal Church (MEC), The Methodist Protestant Church (MPC), The Methodist Episcopal Church, South (MECS), and their later union into The Methodist Church (MC). The broader "Methodist" branches of The Evangelical Association (EA) and The United Brethren Church (UBC) will also be considered as appropriate.[16]

A. Separation from an Anglican Context

The beginnings of American Methodism are intricately intertwined with the extended ministry of Francis Asbury, from his appointment as the first superintendent in 1772 until his death in 1816. Asbury was without question the most immediate mentor of the first generation of American preachers. His influence in this capacity, in specific regard to Wesley's model of theological activity, must be judged ambivalent.

On the one hand, Asbury valued Wesley's basic theological stance. He praised Wesley's works for the spirituality they conveyed, and even called him the "most respectable divine since the primitive ages."[17] Yet, as this quote suggests, Wesley's theological writings were for Asbury more the "standards" provided by an esteemed founder than a model to be emulated. When this attitude is combined with his lack of formal theological education, it is not surprising that Asbury made little attempt to publish first-order theological materials himself. While he embodied some dimensions of Wesley's model of pastor-theologian, he voluntarily renounced most dimensions that involved literary expression, and enforced on his American preachers the controls over publication that Wesley had established.[18]

Even more important to our story is the way that Asbury participated in the separation of early American Methodism from the theological context of its origin. The beginnings of this separation are epitomized in Asbury's decision to ignore Wesley's orders and remain with the American colonists during their revolt against British control. The political freedom from England won in that revolt was soon emulated by the organization of the Methodist movement in the new United States as a distinct denomination, severing all connections with Anglicanism. Even dependence upon Wesley was downplayed for a while, reflecting the Americans' disappointment with his lack of support for their revolutionary cause.[19] Among the impacts of this process of cutting attachments was the devaluation of at least three forms of typical Anglican theological activity that had been central to Wesley's model.

1. Liturgy. No form of theological activity received more attention, or was the scene of more debate, in Anglicanism than the development of the standard liturgy in the *Book of Common Prayer.* Wesley valued the practical-theological role of this resource so highly that one of the few items he prepared specifically for the new American church was a carefully edited version, the *Sunday Service.* The American Methodists barely acknowledged this resource, laying it aside in 1792 in favor of a minimal order of worship that continued the "freedom" that had characterized their society meetings. While this "free" worship had an implicit liturgy, there is little evidence of careful pastoral consideration and crafting of its formative impact. Indeed, when there were suggestions in the MEC near the end of the nineteenth century of reappropriating Wesley's *Sunday Service,* the typical response could conceive of no benefit for true religion from liturgy, only its likelihood of stifling the "life" of the worship service.[20] Calls for recovering more formal liturgy in worship did increase with time, though the motivation was not always a conviction of its vital role in shaping Christian character (a common rationale was the concern that Methodists were losing their more sophisticated urban members to the Episcopalians).[21] Only in the 1940s did the MC return to Wesley's precedent and engage in the practical-theological task of crafting a new *Book of Worship for Church and Home.*[22] The extent to which individual pastors have viewed their use (or neglect) of this and subsequent resources as an exercise in practical-theological judgment remains an open question.

2. Creeds. A second major form of Anglican theological activity was determination of a creed that could adequately articulate their distinctive understanding of Christian faith and practice (i.e., the narrative they hoped to instill in their members). Once again, Wesley valued this resource enough to engage in the practical-theological work of producing an edited version for the new American church. Unlike the *Sunday Service,* the American Methodists adopted Wesley's proposed "Articles of Religion" with little question or alteration. Indeed, they established a stringent restriction on any attempt to revise the Articles at the 1808 General Conference. Whatever the benefits of this move, it has effec-

tively stifled the occasional stirrings among American Methodists to
take up the practical-theological task of reworking their established
creed to make it more adequate or appropriate.[23]

3. Sermons. The third relevant form of Anglican theological activity
was production of a standard set of homilies, which stands in some
analogy with the emphasis in the Early Church on catechetical sermons.
The major difference was that the Anglican *Homilies* were designed primarily as templates for clergy who lacked sufficient training for reliable
doctrinal preaching. Wesley bridged this difference in his activity of cir-
culating his written sermons among his societies, since his purpose was
to provide for the practical-theological sustenance and formation of
both his lay preachers and the general membership.[24]

The required reading of Wesley's sermons conveyed to early
American Methodist preachers some of his assumption that sermons
were a serious form of theological activity. Thus, when the *Methodist
Review* began publication in 1818, it included a section called "Divinity"
that was typically devoted to a sermon. But this section was discontin-
ued in 1830, an event foreshadowed by calls for more systematic study
of theology in early issues of the journal.[25] Perhaps in protest of this dis-
continuance, an independent monthly publication of Methodist sermons to serve as expressions of "sound divinity" was launched the
same year.[26] The fact that this venture folded within four years suggests
that Abel Stevens was more representative of the emerging American
attitude in his fiery 1852 series of essays exhorting Methodist preachers
to continue the totally extemporaneous preaching of the Early Church,
which (he believed) was freed from all "sham art" of Dogmatic
Theology.[27]

Notably, Stevens never discussed Wesley's sermons in his series! Even
a more sedate work by Daniel Kidder a decade later, which would
become the first broadly assigned text on homiletics for Methodist
preachers, and which showed more appreciation for doctrinal discourse
than Stevens, paid little attention to Wesley's sermons as models.
Kidder commended Wesley's sermons only for their didactic value,
while praising the more extemporaneous sermons of Fletcher as the
model for a blessed ministry.[28] It was not far from Kidder to the next
widely assigned text on homiletics for Methodist preachers, which
began with the motto: "In preaching, the thing of least consequence is
the sermon."[29] The conception of preaching, or published sermons, as
centrally concerned with theological formation was fading fast! Indeed,

by 1905 the reviewer of a book on the doctrine of the Holy Spirit in the *Methodist Quarterly Review* found it necessary to say that his observation that the book was a series of sermons was not meant as a disparagement.[30]

B. Formation in the Crucible of Calvinist Debates

If severing their Anglican connections distanced American Methodists from some forms of Wesley's practical-theological activity, their resulting independent status reinforced the tendency to disregard Wesley's model of theology. This is because the move to independence required them to interact even more with their pluralistic theological setting. Within this pluralism, most major non-Methodist voices inclined toward one form or another of the Reformed theological tradition. This was particularly true of voices prominent in the religious press and theological education. As a result, Methodist theological attention was increasingly focused on issues resulting from internal Reformed influence and external Reformed critiques. For example, the presence of Reformed alternatives helped fuel internal dissension over the decision to retain episcopal polity, provoking some of the first indigenous publications by American Methodists (and the eventual MPC split).[31] Even clearer is the way that Reformed critique provoked Methodist apologies for their message of God's universally available saving grace and the vital human role in responding to that grace. The first doctrinal monograph by an American author published by the MEC book agents (in 1813) was devoted to this agenda, and it remained one of the most frequent subjects of publications through the next fifty years.[32]

Such prominence of controversial dialogue with their Reformed neighbors inevitably affected the development of nineteenth-century American Methodist theology. My focus remains on the ways that it affected the professional practice and forms of this theology. But to explain this effect, I need to point out a subtle change from Wesley in some basic assumptions of American Methodist theology, a change that arose directly through debates with the Calvinists.

1. Change in Moral Psychology. The change to which I am referring concerns the assumptions that one makes about how humans are motivated to make moral choices and are enabled to put those choices into action, issues discussed under the heading "moral psychology." Much of Christian tradition has been dominated by an intellectualist stance on this issue—conceiving virtue as primarily a matter of reason suppressing the distractions of the (irrational) passions in order to effect morally free and correct acts of will. Such assumptions reigned in early Anglican moral thought, but the eighteenth century witnessed an aggressive challenge to them.[33] This challenge drew upon such diverse currents as the empiricist turn in English philosophy and pietist reactions to deistic reductions of religion to mere reverence for the truths of natural revelation and reason. What these diverse streams held in common was the insistence that reason alone was not sufficient to motivate or enable moral action (or spiritual life). Their alternative highlighted the indispensable role of our affections or passions in engaging our will and inclining it toward specific actions. Of importance, they insisted that these affections are not simply epiphenomena of rational choices, they are an independent aspect of the human psyche.

Wesley joined those who were turning from the reigning intellectualist moral psychology in preference of a model that had a deep appreciation for the contribution of the affections to human willing.[34] As one expression of this, his anthropology directly equated the human "will" with the affections. In their ideal form, on Wesley's understanding, the affections integrate the rational and emotional dimensions of human life into a holistic inclination toward particular choices or acts. Moreover, while provocative of human action, the affections have a crucial receptive dimension as well. They are not self-causative, but are awakened and thrive *in response* to experience of external reality. In particular, it is only in response to our experience of God's gracious love for us, shed abroad in our hearts by the Holy Spirit, that the human affection of love for God and others is awakened. This grounds our holiness and salvation in God's gracious prevenience. But it also leaves a place for our integrity, since our initial experience of God's love awakens in us only the "seed" of every virtue. These seeds mature and take shape as we responsively "grow in grace."

One way to describe such responsive growth is that our affections are progressively habituated into enduring dispositions. Wesley appreciated the way in which such habituated affections brought greater consistency to human action. Yet, he was also aware that some contemporary advocates of an "affectional" moral psychology (particularly David Hume) portrayed the impact of the affections on our actions as deterministic, thereby undermining human freedom. To avoid such implications Wesley carefully distinguished the human faculty of liberty from the will. He understood liberty as our capacity to enact (or refusal to enact) our desires and inclinations. This capacity allowed him to insist on the crucial contribution of the affections to human willing without rendering such willing totally determined.

Whatever its merits, Wesley's response to Hume's determinism was destined to have far less influence than that of Thomas Reid. Wesley had developed an alternative form of affectional moral psychology, while Reid championed a repristinated intellectualist moral psychology.[35] Central to Reid's argument with Hume was the insistence that the psychological faculty of the will should not be identified with the affections, but was instead our unconstrained *rational* ability to choose between (or suppress) the various stimuli that motivate us toward action. The importance of Reid to our topic is the breadth with which his response to Hume was adopted in American circles to critique the theological expression of a deterministic affectional moral psychology in Jonathan Edwards. Even revisionist Calvinists turned to Reid in their search for a more "compatibilist" account of the relation of divine foreordination and human action than that of Edwards.[36] This makes it less of a surprise that early American Methodist attempts to articulate their "noncompatibilist" defense of human integrity against all Calvinist camps also invoked Reid's intellectualist assumptions.[37] Opposition to determinism had become so identified with Reid's approach in their setting that they failed to recognize that Wesley's understanding of human action and liberty had been framed instead within an affectional moral psychology.[38]

2. Intellectualist Model of Religion. Whether conscious or not, the American Methodist rejection of Wesley's affectional moral psychology in favor of the intellectualist alternative had a critical impact on their other theological assumptions. The most relevant case is the nature of religion. In keeping with his psychology, Wesley understood religion to be most properly a matter of the affections; in particular, true religion was epitomized in holy tempers (i.e., dispositions) toward God and other persons.[39] To put an edge on this point, he once argued that "orthodoxy, or right opinions, is, at best, but a very slender part of religion, if it can be allowed to be any part of it at all."[40] This polemical claim must not be overplayed.[41] Wesley's contention was simply that *mere* intellectual assent will not lead to holy living, because human actions spring more properly from the affections. He was not intending to suggest a total disjunction between intellectual understanding and the affections. In fact, he was quite willing to agree that right opinions *generally* help promote the development of holy tempers. What he rejected was any intimation that *only* right opinions can contribute to this development, or that proper affectional disposition is a simple *reflex* of proper intellectual belief.

It was precisely such intimations that became increasingly common among Wesley's American descendants. In keeping with their adopted moral psychology, nineteenth-century theologians broadly portrayed the affections as inherently irrational, needing regulation by the more primary human faculty of the understanding. On these terms, the essence of religion became the intellectual truth that it delivers. Likewise, proper affectional disposition and correct action became mere reflexive functions of being intellectually persuaded of this truth.[42]

One can easily wonder how early American Methodist theologians could appropriate this intellectualist model of religion so broadly, in the face of Wesley's pointed critiques of it. Part of the answer is to recognize that these critiques were contextualized in Wesley himself. His overall view of reason is quite positive. Far from portraying it as demonic, he continually praised the benefits that reason brings to the religious life. He simply insisted that one must also acknowledge its limits.[43] As such, the move from Wesley toward an intellectualist emphasis was one of degrees, not total reversal; proponents had only to diminish the limitations of reason.

This move was made easier for American Methodists by the fact that John Fletcher was already sounding a more intellectualist note (perhaps reflecting his continental training). While Fletcher could repeat Wesley's affectional language, he more typically gravitated to a model of the will as the power of rational self-determination, exercised to control the affections and other irrational motivations.[44] The corollary of this was that Fletcher identified intellectual belief as the ultimate principle of all human action, and contended that if we can change a person's assent from a lie to the truth, that person's dispositions and actions will automatically follow suit.[45] The importance of Fletcher to our story is that his writings were given a place directly alongside those of Wesley from the beginning in American Methodism. In fact, they took on greater prominence than Wesley's works in the specific debate with Calvinism.[46] Thereby, they legitimated the intellectualist model of religion as "Methodist."

If Fletcher's lone voice threatened to offset Wesley's affectional model of religion, imagine the impact of a chorus of voices in agreement with Fletcher! That is exactly what the typical Methodist preacher encountered in his theological training as the nineteenth century progressed. Various components contributed to this chorus, but its core was the textbooks for the nineteenth-century discipline of moral philosophy that were assigned reading. These texts unanimously adopted, and systematically defended, the intellectualist moral psychology of Reid and his disciples (with its attendant implications for the nature of religion).[47] It was understandably hard for the affirmations of an affectional model scattered through Wesley's various practical-theological writings to be heard over the regimented harmony of these texts.

3. Emergence of Methodist Scholasticism. How did the moral psychology that American Methodist theologians were appropriating through their debates with the Calvinists reinforce the tendency to dismiss Wesley's model of practical theology? The current intellectualist model of religion included certain assumptions about the forms and methods of theological activity necessary for providing the requisite rational assurance that one's beliefs are true. A good indication of these assumptions can be gained by considering a Calvinist critique of initial American Methodist theological publications. In an address to the 1852 Presbyterian General Assembly, E. P. Humphrey argued that Methodist theology was unworthy of serious consideration because it

> has yet to be reduced to a systematic and logical form.... We have its brief and informal creed in some five and twenty articles; but where is its complete confession of faith, in thirty or forty chapters? ... Where is its whole body of divinity, from under the hand of a master, sharply defining its terms, accurately stating its belief, laying down the conclusions logically involved therein, trying these conclusions, no less than their premises, by the Word of God, refuting objections, and adjusting all its parts into a consistent and systematical whole?[48]

What Humphrey was here assuming as the standard against which Methodist theology came up short is a scholastic theology—that is, a textbook that provides a comprehensive and carefully organized survey of a tradition's truth claims, defends any controverted claims polemically, and provides rational grounding for the whole. Wesley had not provided such a work for his Methodist people. His American descendants could have taken this as warrant to question the preeminence being given this specific form of theological activity by their critics, but

few did so.[49] Their adopted intellectualist model inclined most instead
to consider the lack of such a resource a major deficiency in Methodist
theology.[50]

It was not long before some brave souls set out to fill this deficiency.
The trailblazer was Richard Watson, who published his multivolume
Theological Institutes in 1825–28.[51] While Watson was a British Methodist,
he is relevant to this study because his *Institutes* was the most common
theology text on the course of study for elders across the breadth of
American Methodism from its introduction in 1830 through most of the
remainder of the nineteenth century.[52] Part of the reason for this enduring place was that Watson resonated with the intellectualist conviction
spreading in American Methodism. He, too, had opted for an intellectualist moral psychology (apparently drawing on Reid) when searching
for an alternative to Edwards's deterministic account of the affections.[53]
The resulting scholastic character of his theology is evident already in
the subtitle: "A View of the Evidences, Doctrines, Morals, and
Institutions of Christianity." The drive for comprehensiveness is obvious. Also striking is the leading role for "evidences." The work opens
with a rational apologetic for belief in God and acceptance of Christian
revelation, clearly assuming that these foundations must be established
before consideration of the Christian worldview itself can begin. Finally,
the work is punctuated throughout with polemic defenses of disputed
Methodist claims.

While Watson was rapidly and broadly embraced in American
Methodism, there were a few who expressed reservations. For example,
there was some debate as to whether Watson's "evidences" leaned too
heavily on providing rational justification for accepting Christian
Scripture as revelatory, or not heavily enough.[54] There was also an occasional complaint about the amount of polemical argumentation in such
a scholastic theology, preferring the simple positive exposition of doctrinal beliefs.[55] It is quite revealing, however, that the only voice in a
Methodist publication protesting the very enterprise of developing a
comprehensive survey—rather than sticking to creeds and other first-
order forms—was a guest editorial by a Protestant Episcopal (i.e.,
Anglican) bishop.[56]

The more typical complaint about Watson's *Institutes* was that the
work's length and labored argumentation made it inaccessible to
laypersons and beginning candidates for ministerial orders. This concern sparked the first American ventures in survey texts of Methodist

theology: in 1840 Amos Binney published a brief *Theological Compend*, which was aimed at use by families and Sunday schools (but made its way into ministerial courses of study at times); and Thomas Ralston contributed a somewhat longer survey of the *Elements of Divinity* in 1847, geared specifically to beginning candidates for ministry.[57]

Though he showed no awareness of them, these two "popular" surveys would have been ridiculed in Humphrey's estimation of Methodist theology even more sharply than he had dismissed Watson for being insufficiently comprehensive and lacking systematic organization. Often in direct response to this dismissal, most American Methodist writers after 1852 focused their energies on providing a more rigorous "scholastic" text than that of Watson.[58] The prime example is Samuel Wakefield's *Complete System of Christian Theology*, published in 1862.[59] This text was explicitly a reworking of Watson, partly to provide a less labored style. But its main agenda is evident in its title and its additions to the subtitle; Wakefield's version claimed to provide "A Concise, *Comprehensive* and Systematic View of the Evidences, Doctrines, Morals and Institutions of Christianity." American Methodist Scholasticism had reached its stride!

It is no accident that Wakefield's editing of Watson included giving greater clarity and prominence to the intellectualist moral psychology present in the original.[60] This psychology, and its correlated model of religion, propelled the growth of Methodist scholasticism. It also fostered a significant narrowing of Wesley's model of theological activity. Wesley's model embraced the range of activities that awaken, strengthen, and shape Christian character. On his terms, the crafting of structures like the class meetings was as much an exercise of practical-theological judgment as was editing of a doctrinal catechism. But under the terms of an intellectualist model, "theology" was equated more exclusively with doctrinal instruction and apologetics. When such theology was pursued according to strict scholastic assumptions, it sought to provide a comprehensive survey of timeless truths, all rationally demonstrated. And even in those rare cases in the second half of the nineteenth century where some of the scholastic assumptions were questioned, the intellectualist focus of Methodist theologies on formal doctrinal instruction and apologetics remained.[61]

C. Institutionalization of Ministerial Education

A third major factor that influenced American Methodist understandings of theology during the nineteenth century was the increasing institutionalization of theological education. Some of the directions chosen in this process further displaced Wesley's model of practical theology.

1. Transitions in Ministerial Education.[62] Given their lay status within Anglicanism, there were no formal academic prerequisites for the initial generation of American Methodist preachers. The training that they received was mainly through apprenticeship. Each recruit was teamed for a period with a seasoned itinerant—to benefit from the veteran's model of effective exhorting, his advice on means of discipline, and his introduction to reliable sources of food and shelter. In addition to gaining a grounding in these basic skills of itinerant ministry, there was also some expectation of the fledgling preacher to engage in independent study of theological works like Wesley's sermons and Fletcher's apologetics. During the founding period of Asbury's leadership, however, there was little accountability for this expectation, and even less pressure for reading beyond these standard works.

Concern to provide more direction to the independent study of fledgling preachers became public immediately following Asbury's death. While this concern encountered some resistance, it led to the adoption of an official course of study for candidates for elder's orders in each of the direct branches of Methodism during the second quarter of the nineteenth century (and the UBC and EA shortly later).[63] Though more explicit in its listings, this course was still designed for independent study, to be pursued over a series of years in the midst of ministerial apprenticeship and practice. At its initiation, there were few stipulations for supervision and examination of candidates. Moves to formalize this process multiplied toward the end of the nineteenth century, eventuating in standardized exams by the early twentieth century.

The other way to formalize independent study, of course, is to shift it into academic institutions. There was strong peer pressure for Methodists to move in this direction, matching the practice of many of their denominational competitors. But while this option for education of Methodist ministers had scattered proponents from the beginning, there was widespread resistance to contend with initially. Among the common fears were that any move to require formal academic training of prospective ministers would (1) encourage erroneous doctrinal speculation, (2) unduly eliminate as ministerial candidates some who had a divine call, (3) create a shortage of available itinerants, and (4) produce elders unable—or unwilling—to minister to the lower classes.[64] It is also clear that many of the initial generation of traveling preachers viewed the mounting call for more academic training as an implicit devaluation of the contribution they had made to the church.

Whatever their source, these hesitations about ministerial education did not reflect a Methodist rejection of education in general. In fact, few were more prolific than Methodists in creating colleges during the nineteenth century. But unlike their earlier New England counterparts, Methodist colleges did not originate primarily for ministerial education. They were designed for the moral, cultural, and vocational education of all Christian citizens. It was in fulfilling this larger goal that they contributed to the sense of need for more formal education of ministers. There was increasing concern that Methodist preachers were losing the ability to relate to (and have the respect of) their academically trained congregations![65] In response it became common by the mid-nineteenth century for the various Methodist groups to encourage (though not require) their prospective ministers to attend colleges as part of their preparation. With the emergence of specialized theological institutes or seminaries in the latter part of the century, there was also wide adoption of the policy of allowing graduation from such a formal program to satisfy the requirement of the course of study. Even so, the course of study technically remained the standard route for ministerial education until 1956, when the MC decided to make seminary education the required standard (continuing course of study only as a very restricted optional route).

Thus, the saga of Methodist ministerial education led from almost exclusive reliance on apprenticeship to being largely confined to a formal academic setting. There is at least room to question whether this move involved distancing of theological reflection from the praxis of the Christian community, in direct contrast to Wesley's practical theology. Daniel Curry raised this suspicion with characteristic vigor in 1886, charging that pursuing formal theological education detracted ministers from the work of preaching the pure and simple gospel to common folk, replacing it with "bookish" concerns and academic ambitions.[66]

2. Adoption of Continental Fourfold Curriculum. Curry appears to have assumed that seminary education per se inappropriately separates theology from the daily praxis of the Christian community. While this broad charge is insupportable, the specific curricular form adopted by the emerging Methodist seminaries has proved liable to this tendency. Virtually all earlier seminaries and divinity schools founded in North America had organized around the fourfold curriculum currently advo-

cated in the continental European discussion of "theological encyclopedia" (i.e., Biblical Theology, Historical Theology, Systematic Theology,
and Practical Theology).[67] In their drive to catch up, Methodists followed suit. Indeed, one of the ironies of nineteenth-century theological
education is that the "backward" Methodists played a prominent role in
popularizing this continental curricular model.

This irony is explained in part by a connection the American
Methodists had formed with the foremost arena of continental theological debate—Germany. While natural roots for this connection lay in the
EA and UBC, the MEC was prominent in the initial contacts.[68] This was
because the MEC had been fortunate enough to attract Wilhelm Nast, a
native German who had studied for the Lutheran ministry before emi-
grating to the United States. Nast took leadership in MEC ministry
among Germans, including an 1850 mission to start Methodist work in
Germany itself (the same year as EA contacts). John McClintock accompanied Nast to scout this project, and came home convinced of the preeminence of German theological training. He subsequently helped
entice William Warren and John Hurst to pursue postcollegiate studies
in Germany. These two ascended quickly to the presidencies of the
schools of theology at Boston and Drew respectively, and standardized
the preference for faculty prospects to have studied in Germany.

On a broader scale, McClintock was committed to upgrading the level
of theological scholarship in America—to match the German standard.
His main venture in this regard was launching a multivolume encyclo-
pedic survey of biblical, theological, and ecclesiastical scholarship.[69]
The articles were prepared by American (and a few British) scholars, but
highlighted German contributions in the area of theological method.
Notably, the article on the discipline of theological encyclopedia lamented the lack of a proper book of this genre in English, citing this as part
of the reason for the neglect of English theological work in Germany.[70]
A first attempt to address this lacuna was the posthumous publication
in 1873 of McClintock's own inaugural lectures on theological encyclopedia at Drew.[71] Then in 1884 John Hurst teamed with George Crooks
to publish through MEC auspices the first English translation of the
most influential German theological encyclopedia, supplementing each
section with a bibliography of relevant English works.[72]

With all of this interest in the fourfold theological encyclopedia, it is
little surprise that this curricular structure defined the seminaries
emerging throughout the Methodist family and came to dominate even

the course of study by the end of the century.[73] The problems inherent in this structure also progressively permeated Methodist theological education. While the identification of distinct theological interests like biblical studies or pastoral care is hardly illegitimate, the tendency of this specific model was to fragment theological education by striving to establish clear disciplinary borders between each interest and urging that these borders not be crossed. The theological status of the resulting disciplines was also called into question when theology "proper" was identified as only one of the four (Systematics).[74]

The impact of this structure can be illustrated by contrasting the discipline of Practical Theology with Wesley's "practical theology." In Wesley's case we were not dealing with a specific discipline, but with the overall character of his theological activity. He kept consideration of Christian praxis at the center of theological reflection, integrating his interaction with the whole range of theological interests around this touchstone. By contrast, Practical Theology was rendered an "application" discipline in Methodist theological education—that is, it was reduced to applying to Christian life the truths previously established by Systematics, and limited at first largely to technical considerations of preaching and evangelism.[75] While its focus of application broadened somewhat over time to include pastoral care and social action, its derivative theological status has only recently been seriously challenged.[76] It has thus served as a graphic symbol of a growing dichotomy between "theory" and "practice" in American Methodist theological education.

3. The Professional Systematic Theologian. A major factor contributing to this increasing dichotomy was the professionalization of the office of theologian that took place in the last quarter of the nineteenth century. This office had been initially defined by Wesley, who integrated doctrinal reflection with pastoral oversight of his Methodist movement. While Francis Asbury laid claim to this "episcopal" teaching office in the American church, his focus on administrative issues set a precedent that marginalized the teaching role in later episcopal practice. The teaching office effectively passed to the book stewards and journal editors, who could define Methodist doctrine by their publication decisions.[77] The most successful editors were those skilled in confessional apologetics—for example, Nathan Bangs, Albert Bledsoe,[78] and Daniel Whedon. Their move to prominence elevated a model of "theology" that, admitting its importance in its place, lacked the first-order forms and formative focus of Wesley's practical theology.

As the newly founded seminaries subsequently gathered steam, they garnered an increasing share of the *de facto* teaching office. Since they were devoted to training for pastoral ministry, these institutions seemed promising arenas for recovering a model of theology that reintegrated doctrinal reflection with Christian praxis and formative pastoral concern. This promise was heightened by the fact that the initial professors of doctrinal theology at these schools typically came to teaching (mentoring) late in life, bringing with them extensive pastoral experience.[79] Unfortunately, this potential for integration would soon dissipate. The countervailing pressures of the lauded continental model of the academic theologian proved too strong.

One of these pressures was for scholars to train specifically for an academic vocation and to devote their entire career to it. The second generation of doctrinal theologians in Methodist seminaries were already approximating this pattern.[80] By the third generation, many considered it self-evident that spending one's entire career in teaching was superior to "coming to theology" *(sic)* late in life from the parish![81] If early American Methodists had been prone to distrust those who spent time in the academy, Methodist theologians were now prone to dismiss those who spent too much time outside it.

Alongside this progressive isolating of the theology professor within the academy, the continental model also pressed—as noted earlier— toward the isolation of the four major areas of theological concern from one another. The impact of this pressure in American Methodist circles was signaled by the shift from producing scholastic compendiums (which could include biblical and historical sections) to observing the disciplinary restrictions of Systematic Theology. Major theology texts across the spectrum of the movement that were published in the thirty years following the appearance of McClintock's theological encyclopedia all adopted this narrower focus.[82] From this point on, only the most gifted scholar would dare teach or write in more than one area of the theological curriculum, and even these exceptional folk (like Henry Sheldon) carefully observed the disciplinary boundaries within their various published works.[83] Protests against the separation of doctrinal theology from biblical studies, and revisionist attempts to bridge this gap, were both quietly ignored.[84]

The fragmentation went further yet. The fourfold model technically included the areas of dogmatics, polemics, apologetics, and ethics in Systematic Theology. But with professionalization came the pressure for each of these to become a separate specialty. Thus, many of the systematic theologies just mentioned purposefully restricted themselves to dogmatics or doctrinal theology.[85] Separate volumes of apologetics were left to other specialists,[86] and Christian ethics began to enter the curriculum as a distinct theological discipline.[87] This latter development was the most significant (in comparison to Wesley) because theologians were now theoretically trying to separate consideration of what Christians believe from consideration of how they should act.

A final pressure of the continental model that deserves attention is its demand for systematization in doctrinal theology itself. Concern with establishing systematic connections between doctrines was not unique to the continental model. Nineteenth-century British and American theologians emphasized this role as part of their argument that theology qualified as a (Baconian) science. Methodists were no exception.[88] But through the influence of Schleiermacher and Hegel, a distinctive approach to systematization came to characterize the continental model. It was no longer enough simply to show that the various Christian doctrines were congruent. The goal became to demonstrate that they were all entailed in (or derived from) a single idea or principle. The introduction of this conception of systematization into American Methodist theology is easy to locate. Upon completing his studies in Germany, William Warren was invited to remain and teach at the theological institute Methodists had established in Bremen. In 1865 he published the introductory volume of a planned systematic theology to use in his teaching. This volume mapped out his proposal that Methodist theology should be unified by organizing all doctrines around the systematic principle of perfect love—that is, the distinctive Methodist conception of the interrelationship of God and humanity.[89] While Warren's project was never completed, being interrupted by his return to take the presidency of the school of theology at Boston in 1867, his proposal proved influential on the direction of subsequent American Methodist theology.[90] There was an increased focus on the internal consistency of the System, often at the expense of reciprocal interaction with the (messy) life and issues of the community of faith in the world.

It must be admitted that each of the developments that we have been considering had benefits. The professional Methodist theologian could bring more time, more precise focus, and greater scholarly resources to his or her reflection. But these benefits came with the trade-offs of specialization. One obvious trade-off was the reshaping of "theology" into an academic product, distinguished sharply from those forms of literary activity that most directly awaken and shape spiritual life (e.g., hymns, sermons, and liturgy).[91] It became increasingly rare for theologians to write for the laity; they wrote for the academy. Of course, pastors-in-training were part of the academy, so one might assume that academic theologians addressed congregations indirectly through their pastoral "apprentices." But the reality is that the division of labor broadly assumed in the academy mitigated against apprenticeship. Professional theologians were considered to cultivate theology as a science for its own sake, while pastors simply applied the results of this science to the congregation.[92] There was little rationale for training pastors in the "science" of theologizing, and little reason to assume that theologians had the experience to mentor in application!

The defining characteristic of Methodist theological education at the end of the nineteenth century was how seldom these trade-offs were noticed, let alone lamented. It is small wonder that by mid twentieth century the seminaries (and professional systematic theologians) had lost any *de facto* role that they held earlier in the teaching office of the church.[93]

4. Impact on Wesley as Theological Mentor. It is also a small wonder that by the turn of the century academic theologians hardly knew what to make of Wesley as a theologian. On the fourfold model most of Wesley's theological productions would fall within the application discipline of Practical Theology, which is precisely the realm to which a few restricted his interest and abilities.[94] Others rejected this narrow classification, allowing that Wesley combined aspects of the professional theologian with those of the practical Christian teacher.[95] But this concession only heightened the problem. What serious theologian would overlook these boundaries? And why did Wesley never undertake the central theological task of a Systematic Theology? Some of his academic descendants were inclined to excuse Wesley on the basis of his misfortune of training in the methodological backwaters of Anglican theology.[96] Others appealed to a supposed principle of historical development—that revivals of Christian life inevitably focus on immediate ministry, while creative epochs of theological science necessarily follow and consolidate these revivals.[97] In either case, the departure of later Methodist theologians from Wesley's model of theological activity was neatly justified; after all, Wesley had not been a "real" theologian!

With an attitude such as this, it is little surprise that Wesley's *Notes* and *Sermons* were disappearing from the course of study by 1900.[98] The result was that Methodist pastors (and future theologians) were exposed less and less to Wesley as a mentor even in doctrinal claims, let alone in theological method. By 1909 Olin Curtis—who had been teaching Systematic Theology for twenty years in Methodist seminaries—could concede that he had only recently examined the fourteen volumes of Wesley's *Works* and had been astonished by the level of Wesley's doctrinal concern![99]

D. Coming of Age in Twentieth-Century North America

As the example of Curtis suggests, North American Methodist theologians were in a very different situation entering the twentieth century from the one they had been in a hundred years before. Any perceived restrictiveness of loyalties to past theological voices and models had been neutralized. They were free to embrace the latest currents in culture and theology. And they were quick to take advantage of this freedom. Methodists assumed leadership roles in the range of innovative programs and reactions that have characterized twentieth-century North American theology.[100] Methodist theology had "come of age"!

But had it also become captive to the "spirit of the age"? With the benefit of what perspective we can have on such recent developments, it seems that this was too much the case. By the turn of the century the Enlightenment assumptions that permeated North American culture, and that had been creeping into Methodist theology for some time, were broadly championed by Methodist theologians. The experience of North American churches through the twentieth century would evidence that some of these assumptions (such as the individualism noted in the introduction) were inimical to Christian faith.[101] I want to draw attention to how some of them also have mitigated the likelihood of recovering Wesley's practical theology through most of the century.

A fundamental assumption of the Enlightenment was the superiority of modern knowledge and methods over traditional truth-claims. This assumption was blithely endorsed by Randolph Sinks Foster (a former theology professor and current MEC bishop) when he began a multi-volume series of *Studies in Theology* in 1891 with the claim "We know more today than our fathers a hundred years ago. We have truer beliefs than they had." It is little wonder that Foster almost never interacts with Wesley in his series![102] His precedent would be widely emulated in twentieth-century Methodist liberalism.

Another relevant Enlightenment emphasis was optimism about humanity. In psychological terms this entailed the inherent goodness of human nature. Moral failures reflected simply the inadequate use of reason to control our passions and appetites. Enduring moral defects were accounted for as the product of negative experiences and habits, or as reactions to the imposition of repressive social constraints upon the individual. An indication that these themes were penetrating Methodist theology by the turn of the century is provided by Henry Sheldon's insistence that while the church may have some effective instrumentality in nurturing Christian character, it has no sovereign prerogative in its production—that belongs to the individual.[103] This helps explain why twentieth-century Methodist theology has largely undervalued the role that Wesley assigned to the church in shaping (imposing?) holiness on individuals' lives through its communal support and first-order forms of practical-theological activity.[104]

In historical terms the optimism of the Enlightenment involved a conviction of the evolutionary progress of humanity, not only physically but socially and morally as well. The presence of this conviction within early-twentieth-century Methodist circles can be illustrated by James Mudge's choice of motto for a book on Christian Perfection: "Progress is the law of life, man is not man as yet."[105] To be sure, such a bald assertion would not pass unchallenged in the broader Methodist community. But the very attempt to reject it contributed to its impact on the form and agenda of twentieth-century Methodist theological activity. This is because Enlightenment critics, assuming the progress of humanity as a self-evident norm, had begun to judge the value of cultural expressions by their contribution to (or debilitation of) that progress. When this test was applied to religion it called forth a distinctively modern form of apologetics. Respondents tried to demonstrate that certain religious convictions were fundamental for establishing the value of human life and for driving the progress of human culture. Many also vied to convince that their particular religious tradition was the most beneficial in this regard. American Methodists began dabbling in this modern apologetic enterprise as early as 1881, when Daniel Dorchester justified the rejection of scholastic forms of theology (whether compendiums or Systematics!) by some progressive Protestants on the grounds that they were simply removing the obscuring husks of dogma and allowing the pure Christian faith in *humanity*, God, Christ's divinity, and *ethical order* to shine through.[106]

Dorchester's claim can serve to mark the emergence of a major transition in the focus of professional American Methodist theological activity.[107] This focus had earlier been primarily internal to the faith community, seeking to clarify the Methodist doctrinal stance among its adherents and to defend this stance against the attack of other Christian traditions. But now the focus was broadening to incorporate an external concern, the defense of religion before its "cultured despisers" in modern society. As Dorchester had hinted, this change in focus had direct implications for the form of theological productions. Henry Sheldon can serve again as a pivotal example. After issuing *System of Christian Doctrine* in 1900, Sheldon's next publication on doctrine was *The Essentials of Christianity*.[108] The echoes of Adolf Harnack were not accidental! Sheldon had become convinced that the present setting had less need of a comprehensive system than of a shorter "interpretation" of Christianity that could demonstrate its positive value for human individuals and society (i.e., a modern apologetic).

Sheldon was not alone in this decision. With the turn of the century the production of major Systematic Theologies virtually ceased among mainline American Methodists.[109] Those assigned to teach Systematic Theology turned to producing introductions and interpretations of Christian belief (or of individual doctrines), all with a modern apologetic slant.[110] What differences there were among these various projects revolved around disagreements over which methods and emphases were most appropriate for this apologetic agenda.

1. Liberalism: The Turn to Experience. The largest chorus of voices on such issues at the turn of the century gathered under the banner of "liberalism."[111] Liberals were convinced that Methodists had avoided for too long a rethinking of their doctrinal beliefs in light of the advances of modern learning. They tried to initiate this process by introducing modern methods and conclusions into the curriculum of Methodist colleges and seminaries. The response was often quite heated. A particular flashpoint concerned the application of modern historical-critical methods to Scripture. There was also the infamous debate over evolution. For present purposes, however, the most interesting point of contention was the passing appeal to Wesley by some Methodist liberals precisely to endorse the Enlightenment assumption of the superiority of modern knowledge and methods over traditional truth-claims. As one proponent put it: "Back to Wesley is forward into the spirit of what is best in the twentieth century!"[112]

To understand this claim, it helps to note that the specific weakness that Enlightenment critics decried in traditional approaches to knowledge was their identification of truth as conformity to particularistic authoritative canons. In contrast to such "confessionalism," Enlightenment thinkers insisted that truth-claims should be based on criteria that are available to any person at any time—with reason and empirical experience being the most broadly accepted examples. The appeal to experience drew the particular attention of Methodist liberals. They saw correlations with the emphasis on experience by both Wesley and later Methodists. They began to tout as a virtue of Methodism that, unlike other confessional movements who forced ill-fitting traditional dogmas *upon* present experience, Methodists had allowed their theology to flow naturally *out of* religious experience.[113]

Building on this supposed precedent, many Methodist liberals championed a modern "empirical" approach to theology.[114] The most influential advocate was Harris Franklin Rall (son of an EA pastor and professor of theology at Garrett).[115] Rall insisted that Christian theology was not meant to be the master of religious life, but its servant; it was not meant to determine from external sources like Scripture or dogma what religious experience ought to entail, but to set forth what is implicit in Christian religious experience itself and then develop the theological conceptions that this experience entails. Rall was confident that the outcome of this process would accord with the essential teachings of the Bible. More important, he believed that it was the most effective way to make evident to modern persons how Christian faith addressed their needs.[116]

What Rall and others were advocating as the model for theology was, of course, a *Glaubenslehre*—a phenomenological description of the convictions of the present religious community. In their claim that this model was characteristically Methodist, they were reading Wesley too much through the eyes of Schleiermacher (or his progeny, Ritschl).[117] Wesley would share their contempt for a dogmatic theology imposed upon people without consideration of their specific needs and situation. But he would not be content with an alternative where doctrine is derived unilaterally from Christian experience. This is because Wesley would not share the apparent assumption that Christian life emerges "naturally" into authentic forms, an assumption often expressed by Methodist liberals in specific disparaging contrast with any who would maintain a necessary role for formative disciplines or institutions.[118] As long as this assumption reigned, there could be little hope of these theologians appreciating or recovering the formative interaction of Christian tradition with present experience that characterized Wesley's practical theology.

2. Boston Personalist Philosophy of Religion. The most prominent school within Methodist theology through the first half of this century, and the one that Methodists were most identified with in other circles, was Boston Personalism. This school was part of the larger liberal chorus, but placed a special emphasis on the philosophy of religion. Whereas many Methodist liberals distrusted philosophical speculation and limited themselves (in theory) simply to describing Christian experience, Borden Parker Bowne—the father of Boston Personalism—saw such empirical work as preliminary to the crucial task of providing metaphysical justification for Christian faith. What Bowne is best known for is his defense of a type of neo-Kantian idealism, which he named "personalism," as the metaphysic that is most appropriate to Christian faith and most adequate by modern standards.[119] While this metaphysic itself would fall into disfavor by midcentury, two of the implications for theology that Bowne and his followers drew from their philosophical work merit our attention, partly because of their continuing influence in Methodist circles.[120]

One of the defining characteristics of Boston Personalism is the way that their neo-Kantianism reenforced the rationalism and individualism already present in much Methodist theology. This effect was purposeful, in that personalists self-consciously built their theology upon (neo-Kantian) psychology. On these terms, religious formation was basically equated with moral education, with religion having at most the extra benefit of a more powerful intellectual motive for obedience (viewing the moral law as the will of God) and some added emotional warmth.[121] But religion as traditionally understood and practiced also had many features that were considered to threaten its moral potential. As such, a major theme in Boston Personalism was the need to rationalize and moralize modern religion by purifying it of all mystical and ceremonial overlays.[122] Among these "overlays" were many of the first-order activities and forms so central to Wesley's practical theology! It is little wonder that personalists found it hard to value Wesley's concern for these matters.

This difficulty was reinforced by a shift in the identification of the most essential aspect of theological activity. With personalists the emphasis moved from doctrinal theology itself to "meta-theological" issues concerning the philosophical grounding of both religious belief and doctrinal claims.[123] This shift was at the root of their dissatisfaction with the approach of other liberals like Rall. Personalists insisted that the (apologetic) theological task should not be limited to articulating Christian experience; the most crucial dimension of this task was the use of reason to construct "foundations" for that experience.[124] For Albert Knudson this ultimately meant the identification of the task of Systematic Theology as the construction of a philosophical theism.[125] On such a definition, Wesley's first-order work would inevitably come across as characterizing at best an evangelist, hardly a theologian.[126]

3. Neo-Orthodoxy and Neo-Wesleyanism. The apologetic strategy of Boston Personalism, like that of Methodist liberalism in general, was explicitly revisionist. In order to demonstrate the value of Christian faith to modern persons, it was often judged necessary to adjust traditional Christian commitments to fit the constraints of current thought.[127] But this assumed that current thought was fully compatible with the essentials of Christian faith. Through the initial decades of the twentieth century a significant minority challenged this assumption. This minority multiplied dramatically as the warning sirens of continental Neo-Orthodoxy found resonance in North America between the World Wars.

The best representative of the Neo-Orthodox agenda in its North American Methodist guise is Edwin Lewis. A survey of his works makes clear that he was as concerned as anyone in his day to offer a modern apologetic. He was simply convinced that traditional Christian commitments to such things as the reality of a supernatural order addressed the needs of modern persons more adequately than any revised alternative could.[128] The true apologetic task, for Lewis, was finding ways to proclaim these traditional commitments so that it is more evident how they answer the questions that modern persons are asking (i.e., the best apologetic was a good dogmatic!).

In its broader expression Neo-Orthodoxy was characterized by a renewed interest in the theology of the Magisterial Reformers (especially Luther and Calvin). As Methodists jumped in, they naturally developed a parallel Neo-Wesleyan interest.[129] But this did not foster an immediate recovery of Wesley's model of theological activity. The reason is that the major agenda of the studies of Wesley at this point was to emphasize his similarities to the Magisterial Reformers. Those pressing this agenda found it necessary to concede at the outset that Wesley was not a "real" theologian—like, say, Calvin![130] Their desire to recover Wesley's *doctrine* to proclaim, distracted them from the suggestion of Wesley's theological *practice* that awakening and nurturing Christian life requires much more than proclamation.[131]

It bears adding, however, that the neo-orthodox interest in Protestant roots was part of a larger concern with confessional identity and connections stirred by the emerging ecumenical dialogue. It was out of this broader dialogue that some theologians, notably Albert Outler, began after midcentury to encourage their fellow Methodists to recover their Wesleyan tradition in its own right, not filtered through a standardized Protestant screen.[132]

4. Process Theology. Before tracing further Outler's suggestion, a development in philosophical theology deserves brief notice. As the personalist metaphysic faded from favor at midcentury, a new philosophical theism, built on the metaphysic of Albert North Whitehead, assumed its place of prominence. While this "process theology" has not been as closely identified with Methodism as was Boston Personalism, it is striking how many Methodists have played a significant role in it— beginning with Schubert Ogden and John B. Cobb Jr.[133] Sparked in part by the renewed concern to connect with tradition, many of these Methodist participants have reflected on the similarities between their Wesleyan roots and their process commitments.[134] For one stream of process theologians (epitomized by Cobb) these similarities have grown to include an emphasis on renewing practical theological reflection in the church.[135] For the other major stream the defining task of a modern (apologetic) theology remains the construction of a philosophical metaphysic.[136]

5. The Challenge of Contextual Theologies. Their concern to construct such a metaphysic places the latter stream of process theologians in tension with what has emerged as the dominant trend in North American theology over the last thirty years. This trend is the insistence upon the inescapable contextuality of all theological reflection, in direct challenge to the earlier Enlightenment desire that all truth-claims be universally demonstrable and universally applicable. This Enlightenment desire has itself been contextualized, and its desirability called into question.[137]

One impetus toward the more positive valuation of the contextuality of theology was the ecumenical dialogue, as it struggled to discern the authentic relation of the various Christian traditions to one another. The most significant impetus, however, has been the entry of "other voices" into the enterprise of academic theology—which was previously a European and Euro-American male stronghold. This entry was accompanied with predictable ferment, which at times has served to exacerbate the separation of academic theology from the ongoing life of Christian communities.[138] But overall, as noted at the beginning of this study, the impact has been to cause a rethinking of the essential nature of theology, looking for ways to relate it more integrally to the praxis of specific communities of faith.

As the reigning model of academic theology has been called into question, Methodist theologians have been freed to reconsider earlier forms of theological activity. At least one, Thomas Oden, has seen the eclipse of the Enlightenment as justifying a return to producing a lengthy Systematic Theology.[139] By contrast, Albert Outler found this transition a fruitful time for reappraising Wesley's model of theological activity. At first, this meant only defending Wesley's "folk theology" as a legitimate supplement to academic theology.[140] Eventually, Outler was insisting that Wesley's theological model was an authentic and creative form in its own right, which need not be compared negatively to academic theology.[141] Some others have gone further yet, suggesting that Wesley's model should be valued (and recovered!) as a more primary expression of theology than what characterizes present reigning academic models.[142]

IV. Lessons Toward a Recovery of Practical Theology

With this renewed interest of professional theologians in Wesley's model of theological activity our historical investigation has come full circle. My remaining task is to suggest a few lessons from the saga just sketched for those hoping to recover something like Wesley's practical theology.

The first lesson is simply that we Methodists need to overcome a persistent bad conscience about our theological identity. For too long we have been preoccupied with winning theological respect by conforming to the academic expectations of Reformed Scholasticism, or continental Systematic Theology, or German liberalism with its *Glaubenslehre,* and so on. There are undeniably benefits that we have gained, and continue to gain, from dialogue with these and other theological movements, but we have typically failed to see (or offer) what valuable insights we might bring to such dialogue ourselves.

As an example of such an insight, the second lesson that I would suggest Methodists draw from their history is the importance of continually affirming that the life of the Christian community in the world (which
includes the academy), rather than the academy per se, is the proper
arena for defining the nature and task of theology. This identification
would certainly not rule out such activities as defenses of theological
methodology, apologetic dialogue with modern science, or construction
of philosophical metaphysics; but it would resist the current tendency in
the academy to identify theology almost exclusively with these under-
takings, devaluing traditional first-order activities aimed at nurturing
and shaping the Christian worldview in believers' lives.

There is another lesson that I believe the distinctive saga of Methodist
theology can offer to the entire Christian community. Wesley's emphasis on first-order activities that form the Christian worldview in believers' lives was integrally connected to his affectional moral psychology.
As this moral psychology faded in American Methodism, so did the
concern with many of these first-order activities. Under an intellectualist moral psychology it often seemed that all that was needed to "make"
Christians was a cogent rational summary of the Christian faith. And
under the optimistic (indeed, romantic) psychology of the Enlightenment, this could be reduced further to merely a reflective account that
raises consciousness of the native faith within each of us. If contemporary North American Methodist churches—and their Christian siblings—are to provide the character-forming influence that our culture so
badly needs, I am convinced that they must challenge these optimistic
and intellectualist psychologies that continue to permeate this culture.[143] We need to recover the insights into human nature embedded in
an affectional moral psychology like that of Wesley. Some progress in
this regard can be discerned in the renewed interest in character ethics,
but there is still much work to be done.[144]

The final lesson that I would mention relates to the structures of professional theological education. I am obviously sympathetic with the
current calls for theological education to focus more on producing
"practical theologians." The preceding historical survey should make it
clear that this shift in focus will necessarily involve changes in instruc-
tional curriculum and structures. For example, the current fragmentation in the self-understanding of the various theological disciplines can
only be overcome by curricular changes that encourage individual faculty members to interact across the range of disciplinary concerns and

the corporate faculty to teach in integrative situations.[145] Likewise, the distance between the academy and the church can be bridged only as the dimension of apprenticeship is made more integral to the structure of theological education. In part this will mean cooperation between schools and churches, as local congregations and pastors help mentor theological students.[146] But it should go further than this. Instructors in theological disciplines ought to be mentors in first-order theological activities as well. Their involvement in some form of first-order ministry is desirable for nurturing their sensitivity to the practical-theological dimension of their specialized discipline. Undoubtedly, many faculty have such involvement "on the side." But as long as it remains ancillary to the expectations and reward system, it is not likely to transform the underlying self-understanding of the theological academy. I believe that it is time to talk seriously about such notions as partial-load assignments or fully supported sabbaticals for theological faculty in parish and other ministry settings.[147] Maybe then we can counterbalance the current academic emphases with Wesley's emphasis on the pastor-theologian actively shepherding a community of faith in the world!

This is what I want to do!

J. Steven O'Malley

Steven O'Malley's essay represents an important contribution to American Methodist understanding of the way in which the Evangelical Association and the United Brethren in Christ dealt with doctrinal issues. He shows the way in which they shaped their Confession of Faith, and in turn how the Evangelical United Brethren tradition influenced contemporary United Methodism. Randy Maddox argued that American Methodism largely failed to tap its Wesleyan heritage. The church tended to ignore its inheritance, including the Articles of Religion, as revised by John Wesley. O'Malley suggests that within the distinctive German traditions that produced the EUB, there was continuing engagement with doctrinal issues because the General Conferences were empowered to revise the Confessions. This essay is a reminder to us that our doctrinal statements tell us a great deal about the communities that create and affirm them. O'Malley further argues that the distinctive contribution of the EUB Confession has not been sufficiently appreciated by United Methodists as they seek to better understand and interpret doctrinal standards.

Perhaps the major issue suggested by this essay has to do with the significance of doctrinal statements within Methodism. Are they normative because they are embraced within the constitutional part of the *Discipline*? How can we not acknowledge their normativity given the status of their location in the *Discipline*? Contemporary theologians differ in the use to which they put doctrinal statements. Are they historical artifacts of little interest or significance, or are they vital witnesses to the essentials of the Christian faith? How necessary are they for theology in our time? Is it worth it for the church to struggle with its theological heritage? Are there limits beyond which theological revision may not go? Historical understanding of the way in which the churches have dealt with these matters helps us to better deal with contemporary realities.

The Distinctive Witness of the Evangelical United Brethren Confession of Faith in Comparison with the Methodist Articles of Religion

J. Steven O'Malley

Introduction

The United Methodist *Discipline* has referred to the *Confession of Faith* (CF) of the former Evangelical United Brethren Church (EUB) as a document possessing distinctive ecclesial and soteriological traditions that reflect the "modified Calvinism of the *Heidelberg Catechism*" (1563).[1] However, little explanation is offered to indicate precisely what those distinctives constitute, or how its witness may be viewed as complementing the position represented by the Articles of Religion (AR) of the former Methodist Church.[2] In addition, discussions of United Methodist beliefs have often been limited to the AR,[3] thereby failing to engage the church with the witness of the CF, despite the fact that both documents carry the status of being normative statements of faith for the denomination.[4]

The CF is a 1962 revision of the *Confession of Faith* of the former Church of the United Brethren in Christ (UB/CF), dating from as early as 1789; and the *Articles of Faith* of the former Evangelical Church (AF/Ev.), dating from 1809. The CF of 1962 represented an effort to conflate the content of these prior documents, and to express that content in twentieth-century English. Both of these documents were originally written in German and were translated into English at later dates.

Bishop William Burt Pope's dictum that doctrine was neither foundational nor unimportant in the inception of Methodism[5] is probably applicable to the CF (and its predecessor documents) as well as to the AR. Nevertheless, both the CF and the AR provided a link with the apostolic, universal church. Both were received as summations of Scripture and as guidelines to its use. Both were means of affirming denominational self-identity and helped to undergird their spiritual life as the people of God. Both served as ordination and disciplinary standards for the denominations they served. Finally, both have made important legal contributions in church unions, such as those of 1939 (Methodist) and 1922 (Evangelical), 1946 (EUB), and 1968 (UMC).[6]

Denominational ambivalence toward both of these documents has been seen in the tendency to allow them to remain somewhat in the background of the life of the church, despite the fact that they have legally been held in perpetuity by action of the General Conferences.

In explaining this point, Stein cites two observations that would appear to be more applicable to the AR than to the CF. First, it is asserted that these documents have not commanded personal loyalty that springs from the heart of the faith.[7] While that may be an accurate description of their function in the later institutional life of the denominations, particularly in Methodism, it is probably less descriptive of the early history of the predecessor documents of the CF—the United Brethren *Confession of Faith* and the Evangelical *Articles of Faith*. Second, it is asserted that they omit several key doctrines that were essential to the early life of Methodism.[8] While this point is applicable to the AR, it does not apply to the CF, nor to its predecessor documents.[9] These considerations further underscore the need for a study that would address the question, What, then, has been the distinctive witness of the CF, and its predecessor documents, in the light of its particular historical and theological context?

The Origin and Development of the United Brethren Confession of Faith

The United Brethren in Christ, as well as the Evangelical Association, represented the largest North American denominations that were formed in response to the revival activity among German Americans who were primarily residing in Pennsylvania and Maryland during the Revolutionary War era and its aftermath.

It was presumed by the earliest UB historian[10] that the UB/CF was composed in its earliest form by Philip William Otterbein (1726–1813) for use in his Baltimore parish.[11] He had been reared and ordained to the ministry within the Pietistic center of the Reformed Church in Germany. Its principal symbol was the *Heidelberg Catechism* (1563), an irenic statement of faith that mediated between the high, supralapsarian Calvinism of Geneva and Lutheranism, particularly of the conciliatory, Melanchthonian variety.[12] The Herborn Academy, where he and five of his brothers were educated for the ministry, had become known for its anti-scholastic, life-centered approach to teaching the *Catechism* "without bondage to its words and form."[13]

At Herborn, Otterbein's principal theological textbook was a compend of the writings of the great federal theologians F. A. Lampe (d. 1729) and G. Vitringa (d. 1722). They interpreted the 129 questions and answers of the *Catechism* as a progressive order of salvation *(Heilsordnung),* whose steps must be ascended by every pilgrim-believer as a *scala paradisis.* Only by completing this ascent can full salvation be secured. Only then can one confess with personal assurance the affirmation of Question 1:

Q: What is your only comfort in life and in death?
A: That I belong to my faithful Savior Jesus Christ.

Lampe's commentary on the *Catechism,* his *Milch der Wahrheit,*[14] was in such popular use in the Rhineland and in the Middle Colonies of North America that it was often used by pastors and the heads of families in place of the *Catechism* itself. His interpretation relied on the federal theology of the Dutch theologian Johannes Cocceius (d. 1669), with emphasis given to the subjective personal benefit of the covenant relationship as it progressively unfolds in the life of the believer. Lampe linked this historical *(heilsgeschichtlich)* outlook with the imagery of bridal mysticism and millennialism—both themes that had previously been excluded from state church *(landeskirchlichen)* theologians. His work also showed the imprint of the "precisionism" of a Dutch biblical theologian, G. Vitringa (d. 1722), with emphasis given to a strict delineation between the converted and the unconverted, and to the use of small conventicles for the nurture of awakened church members within his parish at Bremen. All of these themes are reflected in the surviving records of P. W. Otterbein's ministry, that came to fruition in his American mission service (1752–1813), and especially in the Confession of Faith he prepared for use in his Baltimore parish.[15]

Although the Otterbein-Boehm movement can be traced from their historic meeting at Isaac Long's barn in 1767, formal organization did not begin until 1800.[16] In 1813, the *Confession,* along with the rules of discipline, were ordered published, and this task was completed in 1814. In this German manuscript version, it will be noted that the first article speaks in Nicene terms of the Godhead, but also gives attention to the activity as well as the being of God. He is known not only as Creator but also as the One who providentially orders all creaturely activity—

especially the historical affairs of humanity. The third paragraph likewise addresses the Person of the Holy Spirit in Nicene terms, with due
reference to the Western filioque clause. However, more attention is
devoted to the activity of the Holy Spirit, which is described largely in
terms of personal, entire sanctification. The second paragraph, on Jesus
Christ, speaks of him in the Chalcedonian terms of very God and man,
but once again, the emphasis falls upon his completed historical work as
Redeemer. Further, this statement asserts the universality of Christ's
atoning work, over against the limited atonement doctrine of the Canons
of Dort (1608). P. W. Otterbein had been obliged to give assent to the latter when he was examined by the Synod of Amsterdam as a young
missionary recruit to America. However, he later left written evidence
that he had distanced himself from that position.[17] Here is also to be
found an affirmation of the competence of the human will to embrace
the gospel of Christ, over against the high Calvinist tenet concerning
total human depravity. This emphasis enables Otterbein to embrace a
synergistic view of redemption that accords with Wesley's Anglican heritage. Unlike the Chalcedon Creed, his paragraph on God the Son has a
clear eschatological reference, as it summons hope in Christ's return as
judge on the last day. In his ministry, Otterbein explained this expectation in postmillennial terms, thereby showing the influence of Lampe.[18]

Paragraph 3, concerning the Holy Ghost, follows the traditional
Western view of his double procession (the filioque clause). However, as
in the discussion of the Father and the Son, more attention is given to
the Spirit's operation than his being. Unlike the *Apostles' Creed*, the
Confession links the Spirit's work to the sanctification of the believer.
This paragraph departs from older Reformed doctrine by clearly affirming entire sanctification as a necessity, and not as merely an option.
Although Otterbein had developed a personal friendship with Francis
Asbury by the 1780s, when the *Confession* was probably first composed,[19] there is little basis for concluding that this statement represented a Wesleyan doctrine of sanctification. The content of the statement is
a virtual restatement of the doctrine of sanctification that Otterbein had
exposited in his published sermon of 1760 on "The Salvation-Bringing
Incarnation." In that sermon, preached at York, Pennsylvania, several
years before the arrival of the first Methodists to North America,
Otterbein asked:

> But is it possible for a man to come to a complete victory over sin through
> Jesus Christ? (Answer) Who is mightier, Christ or the devil? In the gospel we

are given all kinds of divine strength for life and godliness (Titus 2:11-12). . . . Hence, . . . "I can do all things through Christ. . . ." Thus it is an obvious error to imagine that one cannot in this life be freed from sin.[20]

The most developed statement concerning the *ordo salutis* is in the fourth paragraph, where it is joined to the article concerning the Bible. Whereas the Methodist AR (Article 5) speaks of the Bible as containing "all things necessary to salvation," so that what is not "read therein" or "proved thereby," is not to be required to be believed; here it is presented as the "true way to holiness," and as a guide *(Richtschnur)* for the pilgrim-believer to follow, "under the influence of the Spirit of God."[21] Georg G. Otterbein had written that the Bible is the source of truth, and the *Catechism* directs us to that order of salvation *(Heilsordnung)* found within the Bible.[22] This order corresponds to the tripartite division of the *Heidelberg Catechism*, which affirms that the three things to be known (that is, to be appropriated into one's life) are as follows: first, the greatness of my misery (sin); second, the wonder of God's provision for my redemption in Jesus Christ; and third, the gratitude I owe God for such a redemption, which is the life of good works in joyful fulfillment of the law.[23] Following this *ordo*, the fourth article of the *Confession* explains the "true way" to our salvation contained in the Bible. These steps are repentance, faith in Christ, forgiveness, and the acceptance of discipleship *(Nachfolge Christi)*. This *ordo* is restated in Article 5, which summarizes the content of the biblical revelation as "the fall in Adam and salvation through Jesus Christ," and this is identified as the message of the Christian mission to the entire world. This missionary impulse was first brought home to Otterbein at Herborn, where he had been recruited in 1752 as a missionary to the New World.

The last article concerns the "outward signs and ordinances," which are briefly cited as baptism and the "remembrance of the Lord" in the Lord's Supper, both of which are "recommended." In addition, the washing of feet is provided for because of the prevalence of Mennonites in their early fellowship.

This UB Confession was terse, earthy, and suited for an informal fellowship of "awakened" German revival preachers. There is no reference to "Church" *(Kirche)*, seeing that the movement had adopted the title of "United Brotherhood in Christ Jesus."[24] "Church" carried the negative connotation of the persecuting state churches of Europe. The early UB minutes spoke of their identity as an "unpartisan" *(unparteiische)* brotherhood, "free from sin and a party spirit."[25]

They conceived of this fellowship as a new redemptive order that was breaking into this fallen world, as an end-time event. This new order had been dramatically enacted in Otterbein's exclamation "wir sind Brüder" to the startled Mennonite, Martin Boehm, at the Long's barn meeting on Pentecost, 1767. Their credo brought together elements of classical Christian doctrine (e.g., the statements on the Trinity and Christology) with a Reformed Pietist soteriology. Further, it included aspects of Anabaptist theology (e.g., the theme of "Nachfolge Christi" and the washing of feet). Baptism and the Lord's Supper were explained with sufficient breadth to be acceptable to the "awakened" from both the Mennonite and the Reformed backgrounds.[26]

Whereas this early CF of the United Brethren was terse, less technical, and earthy in its expressions, the AR was formal, more reflective of the technical language of the ecumenical creeds, and less capable of being understood by the lay folk who would constitute the heart of the M.E. Church. The CF was appropriate for a movement of awakening that did not at first aspire to attain a full-blown ecclesiastical status.[27] The AR, as abridged by John Wesley from the 39 Anglican Articles of Religion, was intended for a movement that was about to become a church, and an "Episcopal" one at that! In addition, the CF was written in the first person plural, indicating that it was a normative statement, commanding personal loyalty at the heart of their faith. The AR, written in the more impersonal third person, was intended to define the outer perimeters within which faith and order and life and work could proceed.

The early CF and the AR share much common ground, especially in soteriology, but each has its own distinctive set of factors that influenced its formation. For the CF, these factors included the irenic Reformed theology of the *Heidelberg Catechism*, reshaped by the Pietists' special soteriological interests, Anabaptist theology, and the ethos of German-American revivalism. As A. W. Drury, leading UB historian of the last century, stated, "The Confession was not framed directly out of any existing creed, but was developed and compacted by a mind familiar with the form and content of the ancient creeds."[28] For the AR, the chief constitutive factor was John Wesley's commitment to the tradition of Anglican theology and episcopal polity. Hence, the AR retains a clearer balance between catholic and evangelical tendencies. Wesley had hoped that the latter would be augmented by his inclusion of his *Sermons* and *Notes*, although these did not attain the same normative status as did the AR.[29]

In 1815, the early CF was revised and enlarged by the first General Conference (UB), which then represented the Eastern and the Miami annual conferences. The minutes stated that "The Confession of Faith (*Glaubenslehre*) and the Discipline (*Zuchtordnung*) were considered; somewhat enlarged, some things omitted; on the whole improved, and ordered printed."[30] This revised CF, that appeared in the first published *Discipline* of 1816, contained several additions that strengthened its exposition of classical Christian doctrine.

In paragraph one, the word *triune* was added before "God created heaven and earth." The discussion of the Incarnation on paragraph two is enlarged by adding "that He by the Holy Ghost assumed his human nature." This contains an apparent trace of the Mennonite doctrine in which, according to Menno Simons, "the human nature of Christ was formed immediately by God through the Holy Ghost in the womb of the Virgin Mary."[31] The likelihood of such an influence is attested by the fact that the former Mennonite element probably represented the largest contingency in the early United Brethren, including two of the first three bishops (Boehm and Christian Newcomer). The problem of Menno's Christology was its tendency toward Docetism, which corresponded to his advocacy of a strict separation between the "true church" and the world. Among the early United Brethren (and Evangelicals) there was a pronounced emphasis upon avoidance of "worldly" behavior,[32] but not so much as a precondition for salvation as a testimony to the fact that one's identity was no longer with this world but with the Savior who had been encountered in the new birth.

Another addition that appeared in the second paragraph of the revised 1816 CF is the assertion that salvation depends not simply upon their will (1815) but upon whether "they with faith in him, accept the grace proffered in Jesus."[33] This new construction is less susceptible of being interpreted in a Pelagian manner and is now more compatible with a doctrine of prevenient grace, enabling the response of the will to Christ. The new statement concerning Christ's continuing intercession at the right hand of the Father, a theme omitted from the AR, actually strengthens the Reformed influence that comes from the *Heidelberg Catechism*.[34]

A significant alteration is to be found in paragraph three of the revised CF, where the divine Personhood of the Holy Spirit is accentuated, and then a new description is given of the *ordo salutis* that is actualized in the believer through the Holy Spirit. Whereas the original CF spoke only of the Spirit's sanctifying work, balanced attention is now given to justification and sanctification, although the explicit discussion of the need for entire sanctification, which was prominent in the 1814 text, has by 1816 fully disappeared! In its place, there is a reference to the Augustinian theme of illumination, as being the basic sign of the Spirit's indwelling presence within the believer.[35]

The fourth paragraph, concerning a "holy church," is a wholly new entry in 1816. It follows the wording of the Apostles' Creed, omitting the adjective "catholic," and it follows the precedent of Question 54 of the *Heidelberg Catechism*.[36] As Drury noted, the doctrinal references in this paragraph are titles for doctrines rather than expressions of particular doctrines.[37] The 1814 *Confession* still adhered to the pre-ecclesial, lay-movement phase of the United Brethren movement, whose participants hoped to retain their relationship with their traditional church traditions while simultaneously sharing in a "higher unity in Christ" by virtue of the new birth.[38]

After the affirmation of the Bible as the "true way" to our salvation (paragraph 5), the *ordo salutis* has been altered in the 1816 text. The original statement placed repentance before faith, but now it is "faith in Jesus Christ, [and] true penitence." The revised statement adheres to Calvin's *ordo*, which reverses the Roman Catholic *ordo salutis*, inherent in penance, by stressing the primacy of the Word in awakening saving faith, which is followed by lifelong repentance.[39]

In the last paragraph, the sacraments are no longer merely "recommended," but rather they are "to be in use in all Christian societies," and their obligatory nature is "according to the command of the Lord Jesus." They are also now designated as "means of grace," and not merely "signs and ordinances" (1814 text). These changes reflect the growing denominational self-consciousness among the United Brethren. The mode of administering both baptism and the Lord's Supper is left "to the judgment of every one."[40] The recognition of a plurality of modes of baptism had been *de facto* in operation from the beginning, as a reflection of the differences between the Otterbein (Reformed) and Boehm (Mennonite) segments of the movement. What was more important was the inward baptism in the Holy Spirit, which could be externally expressed in a variety of modes.[41]

The 1817 revision altered the reading of the paragraph on the Holy Ghost to delete the filioque clause and to add an allusion to John 16:13 that affirmed "he comforts the faithful and guides them into all truth."[42]

With this addition, the statement regarding the Spirit's work of justifying and sanctifying is omitted.

After 1817, the changes made were fewer and less substantial. In 1825, a statement was adopted that forbade preachers to disallow the mode of baptism used by their fellow preachers.[43] The 1833 General Conference forbade further changes either in the CF or the rules of discipline.[44] Since it was left to the secretary of the General Conference to record any revisions in the conference minutes, and then to include these in the published *Discipline,* that official actually served as the authorized reviser of the CF.[45] It was perhaps due to the power of the secretary that additional minor alterations occurred in the CF in 1845 (in the German CF) and 1857 (in the English edition). By the latter date, English had become the prevailing language in conference sessions.

In the latter half of the nineteenth century, two divergent schools of interpreting the CF and the church constitution appeared. The so-called "liberal" school spoke disparagingly of the irregular manner in which changes in the CF and the constitution had been made. The historian A. W. Drury, representing that faction, criticized the way in which motions to amend these documents were made on the floor of General Conference until 1857.[46] The CF and the constitution were each read aloud by a designated person and amendments were proposed and adopted in the course of the reading. That this practice violated the restrictive rule of 1833 is an indication of the loose regard for rules of order among the early United Brethren.[47] In 1861 and 1865 the CF and the constitution were referred to a committee on revision, but it appears that their recommendations were not permitted to come before the General Conferences for a vote. No consideration of the question of revision was permitted between 1869 and 1885. Drury concluded that this hesitancy was due to a fear that changes would be made in the long-revered stand of opposition to secret societies. That stand, together with a long-standing antislavery stance,[48] reflects the ecclesial understanding of the early United Brethren: they were to remain an "unpartisan" *(unparteiische)* fellowship, and not become a new sect.[49] There were to be no divisions among the members of the Brotherhood, either because of secret society (especially Masonic) oaths, or because of the enslavement of fellow human beings by any member of the Brotherhood.[50]

Those who desired to retain the early, noncompromising stance on these matters organized themselves as the so-called "radical" United Brethren, under the leadership of Bishop Milton Wright (1828–1917), the father of the Wright brothers of aviation fame. In 1885, the liberal wing of the General Conference proposed creating a "church commission" of twenty-seven persons (clergy and lay) to prepare a new constitution and a new CF. The constitutional change was necessary for amending the prohibition against secret societies, but the proposed revision of the CF came as a surprise to the radical leaders, who perceived that the CF issue was raised to obscure the liberals' true agenda of abolishing the rule on secrecy.[51]

The constitutional crisis came to a head at the General Conference of 1889, when a revised and greatly expanded CF and church constitution were approved following a referendum of the members of the annual conferences. The constitution was ambiguous in its stipulation that a change in the constitution and the Confession required a two-thirds approval of the membership. Did that mean two-thirds of the total membership or two-thirds of the voting church members? The 1889 General Conference accepted the latter option and when 46,900 out of 54,250 voting members approved the revised documents (from a total church membership of some 200,000), these were authorized by the General Conference.[52] The minority or "radical" faction, led by Bishop Wright, withdrew to form The Church of the United Brethren in Christ, Old Constitution.

Both sides appealed to different segments of United Brethren tradition to make their case. Wright appealed to the "old standards" over against the rise of "prosperity" Christians, and he saw a perverse collusion between liberal theology, lax and accommodationist ethics, and Freemasonry. The "old" constitution of 1841, which had banned secret societies, was now being overturned. The "liberal" wing had proposed a substantial revision of the Confession of Faith, as well as a new constitution they thought was suitable for a more urbane, cosmopolitan age. They had forced the issue by interpreting the "two-thirds majority" provision of the old constitution to mean two-thirds of all voting members in a church referendum, and not two-thirds of the total membership.[53] The "old" CF taught the necessity of faith, repentance, regeneration, and an indwelling Savior, but Wright perceived that Freemasonry was teaching salvation by charitable works.[54] He believed Christ's kingdom would appear on earth, in a postmillennial manner, as the reign of righteousness on earth through the moral impact of regenerated Christians. They would participate in a "universal Pentecost" that would complete the world's salvation and thus usher in the

Millennium."[55] Interestingly, one of the few extant letters of Philip William Otterbein was in Wright's possession—a letter on the millennium, in which Otterbein stated that "there is in prospect a more glorious state of the church than ever has been, and this we call the millennium."[56] Not only was there congruence between the postmillennialism of Otterbein and Wright, there was also similarity between Otterbein's call for a nonsectarian, nonpartisan (*unparteiisch*) fellowship of brethren united in Christ and Wright's continuing stand against secret societies.

Nevertheless, the liberal majority among the United Brethren was also developing its version of interpreting the CF and the history of its interpretation. Drury, who was perhaps its leading academic spokesman, argued that a major revision of the CF was needed because (a) most of the alterations made in the CF after 1815 were detrimental and not helpful, and this was because "the mixed and untrained elements, often influenced by narrow prejudices, that came into control of things about 1815, were not suited to making improvements in the creed."[57] It is indeed true that those UB leaders who followed Otterbein lacked his extensive theological training since they were products of the frontier revivals, and they generally stood opposed to the formal training of preachers. (b) The initial use of the German language, followed by a stressful transition to English, further impeded progress in transmitting the CF. (c) Reverence for these "fathers" of the church ought not prevent us from realizing that, being "unlearned men," they were incapable of "anticipating the wants of the future" and that their method of revising the CF [i.e., by simply approving amendments offered from the conference floor] was "wholly unfavorable." (d) Drury further argued that revision of the CF and constitution was needed because of the unclear "legal character" of the CF. Although the church has never been "latitudinarian in doctrine, it never by any authoritative act determined the use to be made of the Confession, or the extent to which subjection to its teachings was required."[58]

Like the Methodist AR, the UB/CF never required the formal consent of the laity, for whom there was only the requirement of an affirmative response to the question, "Do you believe the Bible to be the Word of God?" Only twice were questions concerning the CF for clergy introduced into the *Discipline*.[59] Otherwise, there was no required subscription to any of its doctrinal statements, save this general accommodation that has appeared in every UB *Discipline* since 1815:

> After mature deliberation, they [members of the Conference of 1815] presented to their brethren a *Discipline* containing the doctrines and rules of the

church, desiring that they, together with the Word of God, should be strictly observed.[60]

Finally, liberal UB spokesmen contended that the "moral force" of the old CF, while generally felt, was never intentionally communicated. To the year 1889, no exposition of it had been attempted, nor was it used in instruction, except when a preacher occasionally read from it in a service of worship. In the few instances where preachers were expelled on grounds of doctrinal heresy, the CF was not sufficiently explicit to serve as a guide in assessing the doctrinal view that was under examination.[61]

Hence, the liberal party concluded that the revisions of the CF and the constitution of 1889 were justified and necessary. The restrictive rule contained in the constitution of 1841 had stipulated that the General Conference could not "change or do away with the Confession of Faith as it now stands,"[62] but this same constitution had stipulated the "two-thirds" proviso, which was retained in the revised constitution adopted in 1889. To be sure, the liberals were interpreting the two-thirds to refer to those voting, and not the total membership. These liberals appealed also for precedent to the Methodist Episcopal Church, which Drury argues had "twice amended the general rules," under a provision for changing the restrictive rules themselves.[63]

These arguments were intended by the liberals to buttress their case for revising an "unserviceable" and neglected CF, "along with the demands of our times and a living Christianity."[64] Conservatives like Wright viewed such arguments as merely foil for an effort to revoke the secret society clause. At least one liberal spokesman was candid enough to address this issue explicitly. In an article on Philip William Otterbein, which also appeared in the *UB Quarterly Review*, E. W. Curtis criticized the UB founder for his "antisecrecy opinions," whereby

for three quarters of a century, members of secret orders were not admitted into the fellowship of this Church. This together with the lack of organization and the transition from the German to the English, retarded our progress so that many other denominations have outgrown us. Frequently our ministers have gone into new communities and held great revival meetings with large numbers of converts, nearly all of whom would become members of other churches. The converts were members of secret orders and could not unite with us. In this we followed Otterbein too long . . . in 1889 . . . the General Conference declared that old law repealed by the general vote of all the members of the denomination. Since that time, we are prospering generally in the cities and towns, and few religious bodies are growing so rapidly. Now we usually receive our converts into the Church. We string the fish we catch. We shock our wheat. It took nearly a century to correct the mistake.[65]

Hence, the liberals were willing to critique their founder, and the old standards, for the sake of success. For them, the early UB "unsectarian" *(unparteiisch)* ideal meant an open attitude toward persons who sought regeneration in Christ, regardless of their masonic preferences. For them, this attitude was in accord with the spirit of Otterbein, whose "union revival meetings"[66] were advocated in the days "when sectarian walls were as high and immovable as the Alleghenies."[67] For them such an outlook would best preserve the intent of the affirmation in the old CF, "that all men through [Christ] may be saved if they will."[68]

An examination of the new CF, which was adopted at the cost of a denominational schism in 1889, will indicate the extent to which the new standard departed from the CF of 1841, which had remained in use.[69] In place of the original six paragraphs, the new CF contained thirteen articles. The articles on the Trinity and creation are virtually unchanged. Article III on Jesus Christ adds a statement on Christ's incarnation through Mary. Article IV on the Holy Ghost balances the previous emphasis on his "comforting" role (an allusion to Question 1 of the *Heidelberg Catechism*) with his convicting activity: "He convinces the world of sin, of righteousness, and of judgment." Article V on the Holy Scriptures is shortened by the removal of the *ordo salutis*, which stood at the close of that paragraph in the older CF. That *ordo* had, in turn, reflected the structure of the *Heidelberg Catechism*, as previously noted. The effect is to lessen the connection between the Bible as the "guidebook" for the pilgrim and the actual steps of faith, repentance, forgiveness, and discipleship. The sixth article, on the Church, is an expanded article that identifies it as the *communio sanctorum*, where the marks of Word and sacraments are present and its purpose in worship, nurture, and mission is recognized. The discussion of the sacraments (Article VII) remains brief, with emphasis given to the respect for "individual judgment" with regard to the mode of baptism, the manner of observing the Lord's Supper, and the example of foot washing. Significantly, the baptism of children is left to parental judgment. The new articles (VIII to XI) develop the aspects of the *ordo salutis* that had previously appeared in Article V: depravity, justification, regeneration and adoption, sanctification. Article XII (Of the Christian Sabbath) locates within the CF an issue that had previously been discussed under the "duties of church members."[70] The final article ("Of the Future State") continues the theme of the general resurrection and judgment, which had been introduced in the article on Christology (Article III).[71]

In retrospect, the CF reflects some of the catholic themes that are prominent in the AR, especially in the doctrines of the Trinity, Christology, and human depravity. It also reflects certain of the Reformation emphases, which are also found in the AR, particularly in the authority of Scripture and in the doctrine of justification. In those areas, both documents bear the imprint of the *Augsburg Confession* (1530 and 1540), which first gave those Protestant themes their definitive form. However, as H. M. DuBose recognized,[72] the AR are not particularly Methodist in content, since they represent John Wesley's abridgment of Cranmer's Thirty-nine Articles as intended for the newly constituted Methodist Episcopal Church.[73] What is distinctive about the CF of the United Brethren is the presence of those unmistakable traces of the *ordo salutis* of the *Heidelberg Catechism*, as interpreted through the step-wise "Heilsordnung" of the Reformed Pietists (Lampe and Otterbein). In addition, there are telltale marks of an Anabaptist-Mennonite ethos, including references to discipleship *(Nachfolge Christi)* and foot washing.[74]

The Origin and Development of the Evangelical Articles of Faith

Less attention will be given to the early history and content of the AF insofar as it represented a German translation of the Methodist AR, with certain deletions and two important additions. Its intended author was Jacob Albright (1759–1808), the founder of the *Evangelische Gemeinschaft* (Evangelical Association), since he was directed by the conference of 1807 to prepare a formal *Discipline* for the new body. By this time, Albright, a Pennsylvania-German farmer and tilemaker, had undergone a profound conversion through the ministry of a U.B. lay preacher and a Methodist class leader.[75] His prayerful supplications that God would send evangelists to work among the Germans resulted in his discovery of his own call to preach in 1791, despite his lack of education or recognition by any existing church body.[76] This call had resulted in Albright's ordination in 1803 by the resolution of his converts (without ecclesial ritual), and his election as bishop in 1807.[77]

Albright had preferred the Methodist episcopal plan of church order,[78] and so it is not unusual that its *Discipline* would be the model used by Albright's capable assistant, George Miller (1774–1816), to whom fell the task that had been assigned to Albright after that founder's death the following spring. Miller adopted the Methodist *Discipline* and AR as they had been rendered into German by a physician, Dr. Ignatius Römer of Middletown, Pennsylvania.[79] After considerable alterations of the *Discipline,* as well as less extensive changes in the AR, the Evangelical *Discipline* was prepared and adopted by the annual conference of 1809.[80] Without the work of Miller, the literary record of the beginnings of the Evangelical Association would be virtually nonexistent. His *Thaetiges Christenthum* (*Practical Christianity,* 1814) consists of a practical exposition of the early doctrinal emphases and worship life of the Evangelicals.[81]

In its content, the AF has reduced the twenty-five Articles of Religion to nineteen articles. Six polemical articles against earlier Roman Catholic practices were deleted, plus one that had been directed against the Anabaptists.[82] Then, one article (XIX) is added, "Of the Last Judgment," which was probably derived from the Lutheran *Augsburg Confession.* Inexplicably, the AR fails to devote an article to eschatology. The AF deletes certain names and technical terms used in the AR, such as "Pelagians" (AR Article VII); and "transubstantiation" (AR Article XVII).

The most noteworthy addition to the AF is the extended, six-page supplement to the AF in the second chapter, entitled "The Doctrine of Entire Sanctification and Christian Perfection," which is almost as long as the first nineteen Articles together. The precise source of this essay is uncertain.[83] It is not to be found either in the English Methodist *Discipline,* nor in Römer's German text. In content, it appears to paraphrase themes found in Wesley's and Fletcher's discussion in their doctrinal essays on Christian perfection, which Miller had read and rendered in part into English.[84] It is also instructive to read this chapter in the German in the context of Miller's discussion in his *Thuäetiges Christenthum,* which shows a common usage of terms that are characteristic of the older German Pietists, whose literature was plentiful in the environment of Pennsylvania in 1800.[85]

For example, there is a pronounced use of such expressions as "one must be grounded deeply in God, and love him in truth from the depths of one's heart, soul, and all one's powers."[86] To be "grounded" in God from the "depths of the soul" is a clear reflection of the thought and language of the Reformed Pietist Gerhard Tersteegen, and of the older tradition of Rhineland mysticism rooted in Tauler.[87] This influence continues to be evident as Miller describes Christian perfection as the result of "true wayfaring and following after the Lamb," until it is brought to fruition through "the powerful influence of grace from the divine Spirit in the soul."[88]

The issue at stake here deserves our special consideration. The *Discipline* was a book read devotionally in homes, along with the hymnal and Bible. As long as it was being read in the German, the essentially Wesleyan doctrine of sanctification was being communicated in the genre of German Pietism. When Evangelicals changed to the use of English, which slowly took place during the last half of the century, Evangelicals were belatedly introduced to a more "Wesleyan" portrayal of that doctrine. Likewise, they were now brought to terms with the catholic language of the theological, christological, and anthropological articles in the AR, which was also part of the Methodist legacy to the Evangelicals. And yet, there remained something of the older Pietist ethos that was virtually inbred into the lives of later generations of Evangelicals, who also clung to their German ethos much longer than did the United Brethren.[89]

This German ethos was further strengthened by the Evangelicals' decision to return to the "Fatherland," by establishing in 1850 a strong mission effort in Germany. There a meeting took place between the spirituality of German-American Evangelical missionaries, who entered this field (including Sebastian Kurz, J. C. Link, J. P. Wolpert, and others) with the indigenous Pietist-influenced communities of Württemberg, where the message of these Albright preachers was first heard in Europe. The result of this interaction was a new breed of spirituality, which was exemplified by a generation of indigenous Evangelical leaders in Germany and Switzerland. The outstanding figure in this new leadership was Gottlob Füßle, hymnwriter and church editor in Stuttgart from 1868 to 1916. His exposition of the Evangelical doctrine of entire sanctification was unmistakably couched in the terminology of the German Pietists, notably Tersteegen.[90]

The doctrine of entire sanctification was prominent in the preaching of Evangelical itinerants from the early days of Albright and Miller. It was the theme that became grandly incarnated in the prodigious itinerant ministry of the denomination's preeminent missionary bishop, John

Seybert (1791–1860), as represented in his extensive (and yet unpublished!) *Journal*.[91]

In the latter half of the nineteenth century, Evangelicals became embroiled in internal debate and division (1891), in which the doctrine of entire sanctification was a major issue of contention. It erupted in 1856 when a Pennsylvania presiding elder named Solomon Neitz (1821–85),[92] published a pamphlet entitled "Christian Sanctification according to Apostolic Teaching." It was a momentous event for two reasons. First, it rebutted an extreme article that had appeared in the church paper, *Der Christiliche Botschafter*. This anonymous article (thought to be the work of W. W. Orwig) had boldly asserted that persons who had been justified but not entirely sanctified would be eternally lost.[93] Second, in refuting this position, Neitz's article essentially rejected the Wesleyan position reflected in the Evangelical *Discipline* by denying the possibility of Christian perfection, arguing instead that sanctification, like justification, is gratuitously imputed to a believer but it is never imparted, nor is there ever an annihilation of the root of sin in the believer.[94]

After open debate erupted in 1859 on the floor of the East Pennsylvania Conference between the principals, Orwig and Neitz, the matter was carried by Orwig to the General Conference of that year. Although a resolution was passed declaring that Neitz was not in harmony with the position of the denomination, he was not censured—an omission that served to fuel the controversy.

The cleavage that had erupted eventually contributed to the division of the denomination in 1891 and the adoption of differing Articles of Faith by each of the two rival bodies. The issues that contributed to this division were complex, involving also the use of German versus English, and personal disputes among leaders.[95] Briefly, Orwig was elected bishop in 1859, but Neitz's supporters prevented Orwig's reelection in 1863. However, they were unable to receive secure the election of Neitz himself. Rather, a young Orwig supporter from Illinois, J. J. Esher, was elected, and he now became the aggressive spokesman for the Evangelical (or Wesleyan) doctrine of sanctification. The controversy between Orwig and Neitz erupted again in the General Conference of 1867, with the bishops joined in opposition to Neitz.[96] Church editor Rudolph Dubs was soon drawn into the fray due to his printing of a piece by Neitz that satirized his opponents.[97] Of the three new bishops elected in the 1870s, two (Reuben Yeakel and Thomas Bowman) were allied to Esher and were also antagonistic toward the third, the former pro-Neitz church editor, Rudolph Dubs. A series of church trials began in 1889, with the suspension of Bishop Dubs being one outcome.

By 1891, when two rival General Conferences were convened,[98] personal antagonisms overshadowed the issue of sanctification as a basis for contention. These rivalries had polarized the clergy and much of the laity. As congregations and conferences divided, the trust clause of the Evangelical Association had been upheld in church and civil courts, with the result that the pro-Dubs minority (representing two-fifths of the total membership) reorganized on a more congregational basis as the United Evangelical Church.[99] It is noteworthy for this study that the new AF adopted by the latter body significantly revised and expanded the earlier AF of the Evangelical Association. As Harold Scanlin has shown in a definitive article,[100] the 25 Articles in the new United Evangelical AF were taken practically verbatim from the *Doctrines of American Methodism* (1887) of Milton S. Terry, who was then Professor of Theology at Garrett Biblical Institute near Naperville, Illinois, where the new church organized and adopted its AF and *Discipline* in 1894. The six new articles included one emphasizing a distinctive Wesleyan doctrine (No. 10, "Of the Witness of the Spirit"), two articles emphasizing distinctives of the new polity of this church (No. 20, "Of the Ministry," and No. 23, "Of Church Polity"), and one reflecting Terry's missional emphasis (No. 25, "Of the Evangelization of the World").[101] The new essay on entire sanctification, which was in substantial agreement with its antecedent, is dominated by an extended citation from Wesley's treatise on *Christian Perfection*.[102]

For the reasons cited, it may be argued that the United Evangelical Church was amenable to more innovative views of church authority and doctrinal expression and, as Heisey has shown, to a greater use of English rather than German.[103] In support of the latter point, it may be noted that the major exposition of the older statement on sanctification in the Evangelical Association was contained in a three-volume systematic theology written in German by Bishop Esher after the division.[104] It was never translated into English.

These two divisions of the denomination were reunited in 1922, in light of the virtual cessation of the use of German in the era of World War I and the passing of the older leaders. Three significant doctrinal additions were now made to the *Discipline* of the newly constituted Evangelical Church. Articles 9-11 of the former United Evangelical AF, which reflected the words of Terry, were now printed at the head of chapter 2, which was the essay on Christian perfection that followed the 19 Articles of Faith (chapter 1). These articles concern regeneration (Article 9), the witness of the Spirit (Article 10), and sanctification (Article 11). The title of the chapter has changed from "The Doctrine of Entire Sanctification and Christian Perfection" to "The Doctrines of Regeneration, Sanctification, and Christian Perfection"—the doctrine of the witness of the Spirit being presented as an aspect of regeneration.[105]

In retrospect, the Evangelical AF is not so much the creative mix of diverse traditions (as was the CF of the United Brethren). It mediated the catholic/evangelical balance of Anglican tradition in the German idiom, plus an article on the Last Judgment. This was supplemented by an essay that summarized the distinctive features of the Wesleyan *ordo salutis*, again mediated through a German—and especially a German Pietist—idiom. The later English version of the AF included a supplement, contributed by the United Evangelical faction, which has been traced to the thought of Methodist theologian Milton Terry.

The Formation of the Confession of Faith of the Evangelical United Brethren Church

The uniting General Conference of 1946, which joined the Evangelical Church to the Church of the United Brethren in Christ, initially decided to publish the doctrinal standards of the two former denominations side by side in the *Discipline* of the new church.[106] This *Discipline* did not provide restrictive rules forbidding alterations or deletions from the doctrinal standards, as was the case in the Methodist *Discipline*. Unlike the latter, there was no comprehensive constitution. Instead, there were a series of constitutions for the several structures and agencies of the denomination, and each constitution typically concluded with the statement "This constitution can be amended only by the General Conference."[107]

It was on this basis that the 1958 General Conference authorized the Board of Bishops "to conduct a study of the respective confession of faith of the two former communions, with a view to combining both statements into a unified creedal statement of belief."[108] This action was predicated on the assumption that the former communions "were American born with their origins in a rebirth of spirit and not in a theological revolt"[109] and that "In all the basic and enduring elements of faith and ecclesiastical organization they are alike."[110] The authors of the revised CF were charged not to alter the content of either of the preceding doctrinal standards.[111] They were to represent its content in an integrated manner, restated in contemporary language. It was further decided to continue the first person plural, confessional format of the United Brethren CF.

The CF adopted at the 1962 General Conference in Grand Rapids, Michigan, was the result of this project. It was declared to be "a continuance of" and the essential equivalence of the predecessor doctrinal statements.[112] The form and content of those earlier standards are visibly reflected in the new document.[113]

Vestiges of the *ordo salutis* of the United Brethren CF, which has been traced by way of Otterbein through the Reformed Pietists, to the *Heidelberg Catechism,* are apparent in the sequence of "Reconciliation Through Christ" (Article 8), "Justification and Regeneration" (Article 9), "Good Works" (Article 10), and "Sanctification and Christian Perfection" (Article 11).[114] Article 8 (EUB/CF) affirms that Christ's death is "sufficient for the sins of the whole world," reflecting Article 3 (UB/CF 1889), that Christ "is the Savior and Mediator of the whole human race." Article 9 (EUB/CF) alludes to the "federal" theme[115] of the renewal of the "imago Dei" through our regeneration in Christ, which is taken from Article 10 (UB/CF 1889). To say that the purpose of regeneration and adoption is for the believer to be "enabled to serve God with the will and the affections" recalls Part III of the *Heidelberg Catechism* as well as Article 10 (UB/CF 1889).[116] This similarity to that *Catechism* is strengthened by the statement that good works necessarily "spring from a true and living faith," which is taken from Article 9 (UB/CF 1889). Sanctification (Article 11, EUB/CF) is portrayed in the language of the pilgrim ascending the *Heilsordnung,* when it states that the reborn are "enabled . . . to strive for holiness without which no one will see the Lord." This is comparable to Article 11 (UB/CF 1889).[117]

Other similarities to the CF of the United Brethren are found in Article 3 (EUB/CF), where the convicting, comforting, and guiding work of the Holy Spirit is affirmed (see Article 4, UB/CF 1889). The statement on the Holy Scriptures (Article 5, EUB/CF) again recalls the older *Heilsordnung* theme, in that the Bible "reveals the only true way to our salvation," and hence is our "only rule and guide in faith and practice." The older UB/CF had spoken of the Bible as the guidepost ("Richtschnur") for the believer to follow as a pilgrim toward God's Kingdom (see also Article

5, UB/CF 1889).[118] Also, the church (Article 5, EUB/CF) is defined in terms of the universal spiritual body of persons regenerated in Christ (compare with Article 6, UB/CF). By contrast, the AR (Article 13) defines the church, from the Anglican parish perspective, as the visible congregation of believers. Finally, Article 14 on the Lord's Day (EUB/CF), another reflection of the Pietist legacy, is the successor to Article 12 ("Of the Christian Sabbath," UB/CF 1889).

The legacy of the Evangelical AF is most evident in the discussion of "Sanctification and Christian Perfection" in Article 11 (EUB/CF), although the original twelve-paragraph discussion is now reduced to three paragraphs in this Article. Since the AR contains only the brief supplemental paragraph on sanctification, which was introduced through the Methodist Protestants in 1939, EUB Article 11 stands as the most explicit discussion of the historic doctrine of sanctification in the current (1992) United Methodist *Discipline*.[119]

Other influences from the AF are infusions of its Anglican terminology, that served to enhance the compatibility between the EUB/CF and the theological tradition of Methodism, with whom the EUB would unite in only six years after the adoption of the 1962 CF. Instances of Anglican influence, by way of the Methodist AR and the Evangelical AF, are primarily in the areas of the doctrine of the Trinity (Articles 1-4, EUB/CF, compare to Articles 1-4 of the AF), original sin (Article 7, EUB/CF and Article 7 AF), and the sacraments (Article 6, EUB/CF and Article 14, AF). However, the second paragraph of Article 6 (EUB/CF), concerning the need for baptized children to be "led to personal acceptance of Christ and by profession of faith confirm their baptism" serves to reinforce the EUB revivalist heritage, whereby the experience of the new birth, and not baptism per se, is the sine qua non of Christian identity.[120] The EUB Articles on worship (13), property (15), and government (16) are also derived from the AR and the AF (16, 17, and 18). The distinctive AF article on the last judgment (19) is carried over as Article 12 in the EUB/CF.

Conclusion

The attempt of the theological study commission of 1968–72 to address United Methodist ambivalence toward its doctrinal distinctives has itself come under criticism. Its effort to define *theology* as being primarily a never-ending dialogical activity has been countered by the criticism that disregard of the normative importance of the foundational documents can only encourage instability in the life of the church.[121] This concern, expressed in 1976, seems to have been warranted by the subsequent decline of the denomination in numerical terms as well as in its overall vitality. In this situation, the EUB Confession of Faith exists as the lesser known and underutilized of our two foundational statements.

This study represents possibly the first attempt to substantiate in what way the EUB/CF was the successor to the UB/CF and the AF, not just in legal terms but in light of its theological content and historico-religious ethos. The AF of the Evangelical Church had a lifespan of 137 years. The life of the CF of the United Brethren in Christ was 131 years. By contrast, the EUB/CF had a lifespan of only 6 years until the denomination it represented was united with its Methodist counterpart to create a new communion. For its part, the Methodist AR has had a continuous life since 1784.

The tendency for United Methodists to overlook the CF in discussions of their doctrinal standards has been shortsighted for at least two reasons. One, it has not enabled them to recognize the broader (i.e., continental Reformation and Pietist) traditions in which United Methodism was shaped. Second, since the AR was not supplemented by Wesley's *Sermons and Notes on the New Testament* in the Methodist *Discipline,* it has meant that distinctive Wesleyan themes, which are well represented in the EUB/CF, have also been overlooked.

To be sure, the history of the antecedent standards to the EUB/CF not infrequently became the source of polemical strife and even church division. I hope that its reappropriation through informed study and reflection in local congregations may become a means of enhancing our sense of catholicity as a people of God and our commitment to the evangelical distinctives that once defined and energized us in mission.

L. Gregory Jones

Questions of identity and mission have received a great deal of attention in recent discussions of theology within the United Methodist Church. To what extent do theologians understand themselves to be working within a church context, let alone a denominational setting? Is there any meaning to talk of United Methodist theology in a time when there is so much fragmentation in the church and disagreement about what it means to be a United Methodist? Greg Jones argues that it is worth the effort to attempt to define the shape and purpose of theology within United Methodism. He reviews the work that has been done in recent years and concludes that among the various proposals perhaps the best is thinking of Methodism as an evangelical order within the church catholic. The particular contribution of Methodism, he argues, is emphasis on scriptural holiness. Toward the end of the essay Jones makes some suggestions of structural possibilities for theological and ecclesial renewal.

Readers will want to think about how the structural possibilities could be realized. Do the realities of the United Methodist Church, particularly its corporate wealth and the social and economic status of its members, allow for the institution of scriptural holiness as Jones describes it? Do the differences in thinking about what constitutes scriptural holiness prohibit enough shared agreement to make specific claims about theological identity and mission meaningful? These are some of the questions that will continue to vex United Methodists as they struggle with the issues raised by this essay.

What Makes "United Methodist Theology" Methodist?

L. Gregory Jones

In recent years there has been considerable discussion and debate about what constitutes the identity and mission of the United Methodist Church in general, and United Methodist theology in particular. These discussions have ranged from formal study commissions appointed by the General Conference to the ongoing work of the Oxford Institute of Methodist Studies, from various declarations to recent disputes and debates about the use of general church funds for this or that purpose.

In one sense, we should not be surprised by the felt need for attention to issues of identity and mission in The United Methodist Church's life. After all, a crucial part of any tradition's ongoing life is conversation and argument precisely about its identity and mission. And, indeed, ever since the earliest days of the Methodist movement, or of the Evangelical and United Brethren movements, there have been arguments about the content and shape of their identity and mission.

However, at this juncture questions about the identity and mission of United Methodism are taking on renewed urgency, an urgency felt (albeit in different ways) across the theological divides of the Church. I want to take up a particular angle on these questions, focusing on the shape of United Methodist theology. This decision echoes Dennis Campbell's important suggestion in his keynote address inaugurating the Duke-Lilly study that United Methodists need to maintain the priority of theology in both our diagnoses and our prognoses. That is, I focus on the importance of United Methodist theology because I am convinced that theological concerns go to the heart of many of our most troubling issues within United Methodism, particularly in that area covered by this Lilly study—American culture. Even so, understanding why it does so will only become apparent toward the end of this paper.

We urgently need a *clarity of purpose* about United Methodism's identity and mission. Of course, at our best, United Methodists have never tried to be distinctive—if by distinctive we mean having some treasure or self-understanding that no one else can share. Yet we have had distinctive emphases, both in the content of our theological convictions and in our organization for mission and service, which have—once again, at our best—enabled us to make a distinctive contribution both to the larger Christian tradition and in wider social and political contexts.

For reasons rooted both in cultural shifts in the U.S.A. and in ambiguities in our own ecclesial heritages, many people across the theological divides sense that we are coming to a crossroads, a crossroads that requires a recovery or discovery of United Methodist identity and mission. For example, a decade ago Thomas Langford closed his book *Practical Divinity,* a study of "Theology in the Wesleyan Tradition," by noting that "the future of the tradition is not clear." And he asked the following questions: "Has the Wesleyan tradition already made its contribution? Has the time come for the tradition to be dispersed into the broader Christian stream? Or in contrast: Is there significant reason for the tradition to continue? Is there a role within Christian ecumenism for a continuing Wesleyan tradition?"[1]

I am convinced that there is significant reason for the Wesleyan tradition of theology to continue, and for The United Methodist Church more generally to offer a distinctive witness both within the larger Christian tradition and in the wider social and political contexts in which we find ourselves. Further, I am convinced that United Methodism still has significant resources on which to draw in order to do so. But we need honestly to diagnose our contemporary situation and to offer prognoses for recovering and discovering our identity and mission.

Hence, I want to identify, and briefly explore, four subthemes related to our need for greater clarity of purpose, and more specifically to identify why issues of *theology* are at the heart of those questions: these have to do with (1) cultural shifts, (2) ambiguities in our ecclesial heritages, (3) the distinctive shape of United Methodist theology and life, and (4) structural possibilities for renewal.

I. Cultural Shifts

Many people have noted that diverse Christian traditions seem no longer to have distinctive identifying marks, at least to the extent they used to have. This can be put positively, in the sense that the twentieth-century ecumenical movement, along with many liturgical reforms and emphases on social witness, have produced congregations and worship patterns and social commitments across traditions that are more similar than dissimilar. Such convergences generate signs of unity that defeat the differences that divide Christians from one another, and enhance the church's witness in specific social and political contexts.

On the other hand, this relative lack of distinctive marks is often—and perhaps increasingly—the result of a failure of churches to articulate clearly for and with their members a vision of the church's identity and mission, United Methodist and otherwise.[2] But insofar as churches fail to articulate such a vision, and to provide the practices and education for people—laity and clergy alike—to become equipped to claim that vision, it becomes difficult if not impossible to engage in conversation, argument, and witness about Christian identity and mission because people lack the resources to do so. Indeed, we run the risk of replicating or exacerbating the worst tendencies of the culture that surrounds us—including, in our time, ignoring the racism and sexism that pervade people's lives and our communities and our churches; ignoring specific neighbors, particularly the poor; and giving in to the temptations of consumerist models of church life, "sound-bite" politics, and social witness reduced to partisan politics.

In this sense, Christians across the traditions face a theological crisis. This is particularly true in the U.S., where there is an increasingly pervasive lack of the background formation necessary for Christian theological reflection. Recent generations, particularly in the U.S., could presume that even unbelievers would be familiar with the basic content of the gospel; the unbelievers just didn't believe it to be true—perhaps, at least in many cases, because of the distortions and corruptions in churches' practices and understandings. However, we can no longer presume even that believers are familiar with the content of the gospel. This is seen both in local congregations of diverse traditions and in the larger culture. This has sometimes been characterized by terms such as "biblical illiteracy," an "ignorance of the Christian tradition," and even a lack of awareness of basic terms and practices of Christian faith and life.

Further, people currently lack a sense of the importance of theological reflection for Christian life. This is true within ecclesial contexts, where theology is too often presumed (at best) to be the domain of "professionals" rather than a task incumbent upon all believers; it is true within professional Christian theology, where "theology" is too often taken to be one subdiscipline that students are expected to take as distinguished from biblical studies, historical studies, or practical areas of inquiry; it is also true within the contemporary academy, where theology is often marginalized (by both its proponents and its opponents) as a questionable area of inquiry. In short, if even believers are dubious about the significance of theology, then we can hardly expect issues of theological conviction and inquiry to become central to Christian life and faith, much less public discussion and debate.

These sorts of problems have been identified (albeit in diverse ways) by a variety of recent commentators, including sociologists, historians, and theologians. These commentators—from a variety of perspectives—have noted the trivialization of theology, and of Christian commitment, even among believers. For example, Robert Wuthnow's study of small groups in America, *Sharing the Journey,* found that two-thirds of the small groups in America are Bible studies; even so, people in these Bible studies do not typically gather primarily to learn about God (that ranked seventh on a list!), nor do they actually increase their knowledge of the content of the Bible. Indeed, according to Wuthnow, participants often use the Bible in utilitarian ways and adopt wooden forms of interpretation (e.g., the Bible "worked" to help me get a job; thus it must be true).[3]

Further, George Lindbeck has recently noted that it would be difficult, if not impossible, for American people to understand Lincoln's Second Inaugural or Martin Luther King Jr.'s "I Have a Dream" speech in our contemporary cultural context; sadly, it may be almost as true in ecclesial contexts as well. Anecdotes about seminary classes needing to attend to basic catechesis are becoming commonplace at professional conferences.

The problems are not unique to either "conservative" or "liberal" congregations, Protestant ones or Catholic; they tend to cross theological borders and ecclesial divisions. Even contexts such as African American churches, which have perhaps maintained stronger practices of formation and scriptural nourishment in the past, are increasingly beset by these problems. To be sure, there are important differences in how we should diagnose the problems in these different contexts, as well as the prognoses we should offer for reclamation. But, at this point, the problems and issues overlap more than they diverge.

Though the predicament is increasingly shared across the traditions, it is a particular problem for United Methodists. For United Methodists have, both theologically and institutionally, emphasized the central role of *all* believers—laity and clergy alike, men as well as women, people from diverse ethnic heritages—in the activity of theological reflection. But we have not adequately attended to broad cultural shifts that have diluted and diminished both the theological importance of, and the institutional resources for, such reflection. Nor have we adequately interrelated the distinct but complementary contexts of theological reflection—for example, gatherings in specific communities, broader ecclesial structures, and intellectual debates in academies. As a result, many Christians—across the board, and in large measure independently of their "conservative" or "liberal" leanings—are insufficiently able to articulate a clear and coherent vision of Christian identity and mission, much less with a United Methodist angle on it.[4]

II. Ambiguities in Our Ecclesial Heritages

This difficulty is compounded by difficulties created by ambiguities internal to United Methodism's own conception of its identity and mission. In many ways, United Methodists now lack both the specific Christian practices that have given particular shape to our vision of the Christian life *and* a clear sense of how that vision fits with, and contributes to, the larger Christian tradition. At least in part, this lack of clarity, and the loss of our distinctive practices, is bound up with ambiguities in our complex ecclesial heritages.[5]

It is by now a commonplace that Methodism began in England as a reform movement, a movement that only gradually became a "church."[6] Perhaps at least partly because of the ambiguities about our origins, there have often been anxieties—as well as specific proposals—about what *distinctively* Methodist contributions might be made to the larger Christian tradition as well as in wider social and political contexts. These issues have been exacerbated by the sad legacies of our historical divisions over race, legacies that continue to haunt us into the present.[7]

Conversely, there has also been some uncertainty—or, perhaps more accurately put, unresolved controversy—about what provides a sense of unity among United Methodists and other Christians. More specifically, these debates typically concern the place of doctrine or doctrinal standards in the Church. These controversies took on renewed prominence in the 1980s and came to a head in the debates surrounding the revised section of the *Book of Discipline* on "Doctrinal Standards and Our Theological Task" adopted by the 1988 General Conference. Further, they have recently resurfaced in debates about the perceived need, and the opposition to that perceived need, for a "confessing movement" within The United Methodist Church.[8] There remains considerable ambiguity about how doctrine and theology ought to be understood in relation to each other.

Both of these sets of issues, namely the relations between a "movement" that gradually becomes a "church" on the one hand, and the relations between "doctrine" and "theology" on the other, are interrelated. They press questions about what United Methodists share in common and what we might have distinctively to contribute theologically to the larger Christian tradition. And, in so doing, they require us to focus on the potentially diverse and perhaps incompatible needs of a movement and those of a church—and, as a consequence, press uncomfortable questions about the ecclesial presumptions of United Methodism's understanding of doctrine and theology in relation to the whole Church.

In one sense, Methodism's origins within the Church of England provided a great deal of freedom for Methodist theological reflection. The Doctrinal Standards of the Anglican Church were relatively clear, and there was a well-established tradition of ecclesiological self-understanding within the Church. Hence, the early followers of the Wesleys could engage in that crucial task of, to use the more recent formulation of our 1992 Discipline, "the testing, renewal, elaboration, and application of our doctrinal perspective in carrying out our calling 'to spread scriptural holiness over these lands.'"[9] Further, the theological reflection of those Methodists was embodied in ongoing gatherings of Christians, and specifically in the varieties of Christian conference. What was distinctive of the early Methodists was, at the very least, as much their emphasis on the communal shape of theological reflection as on specific content—though that content was often explicitly important, particularly in disputes with both Moravians and Calvinists.

And this theological exploration within community has also characterized Methodist theology at its best. However, our emphasis on the communal shape of theological reflection has too often diluted either the content of the gospel or its concrete power for ministry and witness—or both. For example, the structure and argument of Langford's *Practical Divinity* reveal considerable difficulty in identifying what, if anything, Methodists—or, more broadly in his terms, Wesleyans—have shared substantively in common. Langford suggests some general "distinctives," but they are so broad as to have been widely shared among most Christians. His analysis suggests either a remarkable diversity or a troubling cacophony. M. Douglas Meeks describes it in the former terms. He writes:

> As Langford's analysis shows, it is much easier to demonstrate the irenic ecumenism, fructifying tolerance, and generativity of a healthy pluralism in Wesleyan theology than it is to track down its distinctive characteristics which promise actually to provide a concrete shaping power for the future of theology, church, and world.[10]

On the other hand, those more troubled by the lack of a distinctively Wesleyan or "United Methodist" shape to theological method and substance, and who find more cacophony than diversity, are more likely to focus on the latter part of Meeks's observation: the need for distinctive characteristics that "promise actually to provide a concrete shaping power for the future of theology, church, and world."

It is not simply in the interests of my own irenic ecumenism or fructifying tolerance that I want to suggest that both sides are partly right, and both partly wrong. Rather, I think United Methodist theology is best articulated when it embodies both a clear sense of doctrine, including distinctive ways of providing "concrete shaping power for the future of theology, church, and world," *and* a plurality of specific theological proposals. We have mired ourselves in the mud by thinking that we must choose an either/or, a choice that becomes even more pernicious when we think in terms of either being a "movement" or a "church."

That is, those who stress the importance of theological creativity are also often the people who want to emphasize our origins as a movement, our sense of the importance of Christians gathering together to explore and engage in theological reflection in the context and wake of their own experience. Conversely, those who stress the importance of specified doctrine, and of doctrinal standards, are also often the people who emphasize United Methodism's "churchly" status, the importance of maintaining continuity with—and fidelity to—the larger Christian tradition.

Almost assuredly, there are matters of emphasis and degree here. And, clearly, there is a temptation for those who want to stress our iden-

umc as mort. v. church

tity as a "movement" to focus most clearly, if not exclusively, on the "practical" dimensions of doctrine and theology. Conversely, there is a temptation for those who want to stress our identity as a "church" to focus most clearly, if not exclusively, on the priority of catechesis and of learning doctrine rather than engaging in communal, theological reflection. But while there will inevitably be diverse interests and ongoing arguments about how to articulate the relations between doctrine and theology, we need greater clarity of purpose about their mutually enriching significance in the context of our ecclesial self-understanding.

Put more bluntly, I think the ambiguities of our ecclesial heritages have now become conjoined with cultural shifts to create anxieties, confusions, and distrust that are threatening to polarize people within the Church. John Cobb, a United Methodist theologian well aware of the cultural shifts and the political polarities within contemporary United Methodism, has admirably attempted to articulate a Wesleyan theology that could provide a "shared basis" on which people could move forward in terms of theology and mission.[11] There is much to value in Cobb's proposal, particularly the seriousness with which he engages Wesley as a theological resource for contemporary theology. Arguably, to have a scholar with Cobb's wisdom and irenic temperament engaging the Wesleyan theological heritage is itself a significant means of reducing the possibilities of polarization within United Methodism.

Even so, Cobb's perspective is significantly weakened both by his failure adequately to articulate the relations between doctrine and theology, and by his lack of more serious attention to the ecclesiological issues ingredient in theological reflection. Indeed, the greatest strength of Cobb's perspective, its engagement with Wesley, is also its greatest weakness—it engages only Wesley's thought, and not the practices or the doctrines of the larger movement of the people called Methodists—both in relation to the eighteenth-century context, and in terms of contemporary United Methodism.

This is particularly the case given some internal inconsistencies in Cobb's evaluation of Wesley's views on doctrine. Curiously, Cobb indicates in a note that he does not disagree with Thomas Oden's emphasis on doctrinal standards in Wesley's life and thought *in terms of Wesley himself*, implying that their differences are over the contemporary relevance and appropriation of doctrinal standards.[12] Yet in the text of his argument, and particularly in dialogue with Jerry Walls's interpretation, Cobb minimizes the role of doctrine in Wesley's thought—he makes only brief reference at all to the role of the Thirty-nine Articles, or Wesley's own Sermons and Notes as standards Wesley proposed (and largely set) for the Methodist movement. As a result, despite his avowed agreement with Oden, Cobb fails to provide a fully balanced account of Wesley's theology because of his inadequate interpretation of the role of doctrine in Wesley's life and thought. This inadequacy concerns both those doctrines whose importance Wesley assumed as settled and those doctrines he explicitly invoked in his own writings.[13]

Further, beyond the confines of Wesley's theology, Cobb fails adequately to analyze what normative role doctrine does, or should, play once the Methodist movement establishes itself as a church separate from the Church of England.[14] This is so in relation to Cobb's neglect of the developing relationships between doctrine and discipline in the Methodist traditions of the nineteenth and twentieth centuries, his neglect of the role of doctrine in the Evangelical and United Brethren traditions, and his lack of adequate attention to the *Book of Discipline*'s understanding of the relations between doctrine and theology in the contemporary United Methodist Church.[15]

Hence, despite the significance of Cobb's dialogue with Wesley in relation to contemporary theological issues, his proposal is inadequate as a means of providing a "shared basis" on which contemporary Wesleyan theology can move forward and avoid the destructive divisions and polarizations that are sowing the seeds of our own destruction.

To be sure, it is undoubtedly the case that some of my disagreements with Cobb's proposal have to do with theological method; Cobb's method retains a neoliberal theological practice of "dialogue" with the tradition (and a heightened appreciation for reason and experience), whereas my own argument gives greater weight to the theological practices of lived Christian communities in theological exploration and argument (and hence a heightened appreciation for Scripture and tradition, understood as living realities rather than static categories). Even so, those disagreements are not crucial to the point at hand.

The fundamental problem with Cobb's proposal, at least in the context of this essay, is his failure to develop a clear account of the relationship between doctrine and theology and an account of the ecclesial presumptions, practices, and convictions that are reflected therein. As a result, Cobb fails to locate a "shared basis" for a contemporary United Methodist—much less more broadly Wesleyan—theology that can "move us forward." This is so quite apart from any specific substantive differences that people might have about how best to engage or appropriate Wesley's theological convictions and practices for contemporary theology.

By contrast, I want to suggest that the divisions and polarizations within United Methodism can be ameliorated, and shared ground can be advanced, through greater clarity about—and more specific explorations of—the relations between doctrine and theology for a movement that now clearly has become established, at least in some sense, as a "church"—and one that has predecessor bodies in the Evangelical and United Brethren traditions. This is particularly the case in relation to reflection on God—we need both the grounding in doctrine that focuses our attention on the work of the Triune God, and the sorts of theological engagement that enable us to attend to the work of God's Spirit among us—and to discern God's Spirit, the Spirit conforming us and the world to Jesus Christ, from other "spirits." There are significant resources in Part II of the current *Discipline* for doing so. But such texts are insufficient unless they are given life in specific practices and in a broader ecclesial vision, grounded in doctrine, that animate particular communities of Christian theological engagement and discourse.

Space does not permit a full exploration of these issues; however, I want to indicate the broad contours of a proposal for a distinctively United Methodist ecclesiological vision for doctrine and theology.[16]

III. The Distinctive Shape of
United Methodist Theology and Life

In recent years, Albert Outler and Geoffrey Wainwright have proposed that Methodists (United as well as British) ought to understand ourselves as an "evangelical order within the church catholic."[17] Such a description provides, I think, some very crucial distinctions that can help provide that clarity of purpose we so urgently need.

First, it provides a clear reminder that we are a part, not the whole, of the Church; likewise, it indicates the importance of our being located in relation to what is shared in common among Christians more generally. In this sense, we need to hear the *Discipline*'s indication that we stand "continually in need of *doctrinal reinvigoration* for the sake of authentic renewal, fruitful evangelism, and ecumenical dialogue."[18] This is so in any time, as we face the continual task of learning and appropriating

Christian doctrine and the doctrinal heritage for ever-new situations. For Methodists, this has often been carried as much by our hymns and spirituals as by other practices; but we have not adequately passed this practice on to future generations, much less other practices by which doctrine is learned and extended and transmitted. The introduction of *Songs of Zion* and the 1988 *Hymnal,* with their remarkable diversity and structure, has certainly helped; but much more needs to be done to reclaim the doctrinal significance of our hymns and the practice of singing the faith.

That is, the need for doctrinal reinvigoration is particularly crucial in our diverse contemporary cultural contexts, a time in which so many United Methodists—lay and clergy alike, ordinary and professional theologians included—are in need of much more profound catechesis and formation in the faith. I mean this not in a passive sense of being given instruction, but in the more classical—and hence radical—sense of being nurtured in the faith's content and its patterns of thinking, feeling, and acting so as to see and understand all things in their relation to the Triune God. We do this through particular practices—of singing and praying, of serving and witnessing, of repenting and forgiving. On the whole, and despite some pockets of hope, we are currently doing an abysmal job of locating our conversations and arguments in relation to the fullness of the Triune God's work among us. And this is true more often than not across the board, from local congregations to boards of ordained ministry, from our patterns of educating Christians to our varieties of gatherings for "Christian conference."

Second, understanding ourselves as an "evangelical order" provides a reminder that we have distinctive ways of envisioning both doctrine and its relation to the theological task. That is, for Methodists our focus is on "practical divinity." Here Cobb's emphasis on the Wesleyan tradition's emphasis on the transformation of life is important. Yet, we make a mistake if we think that all doctrine is somehow "practical," or if we collapse the whole of theological engagement into a reductive understanding of "practical theology." However, it is part of Methodism's distinctive vision to *emphasize* the practical—the end of transformed and transformative living in service to God. More specifically, I think this suggests that Methodism's distinctive *charism* as such an evangelical order is "holiness," or, to use more specifically Wesleyan terminology, "scriptural holiness."[19] It needs to immediately be added that we must understand there is no personal holiness that is not also social holiness.

We must be vigilant both in refusing to allow holiness to be transmuted into sanctimoniousness, and in refusing to allow holiness to be reduced to personal moralism. The Methodist record on many issues is, admittedly, rather mixed (in part, at least, a continuation of the complexities of Wesley's own views and mixed record); even so, there is a clear context for both doctrinal and theological reinvigoration—theological exploration and argument whose effects can and ought to be faithful to the tradition and transformative for specific people as well as for broader social structures. We have too often been a mirror of the culture rather than a window enabling people to glimpse God's kingdom more clearly.

Indeed, we might extend the claim about our *charism* of holiness one step further, specifying that scriptural holiness cannot be discovered or nurtured unless it has a special concern for the poor—for neighbors near and far.[20] This can be understood in a reductive sense (i.e., theology must always and only be focused on the poor), but it need not be so; and, indeed, some very significant theological contributions have been recently offered to the larger Christian tradition by people within the Methodist traditions—including the range of discussions at the 1992 Oxford Institute of Methodist Studies, whose theme was "Good News to the Poor in the Wesleyan Tradition." More generally, when we envision theological reflection and Christian life with at least a distinctive focus on the needs of specific, concrete others—and, most particularly, those among us who are disadvantaged—it provides a powerful, and transformed, context for our theological reflection in other areas and on other issues. Concentrating more of our attention on holy living, both by showing forth exemplars and in struggling to discern sanctity from sanctimoniousness, can help provide a context for our discernment about many of the issues currently facing the Church.[21] In this sense, we need to reclaim the importance of *testimony*, of learning to tell the stories of what God's Spirit is doing in our own—and one another's—lives. Examples of this can be found in Wesleyan class meetings, African American practices of "testifyin'," and in the significance of lifting up the lives of saintly people both in our midst, among the heritage of the people called Methodist, and in the wider Christian tradition.[22]

Third, we need to reclaim a significant sense of discipline—in both our ecclesial self-understanding and in our theological reflection—if we are to be able to embody the charism of scriptural holiness as an evangelical order within the church catholic. Richard Heitzenrater's recent study of *Wesley and the People Called Methodists* provides a compelling narrative of how the early Methodists' discipline provided both the structure and the support for deepened theological understanding and radical discipleship. Indeed, the "ordered" character of the Methodists' life together was what enabled them to be open and in service to the world in remarkable and transformative ways.

Moreover, Bishop Kenneth Carder has rightly suggested that one problem with our church is that we have substituted "demographic extrapolation" and sociological explanation for "eschatological expectation."[23] We lack the discipline in our theological reflection, and in our life together, to enable us to separate the wheat from the chaff of the social sciences. This is not to deny the need for careful social analysis, accurate diagnoses of contexts, and thoughtful strategic planning; but it is to suggest the specific theological shape in which this ought to be done. Indeed, we need to confess and repent of our temptations to believe that sociological analysis can be substituted for doctrinal clarity and theological argument, rather than recognizing social analysis as one important element within a more determinative theological landscape. That is, we have too often failed to be sufficiently animated by the gospel, and by the doctrines and theological claims that articulate the gospel's shape, in order to embody genuinely transformative living.

At our best, United Methodists have not been so much interested in "organization" as in providing structures and practices to enable disciplined, Christ-formed, and Spirit-led living. But we have allowed the notions of an "order"—that disciplined community whose *charism* ought to provide a distinctive contribution to the church catholic—to become fascinations with sociological technique rather than theological wisdom embodied in scriptural holiness. We need to reclaim and rediscover, for example, the formative and transformative power of class meetings, of the significance of "Christian conference" as a means of grace, and of the power of social witness in creative practices and institutional structures—practices that, at least in contemporary contexts, are found far more frequently in places like Latin American base communities than in U.S. Methodism.

Yet, given the cultural shifts of recent years as well as a clearer articulation of our place within the church catholic, we need to think more carefully, and more basically, about what seekers—including those Wesley termed "serious seekers"—and new Christians need in order to become acquainted with what being a follower of Jesus Christ entails on the one hand, and actually learn to become such a follower on the other. Here we need to reclaim our own strengths in terms of specific *practices* of Christian discipleship, examples of which are found in the General Rules, which give shape and form to Christian life. They are practices centered on the work of the Triune God, which require ongoing education and formation, and which involve us in mission in the world. They include such practices as showing hospitality to strangers, of searching the Scriptures, of engaging in struggles for forgiveness and reconciliation through accountable discipleship, of prayer and fasting, of visiting the sick and those in prisons, of engaging in prophetic critique of injustice, of keeping the Sabbath holy, of hymning the world to God.

Further, they require a reclamation of distinctive practices of education in theology (including catechesis, specifically learning doctrine), recognizing that education in theology also involves reflecting on particular practices of discipleship, and that we thus have a great deal to offer to the world about the kind of education and formation people need in order to flourish. Again, Wesley and the Methodists in the eighteenth century recognized the central importance of linking "vital piety" with "knowledge" (as one of Charles Wesley's hymns puts it), and they both started and nurtured educational institutions to provide instruction and opportunities for reflection—from young children to older adults.

In this sense, envisioning United Methodism—and United Methodist theology—as an evangelical order within the church catholic, an order whose *charism* is scriptural holiness and focused particularly both on the needs of the poor and the central importance of education, will require shifts and changes among all of us. Those who rightly stress the importance of doctrine, and of personal conversion, will need to reclaim the significance of the church catholic and missional commitment on behalf of the poor; those who rightly stress the importance of practices of social witness and openness to the world will need to reclaim the significance of doctrine; and those who rightly stress the importance of careful social analysis will need to reclaim the priority of a comprehensive theological vision nurtured through sound and imaginative practices of education. There is no one doctrine, no one feature, no one social institution, that distinguishes United Methodism from other Christian traditions. Even so, I suggest that it is the constellation of these themes and practices, signified particularly though not exclusively by the notion of scriptural holiness, which best locates both the theological and the ecclesial self-understanding of what Methodists have sought—and, so I would suggest, should now continue to seek in transformed ways—to embody.

Obviously, spelling out these claims would require a much more robust account of the church, and of theology in United Methodism, than could possibly be provided in one essay. Even so, I think that United Methodism has already within it significant structural possibilities for renewal, grounded in our tradition's contributions over the years to American culture. Hence, I conclude by offering—albeit in remarkably brief and overschematized form—some suggestions for the resources from which United Methodism can draw for renewing our theological and, more specifically, our ecclesiological identity.

IV. Structural Possibilities for Theological and Ecclesial Renewal

The first indication of our structural possibilities for theological renewal is that, despite our internal dissension and anxieties about declining membership, we still have a vast set of institutional networks on which to draw. Our task is less to develop new institutions than it is to claim and re-claim them for a distinctively Christian witness—this is as true of our hospitals and nursing homes as it is of our institutions of higher education and our soup kitchens. But in each case, we need a clearer theological articulation of their identity and mission as United Methodist institutions. So, for example, when one United Methodist bishop went to dedicate a new United Methodist hospital, he indicated that its Christian identity ought to make a difference in everything it does—from personnel to its financing to the kind of care that it offers. Doing so should reflect our commitment to the poor as well as the theological significance of such practices as hospitality.

Similar possibilities exist for reclaiming the centrality of a United Methodist vision of education, from our mission schools to our colleges and universities, including theological and graduate education. This includes attention *both* to the great heritage within United Methodism's witness to, and involvement in, American culture through education *and* the distinctive possibilities for developing a United Methodist vision of theological teaching and learning in diverse settings of education.

More generally, this focus on the theological identity and shape of our institutions, and the practices housed by those institutions, requires that we give up false dichotomies about, for example, either "small groups" or "large institutions," either "local needs" or "bureaucratic structures," either "town and country" or "urban" settings, either "mission-evangelism" or "social justice." We need instead to see how they are necessarily interrelated, and to provide theologically informed, disciplined yet creative explorations of how we can best mobilize our structural resources to enhance Christian practices and Christian witness in diverse contexts and concerning irreducibly diverse needs and issues.

Second, United Methodism in American culture has within it structural resources for the kinds of interactions among Christians that we desperately need if we are to enable significant practices of theological inquiry. As Marjorie Suchocki has emphasized, theological education is a task needed not only for the clergy, but for all Christians; we cannot afford, either for theological reasons or institutional ones, to presume that only clergy are theologians or are the only ones in need of theological education.[24] But such schooling in doctrine, and in patterns of thinking, feeling, and living as Christians, requires a more comprehensive vision of what kinds of education we need, and how those diverse kinds should be interrelated—ranging from small gatherings of seekers to Sunday schools, from specific practices of discipleship to broader theological commissions, from reflection on engagements in the world to careful study of the traditions we inherit as well as the findings of other disciplines. We have, at least in principle, many of the structural resources necessary for better engaging in these diverse practices; but coordinating and integrating them will require extraordinary imagination and energy—cultivated in a spirit, or more accurately Spirit, of discernment. It will also require the cultivation of better forums, and better outlets, for theological discussion and argument. *The Circuit Rider* just is not sufficient for the task.

Third, we need to examine where our structural resources need to be more clearly articulated and developed to enhance our theological identity and mission. One step is to make clearer the theological vocation of all Christians in and through Christian conference, including the place of clergy and bishops as *teachers* (both in words and in our lives)—and of a sense of the importance of the teaching office of the Church. Some work on this has been done in recent years, but much more is needed.[25] Similarly, the Church ought to cultivate more clearly the importance of its professional theologians for its ecclesial and theological self-understanding and mission—ranging from claims upon our time to investments in our education, from a clear sense of the crucial though limited significance of the professional theological task to changes in deployment (and the descriptions of the appointment) of those professional theologians who are ordained. At present, it is regrettably the case that United Methodist theologians are defined more by the habits and theological methods of the institutions where they receive their graduate training than by any clear formation within United Methodism (even when the people went to a United Methodist seminary or graduate school).

At their best, United Methodist theology and The United Methodist Church hold together diverse though complementary themes that are often separated from one another: justification and sanctification, grace and responsibility, evangelism and social witness, Christ and the Spirit, life centered in the Triune God and specific personal experience, evangelical commitment and a catholic spirit, doctrinal clarity and theological creativity. However, at their worst, United Methodist theology and the United Methodist Church have been tempted either to triumphalism (a tendency that goes back to Mr. Wesley himself) or to sundering these themes and practices from one another. We desperately need the clarity of purpose about our identity and mission, and the practices and institutions of formation and education through which we can cultivate such clarity, that will enable us to offer a distinctive witness both to the larger Christian tradition and in the wider society. The task is not insurmountable, but neither is it easy. Yet, if we reclaim a sense of eschatological expectation, of the conviction that the Triune God is actively at work among us, the people called United Methodists, then perhaps we can recover and discover a distinctive sense of—and commitment to—the power of God's Holy Spirit who is, indeed, making all things new.[26]

Michael G. Cartwright

Michael Cartwright has studied the different ways in which the predominantly white Methodist churches and the historically black Methodist churches have dealt with interpretation and practice of their books of Discipline. In this essay he principally discusses the Methodist Episcopal Church, the Methodist Episcopal Church (South), the African American Episcopal Church, and the Colored (Christian) Methodist Episcopal Church in the nineteenth century. The problem he is trying to understand is the way in which the several denominations maneuvered between what their Discipline said and what they taught and practiced. This essay is technical, exploring at length selected specific cases and their interpretations. The payoff comes as the reader begins to see that the differences between white and black interpretations also illuminate the larger problem of what the church says and adopts as teaching, and how it acts on and, indeed, enforces its teachings.

Do the examples from the nineteenth century shed light on these issues at the turn of the twenty-first century? While the specific issues are different, the essential problem is the same. If Cartwright is right, then what insight might we gain about efforts to establish norms for thought and action in the Church today?

How do doctrine and theology inform the way United Methodists actually live in the world today? Do all of the debates about what should be in the Book of Discipline *in regard to what we believe and how we should act make any difference anyway?*

Discipline in Black and White: Conflicting Legacies of Nineteenth-Century Euro-American Methodist and African American Methodist Disciplinary Practices

Michael G. Cartwright

Introduction

At the 1876 General Conference of the Methodist Episcopal Church (North), the "fraternal delegates" representing the Methodist Episcopal Church, South, and the African Methodist Episcopal Church were invited to greet the General Conference at different times. Lovick Pierce, the "fraternal delegate" from the M.E. Church, South, offered greetings that were effusive, even triumphalistic. "As between us, the two great bodies of Episcopal Methodism, there is never to be strife as to which of us shall be the greatest, in this proud sense. But as the apostle requires it, there is a sense in which we may strive to excel..."[1] After reminding those assembled that "we cannot preach holiness unless we are leaders in the experience of holiness," Pierce concluded his remarks with the following exhortation to spiritual unity.

> And finally, let us, as two companies of brothers intrusted with a most precious patrimonial estate, to enjoy as trustees, and enlarge and increase as guardians for an indefinite posterity, see which of us can so use our portion of Methodist capital as to make its per centage of income the test of comparative fidelity, industry and devotion to its polity and principles of operation, as its founders and its fathers turned it over to us. Let us do this as brethren of one heart and one mind, of one great aim and end, and the future will prove that our division into two General Conference jurisdictions was a benediction instead of a deprivation. We will watch over each other only with godly jealousy for a faithful propagation of one undivided Methodism.[2]

By contrast, the Reverend W. F. Dickerson,[3] one of the "fraternal delegates" from the A.M.E. Church, implicitly admonished Pierce and the delegates to the M.E. Church (North) General Conference for the presumptuousness with which they had described the unity of Methodism as comprising only the two predominantly Euro-American branches of episcopal Methodism:

> The African Methodist Episcopal Church is the eldest daughter of the Methodist Episcopal Church. Aye, more than that; not only the eldest, but we think, the most respectable if not the most respected, for we have never transgressed at any time. We, however, throw the mantle of charity around the matter of who is prodigal. But if the calf is to be slain, if organic or permanent union is to take place, we would claim to be the seat nearest our mother's side, the first choice and the best room; and I guess the roll of honor is ours by right also, for we are certainly the most respectful and loving daughter.[4]

It is not clear whether the Colored Methodist Episcopal Church was invited to send its greetings to the General Conference of 1876. However, based upon the complex relationship that the C.M.E. Church shared with the A.M.E. Church and the M.E.C. (North) at that time, it is not merely an idle exercise in speculation to wonder what form such a response might have taken. One wonders what kind of reproach to these "brothers" and "sisters" in the American Methodist family would have been offered by a C.M.E. fraternal delegate who had heard this exchange. The intriguing possibility that there might have been another double-voiced inversion of the parable of the prodigal son, in addition to Dickerson's witty response, displays just how significant the conflict between these four denominations was in the nineteenth century and thereby suggests how complex relations between these siblings of the American Methodist family could be. This incident also reveals that nineteenth-century American Methodists' visions of "re-union" were closely connected to their assessment of the adequacy of one another's disciplinary practices—*through which* they imaged themselves in continuity with their Wesleyan Methodist heritage.

This anecdote about the two "fraternal greetings" (and the notable absence of a third) given at the 1876 General Conference of the M.E.C. suggests a great deal about the multisided relationships that existed between the two historically black Methodist churches and the two predominantly Euro-American denominations in question. What this anecdote does not disclose, but this study will seek to show, is the complex set of issues that arose among these four denominations during the course of the nineteenth century, and the significance of this poignant legacy of segregation for how we understand the relationship of United Methodism and American culture in the past and present.[5] Indeed, as I will explain in the conclusion of this study, there are conflicting assessments (intra-racial as well as inter-racial) between these Methodist "siblings" about *what constitutes* "the legacy" of nineteenth-century American Methodist disciplinary practice.

Scholars of African American religious history have struggled to characterize the complex and shifting relationships that existed between African American Christians and Euro-American Christians in the context of the eighteenth and nineteenth centuries. Several different models for reconstructing similarities and differences have been offered.[6] For example, in the "Prologue" to his groundbreaking study of *Black Religion and American Evangelicalism* (1975) Milton Sernett made the following observation about African American religiosity in antebellum America:

> In matters of work and life, it is true, there were two different worlds in which white Christians and black Christians lived. But in matters of faith and order the Negro Churches reflected the structure and doctrines of Evangelical Protestantism. To borrow an image used by Booker T. Washington, black religion and white religion were as distinct as the five fingers of the hand, but they were one like the hand itself in sharing the Evangelical heritage.[7]

Sernett's intent in making this distinction was to demonstrate that the Black Church—far from being "a fourth faith after Protestantism, Judaism and Catholicism" in American culture—actually *shared* a great deal with nineteenth-century American evangelicals. To use his own words, "The Christian faith . . . is the tie that binds our story together."[8]

In borrowing the phrases of "faith and order" and "life and work" from the twentieth-century ecumenical movement,[9] Sernett obviously was trying to draw a distinction between lived reality and organizational theory, while showing that there was also, in fact, a "tie" that bound white plantation owners and black slaves together in the antebellum period. But as I hope to show, a close examination of nineteenth-century American Methodist disciplinary practice makes it difficult to draw the line in precisely the way Sernett suggests it can be drawn between African American Methodist denominations and Euro-American Methodist denominations. The extant evidence from the four denominations being analyzed in this study reveals *too much overlap* at the level of practice and too many shared conceptions of "discipline" to admit any such neat division.[10]

Therefore, whatever may be said of other denominational traditions of the Black Church, I have come to believe that Sernett's formulation simply is not adequate to explain the significant ways in which the African Methodist Episcopal Church and the Colored (since 1956 "Christian") Methodist Episcopal Church shared more than common "faith and order" with its Euro-American counterparts, the Methodist Episcopal Church (North) and Methodist Episcopal Church, South (hereafter, "M.E. Church, South"). Although I am not yet in a position to offer an alternative, I believe we need a very different set of images to explain the complex ways that these four American Methodist denominational traditions shared disciplinary practices.

In addition to this conceptual issue, there are other reasons why it is difficult to narrate the nineteenth-century legacy of American Methodist disciplinary practice. First, the second great awakening spawned a host of conflicting movements, which in turn influenced how some American Methodists thought about and practiced church discipline. Second, given the splits within Methodism that occurred in the nineteenth century, there is an irreducible diversity that simply cannot be set aside when one is looking at nineteenth-century American Methodism. Third, we have to deal with the divided character of American Methodism, racially and politically speaking, during this period. The question, therefore, I would submit is not *whether* we deal with these divisions, but *how* we deal with them. My approach is to take the racial and political divisions seriously, but not to allow undue suspicion about the politics of nineteenth-century American Methodism to lead me astray in ignoring the significance of nineteenth-century disciplinary practice in general and the ecclesiological significance of the "General Rules" in particular. All of which means, I believe, that we must begin to write the history with the Pan-Methodist denominations in relation to one another even as we also situate these same denominations in relation (synchronically and diachronically) to American culture. I would argue, however, that we should understand this way of approaching the evidence not so much as a "return" to the old style of church history,[11] as the simple recognition that in order to understand the complex relationship between the Pan-Methodist traditions and American culture, we must take into account both the richness and poverty of nineteenth-century disciplinary practice.

A place to begin this kind of study is by asking the question, How was "discipline" conceptualized in early-nineteenth-century Methodism? I will attempt to address this question by discussing discipline both as a practice, or rather a set of practices, and as a rhetoric, that is a "language" spoken by American Methodists. To look at "discipline" as a set of practices is, among other things, to take into account that it was embodied socially and behaviorally in the four groups being considered. To take seriously the rhetoric or "languages" in which the practice of the discipline was described, and in relation to which it was transformed, is to acknowledge the powerful ways that theological language comes to be patterned in relation to (religious and nonreligious) practices. Finally, to consider American Methodist disciplinary practice as both a rhetoric and a set of practices can help with our exploration of another question: In relation to what other American cultural practices and rhetorics (languages) did American Methodist disciplinary practice come to be *reconceived* as the nineteenth century came to an end and these divided American Methodists found themselves in the twentieth century pursuing the quest of a (re-)United Methodism in American culture?

I. "The General Rules" and/as the Discipline of the People Called Methodists

For Methodists at the end of the eighteenth century, the *Discipline* was certainly more than a "body of morals" intended to guide the ethical behavior of the Methodist societies, but it was also *no less* than that. Bishops Coke and Asbury gave classic expression to this conception when they described the "General Rules of the United Societies" as comprising, "perhaps, one of the completest systems of christian ethics or morals, for its size, which ever was published by an uninspired writer."[12] As far as I have been able to ascertain, the bishops' reference to Mr. Wesley as an "uninspired writer"—far from being an ironic comment—appears to have been a reference to the standard of measurement being used to describe the status of these standards of discipleship. The General Rules (after 1789) came to be regarded as "canonical" by virtually all American Methodists. Significantly, this conception of the General Rules as a compact statement of morals shows up in the African Methodist Episcopal Church as well.[13]

Of course, it would be a mistake to regard early Methodist discipline as *only* a body of morals. Wesley's directives in the General Rules and elsewhere made it very clear that the disciplinary practice of the

Methodist societies was closely tied to the pastoral practices and sacramental tradition of the Church of England. For example, the list of the six "Means of Grace" that are commended to the United Societies in the 1743 version of the General Rules are closely linked to the performance of the various rules that fall under the two rubrics of the General Rules: "By doing no harm" and "By doing good of every kind." Wesley clearly envisioned a practice that was empowered by God's grace, and oriented toward the embodiment of holy living, thereby providing the means for the ongoing nurture of the people that God had "raised" in such an extraordinary fashion in the context of the Evangelical Revival of the eighteenth century.[14]

Perhaps it is significant that the one major addition made to Wesley's "General Rules" (1743), the rule on slavery, which was added in 1789, turned out to be the most significant problem of nineteenth-century Methodist disciplinary practice. Between 1792 and 1808, ecclesiastical authority gradually became defined in early American Methodism. First, the 1792 General Conference solidified the authority of the bishops to appoint ministers, thereby resolving a crisis that had been prompted by James O'Kelly's "republican" challenge to Bishop Asbury's authority. The General Conference of 1808 further defined the boundaries between episcopal authority and that of the representative General Conference. Among the six Restrictive Rules that bind General Conference—the only body that can speak on behalf of The United Methodist Church—is the *fifth* rule, which states: "The General Conference shall not revoke or change the General Rules of Our United Societies."[15] With this action, the "General Rules" were given their constitutional status as a text within the *Discipline* of the Methodist Episcopal Church.

This conceptual point about the establishment of the "canonical" form of the General Rules gains more significance when one takes into account the fact that—with one rather striking exception—the General Rules were not altered—in the sense of added to or subtracted from— by any American Methodist body in the nineteenth century. This fact is especially striking, when one considers the number of splits that occurred and the frequency with which moral and disciplinary issues played significant roles in these schisms. The exception that proves the rule, in this instance, is that of the "Reformed Methodists," a group of Methodist New Englanders who were anti-episcopacy, anti-slavery, and—at least initially—anti-war.[16] In making substantial changes to the

"General Rules," the first two *Disciplines* (1814 and 1815) of the Reformed Methodists did what no other denomination (Euro-American or African American) did in nineteenth-century American Methodism.

By contrast, the well-known argument about the application of "the General Rule on slavery" (which began as early as 1785), must be seen as a casuistical dispute about applications and exceptions to be granted within what amounts to a canonical consensus. In point of fact, the rule itself was never deleted, although the publication of the *Discipline* in the Southern region of the Methodist Episcopal Church did omit the statement on Slavery, which in most editions of the M.E.C. *Discipline* after 1816 was printed as the last item in the "Temporal Economy" section.

As a result, throughout the nineteenth century, American Methodists saw themselves as being in continuity with John Wesley and early Methodism without always recognizing the multiple discontinuities that took place at the level of practice (or use) of the "General Rules." In fact, this kind of claim played a central role in the "family saga" about the "rise of Methodism" for virtually all Methodist denominations. For example, in 1829, Methodist Protestants clearly saw themselves as acting in continuity with Wesley, despite the fact that by adopting the "elementary principles" of constitutional law that it did, the M.P. Church arguably can be said to have altered the context of the application of the General Rules.[17] Thus, when the Methodist Episcopal Church, South, split in 1844 from the Methodist Episcopal Church (MEC) over the issue of slavery, it is not surprising to learn that it also claimed to be following nothing but the traditional Wesleyan discipline. Comparable claims can be found in authorized statements of the A.M.E. Church after 1817,[18] and relevant documents of the C.M.E. Church beginning as early as 1887.[19] Part of what made all these appeals convincing was the presence of the "General Rules" in unaltered form alongside the "Articles of Religion" in the book of Discipline of each denominational body.

But, of course, disciplinary practice in the nineteenth century was more complex than these appeals to common heritage would suggest. Both before and after the enactment of the Restrictive Rules of 1808, there was controversy in the Methodist Episcopal Church about whether the General Rules had been retained in their "substance" as well as in their canonical shape.[20] The M.E.C., South, never actually deleted the rule about the buying and selling of slaves from its version of the "General Rules," but it is also clear that the southern church did follow a different disciplinary practice from that of the M.E.C. (North) on this matter. At the same time, however much the M.E.C. (North) might want to claim continuity with Wesley through its use of the General Rules, a case can also be made that the M.E.C. had actually altered the context of the application of those rules when it allowed non-Methodists (such as the German-speaking United Brethren) to be permitted to attend its love feasts. But because the leadership of the M.E.C. (North) could say that they had not violated the fifth Restrictive Rule, which protected the General Rules as a document from alteration, they could effectively avoid facing the fact of the matter, which was that changes had already occurred in the use of the General Rules long before the General Conference of 1808. There can also be no question that over the course of the nineteenth century, the Discipline became something other than the "General Rules." The rhetoric did change and develop in discernible ways: the languages of "ecclesiastical polity," "judicial law," "constitutional law," and "machinery" all jostled together over the course of the century in overlapping and often very confusing ways. But what is also notable is that nineteenth-century Methodists—black and white alike—struggled to hold these additional conceptions of Discipline in tension with the notion of the General Rules as the "discipline" within the book of discipline. As any reader of the literature on the decline of the class meetings soon discovers, the "General Rules" were typically considered as a whole, not as individuated rules.

Related to this problem is the circumstance that at least part of the controversies over slavery (which ultimately led to the schisms with the Wesleyan Methodists and later the Methodist Episcopal Church, South) stemmed from the suspicion (by some) that the General Rules were not being practiced (by others) as John Wesley had intended. There are numerous examples of controversies in which appeals to "the original intent" of the General Rules were voiced by the party to whom discipline had been administered. Not infrequently, these interpretive disputes about the application of the discipline also coincide with efforts to redistribute power (i.e., from bishops to clergy, from clergy to laity, from men to women) in the denomination.[21]

Perhaps if more of the schisms in American Methodism had resulted in significant amendments of the General Rules, then the legacy of American Methodist disciplinary practice could be characterized more straightforwardly, and would therefore constitute less of a controversial conundrum than it has become. But it is no accident that both within the

nineteenth century and since, American Methodist historiographers
have struggled to narrate the discrepancy between the stability of the
canonical shape of the General Rules, which has not changed, and the
actual practice of Methodist discipline, understood as a set of ecclesial-
ly sanctioned behaviors, which has changed a great deal. In this respect,
it is less important to specify the exact locus (e.g., the class meeting, or
the changes over time in the status of "probationary" members) of these
shifts in disciplinary practice as it is to observe that the slippage
occurred in the midst of complex rhetorical practices that highlighted
the continuities in the midst of the many discontinuities. All of which
is rendered even more complex by the fact that the four denominations
in question, which shared a common disciplinary heritage, were separated and/or segregated from one another in ways that also over-
lapped: segregation by race, segregation by region, segregation by
political alignment.

II. The Discipline as "Rhetoric of Separation" and as "Rhetoric of Unity"

From the 1950s until the present, historical studies of the nineteenth
century "class meeting" in Euro-American Methodism have either
taken the form of "jeremiadic histories,"[22] or revisionist claims about
what the "essence" of Methodism is (usually preaching) as opposed to
the presumption that "discipline" is the essence.[23] However, when
African American denominational history and practices are examined,
this is not the kind of pattern that is found. On the contrary, on first
glance, continuities with their Methodist disciplinary practice appear to
be more prominent than discontinuities. And while there are plenty of
examples of disciplinary innovations to be found in historically black
Methodist bodies like the A.M.E. Church, there is also a notable pattern
of conservation of traditional Methodist practices.

Greg Schneider's recent contribution, *The Way of the Cross Leads Home:
The Domestication of American Methodism* (1991), provides a new and
highly interesting way of accounting for the "decline" of the class meeting. Schneider does not change the categories of analysis so much as he
gives a more thoroughly sociological and behavioral explication of both
the decline and the transposition of American Methodist disciplinary
practice within a broader cultural comparison (with the conception of
Southern honor). This model commends itself for the analysis that I am

trying to provide in comparing African American and Euro-American
Methodist practices in the nineteenth century.

Within Schneider's account, "discipline" is discussed as a "rhetoric of
separation" and vividly presented in relation to primary documents
that include diaries and first person accounts.[24] There is no question that
the discipline did in fact function as a language and a practice of separation. However, I would want to argue that the significance of the
"rhetoric of separation" must also be registered in relation to the practice of the discipline as a "rhetoric of unity" in nineteenth-century
American Methodism. Here, I intend to take seriously the documentary
evidence that is available, even as I also take seriously the political background of such documents as "Explanatory Notes" of Bishops Coke and
Asbury to the 1798 edition of *The Doctrines and Discipline of the Methodist
Episcopal Church in America*. More specifically, I would argue that in the
process of assessing how the discipline became what it did over the
course of the nineteenth century, we should be careful that our analytical tools do not prematurely categorize the phenomena in such ways
that we fail to grasp what could have happened given developments
that had already taken place at the beginning of the century.

For example, in their "explanatory notes" appended to the 1798
Discipline, Bishops Coke and Asbury offer the following interpretive
remark about the character of Methodist identity:

> We are but one body of people, one grand society, whether in Europe or
> America; united in the closest *spiritual* bonds, and in *external* bonds as far as
> the circumstances of things will admit. . . . And as our numbers have
> increased exceedingly both in Europe and America, it is necessary we should
> be particularly cautious in receiving strangers into our society, under the pre-
> text of their having been members in other places; as the one end of our
> whole plan is *to raise a holy people*.[25]

This statement provides a significant reminder of the fragility of the
early American Methodist apostolate. Under this understanding, a common disciplinary practice not only provided the basis for maintaining
the "connection" between Methodists in Europe and America (in a time
when national loyalties were making it difficult for Christians in
America to maintain such links) but also enabled Euro-American
Methodists to support their apostolate to "reform the continent."

This sense of unity was also enabled by the early Methodist conception of "Christian Conference" as a "means of grace." For example, see

the discussion in Section XIII "Of the Duty of Preachers to God, themselves and one another" of the 1798 *Discipline*, where the list of "instituted means of grace" concludes with this series of questions about Christian Conference.

> 5. Christian conference: Are you convinced how important and how difficult it is to order your conversation aright? Is it always in grace? Seasoned with salt? Meant to minister grace to the hearers? Do you not converse too long at a time? Is not an hour commonly enough? Would it not be well always to have a determinate end in view? And to pray before and after it?[26]

The advice here, of course, is vintage Wesleyan teaching; it parallels the advice given to the class and band leaders, and provides a way for the preachers to "watch over one another in love." Christian conference, understood as a "means of grace" was present in at least an incipient form at the beginning of the nineteenth century, although, as we will see, it was redirected fairly early on.

To take but one additional example of this disciplinary rhetoric of unity, beginning with the 1798 *Discipline*, a new section appears *"On the Necessity of Union Among Ourselves."* The section begins with a cohortative admonition: "Let us be deeply sensible (from what we have known) of the evil of a division in principle, spirit or practice, and the dreadful consequences to ourselves and others. If we are united, what can stand before us? If we divide we shall destroy ourselves, the work of God and the souls of our people."[27] The discussion continues with a question: "What can be done in order to [sic] a closer union with each another?" followed by seven answers.

> 1. Let us be deeply convinced of the absolute necessity of it.
> 2. Pray earnestly for, and speak freely to each other.
> 3. When we meet, let us never part without prayer.
> 4. Take great care not to despise each other's gifts.
> 5. Never speak lightly of each other.
> 6. Let us defend each other's character in every thing, so far as is consistent with truth.
> 7. Labour, in honour, each to prefer the other before himself.[28]

Whatever might be said about the politics of this matter (i.e., the ways in which a rhetoric of unity could have been abused by the patriarchal and autocratic Bishop Francis Asbury in the wake of the O'Kelly controversy), it should be noted that the sevenfold answer to this question provides a précis of the earlier discussion of "christian conference" as a *means* of grace. In their "explanatory notes" on this section of the *Discipline*, Asbury and Coke comment: "We could write a volume on this weighty subject. Let us preserve our union, and with the Prince of Peace at our head, we shall bear down the opposition of all our spiritual and temporal enemies. We shall imperceptibly gain ground on every hand, and be ourselves from time to time astonished at the progress of the work of God."[29]

In light of these and other remarks by Coke and Asbury, it is also interesting to observe that the section "On the Necessity of Unity" along with its seven accompanying directives about how to obtain a "closer union with each other" was retained (with minor amendments) in every edition of the *Doctrines and Discipline* of the Methodist Episcopal Church from 1785 through 1900. Interestingly, it appears to have been dropped by the M.E. Church, South, beginning with the 1846 *Discipline*. Whether this was done in the awareness of the ecclesiological significance of the split with the Methodist Episcopal Church is unclear.[30] When this section is correlated with the section on "The Means of Grace" (a rubric that did not disappear completely from the M.E.C. until just before its 1939 union with the Methodist Protestant and M.E.C., South), the significance of this "rhetoric of unity" in the Discipline begins to come more fully into view.[31]

Unfortunately, in retrospect, it appears that neither Coke nor Asbury—nor most indigenous American Methodists of that time—had the moral imagination and political creativity to see how to maintain both spiritual and external bonds with African American Methodists in the midst of slavery. Too often, the fellowship extended to African American Methodists by Euro-American Methodists was confined to a notion of "spiritual unity," which was, in actual fact, severely circumscribed by very real political divisions that shaped and redirected the public significance of Euro-American Methodist disciplinary practice. From the struggle at Old St. George's Methodist Episcopal Church in Philadelphia in the 1790s through the early decades of the nineteenth century, there are numerous examples of divergence between rhetoric and practice as Euro-American Methodists placed limits on the extent of their "spiritual unity" in relation to various kinds of external or "temporal" political bonds.

Yet, there is a significant body of evidence to indicate that African American Methodists from the A.M.E., A.M.E. Zion, and C.M.E. traditions have also understood themselves in much the same way as did Asbury and Coke.[32] However, one will not find that evidence by looking for a statement on "the necessity of unity" in these traditions. Rather, as Mary Sawyer's study of the Black Church "contribution" to the ecumenical movement[33] shows, African American Christians such as the A.M.E. Church have consistently seen their efforts for Christian unity in relation to their moral and political stands for justice. Thus, in the years before the Civil War, African American Methodists, like Euro-American Methodists, also sang of "Zion" (and "Bethel") and rejoiced in the spiritual unity that they experienced as Methodists, but they did so in the awareness that, for them, "Zion" included practices of unity that were not always practiced by their Euro-American Methodist counterparts—namely solidarity with their African American brothers and sisters still suffering in the bonds of slavery.

III. The A.M.E. Church Struggle with Slavery

Oddly enough, it was this very emphasis on solidarity with those still enslaved that led to one of the most protracted struggles in the A.M.E. Church at midcentury—the issue of whether someone could be a member of the denomination who, at least technically, held title of ownership of other African Americans. In fact, as late as the 1856 General Conference, the A.M.E. Church was still struggling with the problem of revising its own *Discipline* so that it would be unmistakably opposed to slaveholding. The answer given to the question, "What shall be done for the extermination of slavery" in the first A.M.E. Church *Discipline* (1817) was, "We will not receive any person into our society as a member who is a slaveholder. Any person now a member, having slaves, who shall refuse to emancipate them after due notice has been given by the preacher in charge, shall be expelled."[34]

The General Conference of the A.M.E. Church held in Cincinnati in 1856 engaged in a protracted struggle about this issue. As Gayraud Wilmore explains:

There were still a few black slaveholders in the South and the border states. Some had purchased slaves with the intention of setting them free immediately, but others expected the slaves to "work off" their purchase price before claiming full liberty. The report on the Committee on Slavery proposed to force immediate emancipation or expulsion from the church. It also offered for adoption the policy that no person who was a slaveholder be received into membership in the church under any condition. A minority on the committee objected that in some cases there were extenuating circumstances. They argued that in order not to penalize those who had bought slaves for the purpose of giving them freedom, due notice of expulsion should be given "by the preacher in charge," as already provided for in the Discipline. The minority warned that in establishing the denomination in a new area it was impossible always to know immediately who were slaveholders and who were not until after they had joined the church. Furthermore, there should be a period of "mercy" for such persons, untutored as they might be in the duties of Christians, that they might learn of God's will, repent, and emancipate slaves they may have acquired for whatever reason.[35]

As Wilmore concludes: "Thus in the 1850s, followers of Richard Allen encountered some of the same dilemmas the white Methodists had wrestled with in 1844, despite the fact that the question was presented in Cincinnati more as one of strategy than of principle."[36] In fact, on the floor of the General Conference of 1856, speakers voiced their concern that a state of affairs "*similar to that in the Methodist Episcopal Church* was about to be introduced into the A.M.E. Church."[37]

So protracted was this debate in the A.M.E. Church that it occupied two full days of the General Conference. Bishop Daniel Alexander Payne's account, based on General Conference records, occupies ten pages of text in his 1891 *History of the African Methodist Episcopal Church.* Bishop Payne observed that "the long and heated discussion of the subject" appears to have been prompted by "the fear that the minority report was not sufficiently radical upon the subject of slavery; while, on the other hand, we find that the majority report was too much so, and might interfere with mercy and justice."[38] The final vote was forty votes for approval and twelve in opposition—for the minority report. Although this issue was discussed again at the A.M.E. Church General Conference of 1860, the Report on Slavery essentially repeated the resolution of 1856.

Space limitations do not permit me to offer a full-scale comparison of the similarities and differences between the debate in the Methodist Episcopal Church in the mid-1840s and the debate that preoccupied the General Conference of 1856. The fact that A.M.E. Church leaders at that time and since that time have noted the similarities between the two debates is sufficient for my purposes. However, in asking this question the differences between the A.M.E. struggle and the struggles of the

M.E.C. and M.E.C., South, must be noted; for example, there is no record of the A.M.E. Church ever having justified apparent inconsistencies in its disciplinary practice of the General Rule on slavery by appealing to what God had ordained. The question for the A.M.E. Church was not a matter of principle; it was an issue of strategic implementation. And as such, it was regarded as a matter of import in *both* the spiritual and temporal realms.

IV. The Politics of (Not) Being a "Political Church": The C.M.E. and A.M.E. Churches

From the beginning, one could say that the rather wooden distinction between "the spiritual part" and "the temporal economy" of the *Discipline* never fit comfortably into the practices of the African Methodist Episcopal Church. In 1817, when Richard Allen and company eventually got around to producing a discipline for the nascent African Methodist Episcopal Church, the only substantive changes were those dealing with "temporal" matters, and these largely focused on issues of transfer of deed, and legal incorporation as a denomination in the wake of their having won a series of court battles with white Methodists in Philadelphia over who would control the pulpit and property of the Bethel congregation.[39] However, as Allen often pointed out, it was precisely by means of these kinds of secular maneuvers that Euro-Americans denied African Americans the standing that they believed they were due as children of God, which, of course, had spiritual implications for blacks and whites alike. Therefore, they believed their practice of Methodist discipline was, morally speaking, superior to that of Euro-American Methodists, who had allowed their practice of the "spiritual part" of the discipline to be distorted by racist practices.

Other examples could be offered to show that while the two parts of the *Discipline* were retained, they no longer served the same purpose in the disciplinary practice of the A.M.E. Church. Bishop Henry McNeal Turner's rather *ad hoc* creation of the office of stewardess, a role that, while clearly subordinate to the pastor also displayed pastoral functions, provides a simple but very interesting example. The office of stewardess was described by Turner in *The Genius and Theory of Methodist Polity* as assisting "the stewards, class-leaders, and pastor in managing the spiritual and temporal, affairs of the church."[40] While there is reason to believe that Turner's action involved an attempt to "rein in" or control charismatic authority of women, nevertheless, in a denomination where the "preacher-in-charge," the presiding elder and the bishop exercised considerable authority in the administration of discipline, it is notable that provision was made for the participation of these "mothers of Israel" in pastoral responsibilities.[41]

Actually, this is but one of a number of innovations that emerged in the years after the Civil War, in part as a response to Reconstruction and the so-called Revolution of 1876, and in part as a function of the rapid growth of the African Methodist Episcopal Church, particularly in the Southeastern and Southcentral United States. In certain respects, there are parallels between changes that took place in the A.M.E. Church and the M.E.C. (North), each of which in different ways can be seen to have paralleled as well as played off the new federalism in the United States.[42] At the same time, the M.E.C., South, and the C.M.E. Church had a different assessment of what was happening. Here again, we see that the political conflict among the four churches transpired in the midst of an increasingly complex segregation of practices based upon a common heritage.

Prior to the 1845 split, the Methodist Episcopal Church experienced a great deal of conflict that had its origin in the perception that abolitionists were going beyond the "spiritual" practices of the *Discipline* by becoming involved in a political conflict. During and immediately after the Civil War, this perception was heightened as the M.E.C., South, saw leaders of the Northern Church (like Matthew Simpson) taking advantage of the military situation to gain control of congregations of the M.E.C., South. Conflict about what it meant to be a "political church" reemerged in the last three decades of the nineteenth century between two of the African American Methodist denominations: the A.M.E. Church and the C.M.E. Church. In fact, in the aftermath of the Civil War, all four of these denominational bodies of American Methodism can be seen to have struggled with this issue, and, more important, to have struggled with it in relation to one another. This issue was very complex and, in retrospect, it can be seen to have set up some odd relationships for all four bodies in question, as both the Euro-American and African American denominations reacted to (their perceptions of) one another with mutual suspicion.

Unlike the A.M.E. Church, which in the 1820s found itself struggling for legitimacy against the M.E. Church, the earliest records of the disciplinary practice of the Colored (Christian) Methodist Episcopal Church had little to do with the body from which this group had sprung (M.E. Church, South) in 1870. In fact, apologists for the C.M.E. Church, such as F. M. Hamilton, were very much concerned about the opinions of two different audiences, namely the M.E. Church (North) and the A.M.E. Church. "The idea with many is that the 'Colored M.E. Church [as a noted minister of another Church said] is nothing more than a form without any substance' but they are learning better," said Hamilton in his pamphlet history of the Colored Methodist Church in America (1887) written less than twenty years after the founding of the C.M.E. Church. In particular, Hamilton singled out the "great mistake" of Bishop Matthew Simpson, the M.E. Church bishop who had written one of the earliest accounts of the origin of the C.M.E. Church.[43]

Hamilton attempts to "set the record straight" against those who, like Simpson, doubt the legitimacy of his church's origin, and therefore its claim to membership in the Methodist "family." In typical American Methodist fashion, Hamilton tries to accomplish this purpose by narrating the significance of C.M.E. disciplinary practice as part of the "family saga" of the rise of Methodism in "colored" America. This seventeen-year-old "youngest daughter" of the American Methodist family was not to be set apart from the "great family" of Methodism, argued Hamilton.[44] Hamilton argues that following the division of 1844, "the colored members in the South had no choice what to do, or where they would place their membership. . . . They had not the privilege to go to themselves and organize a 'separate' and 'distinct' body of Methodists."[45] However, once God has brought about a new circumstance in which they have the opportunity to be independent, it now "makes sense" in a way that it never could have while they were still enslaved. Hamilton argues:

> When a man is bound hand and foot his best policy is to remain still, or he may fall and injure himself. But when he is loose and from under restraint he can go where he pleases, do as he pleases, and stay as long as he pleases. What is the use of making an attempt at "kicking" when both feet are in stocks? Better remain still until your chains are taken off.[46]

However much Hamilton's argument about the limited opportunity available to blacks in the South prior to the end of the Civil War may or may not have been somewhat persuasive to African American Methodists and Euro-American Methodists in the North, his appeals to the separation of "Abraham and Lot" in the Old Testament and the separation of Paul and Barnabas in the New Testament as examples to justify the creation of the C.M.E. Church were hardly convincing.[47]

Hamilton concludes the first chapter of his "Plain Account" with several testimonials, including one by Dr. W. C. Dunlap of the M.E. Church, South:

> I believe that the organization of the Colored M.E. Church was under the direction of God, in order that there might be one colored church in the land that would not turn aside for politics or anything contrary to their high calling. In this you somewhat excel the mother. The child in this respect gives the mother an example. I have never heard of your Church or ministers turning aside for politics; I have never heard of political meetings being held in your churches.[48]

The familial language used in this passage recalls the "fraternal greetings" of Lovick Pierce and William F. Dickerson, and also suggests the complex way in which the denominations in question related to one another during the last quarter of the nineteenth century. The C.M.E. Church is regarded as the "daughter" of the maternal M.E.C., South. Meanwhile, the M.E.C., South, is engaged in a sibling rivalry with the M.E.C. (North), which has a long-standing dispute with the A.M.E. Church about the nature of its patrimony. Finally, the A.M.E. Church challenged the legitimacy of the C.M.E. Church on the grounds that this recently formed denomination was leading African Americans back into slavery, a charge that C.M.E. apologists Hamilton, Holsey, and Phillips would repeatedly and indignantly deny.[49]

Thus for Hamilton (using Dunlap's words) to avow that the C.M.E. Church embodies the hope that "there might be one colored church in the land that would not turn aside for politics or anything contrary to their high calling" had a double purpose. This characterization not only attempts to legitimate the C.M.E. Church against those in the northern church who doubt the circumstances of her origin, but also attempts to delegitimate the A.M.E. Church, which is regarded as being a "political" church. Oddly enough, Dunlap's (and Hamilton's) words also recall the "rhetoric of unity" found in early American Methodist texts from 1798 onward, except that in this instance the "spiritual-temporal" contrast has been reinscribed within a context now marked by a new set of segregationist institutions of the post-Reconstruction era. This impression is confirmed by the words Bishop Lucius H. Holsey wrote in his foreword to Hamilton's history.

Divisions upon the subject of Church polity have never affected the germ and inherent life of any of the branches. They all "continue to hold fast to the form of sound words." Upon all those great subjects have agitated and moved the public heart . . . and that have entered the moral and religious arena, there has been a singular, if not a peculiar blending of feeling, thought, and co-operative action, as if the Universal Spirit had stirred and inspired the whole moral mass, and assimilated every sentiment and impulse of the heart to meet the exigencies of the day and face the angry storm of a frowning world. Methodists are Methodists wherever there are any Methodists. True, some bear the name, but disown the life of holiness and purity of character that should distinguish themselves as Methodists; of these we do not speak.[50]

Holsey's indirect speech—"of these we do not speak"—may be regarded as being potentially as important as what he says in the passage just quoted. However, the effect of his words remains largely defensive. Taken together, these examples depict just how protracted the conflict between these four American Methodist "siblings" was at the close of the nineteenth century.

This self-understanding parallels the way the Methodist Episcopal Church, South, related to the A.M.E. Church in the years immediately following the Civil War. As early as 1869, the M.E.C., South, sent representatives to the Georgia Annual Conference of the A.M.E. Church to communicate the "conditions" under which they would "carry out in good faith the terms of amity and alliance agreed upon"[51] with the A.M.E. Church. A.M.E. Georgia Conference records of this exchange of views tersely report: "Cooperation and friendship were pledged . . . but with caution, as was evidenced by the expression, 'Only while we were engaged in our one work.' This was a reference to politics." M.E.C., South, leaders made it clear that the A.M.E. Church "was regarded as a politico-ecclesiastical organization in sympathy with the North."[52] A.M.E. leaders did not consider it an accident that it was in this same context that the M.E.C., South, leaders announced that they intended to "organize an independent colored body in connection with themselves."[53]

What is particularly interesting about this incident is the pattern that begins to emerge thereafter. Several years before this, the South Carolina Conference of the A.M.E. Church felt compelled to address the rumors about its being a "political" church.

Whereas, there appears in some quarters a difference of opinion as to the real status of the African M.E. Church, as it respects other denominations; and some have attempted to place us in a false position, and especially to antag-onize us with that element and power which has brought freedom and suf-frage to our country. And whereas this opinion is falsely based and those who thus position us ... misstate us; more, they misrepresent us. And where-as there are those who terribly complain because we have sought to be friendly, and to treat those respectfully who treat us with a degree of respect, and in the midst of whom we live; and who have aided us and co-operated with us in establishing Churches amongst our people in this Southern region; therefore

Resolved, That, as ministers of the Prince of Peace, we intend to cultivate peace with all men, whether of the North or the South, as much as in us lieth.

Resolved, That we regard those as our enemies—of our race—who seek their division, whether they be from the North or the South, black or white.[54]

As this comment suggests, at least in some precincts, the A.M.E. Church leaders often felt that they were operating alone without allies, encircled by enemies—from both races.

But the members of the South Carolina Conference of the A.M.E. Church did not stop by defending themselves against the charge of being a political church. Taking the offensive, the "Special Committee on the Political Status of the A.M.E. Church" stated its resolve: "That we cannot recognize those as the friends of our manhood who ignore us because we dare to follow the convictions of our mind, and demand of all Christian denominations full and equal recognition of our manhood and the manhood of our race."[55] As this statement implies, the A.M.E. felt the need to state as a precondition to any renewed sense "spiritual unity" between the A.M.E. and other Methodist bodies (including the C.M.E. Church) that such groups had to be standing for full political cit-izenship as the symbol of the full humanity of African Americans.

Over time, this position came to be articulated in the official denomi-national statements of the A.M.E. Church. Thus, in May 1896, when the African Methodist Episcopal Church officially made "God Our Father, Christ Our Redeemer, Man Our Brother" (the saying of Bishop Daniel Alexander Payne) the official motto of the denomination, they not only were restating the position that they had been taking throughout the nineteenth century, but also the denomination was reaffirming the basis for its own stance vis-à-vis Euro-American Methodist bodies.

This is the official motto of the A.M.E. Church, and her mission in the com-mon-wealth of Christianity is to bring all denominations and races to acknowledge and practice the sentiments contained therein. When these sentiments are universal in theory and practice, then the mission of the distinctively colored organizations will cease.[56]

What the 1867 South Carolina Annual Conference resolution and other A.M.E. Church pronouncements do not reveal is how much the charge of being a "political church" stuck to the A.M.E. Church. Throughout the latter part of the nineteenth century, A.M.E. church leaders found that they had to refute this charge over and over again in their dealings with the Methodist Episcopal Church, South and the Christian Methodist Episcopal Church. A.M.E. leaders also faced this problem in the early decades of the twentieth century.[57] Meanwhile, the C.M.E. Church has had a tendency to represent itself (as did the M.E.C., South) as a "nonpolitical" and/or "ecumenical" church. Further, by adopting a spiritualized "rhetoric of unity," which, on some occasions, has appeared to ignore the reality of racial and political divisions in American culture, the C.M.E. Church has sometimes appeared to be supporting segregationist structures.[58]

This conception of its identity, in turn, has shaped the C.M.E. practice of discipline, even as the "political" self-conception of the A.M.E. Church has therefore also shaped its practice of church discipline. Thus, in 1898, C. H. Phillips would remark about the C.M.E. Church: "No new usage or any serious change in Methodist polity or doctrine is likely to find any place among us; we shall follow in the old landmarks, believing as we do, that the simplicity of the system of Methodism will bear the test of generations yet to come."[59] In fact, while there are numerous examples of disciplinary innovations that have occurred in the C.M.E. Church over the past century, there is also evidence of remarkable continuity in disciplinary rhetoric and practice—including uses of the "General Rules" well into the third quarter of the twentieth century.

At the end of the nineteenth century, the four denominations in question were all contesting the emergence of various "political" practices that appeared to go beyond, if not actually transgress, the distinction between "temporal economy" and the "spiritual part" of the discipline. The A.M.E. and the C.M.E. churches represent two different kinds of responses or reactions to the collapse of these categories of disciplinary practice. Thus, American Methodists—black and white—disagreed on the moral adequacy of one another's practices, in part because they disagreed about how, or whether, to draw the line between the spiritual and temporal realms.

V. Twentieth-Century Quest for a "New Discipline" for a Reunited American Methodism

It is striking to notice the very different ways in which African American Methodist denominations and predominantly Euro-American Methodist bodies in the twentieth century have narrated the relationship of contemporary disciplinary practice to nineteenth-century practices. Examination of almost any book of discipline in the A.M.E. Church and the C.M.E. Church will reveal that there is a perception of continuity with their past. In part, this is due to the fact that African American Methodist denominations perceive themselves to be engaged in a continuing struggle against racism (however much they may differ about strategies for combating racism). A prominent example of this would be the continued inclusion of a statement against slavery in all twentieth-century editions of the Book of Discipline of the A.M.E. Church, a practice that began with their earliest Book of Discipline. Although the C.M.E. Church does not have this same kind of disciplinary tradition, their disciplinary practice is by no means devoid of comparably strong interpretive statements.[60] Not surprisingly, where such statements occur, it is in the context of interpreting the significance of the General Rules for contemporary faith and practice.[61] In part, however, this is also due to continuities of rhetorical and disciplinary practices that are distinctive, when compared with the denominational traditions that became The United Methodist Church.

This example stands as a reminder of the very different ways in which African American Methodists confront the issue of changes in disciplinary practice as compared with the predominantly Euro-American traditions. It also reflects the sense in which "discipline" was no longer seen primarily in relation to the General Rules, understood as a significant set of moral and spiritual practices by which "Methodist peoplehood" was to be embodied in life and work. By the beginning of the twentieth century, Euro-American Methodists could no longer overlook the fact that the "General Rules" were no longer serving the purpose that they had been saying they served. In the first decades of the twentieth century, various versions of "Our Social Creed" came to be adopted, and the journey toward the United Methodist "Social Principles" had begun.

From the first quadrennium of the century until the last, General Conferences have faced the specter—and the difficulty—of narrating the moral and spiritual significance of disciplinary change. The earliest, and most striking example of this recognition came in "The Episcopal

Address" given at the 1900 General Conference of the Methodist Episcopal Church. In their discussion of the "Spiritual Life" of the Church, the Council of Bishops made the following observations about the status of church discipline in the Methodist Episcopal Church (North):

> That many changes have occurred in the outward forms of Methodism is obvious. *Which do they indicate, growth or decay?* The class meeting, for instance, is considerably disused: *have fellowship and spiritual helpfulness among believers abated, or do they find, in part, other expressions and other instruments?* The rigid and minute Church discipline of former years is relaxed: *is this a sign of pastoral unfaithfulness, or is it a sign of growing respect for individual liberty and of a better conception of the function of the Church?* The plainness of the early Methodist congregations has disappeared: *is this simply vanity and worldliness, or is it, in part, the natural and justifiable development of the aesthetic faculty under more prosperous external conditions?* The strenuous contention for this or that particular doctrine or usage of Methodism, once common, is now rarely heard: *is this indifferentism, or is it, in part, a better discernment of that which is vital to the Christian faith, and, in part, the result of an acceptance by others of the once disputed opinion?*[62]

The language or languages[63] of this document deserve further analysis. The distinctions that are made (e.g., "outward forms" and inner reality) in relation to the changes over time reflect the attempt by Protestants at the turn of the century to identify some "essence" that stands above history.[64] At the same time, the bishops are not trying to ignore the concerns raised within the church about the possibility of apostasy. The hesitancy of the bishops to assign *any one answer* to the questions they pose in their General Conference address reflects both the uncertainty of the denomination with respect to its own past and the sensitivity of the church's leadership to the challenges of the twentieth century within as well as outside the denomination.

While the bishops did little more than to raise questions for the church's reflection, the stage was set for a revisionist assessment. A few years later, an "instrumental" conception of the purpose of church discipline emerged. This conceptual innovation, which while not unheard of in American Methodism, took shape against the backdrop of a late-nineteenth-century separation between doctrine and discipline. This new construal of discipline appeared first in the "Historical Statement" from the 1904 *Discipline* of the Methodist Episcopal Church.

The Methodist Episcopal Church has always believed that the only infallible proof of the legitimacy of any branch of the Christian Church is its ability to seek and to save the lost, and to disseminate the Pentecostal spirit and life. The chief stress has ever been laid, not upon the forms but upon the essentials of religion. It holds that true Churches of Christ may differ widely in ceremonies, ministerial orders and government. Its members are allowed freedom of choice among the debated modes of Baptism. If any member has scruples against receiving the Lord's Supper kneeling, he is permitted to receive it standing or sitting. In ordinary worship its people are invited to unite in extemporary prayer, but for the Administration of the Sacraments, Ordinations, the Solemnization of Matrimony, the Burial of the Dead, and other special services, a liturgy is appointed, taken in large part from Rituals used by the Universal Church from ancient times.

The sole object of the rules, regulations, and usages of the Methodist Episcopal Church is that it may fulfill to the end of time its original divine commission as a leader in evangelization, in all true reforms, and in the promotion of fraternal relations among all the branches of the one Church of Jesus Christ, with which it is a co-worker in the spiritual conquest of the world for the Son of God.[65]

The traditional Protestant distinction between doctrinal essentials and "matters of opinion" about which reasonable Christians can agree to disagree *(adiaphora)*, now comes to be applied to disciplinary practices. Whereas early American Methodist evangelistic practice was tied to disciplinary practices (cf. the rules for probationary membership, etc.), now evangelistic practice is regarded as separate from disciplinary standards. As if in confirmation of this, at the next General Conference of the Methodist Episcopal Church (1908), the standards of probationary membership were eliminated, thereby giving another level of legitimacy to the emerging consensus about the secondary purpose of disciplinary practices.

Given these changes and parallel shifts that were beginning to take place in the M.E.C. South and the Methodist Protestant Church, it is understandable that the 1939 reunion of the three predominantly Euro-American Methodist denominations, would become the occasion for providing an overview and reassessment of the various changes that had occurred during the nineteenth century. The 1940 edition of the *Discipline* of the reunited denomination—that would be known thereafter as "The Methodist Church"—included a rather striking prefatory comment entitled the "Episcopal Address" (coauthored by Bishops A. Frank Smith, Ernest G. Richardson, and G. Bromley Oxnam), which was printed as the first item just in front of the "Historical Statement."

The Methodist Discipline is a growth rather than a purposive creation. The founders of Methodism did not work out a set plan, as to details. They dealt with conditions as these arose. The Class Meeting, a distinctive feature of the movement, began as an instrument for the collection of funds. It soon revealed its fitness for religious nurture and took that work as its chief aim. The use of laymen as preachers came against Wesley's will, but it was continued because it seemed to be the one effective way of dealing with actual situations. Open-air preaching, always admitted as a "cross" by Mr. Wesley, came partly because the churches were closed to Methodist preachers, and partly because the people who most needed to be helped would not come to regular services in the sanctuaries. Even Conferences gained their origin from the actual need of bringing workers together for consultation and inspiration.

This process of growth showed itself clearly as the Church increased. Conference work was carried on by the asking of what were called "Minute Questions." These were not perfunctory and artificial. They dealt with the effective ways of presenting the deeper phases and duties of religious experience. As new forms of work were developed, new questions were added to the Conference list.

In such a process of adjustment, the *Discipline* became not a book of definite rules, nor yet a formal code, but rather a record of the successive stages of spiritual insight attained by Methodists under the grace of Christ. We have, therefore, expected that the *Discipline* would be administered, not merely as a legal document, but as a revelation of the Holy Spirit working in and through our people. We reverently insist that a fundamental aim of Methodism is to make her organization an instrument for the development of spiritual life. We do not regard the machinery as sacred in itself; but we do regard as very sacred the souls for whom the Church lives and works. We do now express the faith and hope that the prayerful observance of the spiritual intent of the *Discipline* may be to the people called methodists a veritable means of grace.[66]

This is a remarkable statement when compared with documents such as the 1798 *Discipline,* or Richard Allen's revision of the 1816 *Discipline,* both of which contained a very different conception of the significance of disciplinary practice. This modernist apology for Methodist discipline finds its warrant in evolutionary "growth" as opposed to a conception of the "purposive creation" of the General Rules, for example. Not coincidentally, what is notable about the early Methodist class meeting, according to this statement, is not that it provided one of the most significant contexts for the practice of the General Rules, but that it can be seen as the principal example of Methodist pragmatism. The instrumentalist or pragmatic conception of discipline that had first been enunciated in the 1904 *Discipline* of the M.E.C. (North), has now been ratified by a reunited Methodism!

What this document does, in effect, is to transpose the significance of American Methodist discipline, by way of a narrative of progress, as "a record of the successive stages of insight attained by Methodists under the grace of Christ." The focus is no longer about a holy people raised up by God for mission, the embodiment of which is found in their shared disciplines, but rather on the immanence of God as found in the "spiritual insight" of the people. Similarly, whereas American Methodists once regarded the performance of practices like "fasting and abstinence" to be a means of grace (cf. General Rules), now it is the "prayerful observance of the *spiritual intent* of the discipline" that is commended to Methodist people as a "veritable means of grace." This statement is striking not least because it separates performance from intent in a way that early American Methodists would have found downright odd. Finally, it is worth calling attention to the fact that the rules of American Methodism are now to be regarded as "the machinery"; it is the persons ["souls"] which are to be regarded as sacred.[67] Disciplinary practice is now disembodied.

When, less than two decades later, a shrewd observer of the history of American Methodist practices offered his own more scholarly assessment of the changes that had occurred in Anglo-American Methodist disciplinary practice, the accent is entirely on the side of discontinuity.

> *No longer* do we hear the stern authoritative voice of our English founder setting down the strict confines of the strait way a Methodist Christian should follow. *No longer* are we held together by the old class meetings and bands and select societies. *No longer* do we adhere willingly to the strict and unbending discipline of the Rules. Methodist discipline there is, and much of it is written into the many pages of the *Discipline of the Methodist Church*. But it is not the same as it used to be.[68]

As all these examples suggest, in the twentieth century, Euro-American Methodists have chosen to acknowledge the fact that real changes in disciplinary practice have occurred. When, in 1972, the General Rules were accorded the status of "Historical Document" (along with the Articles of Religion and other confessions of faith), the change that was made in the designation was more rhetorical than substantive in as much as the designation marked a recognition of what had already changed in practice. The most significant changes had long since taken place by the time the new canonical setting of the General Rules was effected as part of The United Methodist Church.

Conclusion

This essay began with an anecdote that suggestively depicted the stances of several American Methodist denominations toward one another in the last quarter of the nineteenth century. In light of this study, the remarks of Lovick Pierce and William F. Dickerson can be seen to be significant for several reasons. First, African American Methodist denominations were constituted, at least partially, in response to the perceived discrepancies between the *theory* of Methodist discipline and the practice of the *Discipline* within predominantly Euro-American denominations. Second, despite these suspicions, the perception of a shared Methodist discipline nevertheless served as the means of specifying what "united" these bodies with one another, and thereby also (third) provided a basis for the kind of "fraternal admonition" offered by leaders of African American Methodist denominations to the leaders of the M.E. Church (North) and the M.E. Church, South (as well as to one another). In these ways, then, a rhetoric of "Christian unity" was a prerequisite to the conception of church disciplinary performance for much of the nineteenth century, despite the fact that these denominations existed in separation (and, in some instances, segregation) from one another.

In light of these developments, in retrospect, the prefatory historical articles that introduced the 1939–40 *Discipline* of the Methodist Church can be said to have provided, *at best*, a partial account of the nineteenth-century legacy of division (an account, of course, which was designed to narrate the *re-union* of these three "branches" of Methodism in America) in as much as it did not narrate the divisions in American Methodism that *preceded* the splits with the Methodist Protestants (1824–28) and Methodist Episcopal Church, South (1846). Nowhere do we find any acknowledgment in the "Historical Statement" of the splits with the African American Methodism(s), much less discussion of the schisms of the O'Kelly's "Republican Methodists" of 1792 or the later, but less well-known split of the Reformed Methodists of New England in 1814. Nor is any account given of the complex history and conflict surrounding the formation of the Colored Methodist Episcopal Church in 1870. When one considers that the 1939 reunion was also the occasion at which the Central Jurisdiction (the denomination structure that segregated congregations by race through the late 1960s) was formed, these omissions are all the more to be deplored. These omissions are notable, I would argue, precisely because the groups named bring to mind some of the most difficult-to-narrate problems in nineteenth-century American Methodist disciplinary practice, and point to many of the ongoing struggles in United Methodism. Indeed, I would argue that, in part, the contemporary ecclesiological problematic facing United Methodists in American culture at the end of the twentieth century is entangled with the complex question of how to assess the conflicting legacies of nineteenth-century disciplinary practices.

One of the most poignant symbols of this is the different way(s) in which the "General Rules" are regarded in United Methodism as compared with the historically Black Methodist denominations. Whereas United Methodists no longer think of the "General Rules" as the "discipline" within the [book of] *Discipline,* there is still a sense in which the historically Black Methodist denominations do think of the General Rules in this way. Although there is plenty of evidence of changes in disciplinary practice of the African Methodist Episcopal Church, these changes are not reflected in the language that is used to describe disciplinary practice.

Meanwhile, in the Christian Methodist Episcopal Church, there is evidence of continuity at the levels of both rhetoric and disciplinary practice. Indeed, it is not too much to say that the 1976 "church trial" of an ordained elder in the C.M.E. Church for violation of one of the General Rules might very well constitute the exception in relation to which the twentieth-century practice of church discipline in American Methodism could someday be written.[69] For here is a use of the "General Rules" that appears to stand alone, and one that would seem to have more in common with some early-nineteenth-century American Methodist disciplinary practices than with the disciplinary practice of the United Methodist tradition.

Finally, this example points to the kinds of conceptual, rhetorical, and disciplinary differences that the United Methodist Church, the Christian Methodist Episcopal Church, and the African Methodist Episcopal Church would have to confront in any present or future quest of a (re-)United Methodism in American culture. The recently proposed effort to create a "Pan-Methodist" union between these three denominations (and the A.M.E. Zion Church) is surely a sign of hope. For once again American Methodist denominations are beginning to recognize the significance of all that they share as the people of God in the midst of many differences (visible and invisible). However, based on the foregoing study, no one should be surprised to learn that one of the first obstacles this proposal has confronted is different conceptions of the *locus* ("local" versus "federal" conceptions of connectionalism) and *basis* of the proposal for "organic union."[70] Nor should United Methodist advocates of such organic union be surprised if, in the future, they discover that their own willingness to pursue such a (re-)United Methodism in American culture is met with suspicion, misunderstanding, and substantive disagreement. For, in addition to all of the differences in rhetoric and practice that have emerged over the past century in these denominations, these "brother" and "sister" denominations of the American Methodist family also have conflicting assessments of the value of the legacies they have received from nineteenth-century American Methodist disciplinary practice—in black and white.[71]

A. Gregory Schneider

A. Gregory Schneider, like Cartwright, offers a close historical study of theological issues in nineteenth-century American Methodism. Schneider explores what he calls contrasting bases of identity for some of Methodism's prominent leaders and demonstrates unusual sensitivity to the holiness side. He finds a sharp contrast between those who represent the holiness tradition and those who represent more fully the institutional life of the official church. He uses the term "connectional" to refer to two bishops, Vincent from the Methodist Episcopal Church, and Haygood from the Methodist Episcopal Church, South. The reader will want to ponder the equation of "connection" with "institutional church" and compare this to theological understandings of the term in other parts of our study of United Methodism and American Culture, especially in Volume I: Connectionalism: Ecclesiology, Mission, and Identity. In fact, Schneider's point has less to do with connectionalism as such and more to do with an understanding of the church and its relationship to culture. Otherwise Schneider's essay represents an impoverished view of connection. At base the issues between the leaders Schneider studies have to do precisely with Methodism and American culture. Is culture to be affirmed and embraced as a gift from God, or is it to be rejected as dangerous to the Christian life of holiness?

The insights Schneider's essay offers into the psychology, philosophy, and theology of the leaders about whom he writes are suggestive of the way in which theological affirmations shape both understandings of the church and individual actions. In many ways the essential elements of the contrasting understandings of religious experience and ecclesial relationship to the world continue in our own time within all churches, but especially within United Methodism, because of the great diversity incorporated in the denomination. Disagreements about biblical interpretation, about mission, about institutional life, and about ethical expectations for individuals and community are not new; they are deeply rooted in Methodist history and experience. Do these contrasts embodied in biographical character studies help us deal with the theological problems of mission and identity we confront?

Connectionalism Versus Holiness: Contrasting Bases of Identity for Leaders of Late-Nineteenth-Century Methodism

A. Gregory Schneider

"This great Church," wrote Phineas F. Bresee, "is our mother in some sense, but she is not an old lady to be coddled in the corner, and protected from public gaze." He was answering a woman correspondent who had rebuked him for earlier editorials attacking the Methodist Episcopal Church. The woman wondered that Bresee could speak so harshly in public of the church that was mother to their newly formed Church of the Nazarene. Bresee only grudgingly admitted the maternal metaphor. His next sentence revealed a spirit more feisty than mother love. "This Church is a great army called of God to the greatest work of these late centuries." Her self-proclaimed mission was to spread scriptural holiness over these lands. If she failed at this, she failed her reason for being. And clearly, by Bresee's estimate, the church was failing.[1] Hence his editorial cannonade in the weeks leading up to this reply to his correspondent's rebuke.

Bishop John Heyl Vincent, nationally renowned as the founder of the Chautauqua movement, had been the target of one of Bresee's broadsides. Vincent and a colleague had been holding evangelistic meetings in Denver, meetings that, in the words of Vincent's biographer, were "shorn of the elements that repel the modern sophisticated man or woman." No altar calls, no public testimonies were included. Even the term "revival" was omitted. Vincent became leader of these meetings precisely because of his well-known opposition to the old-fashioned emotional revival.[2] Bresee scorned this "sad travesty," this "Methodist revival with the Methodist methods left out." The substance of his attack focused on doctrinal matters, specifically the bishop's doctrine of sin. But in his mind, and evidently in the bishop's also, the methods were one with the doctrines. The bishop preached a gospel of culture, complained Bresee, little more than a heathen thing where sin was only a habit that could, with enough time, be bleached out of a person by right associations. How different from the gospel of the new birth, which required "the crucifixion of the body of sin, by the power of God!" The "new birth," for Bresee, implied practices like altar calls and testimony where the power of God could be seen, heard, and felt in actual human lives, not just effetely talked about.[3]

These attacks on one of the most prominent Methodist bishops of his day by the founder of what became the largest holiness denomination in the country are the first bit of evidence for the thesis of this paper. The thesis can be most succinctly communicated, perhaps, by suggesting a dichotomy: the evangelist versus the educator. More explicitly, one may say that the differences holiness leaders and mainstream Methodist denominational leaders had with each other were rooted in contrasting patterns of experience and the contrasting self-understandings created by these experiences. Holiness leaders identified with experiences of purity and power, experiences nurtured in practices of personal piety and meetings for testimony and revivalistic evangelism. Connectional leaders, that is, leaders of the two main Methodist Episcopal denominations, identified with experiences of power and effectiveness in organizational activities like benevolence and mass popular education.

Before filling out this thesis, it is important to spell out some parameters of this study and the background to the conflict it covers. The last third of the nineteenth century is the time during which these contrasting constructions of self developed most clearly. The 1850s, when Phoebe Palmer was at the height of her influence, are an appropriate beginning time. The two decades bracketing the turn of the century, when a variety of holiness groups were coming out of the mainstream denominations, are an approximate ending point. The most important early developments in the growth of both mainstream connectionalism and the holiness movement centered in the Northeast. By the end of the period under consideration, however, there were conflicts over holiness in the Methodist denominations in various regions across the country.[4]

Because this is a study of self-constructions, particular persons are as important to specify as are time and place. Two mainstream denominational leaders, among many who might be studied, provide good case studies of connectional identities. John Heyl Vincent of the Methodist Episcopal Church and Atticus Greene Haygood of the Methodist Episcopal Church, South, served their respective denominations in positions like editor, college professor, Sunday school officer, and bishop. They are also clearly identifiable as critics of the holiness movement. On the holiness side, again among many that might be studied, four persons have attracted my attention. John Allen Wood was the originator of the idea of a national camp meeting for promoting holiness and an evangelist of national scope. Joseph H. Smith was a second-generation holiness evangelist who did not "come out" during the schisms of the turn of the century but rather led the movement from within the Methodist Episcopal Church. Milton L. Haney was a leading evangelist in the volatile midwestern stream of the movement. Phineas F. Bresee was the founding leader of the largest holiness denomination to be formed out of the turn-of-the-century independent holiness associations.

The historical background to the conflicts and tensions treated here may be considered under three rubrics: the early Methodist community, mid-nineteenth-century transformations, and responses to the incorporation of American culture in the last third of the century.

In its early decades, American Methodism had pursued its mission through a form of religious community characterized by three essential elements.[5] First, it was a spiritual family bound together by intense feelings of solidarity. Second, this spiritual family enforced firm moral boundaries between its members and those who were identified with "the world." Third, the family shared their experiences of salvation, creating a fellowship that generated a common passion to convert the world from which they set themselves apart. These three characteristics were grounded in the early Methodist versions of testimony ritual called class meeting and love feast. The bonds of family were cemented in these rituals, the separation from the world was symbolized in the exclusion of worldlings from them, and the energy for evangelism was generated by them. These rituals of testimony were the building blocks of the revivalistic ethos that pervaded early Methodism. A patriarchy of itinerant preachers superintended the many local communities sustained through these rituals. These ruling "fathers" derived legitimacy among their people from their effectiveness in the rituals of testimony and in the evangelism the rituals supported. The itinerants were pastoral patriarchs whose training by apprenticeship bound them to their spiritual children by ties of common experience.

The world over against which this spiritual family defined itself was a traditional one dominated by patriarchs who demanded deference from their inferiors, a world in which social norms required that high and low alike mind their honor and avoid shame. These traditional demands had based self-worth primarily upon external appearance and physical or verbal performance as these were judged by the watching eyes of the local neighborhood. Traditional norms of honor had been heavily concerned with rank. Issues of rank were generally settled for the upper classes on the basis of family lineage, wealth, refinement of manners, and liberal education, that classically and philosophically oriented form of education that befitted a gentleman.[6] For lower classes these criteria still applied, but were tempered by considerations of sheer physical strength, beauty, or skill, including speaking skills like wit and storytelling. The rituals of such communities were generally rituals of masculine contest like horse races or cockfights, verbal banter or drinking contests, and, when men sought to win their women, dances. The Methodist rituals of testimony helped to create an alternative community of spiritual equality based on the common experience of the evangelical new birth. The abiding inner sense of God's acceptance that resulted from the new birth implied a relative freedom from the shaming eyes of the traditional neighborhood and a greater opportunity for self-governance. This greater freedom was underwritten by the moral boundary between the family of God and the world.

In midcentury Methodism, class meeting was a dying practice, and the pastoral patriarchy was rapidly becoming more managerial, less paternalistic, and less revivalistic. Laity were expressing their evangelical initiatives in two diverging and, eventually, antagonistic trends: the proliferation of voluntary benevolent agencies and the growth of the holiness movement. The pastoral hierarchy of the Methodist Episcopal Church, South, at the General Conference of 1866, signaled its declining interest in paternalistic oversight by officially dropping the requirement of weekly class meeting attendance as a condition of membership.[7] Shortly thereafter, the hierarchy of the Methodist Episcopal Church ratified its natural affinity with the proto-bureaucratic benevolent agencies by, in essence, marrying itself to them at the General Conference of 1872.[8] The holiness movement's weekly meetings for the promotion of holiness centered on personal testimony to the experience of entire sanctification. The weekly meetings for the promotion of this experience were a new, unofficial form of the class meeting. The national camp meetings for the promotion of holiness also gave the love feast a new venue. The old ritual economy of testimony in Methodism took on a new incarnation, but this time *outside* the official channels of the body that had given it birth.

The incorporation of American culture was a general trend that began at midcentury but gained increasing momentum as the century grew to a close.[9] The trend would culminate the Progressive era with its scientifically trained professional managers bent on building a national order on the values of continuity and regularity, functionality and rationality, administration and management. A culture of professionalism undergirded the trend to incorporation. It prescribed careers built on higher education, earning of degrees and credentials, and ever higher levels of accomplishment and recognition in the context of the new ruling bureaucracies. Denominational organization and voluntary agencies in the churches were harbingers of this trend.[10]

The argument developed here interprets holiness and connectionalism as contrasting responses to these trends of incorporation, the former more rejecting of the trend and the latter more accepting. Both responses were concerned to preserve and enhance the unity and power of the Methodist community. Those identified with connectional patterns of association, however, saw the unity and power of the church as consisting in its benevolent activities of missions, social service, and education. Those identified with the holiness experienced its unity and power in their rituals of testimony that fused the hearts of believers and generated great spiritual energy for evangelism. In recent work, I have used the rough dichotomy, "objective selves vs. empowered selves" in an attempt to evoke the self-constructions arising from these differing associational patterns.[11] The present study aims to refine this characterization in terms of contrasts developed under five categories: biography and autobiography, formative experiences, the issue of boundaries, the sense of the divine, and identification with roles.

Biography and Autobiography

From the time Wesley and Asbury wrote journals and published portions of them, there was a tradition of spiritual autobiography in Methodism. The publications of Methodism made available for emulation the patterns of religious experience of notably pious exemplars, not just clergy like Wesley, Asbury, or John Fletcher but also laity like Hester Ann Rogers and William Carvosso.[12] The holiness movement of the nineteenth century took the Methodist penchant for testifying publicly to the work of grace in the heart and elevated it to a *sine qua non*. Those who obtained, but did not give definite testimony to, the experience of entire sanctification as distinct second work of grace would lose this blessing. The practice of constructing an autobiographical narrative around the experiences of grace was widespread, therefore, among all who followed the way of Wesleyan holiness.

Holiness leaders readily wrote autobiographies or provided the grist for biographies structured around their experiences of the New Birth and of entire sanctification. These stories were extensions of their evangelistic witness and were designed to show the supernatural workings of God in the lives of human beings.[13] John A. Wood and Milton L. Haney wrote quite detailed autobiographies that told of how they experienced conversion and sanctification and then how they spent their lifetimes leading others into the same experiences.[14] Joseph E. Smith never wrote his own autobiography, but he did tell his stories of conversion and sanctification enough times to enough people to have them well preserved and to serve as important source material for a theological biographer.[15] Phineas Bresee was a very busy man as he founded and organized the Church of the Nazarene, and he never took time to write his autobiography. But late in life he did spend many evenings recounting his life story to his friend and associate, E. A. Girvin, who took down his accounts in shorthand. These transcripts formed the core of a biography that was published a year after Bresee's death.[16]

In contrast to the continuing interest in testimony and spiritual autobiography that animated the holiness movement, it appears that biographies and autobiographies of the bishops and editors of the church were becoming more scarce. These principal leaders of the Methodist connectional system seemed to no longer be willing to conform their constructions of selfhood to the autobiographical formulas of evangelical testimony. Daniel Curry and Charles H. Fowler were editors of northern Methodism's flagship weekly, the (New York) *Christian Advocate,* and both opposed the holiness movement on this issue. Curry observed that it is one thing to experience the inward workings of the Holy Spirit, another thing to communicate the experience intelligibly. "The faculty of clearly reading one's own mind's operations and of clothing them in recognized language is not the most common mental quality among ordinarily intelligent people." The confusion of meaning arising from different efforts to speak about religious experience resulted in either a war of words, or worse, in Curry's estimation, "the parrot-like utterance of words, without any definite meaning." Fowler echoed this concern over empty and extravagant testimonies, and warned against making the experience of any one person the standard for all. Both men urged that judgments of people's spiritual condition be based on their actions, the fruits of godliness rather than their professions of it.[17]

Of the two bishops that this study focuses on, John H. Vincent was the one who did attempt an autobiography. This work, however, was written in a series of "papers" published irregularly in the (Chicago) *Northwestern Christian Advocate*, and, as Vincent's biographer observed, it lacks form.[18] As the patient reader proceeds through twenty-five rambling installments, it becomes clear that, unlike the evangelist autobiographers, the bishop does not "will one thing," that is the conversion and sanctification of sinners. His eclectic interests, his wish to encompass in Christian faith all of civilization, and perhaps his advanced age make for a diffuse and sometimes repetitious read. Bishop Vincent is all "principles," "themes," and "emphases" and very little story.

Atticus Haygood wrote very little in an autobiographical mode and no full, coherent biography of him was published until 1965 when Harold W. Mann presented him as a harbinger of a political and social vision of "the New South."[19] Mann's treatment of Haygood follows the several official positions he held and, like Vincent's treatment of himself, is primarily topical rather than narrative. This account of Bishop Haygood's life, again like Bishop Vincent's, lacks the focus and coherence, as well as the narrowness, of a life crystallized around experiences of conversion and sanctification and dedicated to bringing others to these experiences.

Formative Experiences

The primary formative experiences for holiness leaders, of course, were their conversions and, especially, their experiences of being "entirely sanctified." These experiences laid out sharp boundaries between before and after in the career of the subject and between carnal and spiritual in the subject's inner realm of motive. They also stressed the motive of complete obedience and total surrender to God in Christ, a totality of commitment that implied the severing of attachments to any part of this world. These experiences, furthermore, were in significant part tests of the conscious will. Holiness leaders consciously chose to seek their religious experiences and these experiences confronted them, in self-examination, with decisive self-denying choices that opened the way to these experiences. Human beings, of course were incapable of saving themselves, but holiness doctrine held that they were fully capable of choosing to be saved, and saved from all sin.

Thus Milton Haney's conversion involved consciousness of his sins "as a deep, dismal cloud" that "obscured everything but the displeasure of God." "There was a period," he reported, "when it did appear the pains of hell had taken hold upon me and I had such of a view of the damnation of the wicked that it has never been erased from my mind." This state of mind was followed, immediately upon conversion, by a radical change: "The change apparent to my sensibilities was the utter and instant removal of my guilty load. . . . I found myself consciously possessed of a new life which I had never known before." Haney played an important role in bringing himself to these states of consciousness. First, he consciously and intentionally attended a New Year's Eve Watch Night meeting in order to "seek religion" and, with a little urging from a friend, responded to an altar call there. Second, when in the throes of conviction for sin, he consciously chose to obey an inner voice he heard telling him to give his hand to the preacher as a sign that he was going to join the Methodist church. He had earlier resisted his impressions that he should make this public gesture. With this last point of resistance surrendered, he passed from consciousness of his sins to consciousness of his new life.[20]

An essential element of the formative moments in the lives of Bishops Haygood and Vincent seems to have been a *rejection* of the traditional revivalistic doctrines and experiences that holiness advocates sought to revitalize. Revivalistic religion was an experience of death and resurrection; it required an experience of darkness and dread that then led into an opposite experience of light and joy. Apparently both Atticus Haygood and John Vincent, in their youth, grew overly competent at imagining themselves in darkness and dread. The gift of moving from this dread to a reliable sense of themselves in the light and joy of God's acceptance eluded them both.

As we have seen, Atticus Haygood did not leave much record of his inner life and struggles. But it was abundantly clear, by the middle of his career, that he did not subscribe to Methodism's long-standing regimen of consciously willed ascetic self-discipline in quest of distinct, publicly identifiable experiences of grace. From this fact and from the documents that are available, Haygood's biographer has inferred that the bishop underwent a "deconversion" from his inherited Wesleyan Arminian faith. This process of deconversion probably happened in the two years leading up to Haygood's "New South" sermon, which brought him to national attention. It seems to have involved a rejection of calculated self-denial leading to a supernatural ecstasy, and an acceptance of a providence that worked through natural processes. Haygood's published works from the 1880s onward, in any case, reflect this more naturalistic vision.[21]

Plausible as it may be, the idea of a definite "deconversion" experience in Haygood's life remains an inference drawn by his biographer. The case for such an experience in John Heyl Vincent's life is much stronger. Although profoundly influenced by a pious mother who was steeped in the devotional literature of holiness, he ultimately rejected what he took to be the morbid, self-centered religion of his childhood. He sought a different map for his inner life, one that pointed out small steps of faith and duty and encouraged the cultivation of the will to make them.[22]

In the twelfth installment of his "Autobiography" he combines accounts of three decisive experiences: his founding of his famous Palestine class, his mother's death, and his fellowship with an alternative dying mentor. The Palestine class was an innovation in Bible study and pedagogy that was crucial to his identification with the role of educator. We will deal with it further below. His account of his mother's death bears most, but not all, the marks of the ritual of happy dying that was the final crisis event, after the new birth, and entire sanctification for the exemplary Methodist saint.[23] His alternative mentor was Henry Hurd, the pastor who had preceded him in one of his early pastoral appointments in New Jersey.

He gives extensive tribute to his mother as one of the two most influential people in his life, and praises her piety and her consistent living of her religion in daily life. He dwells on her death in two consecutive installments of his autobiography, explicitly declining in both to give a full account of her dying experience. Her life, he declared, was a testimony worth a score of deathbed declarations. This is an interesting refusal. Other parts of his account make it clear that his mother struggled to retain her lucidity to the last precisely in order to be able to show her children and neighbors how dying grace is given to the children of God. At the last midnight before she died, in fact, she called her son John to her bedside to read scripture to her in order to steady her mind.

He declares that her smiling face, her looks of love, and "her words at the last" can never be forgotten by those who stood by her that day. Unlike a host of Methodists before and even during his time, however, he refrains from saying exactly what were those "words at the last."[24]

This omission is all the more significant in light of his treatment of the death of the other most influential person in his life, Pastor Henry Hurd. His mother died in 1852. He met Hurd two years later when he discovered what an impact the former pastor had made on the people of his charge in what was then North Belleville, New Jersey. Vincent, who wondered if he was going to make any mark on this pastoral charge, decided he had to meet this man whose name was on everyone's lips and whose picture was on everyone's wall. He sent Hurd a check and invited him to come to visit his people. It seems the young future bishop was hungry for a mentor, for his account of Hurd's visit is almost one of love at first sight. "He came. I saw. And he conquered," wrote the bishop in reminiscence. Again, "He captured me at once. His liberality, breadth, earnestness, and openness of mind attracted me and we became intimate friends."

This man introduced Vincent to a religion of "natural law" in the realm of inner spiritual life. Hurd himself had retired from the ministry due to illness, and had come from a water cure institution in New York. There he had picked up the system of religious thought that he shared with the captivated John Vincent. It was, said Vincent, a mild form of Swedenborgianism, and it stressed "scientific study" of the natural processes by which Christ comes to possess the soul and brings it into harmony with the universe of which it is a part. Vincent counted Hurd as the "most stimulating" of all the friends of his early ministerial life, "especially in the line of subjective spiritual experience." Fifty-six years later, the elderly bishop's imagination was still fired not just with ideas he learned from Hurd but with his image of the man—refined and strong, face and blue eyes full of light, a magnetic voice of rare sweetness, depth, clearness, and force.

It was this man's dying words, not his mother's, that Vincent chose to include in his account of "the most important quadrennium of [his] first twenty-four years of life." Mother Vincent and Henry Hurd both died well, full of the assurances provided by their respective faiths. Instead, however, of the exhortations to shun the world, seek religion, and meet her in heaven that Mother Vincent almost certainly gave at the end, her son gives Hurd's exhortation to authenticity: "Live a true life . . . a true life." Hurd died in October of 1854, and John Vincent wrote in his diary, "He was the best man I ever knew and the best friend I ever had."[25]

It was not until 1856, at another pastoral charge, that Vincent devised his Palestine class. But he had some success as a teacher in the years before he entered the ministry, and during his first ministerial assignments he had split his time between preaching and studying at the Newark Wesleyan Academy.[26] The Palestine class seemed to crystallize his identity. It was as if Hurd's dying exhortation to authenticity granted Vincent the freedom to build a life on his gifts as an educator instead of following the self-denying patterns of traditional Methodist spiritual autobiography urged upon him by his mother's life and death.[27]

Boundaries

Holiness leaders' quest for and insistence upon definite experiences of conversion and sanctification led them also to have a sense of a sharp boundary between believers and the world. This boundary had a dual function. One function was to safeguard the fellowship of believers from unfriendly opponents as they shared their common experiences of what they believed was God's work in their souls. A second function was to signal that there was indeed a difference between being a holy Christian and not being one, a difference so profound as to require an equally profound experience of spiritual crisis and transformation. As John Inskip, first president of the National Camp-Meeting Association for the Promotion of Holiness put it, "But we need a religion sufficiently Divine to cause the world to denounce us as beside ourselves. We must separate from the world if we would influence them. They admire and confide in us most when we antagonize them. To yield is to be subdued, to resist is to conquer."[28]

Such separation from the world was, according to holiness leaders, supposed to be well marked and highly visible. The markers were in the words, dress, and activities that distinguished holiness people from worldly people. Tobacco and alcohol, dancing and theater-going, jewelry and other decorative or showy items of dress—especially on women—were all marks of the world and people regularly gave them up when they were converted or sanctified. Joseph H. Smith took such surrender as a matter of course when he spoke in passing of the fact that his salary on his first pastoral charge was only slightly more than half of what he had spent on cigars when he was "in the world."[29] Indulgence in such items by other Methodist church members, moreover, was the occasion for protest on the part of plain holiness people.

Thus Phineas Bresee picked out for extensive quotation in his weekly, *The Nazarene,* an article by a presiding elder of the South Kansas Conference of the Methodist Episcopal Church that identified a "Crisis in Methodism." The crisis was over holiness and worldliness. When someone accepts a pastor's holiness message, gets the experience, and seeks to testify to it in a definite way, observed the author, "the tendency is to cause comparisons of experience which are not creditable to those not having this grace." Those who testify must then take great care to avoid seeming to be censorious or pharisaical. Indeed, it may not be possible to avoid these appearances. Thus are factions created. The bishops try to harmonize the factions, but their ways of doing so tend to support the lax and unconsecrated while discouraging the really enthusiastic people in the congregations. Bishop Fowler goes so far as to call advocates of holiness "cranks" and to call their desired religious experience "cranktification." "A worldly, card-playing, theater-going, tobacco-using church never gains converts in any considerable degree. But we have gone home from Conference and had that class of members quote from the Bishop's address to prove that our efforts to get them to live pure lives, to consecrate themselves and become soul-winners, was . . . 'cranktification.'" This process of division and the bishops' abortive attempts to heal the split, concluded the preacher, have shorn the churches of much strength and caused "our church to lose its thousands and the Southern Methodist Church to lose its ten thousands."[30]

If holiness boundary-keeping seemed necessarily to imply censoriousness, at least some holiness advocates were quick to point out that the worldly had their own forms of mean exclusiveness. Many of the worldly self-indulgences that holiness folk denied themselves and condemned in others were associated with wealth, refinement, and social respectability. They went with a lifestyle that shamed and repelled the less well-to-do and less refined or, at its worst, rejected them. Thus J. A. Wood remembered that the only congregation that had ever objected to his being assigned to them was one in Windsor, New York, that was quite formal and fashionable. There were some "fastidious" members in the church who had got the impression that Wood was coarse, uncultivated, and not much of a preacher.[31] Phineas F. Bresee was relentless in confronting such fastidious worldliness. His biographer recorded

Bresee's memory of a Methodist church in Iowa where he kept about a quarter of the congregation angry at him all the time, "but not the same quarter, as they took turns."[32] By the time he was building up his Church of the Nazarene in Los Angeles, Bresee was making openness to the poor a hallmark of his movement. "Let the Church of the Nazarene be true to its commission," he declared, "not great and elegant buildings; but to feed the hungry and clothe the naked, and wipe away the tears of the sorrowing; and gather jewels for His diadem." He said he wanted church buildings "so plain that every board will say welcome to the poorest."[33]

These social sensitivities notwithstanding, however, there was a strong tendency among holiness folk to lay emphasis on the minutiae of dress, diet, and conduct rather than on wider social and spiritual forces and principles. As Paul Bassett has demonstrated, moreover, the notions of sanctity and sin implied in the prohibitions of dance, drink, and fancy dress grew increasingly narrow.[34] This narrowness repulsed connectional leaders like Atticus Haygood and John Vincent, who had little patience with the sharp drawing of boundaries of any kind and still less for the holiness style of drawing them.

Haygood took aim at the latter in his last book, *The Monk and the Prince,* ostensibly an account of the career of Savonarola as reformer of Renaissance Florence, but also a critique of the reforms insisted upon by Georgia holiness preachers. Haygood's Savonarola, like his holiness preacher colleagues, was poisoned in the depths of his character by "the bitter-sour distillations of the extremest asceticism." Such asceticism not only made people utterly intolerant of those who did not conform to their dogmas, formulas of speech, or patterns of behavior, it made them spiritually puffed up with notions that they had "the mind of the Spirit" while their opponents did not. Such people, suggested Haygood, were mentally unbalanced and spiritually unhealthy.[35]

John Vincent showed equal hostility, though in a different manner from Haygood, to what he regarded as false and artificial boundaries. He dedicated much of his autobiography to attacking the division of life into sacred and secular, holy and unholy, and, by implication, church and world. "The failure to make secular life as secular life *sacred,*" he asserted, "is to draw a line of demarcation which the Word of God does not draw and to establish two standards of life, one for religious people and another for the nonprofessing." All phases of life in society, be it recreation or business or religious worship, "are so many divinely ordained opportunities for the development of personal character and for the building up of a permanent civilization." To conceive of the religious life as means of attaining personal safety in heaven was to cultivate, under the guise of piety, the vice of selfishness.[36]

The revulsion that both leaders felt against the stark drawing of boundaries seems rooted in their experiences of the revivalistic religion of their childhoods, though Vincent is much more explicit about it than Haygood. Vincent speaks repeatedly of how morbid, anxious, isolated, and just plain bad his youthful religion had made him. He had few friends in childhood because religion made him preoccupied with death and judgment and suppressed a wholesome and spontaneous "boy life." Far from making him a better person, this preoccupation filled him with selfish anxiety to be "safe" by being saved. In adolescence he continued to be a "sensitive, self-centered, morbid" boy, stuck on thoughts of death, judgment, and the terrors of hell. He was hemmed in by convictions that it was folly to love to play and that he needed to constantly engage in meditation, self-denial, and seasons of prayer. These oppressive constraints on his mind and spirit weakened his sense of responsibility for making "a sane adjustment to the immediate conditions of one's life." His individuality and spontaneity were stifled. His life was unreal.[37] Haygood did not go on at such lengths, but he did mention that his ill health as a child combined with his religious sensibilities to make him a wild-eyed, solemn child who expected soon to go out of this world. Moreover, the picture he paints of the young Savonarola is of a morbid youth preoccupied with the sad and dreary expressions of religious art and rejecting of human companionship.[38] It is a picture that resonates with Vincent's self-depictions.

Vincent must have felt the weight put upon his readers by his woeful portrait of his youth. Why say so much about his home training, he asked in rhetorical fashion, especially since it seems to have been to some extent morbid? Because, he replied, it would be impossible to understand many things in his life without these words of explanation about his youth. His rejection of the boundary between secular and sacred was fundamental to his life. He reiterated it in the very last installment of his autobiography, and stressed also a corollary point with which Haygood would also have agreed. When God is present in the inmost soul and the individual assents completely to the divine leading, then all activity, every part of society, indeed, the whole of the cosmos may be made sacred.[39] The center of sacredness, for both leaders, was the sweet and secret communion with God, which makes no part of the world off-limits. If the holiness movement preached a religion that was in many ways a negation of "the world," the religion of people like John Vincent and Atticus Haygood was a negation of the negation.

Sense of the Divine

The sense of the divine presence and activity in the experience of holiness leaders was not nearly so private as it was in the connectional leaders. The presence of God interacting with the believer in consciousness was accepted as a fact that must be testified to in appropriate contexts.

Milton Haney's published record of his sanctification experience gives a clear example of how God in the form of the Holy Spirit, was sensed to be present and active in consciousness. His whole soul, Haney reported, pleaded to be made clean. The Holy Spirit answered his plea by saying two things were necessary: first consecration and then faith in Jesus. He plunged ahead into the entire consecration of himself to God. "The Holy Spirit then probed me with searching questions, asking would I do this, and that, go here or there, and my whole soul said yes." Then came the really hard test. What if, suggested the Holy Spirit, you are never permitted another moment of religious joy, your soul never allowed again to "get happy"? Then will you still be all mine, trust me to cleanse you from all sin, and testify to this cleansing whenever I tell you? Haney believed he had been an "exceedingly happy Christian, and to give up all religious joy. . . . It seemed worse than death." He hesitated. The question was repeated. Then he answered yes with his whole heart. "I then had a clear definite inner sense that I was wholly given to God, and my consecration was a finished fact." The next step was belief, and Haney made "a desperate effort" to believe. All the strain was unnecessary, "for my heart went in advance of my plans, and took Jesus as my complete Sanctifier then and there." He then rose from where he had been kneeling and became conscious of the other Christians around him at the revival meeting. A "brother" asked him about his position with God, and he immediately gave his first testimony to holiness. "I am all the Lord's and I believe the blood of Jesus cleanses me from all sin!"[40]

Haney published his testimony in his autobiography for the same reasons, we may assume, that holiness authors and editors published thousands of testimonies, long and short, in their books and periodicals year after year. As we have observed earlier and as Haney's account makes clear, sharing one's experience was a requirement. Many holiness believers acknowledged that they had once obtained the blessings of holiness but had failed to testify to it, often out of fear of what others might say or think of them. They had therefore lost the blessing.[41] Testifying strengthened the identification of the believer with the holiness community, even as it provided one of the principal means of evangelizing still more believers. The accounts of religious experience provided models for others to follow, and allowed a kind of cross-checking of experience among believers, thus reinforcing the sense of the reality of the blessings they sought.

Testimony, along with singing, prayer and preaching, helped to generate the shared emotional fervor that was a hallmark of holiness meetings. This powerful emotional contagion was understood as a sign of the presence of the divine among, and not just within, God's people. Among the early Nazarenes this atmosphere was known as "the glory," and Phineas Bresee felt it important to get the glory down at every meeting. "Divine personality," he wrote, "manifest upon and in men is the only ministry of power by which salvation fills human souls and sends forth its streams to permeate the world." It was the task of spiritual leaders to "impel the thought, desire and instinct of the people, so that, in unity, with ever increasing intensity, they shall blend their united faith so as to receive the greater measure of His glory."[42]

Camp meetings, love feasts, revival meetings, weekly meetings for the promotion of holiness, and other forms of meetings were all the contexts in which holiness leaders expected to witness the presence and power of the divine. These were clearly *public* meetings in one sense of the term. They were generally open to anyone. Indeed, the public was urgently invited to most of them. But they were not public events like market exchanges or political speeches or even everyday passings on the streets. There was a distinctive social reality created in and through these meetings that set them apart from public reality. This separateness was a corollary of the holiness insistence on the rejection of worldliness and the erection of social behavioral boundaries between believers and worldlings. Holiness believers might indeed have conventionally public and private episodes to their lives, but the meetings and the states of mind cultivated in them were their primary nexus with divine reality.

Location of the divine primarily in such meetings implied an acceptance of the ebb and flow of religious feeling and excitement through the course of a year or a life. During the year holiness believers expected summer camp meetings of ten days or more, winter revivals of as long as six weeks, and various other special meetings, often associated with holidays. Interspersed with these gatherings of large groups would be the weekly meetings of smaller groups in which prayer, teaching, and testimony were bent, again, to the promotion of holiness. The intensity of religious feeling necessarily fluctuated as people gathered and dispersed. Through it all, however, holiness believers sought a constant inner communion with God and a bedrock of faith that endured through all outer and inner fluctuations of feeling. Thus did John Allen Wood testify to the lasting effects of his experience of sanctification: including an annihilation of the distance between himself and God, a more solid tangible sense of spiritual truth and doctrine, and a more complete and habitual triumph over temptation. Another holiness leader, George D. Watson, told of how his holiness experience had imparted a stillness and rest of soul that banished "the long battle of will, all anxiety, all personal ambition, all fret, worry, and care."[43]

Location of the divine in the meetings for holiness promotion implied oral communication as the primary medium of the divine presence. The differences between oral and textual media of communication have profound implications, as Walter S. Ong has shown, for human culture and psychology.[44] The subculture created by the holiness movement had some important continuities with the oral cultures discussed by Ong.[45] Methodist holiness orality involved an empathetic and participatory mode of sharing knowledge. The words of testifying believers issued from the inside of the speaker and penetrated to the inside of the hearers. They did not make room for personal disengagement, distance, or objectivity. They demanded response, not analysis. The testimonies of the saints also reflected oral culture in that they were formulaic and episodic. They relied upon stock phrases easily memorized and recounted episodes of experience in forms that were familiar. The phrases and forms, of course, were derived almost exclusively from biblical exemplars. The assumption was, however, that these phrases and episodes epitomized the life organization of those who used them. The point of the holiness quest, after all, was to conform one's life to what was believed to be the divine pattern.

This paper began with mention of the Denver "Revival" presided over by Bishop Vincent. The patterns of that meeting exemplified the alternative sense of the divine that animated connectional leaders like Vincent. All practices were eliminated that might pressure each individual to testify to an inner work of grace and connect it to a shared spirit of "glory." The intermediate spaces between public and private where holiness religion thrived were squeezed out. Instead there were public "addresses" complemented by hours set apart for private consultation. Profession of faith was done through the sacraments.[46]

Religion for both Vincent and Haygood was personal and private. "The inner power of the will transforms the outward world," declared Vincent. He quoted the biblical aphorism, "As a man thinketh in his heart, so is he" and added, "Here is the secret of life—*within* and not without. Therefore a contented mind is a continual feast."[47] Atticus G. Haygood, in his verbal flogging of Savonarola as a stand-in for Georgia holiness preachers, reminded his readers that the kingdom of God is within and cannot be seen with fleshly eyes. Savonarola was the chief exemplar of that sort of mind that insisted on setting up fleshly standards for discerning the kingdom rendering judgments on other people's states of grace. Such twisted minds would "excommunicate young girls for wearing pretty flowers on their hats and [threaten] with damnation loving and virtuous wives who would not fling into the fanatic's bonfire a tiny marriage ring of pure gold." Haygood seemed to believe that such fanatics deserved to burn in their own fires.[48]

If these connectional leaders found the divine presence only within and in private, they also tended to represent what they found in impersonal and naturalistic metaphors. Thus, when Vincent wrote his book on the inner life, his favored term for God was "first cause." He meant not only the first cause of the classical proof of God's existence, but also the universal moral sense that all humans carried within. Vincent granted that anthropomorphism in speaking of this God was inevitable, but he himself persisted in impersonal references.[49] In his strategic anti-holiness sermon, "Growth in Grace," Haygood grew aggressively literalistic in invoking the idea of growth. Religion is not *like* life, he declared, it *is* life, not art, not acquirement, not a form of things. It is life or it is nothing, and life always means growth, a gradual increase by vital processes. The principles of growth in connection with the divine life within are not, he asserted, accidental analogies. "They are radical, essential, fundamental; they go down into the very heart of the Gospel, and they are the very essence of the divine constitution of human nature." God does not exert power simply upon humanity, but in and through the powers given human beings at creation when God made them in the divine image.[50] In such rhetoric, the distinction between nature and grace, natural and supernatural narrowed almost to the vanishing point.

In similar fashion, such leaders sought to reduce boundaries in time between moments when religion was at low ebb and moments when it was surging upward in revival. Vincent's published critiques of revivalism stressed the need for steady, regular religious effort and development. Day-in, day-out religious endeavor and practice in the home and the Sabbath school should train up every child in the fundamentals of the faith. Pulpit, home, and Sabbath school should set forth evangelical doctrines 365 days a year. There should be patient, unremitting labor twelve months a year, evangelistic proclamation and appeal every week. Then, he insisted, believers will be built up in the faith and sinners will turn to Christ at any time of the year, and not wait for the revival season. Then also would the emotional and physiological reactions that naturally set in after the unnatural excitements of revivals be tamed and moderated. Fewer people would be lost to the depression and disaffection that follow a revival.[51]

Books and all manner of other printed materials were a chief medium of communication recommended by connectional leaders for the effort to transcend the ups and downs of revivalism. Thus Vincent's closing chapter in his anti-revivalist tract, *The Revival after the Revival,* contained the following exhortation to church pastors:

> Consecrate the unoccupied rooms of the church to every-day service. . . . Fill the lecture and class room walls with pictures; spread out tables; put on file the best religious and secular papers; bring in books of the highest class, charts, maps, diagrams. . . . Provide courses of literary, scientific, ecclesiastical, and doctrinal lectures. . . . Let Christ stand in center of all. . . . Thus shall all the lights of sacred story, of secular science, of human thought in the early ages and the latest time, gather around the Cross of Christ.

Then, rhapsodized Vincent, the church would become the center of ten thousand blessed homes, home for the homeless, refuge for the weary, school of culture for the schoolless, light in the darkness, and "the image of the New Jerusalem." On the page facing this concluding gush, moreover, was an advertisement for "Helpful Courses of Reading and Study for Young and Old" offered by Vincent himself.[52]

Vincent's advocacy of books and literate education was, as his biographer observed, remarkable. The bishop was on record as granting that such culture would not save one's soul, but the tenor of his career and his writings raises questions about how deeply he meant or felt this *caveat*. Indeed, at the very point in his autobiography where he tried to express some regret about a neglect in his career of personal religious experience, he suggests that books can be a means of grace. He urged every pastor, young or old, to take a course in religious psychology and even suggested the books for it. The course would not be for intellectual stimulus, he asserted, but rather "a means of grace and of renewed personal surrender to God."[53]

Clearly, for people like Vincent, texts, not oral communication, were the primary medium of the divine presence. When he wrote about personal religion in his own life, he listed authors who had presented the ideas that animated his personal spiritual life.[54] This focus on texts was consistent with his sense of religion as a highly private, interior thing. Reading and writing are essentially private activities, and the meanings inscribed in texts are registered within the silence of individual consciousness. Reading and writing also encourage, or at least create space for, objective reflection upon the world and experience of the reader. They place distance between the writing self and the audience the self addresses. In this space for reflection, an awareness of depth and complexity of character and motive in both self and other can emerge.[55] Persons who have developed such spaces and capacities for reflection may be expected to find unreflective contexts like those of holiness testimony meetings uncongenial.[56]

Identification with Roles

If holiness leaders found the divine presence in testimony meetings and the like, connectional leaders found it in Sunday schools and the like. These contrasting contexts shaped their contrasting identification with roles. The leaders of testimony meetings were evangelists; the leaders of Sunday schools were educators.

The holiness leaders under consideration here were all successful pastors, effective at basic ministerial tasks such as building up church attendance and membership, raising money, and building churches. They all left the regular Methodist pastorate, however, to become full-time evangelists, or, in the case of Bresee, to enter a similar "irregular" ministry.[57] Chief among their avowed reasons was a desire for a wider field of usefulness. The dynamics of revivalistic fellowship constantly generated energy and desire for the salvation of others. Evangelism was the natural response arising from this comingling of one's own salvation experience with that of others. Some of the holiness pastors also encountered opposition in their churches to their holiness evangelism. They found it better to go where their gifts were in demand than to stay where they were constantly opposed. Thus Milton Haney noted how his LaSalle, Illinois, congregation was pleased to hold revivals that won new members, but then "sank back with a will" when he tried to lead congregation and new converts into the second blessing of entire sanctification. The congregation even persecuted the new converts "because they were in advance of them." In his years with this congregation, he found that he was successful as a soul-winner in outlying churches, in camp meetings, and in evangelistic meetings, but that his main congregation remained "settled into their old ruts." Eventually he "determined not again to attempt to pull sinners over the head of a dead membership," and began to pray and look for signs from God that he was to enter full-time evangelism. The signs were forthcoming.[58]

The role and gifts of the evangelist depended upon the particular social context of the revival. These holiness leaders identified constantly with scenes of religious enthusiasm and fellowship in a community of the saved and sanctified. It was a community founded on the common experience of the total surrender of self, and thus all social distinctions were relativized before the God who was revealed on the cross of Jesus Christ. There was a flow of feeling from soul to soul as believers shared their experience, couched in biblical images and allusions, and their fellows recognized and affirmed the selves that thus revealed themselves. The universal human quest for recognition was certainly central to these patterns of fellowship, but the recognition sought was recognition of and confirmation of God's saving action within, something equally available to all, and nothing that was supposed to give special distinction. The sense of life and power that came to people who were able to surrender themselves in the prescribed manner transformed their vision. The holiness folk saw their way clear to eternal life, and they saw also how important it was to stay clear of the fleshly pride, sensuality, and worldliness that lay beyond the boundaries of their special community. They could see such evil especially well when it grew within the wider membership of the church. They could not see in themselves so readily the spiritual pride, censoriousness, sensationalism, and superficiality that leaders of the wider church like Vincent and Haygood saw when they looked at holiness folk.

Vincent and Haygood also started out as successful pastors. They rose to regional and eventually national, even international, prominence, however, through leadership and promotion first of Sunday schools then later of other educational enterprises. After his stint as Sunday school secretary for the Methodist Episcopal Church, South, Haygood served as professor and president of Emory College. He was a strong advocate of an educated ministry and of universal public education, including education of African Americans in the South.[59] Vincent became a major player in Methodist and interdenominational Sunday School work during his pastoral work in Illinois in the 1850s and 1860s. After the Civil War he became secretary of the Sunday School Union for the Methodist Episcopal Church and editor of its paper. He became especially renowned, however, for his efforts at mass popular education, epitomized in Chautauqua.[60]

John H. Vincent's persistence and ingenuity in promoting popular education are so remarkable that his story will be the focus of the efforts here to explain what it meant to identify with the role of educator in his time and contexts. The Chautauqua assembly, held at a camp meeting ground on Lake Chautauqua in western New York, was originally intended as an institute for the study of the Bible and Bible geography and history. The institution arose from the collaboration of Vincent with an Akron, Ohio, businessman and Sunday school leader, Lewis Miller. Miller as president and Vincent as superintendent of instruction built Chautauqua into a kind of summer vacation university where prominent educators and researchers in all fields came to share their knowledge with people from all denominations and all walks of life. It also involved several efforts at year-round learning by correspondence, the best-known of which was the Chautauqua Literary and Scientific Circle (C.L.S.C.). The reach and reputation of Chautauqua grew quickly from its relatively modest beginnings in 1874 when it held its first Normal Class in Bible study and Sunday school methods. When Jesse Hurlbut published his retrospective on the institution in 1921, he was able to fill almost twelve pages of his preface with testimonials and tributes to Chautauqua from U.S. presidents, state governors, foreign ambassadors, prominent journalists, university presidents and professors, and authors and lecturers of national and international renown.[61]

The essence of Chautauqua, however, was contained in the "Palestine Class" that the young pastor Vincent devised while serving in New Jersey in the first few years after the deaths of his mother and his mentor, Henry Hurd.[62] The Palestine Class was a Saturday afternoon meeting open to all, church member or not, and devoted to the study of biblical, or "sacred," history, geography, and biography. Vincent adapted to this class some of the "singing geography" teaching techniques he had used as a teenager experimenting with schoolteaching near his childhood home in rural Pennsylvania. All the Bible places were arranged in songs or chants and were chanted in unison as the teacher moved his pointer around on an outline map that had no names printed on it. This learning game worked, and it attracted a lot of attention. As Vincent recalled, "The simultaneous repetition, the rhythmic movement, and the strong body of sound fixed the whole field of sacred history, biography, and geography in the memory. It made the Saturday afternoon study like a pleasant play and attracted the old as well as the young."

But this was not just fun and games. To ensure thoroughness, he said, Vincent subjected every individual to an examination and was promoted from grade to grade, first a "Pilgrim to Palestine," then, having passed the required examination, he was made a "Resident" and was assigned to one town. The class then held the Resident responsible for all information concerning his or her town. The Resident might then become an "Explorer" of one of the other biblical regions. After that, when interest grew in the historic development of Jerusalem, the Explorer became a "Dweller in Jerusalem," and finally a "Templar." In later classes each "Templar" received a gold medal, and there was even a further distinction of "High Templar."

The Palestine Class, claimed Vincent, "became a delightful fraternity (more nearly a 'sorosis' than a 'fraternity'), and how full it was of enthusiasm!" He mentioned that he still met members of his early classes now and then, and remarked that any of them who read this autobiography of his would "greatly cheer their old teacher by a line of recognition. May we all meet in the New Jerusalem!"[63]

Clearly there are fellowship and inspiration in this context where Vincent found himself as an educator. But it is not of the same kind, some might say not of the same spirit, as the testimony meeting for the promotion of holiness. It is what holiness evangelist Joseph Smith called, in disparaging tones, "educationalism." What are its differences from the spirit of Smith's evangelism? Vincent's educational spirit is competitive, it aims at mastery of content and fact as a means to recognition and elevation and becoming distinguished. The recognition it covets is recognition of accomplishment, with the inference that accomplishment implies character. It aims at the construction of a career with ascending levels of worth and recognition of worth. Evidence of these latter two assertions is in Vincent's reflections on the "Recognition Day" ceremonies performed for those who completed the course of reading and study prescribed by the Chautauqua Literary and Scientific Circle. He noted that enrollment in the C.L.S.C. "institution" with a goal in view appealed to ambitious older people "who still foster 'ideals'" and who "resolve to go on and on and up and 'higher yet'" until they are among those "worthy to be crowned." He read with pleasure the joy and "pride of the right kind" on the faces of those who become the "chosen company" and march in the ceremony under arch after arch and past "flower-scattering maidens." These people recalled to him the "sweet picture of old age" described by Madame de Stael, who said, "When [there is] a noble life and prepared old age, it is not the decline that it reveals, but the first days of immortality."[64] What Vincent offers here, it seems, is a beatification of the culture of professionalism, with its insistence on education and achievement as a measure of character and as a basis for prestige claims. There is, in fact, an echo of the old claims to honor and deference made by the colonial gentry against whom the early Methodists set themselves so strongly.[65]

Another element of difference between the educational spirit and the evangelistic spirit lies in the differing relation each bears to cultural constructs of public and private. What the educational spirit strives for is public, even formal, recognition of a public persona, reserving the inner self for backstage spaces and times. Like all quests for recognition, it requires an audience, but this audience provides recognition at a distance. A mass audience will do, may even be preferred, as long as it offers itself to be fascinated by the honor won by and done to the leading achievers. The evangelistic spirit, on the other hand, requires an audience that can and will draw close and weep or rejoice with the one who shares an inner condition of penitence or joy. Such audiences, and the selves they recognize, must be secluded from norms that call for public reserve and saving face for a public persona. Such secluded audiences can, on certain occasions, be quite large. Love feasts at holiness camp meetings had hundreds, sometimes thousands, in attendance, and individual testimonies were published in periodicals with wide circulations. But such mass moments work best when they are complemented by moments like the weekly holiness meetings where smaller audiences were made of people who knew one another better.

Conclusion

So, what are the implications of this analysis and its rather bleak picture of dedicated and talented members of the same faith communion and tradition attacking and talking past one another? I believe both groups had valid points of criticism against the other and that both had important truths embodied in their ways of constructing self and world. In this conclusion, with some trepidation, I draw the implications by offering some morals to the story. The trepidation arises from the fact that I am offering these largely theological judgments on the lives of some prominent Methodist clergymen when I am neither a Methodist, nor a clergyman, nor a theologian.[66] What follows then, is offered with the invitation to readers to supply their own morals if mine seem wrong.

First, consider what I take to be the connectional leaders' points, with my counterpoints.

1. Yes, efforts at spiritual transformation effected through group dynamics like those of revivalism often result in socially and emotionally coercive environments that bring about superficial changes and set people up for negative reactions in their aftermath. But, there is no true transformation that is not in some way effected and sustained through the spirituality of groups. The body of Christ is real, and it is not merely an aggregate of sincere and authentic individuals.

2. Yes, the life of the Spirit exists deep within individual consciousness (and unconsciousness) and often defies adequate embodiment in human language, especially when the language is organized into set formulas by a tradition of popular discourse about the workings of the Spirit. But, language structures thought, feeling, and spiritual sensibility; in a sense, language creates them. Without the resources of shared language, however formulaic, the reality of the workings of the Spirit will go unnoticed and be lost.

3. Yes, it is vital to aspire to higher levels of achievement in things like education and to cultivate the willpower and character that make possible such achievement. But, neither achievement nor character should be confused with salvation into the kingdom of God. They are the works of human beings and thus are susceptible to pride and other corruptions of a fallen creation.

4. Yes, the rules of dress, language, amusements, and so on, imposed by holiness groups are superficial indexes to spirituality and tempt people to confuse the marker for the reality. But, human beings, at some point in their lives, often at several different points, need visible gestures and markers that differentiate more or less clearly "the Way" from the wrong turns.

5. Yes, every day of the week and every mundane endeavor, in short, all of life, must be seen to have potential for holiness. The sharp division of life into holy and unholy and the stress on getting oneself safely saved can lead to a selfish and self-alienating personal spirituality. The "second blessing" version of this division, furthermore, created a two-class system within the church and thus the grounds for spiritual pride, one-upmanship, and censoriousness. But, there is necessity for a clear boundary of some kind between the church and the world. The claims of the faith imply it, and there remains the sheer pragmatic functional truth that a community with indistinct boundaries will be unable to make convincing its point that it is important to belong to the group.

Finally, consider what I take to be the holiness leaders' points, with my counterpoints:

1. Yes, the powers in the special meetings for the promotion of holiness are exhilarating and effective. But, these powers partake of the fallenness of creation; they are not simply and purely the Holy Spirit at work. Hence the excesses, fanaticisms, and some of the divisiveness that are frequent by-products of such meetings.

2. Yes, it is essential that spiritual people give clear and definite witness to the work of the Holy Spirit in their lives and that their witness be received and tested by others following the same way. But, such witness must be less confined by formulas of language and must have a wider range of venues in which to be given than the forms of witness typically were in holiness weekly meetings, camp meetings, and evangelistic meetings. In particular, venues are needed that are more respectful of personal privacy, more open to doubt and uncertainty, and more questioning of claims of triumph.

3. Yes, evangelizing, that is, proclaiming the kingdom of God, is more important than educational achievement and its concomitant character development, more important than any other endeavor given to human beings. Education, professional career, and the character associated with them can and have become idols. But, the forms of holiness evangelism are not the only way to proclaim the Kingdom, perhaps not the best

way. Nor, therefore, are they to be set up as final arbiters of what constitutes a "sanctified" education or professional life.

4. Yes, an essential part of the Christian spiritual life in a fallen world is self-denial, and people need clear guidelines about what actions, feelings, and thoughts are to be surrendered to and for Christ. But, any such guidelines are fallible human constructions that can be understood and applied superficially and lead to inconsistencies that undermine the credibility of spiritual guidance. More profoundly, such guidelines can also be twisted to work oppressively upon legitimate human needs and impulses, thus making war upon the goodness of God's creation in the name of redeeming it.

5. Yes, the church must be separate from the world, but not in order to present itself as the lifeboat to a drowning world, nor to suggest that people, their personal lives, or the culture at large may be neatly divided between the holy and the unholy. Rather, the boundary must exist in order to make it clear that there is a people who have heard and believed the good news that the Kingdom is at hand and who are trying to learn and embody its ways. The aim of this common life is not purity or perfection, but faithfulness to the life of the Kingdom as practiced and taught by Jesus and the early church and as discerned for these times by those of us who are called to be heirs of that life.

Karen B. Westerfield Tucker

In this essay, Karen Westerfield Tucker explores family and midweek worship in Methodism and finds that these traditions were most characteristic of the movement during the early periods of its development. The mandate and ideal of family worship, and the expectation of midweek congregational worship continued, but changing patterns of family life, social interaction, and communal practice altered the way in which Methodist people and congregations responded. This case study offers an interesting picture of the ways in which the changed circumstances of Methodism brought about different practices through the years. In the early days of the Methodist movement, preachers and members believed that regular and constant observance was necessary to maintain devotion and discipline. As the movement acquired second-generation adherents and became large and popular, discipline was more difficult to maintain. The theological implications of these shifts are of importance. Theological convictions that can be imparted to a small movement are less easily imposed, or maintained, in a large and growing church.

Is the kind of first-order practical theology about which Maddox wrote dependent on devotional practices Westerfield Tucker finds were not sustained as Methodism matured? Is the loss of meaningful family devotion and midweek services characteristic of a church that is missing vital piety? Do Westerfield Tucker's findings confirm some of the insights of Schneider's distinction between leadership that is based in holiness practice and that committed to the growth of institutional religion? Theology and doctrine are taught in part through disciplined devotional life and the reduction of these practices has implications for theology in United Methodism. Is there a theological reason that modern Methodism might wish to recover the tradition of family and midweek worship?

Family and Midweek Worship: Private and Public Devotion in the Methodist Tradition

Karen B. Westerfield Tucker

American Methodists, since the superintendency of Francis Asbury, have opened their *Book of Discipline* to find printed therein the "Nature, Design, and General Rules of our United Societies," a statement often located in a prominent position within the book. Today The United Methodist Church's *Discipline* includes the General Rules with other selected historic texts of the denomination, but the document itself—as well as its contents—remains unknown to most United Methodists. Have the General Rules been retained for over two hundred years simply as a relic of the past? Or has their advice continued to be deemed relevant for each succeeding Methodist generation?

For this study, one instruction provided in the General Rules will be examined as to its interpretation and employment—and "relevance"— among American Methodists: namely, that Methodist Christians should engage regularly in private and public devotion in addition to attendance at Lord's Day corporate worship. Two practices of private and public devotion that have been strongly encouraged by Methodist leaders—family worship and the weekly prayer meeting—serve as the windows for viewing the subject. Primary focus is upon Episcopal Methodist, Methodist, and United Methodist literature, both official and unofficial; material from the Evangelical United Brethren Church and its predecessor bodies has not been examined, though an occasional comment or observation on those traditions has been supplied.

Early Methodist Advice and Practice

From the early days of the Methodist movement, it was John Wesley's expectation that those who sought "to be saved from their sins and flee from the wrath to come" would engage in both public and private worship and devotion: they were to attend Lord's Day worship, offer personal prayer, and practice devotions within the context of the family or extended household as well as in small gatherings outside the domestic environment. Those who aspired to be "altogether" Christians were urged to make "constant use of family prayer," a design known to Wesley from his own childhood, and to set apart time for "private addresses to God, with a daily seriousness of behavior."[1] Like many other matters of Methodist praxis, the notion of frequent prayer within small groups, families, or in one's "closet" was borrowed from Anglican spiritual writers, from the religious societies that proliferated in the eighteenth century, and from the classical Puritan tradition. Dislike of the *Book of Common Prayer* had led the Puritans to promote individual, family, and small-group devotions, and to provide instructions, exhortations, and some written prayer texts for their implementation.[2] Reformed, Puritan, and Nonconformist literary treasures, some written in the late seventeenth and early eighteenth centuries to reverse a perceived decline in the practice of devotion, frequently adorned the reading lists suggested to the Methodist people; and regarding the discipline of prayer, the most notable included writings by Richard Baxter (e.g., *Gildas Salvianus* [1656]) and Matthew Henry (*The Life of Mr. Philip Henry* [1696] and *A Method for Prayer* [1710]). Recommendations for these works are found in various editions of the *Minutes* before John Wesley's death in 1791, and some remain afterward in the British *Minutes* or in the American *Discipline.* An abridgment of Henry's *Life,* other devotional essays, and a few prayer collections were included in Wesley's fifty-volume *Christian Library.*

Prescriptions for Methodist private and corporate devotions were codified in the Rules and Directions provided for the Band Societies (in 1738 and in 1744)[3] and in the 1743 General Rules of the United Societies, which state that it is essential that those who desire to continue in the society attend upon such divine ordinances as "the public worship of God; the ministry of the Word, either read or expounded; the Supper of the Lord; family and private prayer; searching the Scriptures; and fasting, or abstinence."[4] The expectation that these rules were to be followed—even more than forty years after their issuance—is clear from Wesley's 1787 sermon "On God's Vineyard":

> Their [the Methodists'] public service is at five in the morning and six or seven in the evening, that their temporal business may not be hindered. Only on Sunday it begins between nine and ten, and concludes with the Lord's Supper. On Sunday evening the Society meets; but care is taken to dismiss

them early, that all the heads of families may have time to instruct their several households.[5]

Admonitions for private and public devotion should not be surprising coming from a group that saw itself as an evangelical *ecclesiola in ecclesia;* private prayer—particularly family devotions—and small-group public prayer were regarded as supplementary to the regular diet of worship that was expected in the Church of England congregation. But these strictly *Methodist* devotions also served to mark the particular character and identity of the Methodist people in addition to forming and strengthening them in the larger Christian faith. Methodists were charged to "pray without ceasing," and to lift their hearts up to God "at all times, and in all places."[6]

To assist their devotions, Wesley provided the Methodists with a suitable environment—the class and bands meetings—and with prayer texts that could be used alongside the *Book of Common Prayer.* These included: *A Collection of Forms of Prayer for Every Day in the Week,* first published in 1733 and based on the prayer compilation *The True Church of England Man's Companion in the Closet* (1721) made by Nathaniel Spinckes; a second but smaller collection designed for the Methodist societies entitled *A Collection of Prayers for Families* and published in 1744; and a third, *Prayers for Children,* published in 1772. Of course, Methodists were also encouraged, as the Spirit moved, to lift their hearts and voices through the medium of extempore prayer. It is difficult to ascertain the extent to which the printed liturgical resources were actually used by the Methodist people in Britain and North America, even though the number of editions of these works produced surely bears some significance. All editions of these books were published either in England or in Ireland; from 1733 to 1791 at least fifteen authorized editions of *Forms of Prayer* were printed; a twenty-first edition of *Prayers for Families* was published in London in 1809. Determination of American Methodist usage of these prayer collections is particularly problematic. Although there were no American editions of the texts, it is clear that Methodists continued to import devotional material from Britain well into the nineteenth century. However, the titles of Wesley's prayer books generally are not mentioned either in American-produced prayer resources or commentaries, or in American Methodist diaries and journals within discussions on prayer and the spiritual state of the author or others.[7] One might expect, given the apparent American preference for prayer with the eyes closed rather than open (a predilection noted by Jesse Lee),[8] that the printed prayers would not have been as readily accepted by New World Methodists as by their European cousins.

As if these rules, directions, and published prayer collections were not enough (and apparently they were not), the traveling preachers were admonished to encourage private and public devotions in the various communities and homes they visited. Of particular concern was the practice of family religion, and Mr. Wesley himself did not mince words on this matter. Quoting the verse from Joshua 24:15, a scriptural reference that was to provide both the warrant and the injunction for family worship in much of the Methodist (and other Protestant) devotional literature from the eighteenth century on into the twentieth, Wesley recorded:

> I strongly inculcated *family religion,* the grand desideratum among the Methodists. Many were ashamed before God and at length adopted Joshua's resolution, "As for me and my house, we will serve the Lord."[9]

Though viewed as one of *the* essentials for Methodists, actual practice evidently did not improve to the desired extent, for the subject of family worship was spelled out at length in the *Minutes* (especially the *Large Minutes,* both in Question 13 and in Question 33), because of the concern that family religion among Methodists was "shamefully wanting, and almost in every branch." The remedy proposed was that the preachers visit from house to house, instruct the children in matters of religion, and lead prayers in the home as a model for what may be done by the head of the household.[10]

That these efforts were taken seriously is clear from notes recorded in the journals and diaries of the Methodist preachers on both sides of the Atlantic. For example, the American Methodist Ezekiel Cooper, later editor of the Methodist Book Concern, noted his desire to conduct "family duty" when visiting in a home even if the head of the household did not request his leadership.[11] He wrote of the spiritual benefits of family prayer, recording the "gracious visitation" that came on one occasion:

> At family prayer two or three mourners got under distress of soul. A shout soon broke out and continued till near 11 o'clock. The way it came was as follows: soon as family prayer was over two young women went upstairs to prayer. I sent two others up to them. They presently were so affected that others went up also and then others and joined them till their prayer and cries

passed through all the house and all got up in the chamber—the black people also crowded on the stairs to see and hear. Glory to God for this favor![12]

Prayer meetings were also a vital part of Methodist spiritual life during this period and afterward. These gatherings, spontaneous or planned, could substitute for a Sunday morning preaching service or be a regular weekly offering (as, for example, in a city station). The prayer meeting came to be an important component of the Quarterly Meeting, and would be held in the meeting house or in private dwellings.[13] It was the class meeting, which David Lowes Watson has explored in his research, that best enabled the Methodists to be accountable to the disciplines of public and private worship and devotion outside of Sunday morning.[14]

Clearly what is laid out in the eighteenth-century Methodist literature is both the articulation of the *ideal* of private and public devotions and the description of devotional practice as a *record* of spiritual achievement worthy of emulation. Given the continuing attention to the issue of family and small group prayer by direction, sermon, and example, the question may arise of the *degree* to which such practice took hold among the majority of American Methodists during this period. Surely illustrations of disciplined and fruitful devotional practice abound in the literature, but perhaps these persons and families were exceptions and not the rule. On the other hand, the abundance of literature may truly indicate that most of the early Methodists were, indeed, regularly practicing what was believed to be essential to life as a Methodist Christian, and the constant admonitions to private and public devotions were in that case a rhetorical device to encourage the people toward yet greater spiritual goals and discipline.

Nineteenth-Century American Methodist Devotions

Emphasis on the practice of family and midweek prayers continued throughout the nineteenth century, arising no doubt simultaneously from a desire to extol the Christian virtues of prayer and obedience to God's commands, and from a dread that such commendable practices were in danger of disappearing. Family devotions and midweek prayers outside of the setting of the class meeting were seen by clergy and lay leaders alike as all the more vital for the spiritual formation and growth of the Methodist people since the class meeting itself, which had been the forum par excellence for religious nurture among Methodists, was in decline at least by midcentury.[15] Several factors contributing to the waning of the class meeting may be identified: the breakdown of mechanisms of accountability and discipline within the class (and hence, as David Lowes Watson notes, a loss of purpose);[16] classes characterized by routine formalism and loss of enthusiasm;[17] a gradual transition away from doctrines basic to a Wesleyan theology of salvation;[18] and changes in Methodist self-understanding accompanying Methodism's evolution from society to established denomination.[19]

During this period attention focused particularly upon the maintenance of family worship, and the Methodist ideal of the family as an eminently suitable locus for the practice of experimental, social religion continued to be enforced.[20] Proponents argued for the continuation of domestic worship lest the Church lose a generation or more to the forces of wickedness. Encouragement for family prayer now had to come from outside the class meeting, which had for several generations so ably supervised the devotional practices of its members and especially oversaw the devotional duties incumbent upon heads of families. To that end, books and essays by Methodist authors on topics related to family worship and "domestic piety" proliferated in the first two-thirds of the nineteenth century, appealing to Christian parents to fulfill their God-given privilege and duty to establish a "home altar," conduct regular family prayers, and devote attention to the piety and salvation of their entire household.[21] Excuses, such as inconvenience, lack of time, timidity, embarrassment, ignorance, and inability, were in various ways refuted.[22] An anonymous writer in 1821 penned these vehement words for the *Methodist Magazine*:

> O ye, who are intrusted with the care of immortal souls, consider the importance of your charge, and fear with trembling. Should these in the day of eternity rise up and allege, that though you bore the Christian name, you were so far from comporting with the sacred character, that your profession was the greatest obstacle to their embracing it; that your tempers and conduct were so contradictory to the spirit which the gospel enjoins, that taking you for an example they could not admit its pretended excellencies; that your indulgences had strengthened all the innate corruptions of their hearts; that your lack of seasonable and proper correction and instruction, had smoothed the way for the pursuit of carnal pleasures, and the commission of sin without fear: though your name might have stood on the list of every missionary and bible society in the world, and you have had the applause of doing more in various ways than most Christians; will you not be found guilty of neglect-

ing your most important duties, and be condemned not only as the abettors, but as the authors of your children's misery?[23]

Laxity in family duty was not a problem unique to the Methodists. Christian communions, theologically at odds on other matters, encouraged one another on the subject of family prayer. The editors of the *Methodist Magazine and Quarterly Review* in 1836 copied from the British *Wesleyan Methodist Magazine* a pastoral letter of the General Assembly of the Church of Scotland written to "stir up" regular and faithful observance of the worship of God in Scottish families.[24] Indeed, numerous Presbyterian publications are mentioned by Methodist authors, among them James W. Alexander's *Thoughts on Family-Worship,* which applauded the Methodist practice of domestic hymn singing while advocating as well the Reformed custom of domestic psalmody.[25]

In addition to unofficial diatribes by Methodist authors, official and disciplinary language was employed to encourage—and enforce—both family worship and midweek prayer. Listed in the Methodist Episcopal *Discipline,* first under the heading "Of the Duty of Preachers to God, themselves, and one another" and after 1892 as a "Spiritual Qualification" under "Qualifications and Work," were what Wesley called the instituted and the prudential means of grace.[26] Although addressed primarily to the preachers and their own personal practice, therein the preachers were also charged to encourage regular employment of the means of grace among the Methodist people. The very first among the instituted means indicated for consideration and use was prayer:

> Prayer: private, family, and public; consisting of deprecation, petition, intercession, and thanksgiving. Do you use each of these? Do you forecast daily, wherever you are, to secure time for private devotion? Do you practice it everywhere? Do you ask everywhere, Have you family prayer? Do you ask individuals, Do you use private prayer every morning and evening in particular?

Practice of midweek and small group devotions are implied in one of the questions asked regarding use of the prudential means of grace: "Do you never miss your Class?" In another disciplinary paragraph, first legislated in 1852, the implementation of public devotions was put forth in the instruction that the preacher in charge of a circuit was to appoint prayer meetings wherever possible.[27] Evidently, many of the factors behind the decline of the class meeting were also operative in the increasing neglect of both the instituted and prudential means which was, at least by midcentury, becoming a serious problem. In 1864 a provision was added to the Methodist Episcopal *Discipline,* under the specific heading of the "Neglect of the Means of Grace," which authorized the bringing to trial of a church member accused of habitually avoiding "the public worship of God, the Supper of the Lord, family and private prayer, searching the Scriptures, class-meetings, and prayer-meetings." If such a person did not mend his or her ways, expulsion from membership was the recommended solution.[28] The continuing concern of the Methodist Episcopal Church on the issue of neglect was such that this provision was retained in the Methodist Episcopal Church *Discipline* until the 1939 merger, but it is unclear whether or how this ruling was enforced.

Throughout much of the nineteenth century, laypersons generally led midweek and family prayer. For the latter, leadership was expected by the male head of the household with the wife and mother ascribed particular duties for advancing the cause of family religion. Morning and evening were regarded as the best times for services, with the hours chosen dependent upon the availability (and alertness, in the case of children) of the participants. Public and family prayer services were typically doxological, catechetical, and experiential in character. The components of Scripture reading, interpretation of Scripture, prayer (extempore and previously formulated), and hymn singing, which characterized Sunday morning worship, also formed the backbone for family and midweek worship.[29] An evangelical and enthusiastic cast to this same structure, with ample opportunity for public testimony to God's gracious activity in a person's life, also could be found in both family and midweek worship, thereby embracing—and preserving, though in a new way—the revival/camp meeting style. Participation in some form was expected by all those who had gathered for prayer.

Christian nurture and formation—particularly of children—were factors that often shaped the content of both midweek and family worship. Methodist Episcopal bishop Thomas A. Morris advised that children should be given prayers to memorize and repeat at family worship until they were capable of extemporizing on their own.[30] In some of the resources promoting devotions, the stress on catechesis (Bible study and the formal Methodist catechism) and Christian formation (particularly moral formation) seems to take precedence over the pure worship of

God, reflecting instead a concern for the spiritual strength and growth of the individual.[31] Eventually toward the end of the century, as the Sunday school became more firmly established as a Methodist institution, many of the ideals for worship by and with children espoused in the popular literature on midweek and family prayer were, for the most part, transferred to the "opening exercises" of prayer and song employed by the Sunday school department or included within the church school class itself.

Concern for the Revitalization of Midweek Worship

Whereas family religion and domestic worship seemingly constituted the focus of concern regarding Methodist devotional piety during the greater part of the nineteenth century (at least if literary output on the subject is any indication of emphasis), it was the midweek service or the weekly prayer meeting that garnered primary attention during the last quarter of the nineteenth century and in the first three decades of the twentieth century. This shift in stress probably should not be read as a capitulation in face of the less than enthusiastic response to the voices pleading for family worship; indeed, the practice of family prayer continued to be lifted up to the Methodist people as a worthy and suitably Christian endeavor.[32] For example, the 1920 Methodist Episcopal *Discipline* added a new sentence under the heading "Classes and Class Meetings and Units for Prayer and Service" instructing that the class leader, at each Quarterly Conference, was to report the number of families in the class who observed family worship (¶ 61 §2.9). This *Discipline* also included a resolution concerning family worship in the home and legislation for the development of a Family Worship League, the purpose of which was to promote the establishment of a systematic program of domestic worship in each household (¶ 589).[33] The resolution survived unaltered until 1932 (*Discipline*, ¶ 560); it disappeared in 1936.

Particular emphasis came to be placed on the midweek service because, for many, that meeting was seen as the last public stronghold for the vital and enthusiastic revival piety that had for so long characterized Methodism.[34] Values of the prayer meeting advocated by one proponent were that it "teaches democracy, fosters spiritual life, creates Christian fellowship, perpetuates the family altar, stimulates Bible study, and promotes evangelism."[35] As had been the case for family prayer during the first part of the nineteenth century, numerous essays and books were published during this period on the topic of midweek prayer and the prayer meeting. Many offered explanations for the decline in practice, with some resorting to finger-pointing: the laity (and some clergy) blamed the inadequacy of the clergy who by the late nineteenth century had taken over the midweek meeting; and the clergy criticized the secularization and lack of Christian commitment exhibited by their parishioners. An essay by clergyman W. W. King in 1910 cites the following reasons for the decline of the prayer meeting, both at midweek and on Sunday evening:

> Lack of interest in truly spiritual things; waning faith, pressure of business and social life; multiplicity of other church services, and of all kinds of social and business engagements; lack of genuine religious training in the home; abandonment of the habit of prayer; growing formality in the churches; the growth of young people's societies, which in their devotional meetings take the place of the prayer meeting for those who attend; the increased attention to Sunday school work, and the absorption to such a large extent of the energies of the church to build up this service; the missionary societies, whose services are so often wholly, and always more or less, prayer services; the increase in the number of church organizations, the work of which leaves little time for interest in anything else.[36]

It is interesting that this list, which includes the expected attribution of decline to spiritual apathy and the absence of devotional practice in the home, also delineates institutionalization as a cause of spiritual decay, or at least as a precipitating factor in a redefinition of spirituality. Works of charity, mission, and education urged by the gospel and carried out in the institutional life of the church had, in some areas and in some congregations, taken precedence over the intentional and intense discipline of prayer also commended in Scripture. Methodist devotional piety, which in earlier years had been the engine that drove the machinery of outreach, had lost its central place. The transition of Methodism from religious society to mainline Protestantism, the growing liberalism of the denomination, and the impact of the Social Gospel movement each were factors in the redefining of prayer and devotion for Methodist individuals and congregations.

Related to this shift away from the regular practice of prayer was a modification in the theological understanding of the nature of conversion and with it a new definition of *sin*.[37] This new focus was evident in some theological literature and in the practice of worship during the nineteenth century, but by the turn into the twentieth century it had become prominent. No longer was conversion seen as a corporate, public, and yet personal process (both before and after profession of faith) that was strengthened by the gathering of the bands and the class and by intensive formation within the family unit. Conversion had come to be conceived as a private, individual—and instantaneous—event, a notion reinforced by the accent on personal experience found in the camp meeting and in revival worship.[38] Midweek as well as family worship—originally construed in Wesley's day primarily as worship, and secondarily as an opportunity for spiritual refinement in the fire of corporate religious experience—was in general no longer viewed as essential to the conversion process but simply as supplementary. This was a significant transition that brought with it wider implications, such as: a decrease in enthusiastic and experimental religion expressed in a communal setting (since enthusiasm breeds enthusiasm); the loss of a forum for personal testimony (and with it a growing inability of individuals to speak about their faith in public); the privatization of religion (since persons are no longer compelled to state openly their inner experiences);[39] and the placement of organized Christian nurture primarily (and perhaps, in some places, solely) into the Sunday school.

There are indications that the public testimony of faith, which had breathed life into the prayer meeting and envigorated Methodists for so many years, was, by the twentieth century, itself a component contributing to midweek worship's death rattle. The pressure to give each week an inspirational account of personal faith and Christian witness evidently led some individuals to fabricate or overstate their report. Congregational minister Washington Gladden, in his 1898 study of *The Christian Pastor and the Working Church,* points to insincere testimony and the exaggeration of personal faith expressed in the Methodist prayer meeting as a cause of its decline,[40] a sentiment shared by Methodist James Albert Beebe.[41] This loss in the integrity of midweek worship coupled with the inability of some participants to discern between personal comment and faith testimony, and the frequent monopolization of the meeting by a particular individual (termed by George Haller the "prayer-meeting killer")[42] encouraged absenteeism in many churches.

Formalism in worship, often criticized as a cause of many of the problems related to midweek worship, was usually interpreted as a lack of diversity in the shape and content of the service. Variety in practice was regarded as a viable—and by some a divinely ordained—solution to poor attendance at public devotions:

He who made the world likes variety. We see that everywhere. . . . The fact that God's efforts are never formal, neither in nature or grace, in time or eternity, constitutes one reason why men love God's handiwork, why the "old, old story" as experienced in life and related in testimony is ever new, and why we shall enjoy heaven forever.

If our prayer meetings lack variety must we not in frankness admit that they are less than what God desires them to be, and should we not expect that men should fail in enthusiasm for them; and, on the other hand, if we build them as God builds his universe of nature and grace, shall we not more perfectly please him and more surely enlist and hold the interest of men? This question has but one answer.[43]

But the condemnation of formalism was not meant to condone neglect of careful and thorough preparation. In fact, lack of preparation by the leader, be it pastor or layperson, was seen as inexcusable; pastors in particular were chastized for laziness, for not fulfilling their duty, and for using the ever-expanding work of the parish as an apology for negligence. In spite of the best intentions, however, the prescription of preparation often worked against another requisite often delineated for the prayer meeting: shared leadership, following the best democratic principles. Even so, the pastor was usually regarded as the one best qualified to conduct devotional worship, a notion reinforced through the by-now established understanding that clergy, as professionals, had received special practical training for such leadership.[44]

In general, charges of formalism were not levied against the numerous brief addresses, printed prayer texts, orders of service, and other resources that were published to meet the demand for variety. Methodist authors urging the renewal of midweek worship and the prayer meeting often provided such texts and forms as guides and models. Meditations or short essays focusing upon spiritual matters and their relevance to contemporary Christian life (particularly social issues) were published to aid worship leaders whose own spiritual wells had run dry. New gimmicks and plans for organizing the meeting were suggested to attract and retain,[45] although concerns were raised lest the church prostitute itself in exchange for drawing a crowd.[46] While prayer texts and orders for private and public devotions had been available throughout the nineteenth century, publication of this type of resource escalated from the late nineteenth century onward, a phenomenon undoubtedly linked in part to the establishment of fuller orders of worship for Sunday morning and evening that came to be printed in the

Discipline (1870 for the Methodist Episcopal Church, South [Chap. V, Section I] and 1888 in the Methodist Episcopal Church [¶ 43]) and later in the respective Methodist hymnals. The provision of orders for worship, introduced to provide richness to what was deemed a bland prayer meeting, may have, at least in some communities, inadvertently stifled the Spirit-filled qualities so prized in the prayer meeting, and hence contributed to the drop in attendance.

Several factors external to the practice of midweek worship and family prayer undoubtedly had a bearing on their continuing decline. Within Methodism, the relaxing of many social and cultural restrictions in combination with technological developments, such as new forms of public and private transportation (e.g., the trolley and the family automobile), innovations in communication (e.g., radio and television) and entertainment (e.g., the motion picture), and changing patterns of recreation (particularly with the rise of public amusements in urban areas),[47] allowed Methodists to be wooed away from regular devotional practice in the family, at midweek, and on Sunday evening. Prohibitions had been established in 1872 by the Methodist Episcopal Church (*Discipline*, ¶ 340) against such "imprudent conduct" as "dancing, playing at games of chance, attending theaters, horse-races, circuses, dancing-parties, or patronizing dancing-schools," and several of these restrictions survived until the merger of 1939. But new to the 1920 Methodist Episcopal *Discipline* (¶ 69 § 2) was a delineation of "proper" amusements, indicating the now-held belief that "the social and recreational instinct is God-given and, if properly guided, will strengthen rather than injure the spiritual life."[48] "Innocent, clean, and wholesome" sports and activities were urged upon local churches to help foster an appropriate social life. Christian recreation, though an inadequate replacement for private or public prayer, functionally became a "spiritual" resource for individuals and their families.

The alteration of family structures and values concomitant with the urbanization and industrialization of America, and the resultant reformulations of gender roles, definitions, and responsibilities, helped to reorient Methodist devotional piety, especially in the family. By the early twentieth century, many Methodist women rejected the limitations of the "prescribed" vocation of domesticity, and entered more fully into the world outside the home by volunteering in the efforts of social reform (particularly the temperance, women's rights, education, and suffrage movements), seeking employment, completing a college education, or pursuing a professional career. Census figures for 1860 indicate that only 10.2 percent of the female population was employed outside the home, but by the late nineteenth century and especially during the first decades of the twentieth century, women entered the nondomestic labor force in increasing numbers.[49] Although husbands and fathers, as the "head" of the household, had the responsibility of leadership in family prayer, it was the wife and mother who often provided the sustaining support for family religion.[50] With his *and* her absence from the home, maintenance of family worship became more tenuous, and the demands of time and family undoubtedly limited the attendance of some families at midweek worship.

Methodist Family and Midweek Prayer After 1939

The newly created Methodist Church continued to uphold the ideals of midweek and family worship, though without the supports of accountability that had been provided (at least by *Discipline*) in the predecessor denominations. No longer were Methodists to be put on trial for neglect of the means of grace; in fact, the only reference in the 1939 and 1940 *Discipline* to the instituted and prudential means of grace is located in the historic General Rules. Material concerning family prayer is confined to this section, and no particular church officer is named in the *Discipline* as the monitor to oversee its observance. By this time the formerly rigorous regimen of family religion had been reduced in many homes to a once- or twice-daily reading of a prepared devotional booklet at the dining table.[51] But an additional reference to public devotion is found elsewhere in the *Discipline* (1939 and 1940 ¶ 223.11) as one of the stipulated responsibilities of a pastor: "to hold or appoint Prayer Meetings, Love Feasts, and Watch Night Meetings, wherever advisable."

New for Methodists in 1939 (and continued in 1940) is the inclusion in the *Discipline* (¶ 1577) of "Aids to Individual and Congregational Devotion" as part of the section on "Worship and Ritual." While these calls to worship and prayer, invocations, prayers of confession, affirmations of faith, prayers and collects, offertory sentences, and benedictions could be used in the context of midweek worship or the prayer meeting, it is unlikely that they would have been used regularly by individuals or families; leadership by a minister is assumed for the majority of these acts of worship. An order for morning or evening prayer, adapted from John Wesley's *Sunday Service,* is reproduced in ¶ 1576 for both 1939 and 1940, and may have offered a paradigm for some midweek meetings.

Interest in offering devotional resources for the small group, family, and individuals reached a peak in the first official worship book of United States Methodism produced since Wesley's *Sunday Service,* the 1944 *Book of Worship for Church and Home* of the Methodist Church. This worship resource contained seven orders of service for corporate evening prayer, a morning and evening order for "a family or other small group," and one hundred pages of aids for family and personal devotions including a monthly lectionary and a "treasury of prayers." Domestic prayer also received support from disciplinary legislation: in 1948, language urging the practice of family worship was added to the resolution on "The Christian Home" (*Discipline,* ¶ 2021.1); an even stronger statement appeared in 1952 (*Discipline,* ¶ 2021.1) and again in 1956 under the heading "The Christian Family" (*Discipline,* ¶ 2021.1-2). The 1956 resolution, with some modification in content and paragraph numbering, survived until the creation of The United Methodist Church in 1968.

Another worship book was approved by the Methodist Church in 1964, four years before the merger. Unfortunately, only limited resources for public and private devotion were offered in the 1965 *Book of Worship,* though it, like the 1944 book, was designated as a worship book for church and home. Likewise, from 1968 onward the topics of family and midweek worship were not addressed overtly in the *Discipline*; statements on the importance of private and public devotion were replaced with the delineation of local church structures (e.g., the committee on family life) and their responsibilities, though not indicating the spiritual goals of such work.[52] During this time, however, unofficial aids continued to be published by Methodist and other denominational presses.

The most recent official worship resource, the 1992 *United Methodist Book of Worship,* which is *not* designed as a worship book for church *and* home (it is primarily a worship leader's book), has limited materials for midweek worship and corporate daily prayer, and includes nothing specifically designed for family prayer (though the instructions for the services of daily prayer suggest that those services may be adapted for family use). Yet these few official resources for private devotion and midweek worship may not reflect the current interest in midweek or small-group worship that exists within the denomination, or the potential for recovering and reintroducing these historic means of grace.

Midweek worship for the entire congregation is offered currently—in some form—in a minority of churches throughout the denomination. Don Saliers's Lilly Endowment–funded study of the reception of the 1989 *United Methodist Hymnal* found that only one of the thirteen congregations he studied provided a service of corporate worship beyond that of Sunday morning.[53]

In places where midweek worship is celebrated, a variety of forms may be employed, following the allowances for liturgical freedom and flexibility permissible within United Methodism.[54] The service may be one of Word and Table as is found in the current worship resources, which may be abbreviated or adapted. Orders of service based on earlier generations of liturgical resources are an option, as is use of one of the offices for daily prayer located in the *Book of Worship* in the section entitled "Daily Praise and Prayer."[55] These orders are derived more directly from monastic models than from morning and evening prayer as set forth in Wesley's 1784 *Sunday Service*. An order for "A Midweek Service of Prayer and Testimony" is also included in the *Book of Worship*, conveniently located adjacent to the "occasional" service of the Love Feast; prayer, singing, and personal witness characterize both of these services, which were intentionally included in the volume as an invitation to United Methodists to reclaim part of their "enthusiastic" worship heritage.[56] Locally derived constructions may also be used to configure either simply or elaborately the elements of scripture reading, prayer, and hymnody-psalmody, and may or may not include a meditation on Scripture, thereby borrowing the pattern identified in the *Discipline* for Sunday worship in early-nineteenth-century Methodism. Other forms include contemporary "prayer and praise" services, and services of hymn singing and prayer that frame sessions of Bible study. Services are generally held in the evening, although some congregations have daytime services, either at noon or, in a small number of cases, early in the morning to be accessible for working people.

Indications are that the number of congregational midweek services may be increasing across the denomination. One factor in this change may be a desire to introduce evangelistic services (now labeled "seeker services") designed to attract persons who have not yet heard the gospel or who have, for whatever reason, not been faithful to their baptismal covenant.[57] Or, some congregations are opting for a midweek alternative to the "traditional" service on Sunday morning. These services, using "contemporary worship" forms, borrow popular music, arts, and mass media from the culture in an effort to be "user friendly" to the unchurched or to the "baby boomer" or "baby buster" subcultures.[58] Another factor may be the renewed interest in liturgical spirituality and prayer that have been claimed by some United Methodist pastors (often introduced to it during their seminary experience) and therefore enthusiastically conveyed to their congregations.

Along with congregation-wide midweek services, small-group occasions of worship and devotion also appear to be on the rise, reflecting a more broadly based desire within American culture to find spiritual sustenance and support within intimate settings (as Robert Wuthnow's studies have shown).[59] Within United Methodist congregations, devotions are found in specially designated "prayer and share" groups, Covenant Discipleship groups, Bible studies, support groups (e.g., for single mothers), and classes for persons inquiring about the Christian faith. One liability of this format (as Wuthnow acknowledges) has been the tendency in some groups to remake the Christian faith (and hence the worship of God) into one's own (or the group's own) image.

The matter of family prayer is much more problematic. Although many United Methodist Christians believe the reclamation of family worship is essential to the formation of the next generation for worship and discipleship, and among conservatives, family prayer is upheld as a concern for recovery of "family values," yet few offer concrete proposals for its implementation. Regular, routine practice of domestic worship (beyond a casual reading of devotional literature such as the *Upper Room,* or the saying of a blessing at table) is rarely found in United Methodist families. Family worship is occasionally encouraged from the pulpit; it seems to be supported more in those congregations that have a staff member in Christian education whose work is focused in family ministries. Resources for family worship are most readily available during Advent and Lent, but are largely absent during the rest of the year. This is not to say that resources are unavailable from the denomination, but that distribution of these materials and encouragement of their usage aim at these traditionally penitential seasons, which, wittingly or unwittingly, may say something about how the denomination is defining family prayer.

Conclusion

Has the advice in the General Rules on private and public devotion been regarded as relevant for John Wesley's spiritual descendants?

Although it is unclear whether or not advocacy of family and midweek prayer by the Methodist denominations was directly prompted by adherence to the General Rules, it is certain that attempts have been made throughout the past two hundred years to preserve the practice of these two forms of devotion. Yet the degree to which they were stressed has varied according to American Methodism's self-understanding. As a society, Methodism focused intentionally upon a spiritual revival that distinguished it from the surrounding culture even while its broader aim was to convert the populace. Public and family devotions were means toward achieving that goal. The partial success that allowed episcopal Methodism to move from society to mainline denomination also led to its decline as a distinctive body whose standards fell to what was generally acceptable. With the more recent overall crisis of mainline Protestantism, some within Methodism show an awareness of the need to restore devotional practices and the spiritual and evangelistic enthusiasm that marked its first flowering as a society with a mission to spread scriptural holiness throughout the land.

Elliott Wright

As has been shown in the other volumes of this study (especially Volume 2, The People(s) Called Methodist: Forms and Reforms of Their Life*), Methodists during the nineteenth and twentieth centuries were "average" Americans in almost every way. They were not separatist, they were not wealthy, they were not intellectually distinguished, they were "good Americans." Their social location inclined them toward strong support for public education. In this interesting study, Elliott Wright explores in depth and with care the meaning of that support of public education by Methodists in the nineteenth century. During the period of the great growth of public education Methodism gave particular leadership and assumed practical ownership. Superintendents, principals, and teachers were often Methodist adherents. What Wright shows is that American Methodists, along with the other dominant Protestant groups, particularly the Presbyterians and Baptists, saw "public education" as mainline Protestant education. That is the way other religious groups looked at it as well, which was one of the reasons for the development of parochial schools among the Roman Catholics during the periods of Roman Catholic immigration to America in the later part of the century. This study reminds us that Protestant America in the nineteenth century controlled not only the schools, but also the other major institutions of public life. There was a time of shared values when family, school, church, press, and voluntary organizations taught the same things and represented the same values. A good deal of Bible and theology were inculcated through the public schools, even where prayer and devotional life were not allowed.*

Changed circumstances for Methodists now prevail. The greater diversity of religious traditions, changing demographics for Protestants, and new demands on the public order have altered previous realities and made it more difficult, if not impossible, for public education to champion Protestant theology and values. What do these changed circumstances suggest? On the one hand, we may see a time when Methodist commitment to public education will change, particularly due to aggressive movements among independent schools and unease on the part of Methodist people about the quality of public education. Also, the assumption that public education is supplementary to the church in terms of moral education may be breaking down. One of the biggest issues before elementary and secondary education in America has to be with the nebulous term "values." Many church people recognize

Doctrines and Discipline

that the term "values" is empty without some particular content derived from specific moral principles. The home schooling movement in the United States also is a response to these issues. Changes in thinking about public education will, of necessity, bring about new theological understandings of the relationship between Methodism and the public order, indeed, between Methodism and the state. How do the theological concerns of identity and mission expressed by other authors in this collection shed light on the issues here addressed?

American Methodism and Public Education: 1784 to 1900

Elliott Wright

A semiofficial 1964 manual on the social thought and action of the Methodist Church contained a single sentence on public education: "There is strong support of the public schools, and strong opposition to the diversion of tax funds to private and sectarian schools."[1] The halves of that sentence echo but dimly a complex, often noisy interaction in the parallel developments of both Methodism and public schooling in the United States. If strong Methodist support for public schools came to be normative, this was neither axiomatic at the outset nor a common policy in all sectors of what is today The United Methodist Church until around 1900. In fact, Methodist support for public education, that is, free, government-funded elementary and secondary schools, was uncertain in the early decades of the nineteenth century and again in the South after the Civil War. Methodism early on embraced with only minor quibbling, and has sustained, opposition to state support for sectarian schools on elementary and secondary levels.[2] This policy, however, led to conflicts with neighbors, notably Roman Catholics. In the arena of school funding, nineteenth- and early-twentieth-century Methodism was a bastion of nativist, anti-Catholic sentiment.[3]

Methodism and Methodists in the past did more than support public schools. The church and its members also influenced the public system—the stand against state aid to parochial education can be read as a determination to protect a closely aligned institution. The preparation of public school teachers was a self-conscious purpose in the founding of some Methodist colleges. At times, Methodists employed the public schools in support of their causes—especially those of general Protestant morality and specific Methodist temperance.

The goal of this essay is to survey the background and the drama of Methodist public school interaction from the organization of the Methodist Episcopal Church up to 1900. This is a drama of American culture and religion that remains largely ignored in general histories of church, education, and nation. The survey is at points broad and does

181

not attempt to deal with every aspect of Methodist relations with government in the arena of education. It adheres closely to community-based elementary and secondary education. And it focuses primarily on the Methodist Episcopal Church and the ME Church, South, with only passing references to other traditions that comprise United Methodism. This is dictated in large part by the scarcity of primary and secondary sources on the topic outside the ME tradition.

Methodism's role in higher education has been exhaustively studied. Some attention has focused on church-related secondary academies. The theme of Methodism and public schools is likely a less popular theme for several reasons that are themselves part of the story. First, Methodists made little formative contribution to the American concept of religious liberty, and the inherent principle of church-state separation, which provided the context in which common, nonsectarian education flourished. They were not among the midwives of the public school idea itself. While by strong embrace and numerical strength they helped to define the operation of religious liberty and public education, the American heirs of Wesley rarely figure in studies of church-state relations. Second, the public school and Methodism took roots and grew in the same time frame, often appealing to the same segments of society. Each became symbiotic, powerful American institutions, especially on the expanding western frontier.[4] To have raised questions about Methodism and public education in the first half of this century would have been like doubting the centrality of the Bible to Protestants. Third, since World War II, the churches of United Methodism have followed social agenda and accepted church and state trends that move the religious community farther and farther from involvement with public education. Ironically, in the last thirty years a proliferation of "official" denominational statements on aspects of state-funded schools parallel a decline in Methodist action to either bolster or reform what the Methodist Episcopal General Conference of 1972 called "an indispensable safeguard to republican institutions."[5] A postscript to this paper touches upon the twentieth century.

Getting Started: Multiple Educational Possibilities

The public or common school did not become a dominant institution in the United States until more than fifty years after the Revolutionary War. Thomas Jefferson dreamed of a free school system but little came of his 1779 bill to set up a system of Virginia tax-supported boarding schools for deserving boys.[6] The new nation was initially an educational hodgepodge. An uneven system of colonial district, town, and village schools was inherited north of Maryland.[7] Most of the South made do with tutors and private academies. Pioneers along the sparsely settled western frontier had home schooling or nothing, and often put no value on formal education.[8] So much of the motivation for education came from religion and so many of the institutions were church-related that R. Freeman Butts has aptly called the first fifty years of the United States a time of educational "multiple establishments."[9] Many geographically defined schools were controlled by the original or dominant religious group even if and when supported by local tax revenues. (This was especially true in New England.) As the population became religiously diverse, squabbles over religious claims to school funds increased. Methodists were active protagonists in a prolonged conflict over the division of New York City school funds in the 1820s and 1830s.[10]

Education was acutely unsystematized in most places (Boston, beginning in 1818 had one of the first real systems).[11] The basic unit was the grammar school and many students never went beyond that, often for economic reasons. Academies provided formal learning beyond the introductory level. Attendance at school was more or less voluntary outside of New England.

Protestant church–founded private academies—sometimes called "seminaries"—were common in the early national period. The early American Methodists, just getting formally organized in the 1780s, tried to emulate what the Congregationalists, Presbyterians, and Episcopalians were doing as the population spread out. The Christmas Conference of 1784 admonished preachers "to instruct the children in every place" and also laid plans for the ill-fated Cokesbury College. Francis Asbury himself made the first stabs at what would later become a scattered network of Methodist academies. Among these were two schools called Bethel, one in South Carolina and the other in Kentucky, and a Methodist district school in Uniontown, Pennsylvania.[12] Few of these lasted long. A brief history of the founding of Methodism in Uniontown quotes a contemporary as saying the school there lacked "charter or endowment, having to depend wholly on tuition fees for its support" and "soon went down, and was abandoned, involving a few in pecuniary liability to some small amount."[13]

Asbury put little energy into founding schools from the destruction of

Cokesbury College by fire in 1796 until his death in 1816. A lull in general interest in education characterized those same years,[14] decades when Asbury put his emphasis on evangelism and the organizing of Methodist societies and churches. The great circuit rider died on the eve of an educational awakening that would both affect Methodism and be effected by Methodists whose numbers dramatically increased in the first half of the nineteenth century.

The United States was struck by what Bishop W. Ralph Ward Jr. has called an educational "fever" around 1820, and the Methodists caught it too.[15] The General Conference of 1820 said that every annual conference should establish "literary institutions under their own control, in such ways and name as they may think proper."[16] Four years later Sunday schools were heartily endorsed.[17] Methodists would champion the American Sunday School Union's crusade, announced in 1830, to establish such a school "in every destitute place" of the Mississippi Valley.[18]

Separately or alongside the college-level literary institutions were secondary academies. Thirty-four such schools were reported to the 1852 Methodist Episcopal General Conference. *The Early Schools of Methodism,* published in 1886, listed eighty-four academies (past or present) as owned and operated by the ME Church.[19] Thirty-two were in existence in 1922 and fourteen at union in 1939.[20] Some of the nineteenth-century schools were like seeds sown in shallow ground. Others flourished. A number were eventually transformed into public high schools. For example, East Greenwich High School near Providence, Rhode Island, emerged out of Kent Academy, established in 1802 and under Methodist control from 1839 until deep into the present century.[21] Baxter Seminary, initially a missionary school of the ME Church in Putnam County, Tennessee, educated the youth of the Cumberland Plateau from 1908 until it became a county school in 1957.[22] A few early Methodist academies became colleges. Such was the case with Lebanon Seminary, founded in 1818 in Illinois, which grew into McKendree College.[23]

Another notable example of an academy that became a college was the Union Institute in North Carolina, and this school's roots and the relationship of its organizer to public instruction suggest the flexibility of American educational structures prior to the Civil War. Union was the forerunner of Trinity College and Duke University. A local education committee invited Brantley York, a tireless lay preacher and teacher, to help them start a school in 1837. The name "union" was selected because, as York wrote in his autobiography,

> the institution was located between two populous neighborhoods, the one on the south called Hopewell, the inhabitation of which were generally Methodists; the other on the north, Springfield, whose inhabitants were principally Quakers. The object of naming it Union Institute was to unite these two neighborhoods in the interest of the school. This was happily effected.[24]

Union Institute opened with sixty-nine students, who came to class when they could. This was typical of many nonboarding schools, and young and older mixed together in common space. Terms varied from place to place and scholars were not divided by grade level. Fine distinctions were not always drawn between church and embryonic public schools. Brantley York founded and taught in both church-related and citizen-funded schools in five states. He may have "organized more schools than any other man in America";[25] at the same time he was not a typical Methodist circuit rider. He was always a lay preacher, never joining an annual conference and, therefore, had greater flexibility than his ordained brothers.

In an invaluable, singular work on Methodism and public education, available only as a dissertation, Terrell Johnson credits the early Methodist schools, especially in frontier settings, with exerting four significant influences on American education in general. These are: (1) insistence on a demanding curriculum going beyond the rudiments of reading, writing, and counting, (2) the education of women, (3) early childhood education, and (4) moral education.[26] While hardly the originator of these themes, Methodism helped to implant them in the American educational consciousness that came to be embodied in the public system.

Deciding for Public Schools in the North and Midwest

The question of the degree to which Methodism would opt for a parochial system was formally undecided in the fourth decade of the nineteenth century. "Multiple establishments" were being challenged by the concept of "common" tax-supported schools. Should the church continue to found and maintain its own institutions? One of the most vigorous defenders of a parochial system for Methodists was the

Reverend Edmund S. Janes, later a bishop, who in 1839 vigorously argued public schools could never adequately implant Christian morality or introduce youth to the truth of Scripture. Furthermore, he asserted, "education has an important and necessary connection with our missionary work."[27] Janes's sentiments would be heard again in the South after the Civil War.

Missionary zeal was clearly a motivation for many of the academies and colleges. It was a pressing responsibility to educate the youth into the tenets of Christianity and Methodism—and to convert nonbelievers, or Presbyterians, who might happen to enroll. Most of the new Methodist secondary schools that continued to be founded after the public system was in place were mission endeavors, often set up in remote places as lacking in churches as in schools.

Johnson states that the Methodist academy era did not end until the General Conference of 1872 embraced public schools.[28] He is right in an official sense but the General Conference was simply endorsing what rank-and-file Methodists had already chosen in the North and Midwest. The process was gradual but steady and can be detected in formal Church statements back to the early 1820s. An 1824 resolution bearing largely on Sunday schools reflected a concern for general education: "It shall be the duty of every travelling preacher in our Church to keep in mind the importance of having suitable teachers employed in the instruction of the youth of our country, and to use his influence to introduce teachers into schools whose learning, piety, and religious tenets are such as we could recommend."[29] Bishops, in their 1844 address to the General Conference, knew they were speaking to a friendly constituency when asking Methodists to use their influence to assure that the Bible "is universally introduced as a text-book in the *common-school systems* of education in this country."[30] This rhetoric acknowledged the importance of public schools and was also a call to hold fast against Roman Catholic opposition to the use of the King James Bible in those Methodist-attended classrooms. The common, or public, school was an adaptation of the town and village school. This Puritan invention from the 1640s was most highly developed in New England, and Massachusetts was the setting for its transformation from a Congregational Church–controlled institution into a state system emulated elsewhere. Horace Mann and his colleagues went against two centuries of tradition in the disestablishment of the Massachusetts schools, which they accomplished in a ten-year period beginning in the late 1830s. Opposition was substantial. Orthodox Congregationalists concluded that Unitarian Mann was undercutting the foundations of society, and thereby the school issue continued the ongoing conflict between Calvinists and Unitarians.[31]

Methodists, who had twenty-nine Massachusetts congregations in 1800 and 277 in 1858, played little role in the Bay State school conflict.[32] Generally, Methodists and Baptists, as "dissenters" unaligned with either contending theological camp, welcomed the slacking of Congregational control over the schools. They would find it convenient and acceptable to go along with public schools in New York City, where the denomination, along with others, had organized their own institutions. An unsuccessful New York Methodist attempt to win public funds for a charity school in the 1830s was not about commitment to church-based education so much as part of an anti-Catholic ploy. The Methodists were bothered that the Catholics had public support for an orphans' school. The episode fed directly into the Catholic decision to go with parochial education.[33]

Methodist support for and engagement in common schools are evident in the pages of the New York *Christian Advocate and Journal* from 1830 onward. A front-page article on October 8, 1830, admonished care that new common school teachers be men of a "mild, gentle, amicable, conciliating, and affectionate disposition."[34] The paper allowed that interviewers could not scrutinize a candidate's religion too closely but had to consider the matter since each teacher was expected to begin the day with prayer. The *Advocate* worried lest a schoolmaster, once hired, might render God an "unacceptable service" by praying as a hypocrite.[35] The preparation of Christian teachers and a role of clergy in the public system were the topics of a February 1834 article.[36]

The preparation of teachers for common schools was a stated purpose of some of the colleges Methodists founded in the early years. A case in point is Dickinson College in eastern Pennsylvania. The 1835 annual conference resolution founding the school said that the Methodist Episcopal Church "can never fulfill her high destiny until she does her part in providing suitable instruction for the people and sending forth thousands of young men as teachers of common schools and academies."[37] The Methodists of Pennsylvania were equally convinced that the young men most qualified for that task were not in other denominations but "are found mostly among us."[38]

The Methodist Episcopal Church grew far too fast in the two decades

before the Civil War to have provided schools even for its own youngsters. In addition, it was finding itself at home with the educational
ethos of what Martin Marty calls the Protestant "righteous empire" in
the United States.[39] Two primary institutions of this empire were the
common school and the Sunday school, and the moral stance of each
was highly complementary.

In loosening the church hold on the schools of Massachusetts, Mann
did not doubt that one purpose of education was to produce moral citizens and did not challenge the common wisdom that "education must
rest upon religion."[40] His greatest accomplishment, the very foundation
of "common" schools, was to popularize the proposition that a common
core of Christianity morality could serve the children of many denominations. Freeman Butts summarizes:

> Moral education should be based upon the common elements of Christianity
> to which all Christian sects would agree or to which they would take no
> exception. In general, these "common elements" took two forms: namely,
> teaching the common moral virtues of honesty, fairness, and truth, which
> though apparent in the Christian virtues should, however, not be taught as
> sectarianism; and also reading of the Bible as containing the common ele-
> ments of Christian moral but reading it with no comment in order not to
> introduce sectarian biases.[41]

That the common core of Christianity fixed upon included the
Protestant Bible and Protestant morals and mores did not exactly please
Roman Catholics and Jews, but it felt right to the Methodists. Moreover,
as David Tyack and Elisabeth Hansot correctly point out, the pan-
Protestant Sunday school movement, energized by the Valley
Campaign in the 1830s, gave momentum to "nonsectarian" public
education.[42] Methodists, along with many other standard-brand
Protestants, would settle into a two-sphere pattern of education. The
home and Sunday school gave instruction in doctrine and polity; the
public schools underscored a Protestant moral consensus and, in most
places, read the Bible. Some public schools also prayed but this practice
was never universal in American state-funded institutions.[43]

A sense of ease with the arrangement grew as Methodist numerical
growth came to influence the general culture across the nineteenth century. Ruth Miller Elson has identified a shift in the theological message
of school textbooks from the Calvinist *New England Primer* of 1830 to the
readers of the post–Civil War years. "Although the child is told now and
then to fear God, it is more often love that is demanded of the reader."[44]

Can this shift be read apart from the cultural endorsement of the Arminian love theology of Methodism?

Defending and Using the Familiar

Once the Methodist Episcopal Church identified with public schools it was ready to defend the institution, and one of the greatest perceived threats came from "Romanists." What Johnson sees as the formal embrace by the Methodist Episcopal General Conference in 1872 was most essentially a broadside against tax dollars going to Catholic schools. Picking up the tenor of the Episcopal Address, a resolution declared it "hostile to our free institutions and the cause of education" to divide common school funds among denominations.[45]

In opposing the use of public dollars for parochial schools, the Methodist Episcopal 1872 resolution reflected a general Protestant sentiment and also anticipated at least one aspect of a nativist-inspired constitutional dispute that began in the administration of U. S. Grant and lasted into that of Rutherford B. Hayes. President Grant in 1875 proposed a constitutional amendment that would have forbidden the teaching of religious tenets in any public school and disallowing the "granting of any school funds, or school taxes, or any part thereof . . . for the benefit or in aid, directly or indirectly, of any religious sect or denomination."[46] James G. Blaine, then a member of Congress from Maine (and later secretary of state and Republican candidate for the presidency) quickly proposed a constitutional amendment that would have blocked the use of any public money for sectarian education. The House of Representatives passed the measure by a large margin but it was turned back in the Senate.[47] (A blatant nativist, Blaine seems to have gone to great lengths to conceal his own Roman Catholic origins.)[48]

In addition, the 1872 General Conference pledged the church to resist attempts to "exclude from the Common Schools the Bible, which is the charter of our liberties and the inspiration of our civilization."[49] A similar assertion, made in a report on "moral reform," was adopted in 1875 by the General Conference of the Methodist Protestant Church, which in that year had some 53,400 members.[50] These actions reflected a long-standing worry about the secular character of public schools and a simmering conflict between Catholics and Protestants over which version of the Bible was appropriate (as a reader or as devotional literature) in those institutions. Many Protestants interpreted the Catholic displea-

sure with the King James Version as rejection of Scripture itself, and
some Catholics took the position that no Bible in public schools was better than the Protestant version.

The battle over the Bible in public schools had been intense in New
York and Philadelphia at the beginning of the common school era.[51] The
New York *Christian Advocate and Journal* periodically blasted away in the
1830s and 1840s at Catholic (especially Jesuit) intentions to "seize" the
public schools by removing the Bible.[52] This issue resumed with vigor
when Catholic immigration increased after the Civil War. The Midwest
was the new center of dispute, which sometimes led to legal action. A
prolonged conflict in Cincinnati resulted in an Ohio State Supreme
Court ruling (1872) prohibiting Bible reading in the schools of that city.[53]
Catholic disgruntlement simmered in Wisconsin for years. Parents in
Edgerton brought suit in 1886 against the reading of the King James
Version in local schools, and won with a State Supreme Court decision
in 1890. Wisconsin Methodists, who numbered 23,313 in 1880, com-
pared to an estimated 308,000 Catholics, vigorously opposed the suit
and the outcome. They were no doubt less than happy when the
Catholic newspaper described public schools as "Methodist Sunday
Schools under false pretenses."[54]

In the late nineteenth century, the Methodist Episcopal Church and its
people regularly defended public schools and their Protestant ethos
against both Catholics and secularists. They also found ways to use the
institutions for Methodist moral causes, primarily temperance. Training
all of those teachers at Dickinson and other colleges would come to pay
off. The General Conference of 1888 hailed "with joy the enactment of
laws providing for scientific temperance instruction in the public
schools of thirty-four States and Territories, under which six and a half
million children and youth are being taught the evils of alcoholic bever-
ages."[55]

"Scientific temperance" was a prohibitionist ideology that the
Women's Christian Temperance Union caused the thirty-four states and
territories to require in public schools. The WCTU, of course, was a
cause dear to the hearts of many Methodist women. The General
Conference also urged the scrutinizing of textbooks to make sure that
none suggested the acceptability of "moderate use of milder intoxi-
cants."[56] (The school campaign fanned the cause of prohibition ardent-
ly endorsed by Methodism. After repeal, the Methodists were still not
willing to cede the public schools to drinkers. The delegate handbook

for the first General Conference of the Methodist Church in 1940 contained a charge to the new denomination to rekindle the temperance fires beginning with the schools. Delegates were reminded that a "sizeable proportion of the 900,000 public school teachers" and thousands of students were Methodists and, therefore, on-site crusaders.[57] That same report stated that the Board of Temperance had reached 150,000 high school students in the past year.)[58]

A Distinct Situation in the South

As noted earlier, the embrace of the public schools by Methodists in the South was slower. Several states (especially, Virginia, North Carolina, and Louisiana) had given some attention to publicly supported schools before 1860 but true public school systems did not develop until postwar reconstruction. Free, universal schooling was a major plank in the federal reconstruction policy.[59]

Methodist academies and female seminaries had existed in the South before the war and this was the educational approach favored by the Methodist Episcopal Church, South, at its 1854 General Conference; in fact, that conference sanctioned a parochial system like that "which other denominations and particularly the Roman Catholics employ with astonishing sagacity and success."[60] More than forty academies and high schools existed on the eve of Fort Sumter. The education news at the 1866 General Conference was depressing but there was a determination to restore institutions (a few of which survived) and build a network of denominational schools.[61] The Louisiana Annual Conference appointed a committee to redraft a broad plan of church education as early as 1865.[62] The General Conferences of 1874 and 1878 endorsed systems of district Methodist high schools.[63] Methodists in North Carolina "agitated" in behalf of parochial schools from 1881 to 1895, according to a historian of church-state relations in that state.[64] Parochial schools would remain official denominational policy until near the end of the century but, of course, nothing like a comprehensive system ever developed.

One strong supporter of church-based education was Bishop H. N. McTyeire. In 1872, the same year the ME Church officially endorsed public education, the bishop reported that his earlier "hopeful" assessment of the public system had changed because of a lack of religious education in state schools. He continued: "The Episcopalians established parochial schools, and so do the Presbyterians and Baptists. We will have to do so also. Within fifty years I prophesy that our Church will have a school wherever we preach the word."[65] His prophecy proved wrong but he was hardly alone in holding it.

The editor of the Nashville *Christian Advocate* went so far as to propose that citizens pay their school taxes to the three major southern denominations—Baptist, Methodist, and Presbyterian—for parochial education. He complained of being taxed "for the public school fund to educate other people's children, and we have no control over the education that is given them."[66]

Fear that government schools would exclude the Bible was one likely reason for southern Methodist resistance to public institutions. The 1882 Episcopal Address declared that Methodists could not consent to the elimination of "the influence of the Christian religion" from high schools, colleges, and universities. The address continued:

> The Bible must not be excluded, nor must it be denied a place as a text-book in the school that is forming the moral as well as the intellectual habits of the youth of our land.[67]

The bishops went on to warn against Roman Catholicism, and particularly the sending of Protestant children to Catholic schools. They excoriated the idea that Catholic schools were superior to Protestant ones, a notion that seems to have been current among some families seeking to educate girls. When Protestant parents send girls to Catholic schools, said the bishops, "these daughters have abandoned the Church of their father."[68]

If a lack of moral and biblical instruction made southern Methodists leery of public schools, racial reality probably contributed more postwar resistance. The southern states after 1865 had two populations to educate and lacked structures for doing it. For a time, public and private education coexisted, and sometimes competed. The children of the African Americans formerly held in bondage became a particular educational and missionary target of northern denominations, including the Methodist Episcopal Church. Through the Freedman's Aid Society, northern Methodists set up hundreds of schools, some for whites as well as for blacks. The relationship of the races in the educational setup was a thorny issue.

A desire to protect white Methodist youngsters from the reconstruction schools was no doubt a motivating factor in the immediate postwar parochial approach. As northern control ebbed across the 1870s, and white rule was established, the public schools become more attractive to Protestants.[69] Hunter Farish has assembled an extensive collection of southern Methodist newspaper articles and editorials favorable to public schools in the 1880s. Commenting on the situation in 1889, the editor of the *Wesleyan Christian Advocate* (Georgia) said: "For some years now there has been in Georgia and other States but one practicable way to give the masses an elementary education. . . . For some years past, then, opposition to the state public schools has been practically the equivalent of opposition to the elementary education of the masses."[70]

Methodists north and south supported the Blair Education Bill, first introduced into the Congress of the United States in 1881 and reintroduced to no avail up to 1890. This measure, sponsored by Senator Henry W. Blair of New Hampshire, would have provided federal assistance for literacy education through the states, the aid based on the number of illiterate citizens. The practical impact would have been greatest in the South but it had national implications.[71]

The ME Church General Conference of 1884 called the Blair Bill "eminently wise and patriotic."[72] While the southern church does not seem to have officially addressed Blair, Farish notes that "the journal of the Connection warmly espoused the Blair Education Bill. . . . The *Southern Christian Advocate* denounced without reserve the spirit that would oppose the measure because its benefits would be shared by black and white."[73] The bill was decisively defeated by the Senate in 1890, and federal aid for public schools would not become a reality for another forty years.

By 1900, the two major churches of American Methodism were geographically divided but as one in staunch admiration of public education as they experienced it. Few would have disagreed with an 1882 assessment by the Louisiana Annual Conference, speaking of government-funded schools: "It behooves us, therefore, to study carefully the system in its practical operation; to seek in every legitimate way to increase its merits and to reduce, and if possible, to eliminate its objectionable features, where such are found."[74]

Postscript: The Twentieth Century

Little would disturb the amiable relationship between Methodism and public education across the first half of the present century.

Methodist energy would go into various attempts to introduce more religious instruction or moral education into public schools. Methodist congregations across the land took part in the "released time" experiment—students were "released" from public school to attend religious classes—which waxed and waned beginning around 1915.[75]

Methodists continued to champion the Bible in public schools for fifty years after the turn of the century. They often played leading roles in state-level campaigns to *require* or at least assure devotional Bible reading.[76] That effort was successful in thirteen states between 1913 and 1930, and it was one of those state laws—in Pennsylvania—that was at stake in the 1962 Supreme Court ruling barring state-required Bible reading in public schools.

A new day with new issues arrived in the 1960s not only with Supreme Court rulings against required Bible reading and prayer but also with a new awareness of the diversity of American society. The Protestant "righteous empire" of denominational Sunday schools and Protestant public schools lay in the past. While not vanishing from the United Methodist social map, concern for public education *per se* had been overshadowed by civil rights concerns highly critical of inherited educational institutions.

United Methodists would come to agree with the court rulings on prayer and Bible reading, although that was not self-evident in the early 1960s. In fact, clergy and laity were so divided on the issue that the 1964 General Conference was unable to take any action dealing with school prayer. An official of the Methodist Board of Social Concerns would later tell a congressional hearing that the Supreme Court "induced a minor crisis in Methodism." But he speculated that more and more "Protestant Christian people, including Methodists, are recognizing that religious devotions in any organized or formal sense have no place in public schools where students are present by compulsion of law."[77]

The General Conference of 1968 adopted a resolution on church, government, and education that remained in effect in the late 1990s. It affirmed United Methodist support for the "principle of universal public education" and "support for public educational institutions." It also acknowledged the value of private schools.[78] Similar sentiments found their way into the denomination's "Social Principles" in the 1970s, along with the following statement: "The state should not use its authority to inculcate particular religious beliefs (including atheism) nor should it require prayer or worship in the public school, but should leave students free to practice their own religion."[79] The affirmation leaves unclear the question of the locale for student practice of personal religion.

In 1996, the General Conference adopted without debate a seventy-five-page book called "Education: The Gift of Hope," prepared by a task force convened by the Board of Higher Education and Ministry. This document covers the full scope of education—elementary, secondary, and higher, but, interestingly, says very little about the public education as such. Yet it assumes public classrooms as the fundamental locus of schooling. "Education: The Gift of Hope" reads like a well-intended exercise in diversity training but, like the omnibus resolution of 1968, it lacks passion. It wanders through much of the jargon of multi-culturalism and progressive educational reform (notably "learning centered schools") without presenting a convincing case of why Methodists as Christians ought to care about such things. The document concludes with an appeal to each congregation to "develop a plan for concrete involvement in the educational activities of its community, seeking to improve the system and become involved with students"[80]—bureaucratic advice for a bureaucratic age.

Bruce W. Robbins

Bruce W. Robbins has given considerable attention to ecumenical relationships within worldwide Methodism and between Methodism and other churches. In this essay he explores the theological idea of connection. He provides a useful analysis of the way in which the idea of connection has developed in Methodism and the way in which, he believes, the idea has been freighted with meaning in an attempt to "hold us together." Robbins is critical of the efforts to make connection into something more than it is and he uses the Christian theological principle of koinonia *to expand his theological thinking. Robbins suggests that, at least in its origins, Methodism gave less emphasis to Wesleyan distinctiveness than to commitment to sharing in the whole body of Christ.*

Does Robbins's understanding of connection provide a conceptual apparatus for understanding the place of Methodism in the world church? Is koinonia *sufficiently clear to offer a way forward in ecumenical relations? How should we think about the place of Methodism in the wider Christian community into the future? Is it our job to try to keep the Methodist churches distinct in identity and purpose? Do the distinctive emphases of Methodist theology have a place in the future church? Are they dependent on their embodiment in an ecclesial body? Is United Methodism so identified with American culture that it cannot easily contribute to a global Christianity? This essay is both Methodist and ecumenical and reflects on both connection and* koinonia. *We include it toward the end of the volume intentionally because of our conviction that these concerns, that of connection and of the whole body of Christ in the world, will be vitally important to the future of the Methodist peoples in the twenty-first century.*

Connection and *Koinonia:* Wesleyan and Ecumenical Perspectives on the Church

Bruce W. Robbins

Introduction

In an opening paragraph of a sermon on the nature of the Church, John Wesley begins by saying how few people understand what the word *church* means. He continues: "A more ambiguous word than this, the 'church,' is scarce to be found in the English language."[1] For reasons familiar to us all, Mr. Wesley's followers wanted assurance of his faithfulness to the "church," and he sought to provide it. The text he chose for this sermon was the famous ecumenical passage in the fourth chapter of Ephesians concerning the oneness of the body. What is the church?

> The catholic or universal church is all the persons in the universe whom God hath so called out of the world as to entitle them to the preceding character; as to be "one body," united by "one spirit.". . . Two or three Christian believers united together are a church in the narrowest sense of the word. . . . A particular church may therefore consist of any number of members, whether two or three, or two or three millions. But still, whether it be larger or smaller, the same idea is to be preserved.[2]

Since the origin of the Methodist societies, people have questioned the relationships between the "people called Methodist" and between Methodists and those in the wider, Christian church. Even by the end of the first decade, the Wesleys sought greater union and harmony among the societies and asked in a special conference, "How can we unite with each other?"[3] Today, as well, the relationships among Methodists, as well as among those in the wider church, continue to be very much at issue. What holds Methodists together? What makes them unique or distinguishes them within the body of Christ?

The hope of this paper is to examine and ask what perceptions or assumptions we hold, implicitly or explicitly, that shape our thinking about the relationships we as Methodists have to one another as well as to others in the wider Christian community. More particularly, how do our historical understandings of connectionalism and our ecumenical perspectives on the nature of the church today (especially the concept of *koinonia*) affect our outlook for the future? Of course, the perspectives offered in this paper will be far narrower than desired for any adequate response to these broader questions. Specifically, I will examine connectionalism from a historical perspective and then look more closely at its usage within contemporary, United Methodist discussions. And, I shall look briefly at how the popular ecumenical image of *koinonia* is related to connectionalism and how it offers parallel models to the ecclesiological understandings of the "church."

Connectionalism

The words *connexion* and *connectionalism* are central to Methodist identity and history. From the earliest times of the Wesleyan movement, the church has been described as "connectional." Charles Welch, writing on Wesleyan polity, was quoted as saying that connexion "very aptly and felicitously designates the essential and intrinsic character of the Wesleyan body."[4] More recently, a United Methodist *Book of Discipline* (1992) spoke extensively about "the connectional people" and had three long pages specifically addressing what "connection" means. Within studies of the "global nature" of The United Methodist Church there is constant, even overbearing, reference to "connectionalism."

At the same time, little reflection or analysis about "connectionalism" is being developed today. A large *Encyclopedia of World Methodism* devotes only three short paragraphs to the term, regardless of how it is spelled.[5] Other recent publications on Methodist doctrine, theology, or history have little or no reference specifically to connectionalism. Even though it is viewed as foundational to Methodist identity, considerable confusion exists as to what connectionalism means and what role it serves today. This point is well illustrated in the most recent publication on Methodist polity: *Polity, Practice, and the Mission of The United Methodist Church*, by Thomas Edward Frank. Although he does not address connectionalism at any great length, he does point out in various places the confusion over its meaning in reference to other subjects. For example, in the closing paragraphs of the chapter "The Ministry of All Christians," Frank analyzes recent disciplinary changes on connectionalism and asks: "What really does constitute the connection in United Methodism?" He notes that connectionalism is far more than a clergy connection. Yet, he also states that confusing ideas and questions surrounding the term indicate broad and deep issues. Those issues "point to the elusiveness and fragility of the unity of the church."[6]

Origins of Connexion

According to Thomas Frank, the word *connexion* had little ecclesiastical sense to it. Quoting Mr. Rack's *Reasonable Enthusiast,* he says the term could apply to a "trademan's clientele" or to a "politician's personal following" (47). The term fit the Methodists because the group of new adherents had a strong personal connection to John Wesley. However, the term was also important because it was used extensively in relation to religious societies within the Church of England. According to John C. Bowmer (190), those societies were considered legal when they met "in connexion with" a clergyman of the Church of England. Initially, then, the "Methodist connexion" applied specifically to that connection of the adherents with John Wesley even though the term came to bear much greater meaning related to doctrine and relationships. Bowmer extends the term by defining *connexion* as "a number of Societies who have agreed to unite themselves in a common bond of doctrine and discipline, under a common code of regulations and usages, and under a common government" (191). We can see the transition as the "connexion" stands for the greater and greater relationships between the societies (as well as the increased number of societies).

John Bowmer gives further attention to Methodist connectionalism by drawing upon the work of Alfred Barrett. He demonstrates how the connection "was not mere federation, but [it was] a co-ordinated effort and concerted action; but what commended it most to Wesleyans was that, as they saw it, it was scriptural" (191). In the eyes of the early Methodists, the Christian practices of the early church were just like Wesleyan connection. This was seen as true in terms of preaching, care for one another, and even in terms of financial matters. Bowmer cites Alfred Barrett as believing that "under the sanction of the Apostles [in the early church] . . . the initial principle of the church connexion involving central administration was affirmed."[7] These associations further explain the importance of the connexion in building and maintaining the relationships in the early Methodist societies.

Bowmer also describes the three principles upon which the connection was built: episcopé, itinerancy, and mutual help. For the first principle, he cites John Lawson speaking of "Methodist connexional-ism" as an expression of "episcopé."[8] For the second, Bowmer discuss-es the advantages and disadvantages of itinerancy. It was at the heart of Wesleyanism and was demonstrated from John's personal experience. And, regarding "mutual help," Bowmer recalls The Yearly Collection, The Chapel Fund, The July Collection, The Contingent Fund, and other ways Methodists shared resources, with "the strong helping the weak" (195). He concludes by adding other factors to the three principles as further illustrations of the importance of connectionalism, such as the need to "enforce discipline, to maintain sound doctrine and to facilitate expansion" (195).

It may be most important to note how connection was, from its earli-est time, an organizational principle among the earliest Methodist adherents who were part of a larger church, that is, the Church of England. It referred to the particular relationship they had among them-selves as well as their relationship to the Church of England. The Methodists were not, in those early days, a church in themselves. Nor were they a group breaking off from the church, such as a sect.

In Rupert Davies's introduction to "The Methodist Societies" in *The Works of John Wesley,* he recounts the sociological definitions of *church* and *sect*, which had emerged from the works of Weber and Troeltsch. A "church claims to confess objectively the width and depth of catholic tradition, to guarantee the grace of the sacraments," and so on. A "'sect' cuts itself off from the rest as just defined." Davies claims that a "soci-ety" is a "third category of Christian communion" that falls between a "church" and a "sect."[9] Its definition is as follows:

> A "society" acknowledges the truths proclaimed by the universal church and has no wish to separate from it, but claims to cultivate, by means of sacra-ment and fellowship, the type of inward holiness, which too great an objec-tivity can easily neglect and of which the church needs constantly to be reminded.[10]

This is critical to our discussion of connection because of the way the term has its origin in the relationships found in the early Methodist societies. The "connexion" among the members and to the established church is what made the societies unique. "Connexion" applied to non-Wesleyan societies as well. Davies compares the early Methodist United Societies to the Unitas Fratrum, that is, the Moravians. John Wesley was worshiping in such a Moravian society on May 24, 1738. It was the Fetter Lane Society organized by his friend James Hutton (Davies, 6). Societies came and went within the church. However, within Methodism the pattern became established in a powerful way. The strength of the connection within this group of United Societies grew necessarily as a result of conflicts and theological disputes among those associated. The "connexion" provided the cement that held the societies together.

We have seen how the term *connexion* originated in the societies and quickly took on more meaning within the development of the Methodist organization. The organization quickly grew. As early as 1750 and with the publication of *A Plain Account of the People Called Methodists* by John Wesley, the connection was clear in a widespread area of England, Wales, and Ireland. The Methodists had doctrinal identity, a widespread organization, centralized financing, and preachers set apart for specific programs. During this time, it was obvious to critics and members alike that a new organization was forming that would eventually push Methodists from their identity as a renewal society to their emergence as a church.[11] As that occurred in both England and America, the understanding of the "connexion" would have considerable import. In England, a central issue would be the relationship to the Church of England. In America, the question was simpler at first. From the beginning, the Methodists were a church and not a society within a larger "church." However, how Methodists were related to one another in the United States, to other Christians, and to other Methodists across the world would emerge as further challenges to what was meant by the "connection." How unique was the relation between those "connected" in contrast to those connected more generally through the Body of Christ in the Church Universal?

Consideration of the Term Connection

The term *connection* has been foundational to Methodist identity. We need to examine briefly something of the evolution of the term in order to understand contemporary usage. Then we will examine particular usage in the contemporary United Methodist Church. It would be interesting to examine more fully its usage at other points in history (for instance, during the Methodist struggles over abolition and slavery in the Methodist Episcopal Church), but that is beyond the scope of this paper.

In the earliest years of American Methodism, the term *connection* was widely used. Yet, after the formation of the Methodist church in the new United States, the term came to be seen as a holdover from the days when Methodists were a society. At the General Conference in 1816, a resolution required that all references to "connection" in the *Book of Discipline* be replaced by "church," "community," or "itinerancy," whichever was more appropriate for the context.[12] The word was still associated with its usage within the societies.

After the merger of the Methodist Church and the Evangelical United Brethren in 1968, an explanation of our "theological task" as United Methodists could be found in the *Book of Discipline*. Apart from constitutional references, this section did not contain much about connectionalism. But it does offer different language as to what can hold Methodists together. The section, drafted primarily by Albert Outler, refers to a "conciliar principle" but does not define it. We turn to our doctrinal standards in "the presence of theological pluralism" (¶ 69). It also speaks of "newer experiments in ecumenical theology" as a "constructive alternative" to confessional tradition. The emphasis upon relationships among Methodists is overshadowed by the larger ecumenical relationships. The implication is that because of the breadth of Methodist theology and opinion, much diversity is acceptable. There is little emphasis in this section about what might be specifically Methodist in orientation.

However, immediately thereafter, the section addresses the topic of "United Methodists and the Christian Tradition" (¶ 69). Even though there are several pages of discussion on the common heritage and then of the "distinctive emphases" of United Methodists, little mention is made of connectionalism. The only references are in a paragraph on "polity." "Connectional" is mentioned twice in this section: first in terms of a "long tradition of connectional administration," and, second, in regard to a "connectional leadership." Nowhere is connectionalism held up on its own. These paragraphs existed in the *Book of Discipline* from 1972 through 1984.

At the 1988 General Conference, a special committee looked at the doctrinal standards of the church and rewrote much of the language quoted above. At the same time, the General Conference also added far more extensive language about connectionalism in a three-page section called "The Journey of a Connectional People" (¶ 112).[13] It refers to a "connectional principle" (no longer "conciliar principle"), which became a distinguishing mark setting apart Methodists from "normal patterns of Anglican ecclesiastical organization." The "connectional idea is a style of relationship rather than simply an organizational or structural framework." It is said to have deep biblical and Apostolic roots. However, "we are not a connectional people because of biblical or theological or even historical mandates." The section states that the evolution of our polity as "connection" is "a natural response to these elements [biblical and theological roots] in our background and they continue to inform or direct our efforts."

In another point in the same paragraph (112) of the 1988 *Book of Discipline,* the "connectional principle" is defined as "the basic form of our polity":

> It is in essence a network of interdependent relationships among persons and groups throughout the life of the whole denomination. It declares that our identity is in our wholeness together in Christ that each part is vital to the whole, that our mission is more effectively carried out by a connectional life which incorporates Wesleyan zeal into the life of the people.

Following this definition, the section goes on to list the following "essential ingredients" for a connectional principle: Shared Vision, Memory, Community, Discipline, Leadership, Mobilization, Linkage, Affirmation and Stress, and Challenge. The principle is given enormous responsibility for holding Methodism together. Thomas Frank (151) points out how the *Disciplinary* description even "personalizes an abstract principle" when it says, "It is important for connectionalism to bend, to have tolerance in a changing world, to be able to live in the new days ahead of us with freshness and new commitments."

The closing sentence of the section is striking:

> The connectional principle should be interpreted to all our people in new and fresh ways and lifted up with enthusiasm as an effective instrument in our effort to bring the world as we know it closer in harmony with the will and purpose of God as revealed in Jesus Christ.

Notice how much importance is placed on the connectional principle! It is seen as what can hold us together! Yet, there is a significant irony. At the same time that this section was added, *The Book of Discipline* was also changed dramatically in order to strengthen the role of scripture and tradition in the self-understanding of The United Methodist Church.[14] The debate over doctrinal standards was seen as one of the most important actions of the conference. The two emphases juxtaposed to each other seem to turn in two very different ways to engender stronger United Methodist identity.

The 1996 General Conference turned in a very different direction in terms of language about the "connectional people." The dynamic language suggesting the role of the connectional principle as an enabler of harmony was eliminated. In its place two short paragraphs were developed. Connectionalism is described as "not a linking of one charge conference to another," but as "a vital web of interactive relationships" (¶ 109).[15] The role of doctrine is also highlighted as follows:

> We are connected by sharing a common tradition of faith, including our Doctrinal Standards and General Rules (¶ 62); by sharing together a constitutional polity, including a leadership of general superintendency; by sharing a common mission, which we seek to carry out by working together in and through conferences that reflect the inclusive and missional character of our fellowship; by sharing a common ethos that characterizes our distinctive way of doing things.

The differences in the definition of a "connectional people" are striking. Gone are the expectations of connectionalism to bend and have tolerance for the stresses within the connection. Rather, standards, leadership, and the role of conference are emphasized. Thomas Frank writes that the new description continues the church's "seeming resistance to defining exactly what the connection is" while doing little else. "It provides no structural or constitutional explanation, and does not elaborate on what appear to be critical elements of doctrine, polity, and ethos that hold connectionalism together" (152).

In the 1996 *Book of Discipline* there are numerous other references to "connection." Some exist in the Constitution: reference to "any local church in the connection" (¶ 4); the General Conference having power over all matters "distinctively connectional" (¶ 15); responsibilities to the General Conference for "all connectional enterprises" (¶ 15). Other references are scattered throughout the *Discipline*. For instance, the definition of a local church begins by saying that it is a "connectional society of persons" (¶ 203). The district superintendent needs to maintain the "connectional order of the Discipline" (¶ 420.1). The bishop's appointment making demonstrates "the connectional nature of the United Methodist system" (¶ 430.1). This list could be very extensive. A word search indicates that the word *connection* is used 141 times and *connectional* is used 58 times. Many uses have the most general meaning with little specific meaning to them.

Connectionalism and the Global Nature of the Church

Another interesting use of "connection" can be found in the discussions in the Council of Bishops on "The Global Nature of The United Methodist Church." Reports went from the Council of Bishops to the General Conference in both 1992 and 1996 on this subject. In the 1992 report, "connectionality" was seen as one of four important values of United Methodists (the others being locality, globality, and inclusiveness). *Connectionality* is defined as "the vital balance between locality and globality that holds us together and enables us to be in mission together." The bishops' task was to look at the Central Conference structure of The United Methodist Church and make recommendations. The 1992 report was an update to the General Conference of the bishops' work as well as a request for continued authorization to work on this project. The report was accepted, and a resolution was adopted to encourage the bishops to continue.

The 1996 report was far more extensive. The task, as delineated by the 1992 General Conference, had been to find "connectional unity" with "flexibility and freedom for meeting regional needs," and to "maintain a vital global connection." All through the report was the language of connectionalism, defined as "a vital web of interactive and intertwining relationship that enables us to express freely, justly, and in dignity at both global and local levels our essential identity, inclusive fellowship, common mission, distinctive ethos, and visible unity."[16] The importance placed upon the concept of "connectionalism" was overwhelming, especially in regard to a specific, "global" consideration of the church. In terms of "The Journey of the Connectional People," the 1996 General Conference had reduced the usage of the term "connectional" to apply specifically to Methodist identity. By acceptance of the bishops' report, the Conference moved in quite a different direction regarding connectionalism. Are the reports talking about the same principles with the word *connectionalism?* At least in terms of "interactive relationships," the concept is the same. However, in international relationships connectionalism is lifted up as the *only* appropriate model of interrelationship between churches. The following quotation immediately follows the definition of *connectionalism* cited above:

> This means [essential identity at global and local levels], among other things, that we must not allow connectionalism to stop at the national or regional level. Genuine connectionalism cannot be less than global. Moreover, we much not allow our essential identity, inclusive fellowship, common mission, distinctive ethos, and visible unity as United Methodists to be broken up into Humpty-Dumpty fragments which cannot be put together again on a global scale. We must keep and more fully express our global connection. (170)

In its summary, the bishops' report states that it has tried to strike a balance between "global connectionality" and "local autonomy." Rather, it has juxtaposed connectionality to the life and integrity of autonomous Methodist churches throughout the world. For instance, the report says that it would be considered odd at this time "for a church with a national identity or label . . . to be doing mission in another country for the purpose of planting itself there." The reason why this problem would not arise for a global church is "because it is already in almost every country."[17] The hope or expectation on the part of the bishops would be for all Methodists in most parts of the world to become part of one church through connectionalism. This hope is not explicit in the report, only implicit in sections such as the one just cited.[18]

One of the key leaders within the Global Nature study was Bishop Emerito Nacpil. In 1994 he wrote a booklet for use in the Philippines called *A Primer on Globalizing The United Methodist Church*. It is a strong criticism of an autonomy movement in the Philippines called "Autonomy 2000." In section after section of the booklet, globality is contrasted to "mere autonomy." A global church would be connectional and an autonomous church would not. Several pages of the booklet are a direct criticism of Autonomy 2000's claim to be connectional. Any assertion of independence or autonomy on the part of United Methodists in the Philippines is a violation of connectionalism, according to Bishop Nacpil. He claims that national autonomy is at its heart congregationalism rather than connectional. He asks:

> Does not Autonomy 2000 intend to break off relations with and divide and separate from the UMC *connection* in order to establish an independent Methodist Church of and in the Philippines, as indicated in the previous section? If it intends to sever relations from the UMC connection, *why should it affirm the same connection from which it is breaking off?* Is this not insincerity plain and simple? Is there a significant difference between insincerity and dishonesty? (emphasis in the original)

The debate over autonomy has been extremely divisive in the Philippines. Bishop Nacpil's indictment of autonomy as a violation of connectionalism lends weight to a structural definition of *connectionalism* that would mean that any Methodist church not connected to an international structure would be violating connectionalism. The language of the report received by General Conference seems to bear some of the same assumptions as those posed by Bishop Nacpil within the Philippines. Connectionalism is seen as the *only* appropriate understanding of relationships between sister churches across the world. Any other relationship is insufficient and "merely" something else.[19]

Another Recent Use of Connectionalism

In order to demonstrate the breadth of understanding and use of connectionalism, here is another example as different from the structural use of the term as possible. In 1994, Aldo M. Etchegoyen, Bishop of the Argentine Evangelical Methodist Church, wrote a paper for the Council of Evangelical Methodist Churches in Latin America and the Caribbean (CIEMAL) called "Our Connectionality." What does it mean to be connectional? he asks. "Our answer is that it is to move beyond ourselves in meeting others, to dialogue with them, to plan together and travel the same road together."[20] His words expand the term far beyond Methodism to speak of the whole of creation as God's "connectional event." Nature itself lives in connectionality. He reports that the "Latin American Pastoral Task" has been stated as follows: "The connectionality CIEMAL lives implies human interaction in mission, mutual support and cooperation in solidarity for a better, more faithful testimony of Jesus Christ in Latin America." Conversion itself is to live in "connectional relationship with God, with our brothers and sisters and with the community around us." Bishop Etchegoyen has appropriated the traditionally Methodist term for a broader use. God begins the redemption plan. God does it "connectionally" and separates a "Connectionality for Life" from a "Connectionality for Death." To be "anti-connectional" is to "hide from God and from my brother, to break our bond, and to ask: Am I my brother's keeper?" Bishop Etchegoyen uses the term to preach a strong message about interrelationship, about communion with all of creation.

With these examples we have seen a diversity of practice in regard to what *connection* means and how it is interpreted. Originally, it applied to a very special relationship between a society within the Church of England and the clergyman of that church with whom they were "in connexion." However, today, in The United Methodist Church it is used to express an international structural relationship between national churches!

Koinonia

For many years, but especially since the Second Vatican Council of the Roman Catholic Church, the term *koinonia* has stood for a particular model of the church. Recently, it has been highlighted in ecumenical circles, especially at the Seventh Assembly of the World Council of Churches (1991) and at the World Conference on Faith and Order in Santiago de Compostela (1993). It might be helpful to look briefly at this term to see how it contrasts to the discussion of connectionalism earlier in this paper.

In Scripture there is no precise definition for the church, either local or universal. But, from the beginning, there was the awareness of something profound that has come to be described as *koinonia.* The *Dictionary of the Ecumenical Movement* says that in *koinonia* "is expressed the most profound and all-embracing reality which founds and establishes the *ekklesia tou theou,* the church of God." Countless illustrations could be given from Scripture and from the church fathers describing this term and its translations as community, communion, or fellowship. In church tradition, to be in *koinonia* was associated with being in eucharistic fellowship. But it also represented a particularly close relationship between numbers of churches. The term was also used for associations of churches, for monastic churches, and for numerous other collections of churches that have something in common.

The literature is rich and extensive regarding this topic, but a couple of examples may be sufficient to compare *koinonia* and connectionalism. Even though the term was critically important for many early meetings in the Council's life, the World Council of Churches spoke of the importance of *koinonia* in New Delhi (1961) in a special way:

> We believe that the unity which is both God's will and his gift to his church is being made visible as all in each place who are baptized into Jesus Christ and confess him as Lord and Savior are brought into one fully committed fellowship *[koinonia].*

In explaining "fully committed fellowship" the statement goes on to say:

> The word "fellowship" *(koinonia)* has been chosen because it describes what the Church truly is. "Fellowship" clearly implies that the Church is not merely an institution or organization. . . . Such a fellowship means for those who participate in it nothing less than a renewed mind and spirit, a full participation in common praise and prayer, the shared realities of penitence and forgiveness, mutuality in suffering and joy, listening together to the same Gospel, responding in faith, obedience and service. . . . and reconciling grace which breaks down every wall of colour, caste, tribe, sex, class and nation. Neither does this "fellowship" imply a rigid uniformity of structure, organization or government.

Would not such a description apply to the United Societies established by John Wesley? The phrases lifted up here seem similar in thought and intention to the desires of the early societies.

A second illustration of the centrality of *koinonia* can come from the 1993 World Conference on Faith and Order whose theme was "On the Way to Fuller *Koinonia*." Perhaps this conference, more than any other, brought a clearer focus to the church model of *koinonia*. One definition says "*koinonia* signifies this dynamic relationship based on participation in the reality of God's grace."[21] It is the "principle of authentic relationship" that binds communities within the universal. "There is one Church while there are many local churches at the same time" (sec. I, 17).

I raise up these examples in hopes of showing a relationship between connectionalism and *koinonia*. Both of them speak of dynamic relationships within parts of the greater whole. Both of them are used to try to demonstrate a unity among the membership that stems from a gift of God. In one of the earliest documents identifying what it means to be a Methodist, John Wesley's *The Character of a Methodist*, published in 1742, Wesley discards any special characteristics that bind people together within the connection. Not opinions, nor special words, nor actions or customs, nor stress upon any part of the Christian tradition characterizes Methodists. The only mark that identifies Methodists in the connection is the following: "A Methodist is one who has the 'love of God shed abroad in his heart by the Holy Ghost given unto him' (quoting

Romans 5:5)."[22] And, finally, a Methodist has no desire to be distinguished at all from other real Christians, "of whatsoever denomination they be" (42). He concludes by asking, "Is thy heart right, as my heart is with thine? I ask no farther question. 'If it be, give me thy hand.'"[23] After this point we strive together in "fellowship," that is, *koinonia.*

Jack A. Keller, Jr.

Following directly the issues raised by Elliott Wright's study of Methodism and public education is this essay by Jack Keller in which he explores the idea of the church as a community of moral discourse. Methodism has always been concerned with the <u>practical implications</u> of <u>Christian teaching for both the community and the individual.</u> Of particular importance to Methodist understanding from the earliest days of the movement is that the Christian individual is not a moral being unto himself or herself. Only in community are teachings understood and only in community are we judged. There is <u>no such thing as the solitary Christian,</u> and certainly no such thing as an individual moral judgment. All moral judgments are related to the communal understanding. This is one of the key meanings of Christian conference in Methodism. <u>Moral judgments grow out of Christian conference.</u> Keller explores the way in which the church in our time can foster moral discussion in an effort to come to specific recommendations for the community and the individual.

Here is an example of John Wesley's method of theological inquiry applied to the specific needs of persons in community to think about the meaning of the moral life and the way in which decisions are made in regard to belief and action. The questions <u>"How are we to live?"</u> and <u>"What are we to do?"</u> are as old as the Christian faith. Methodist theology in the mainstream has always insisted that the answers to these questions derive from serious mutual encounter with the Scriptures and with Christian tradition as these are apprehended by our experience—as individuals and as the church—and our reason. How does Keller's understanding of the church as a community of moral discourse fit in with the picture of Methodist theology painted by other contributors? How can this model be communicated effectively to help church members deal with moral issues in our time?

WWJD

The Church as a Community of Moral Discourse

Jack A. Keller, Jr.

United Methodists claim a heritage that holds together as complementary goals personal assurance and social witness, personal holiness and social holiness, holiness of heart and holiness of life. We have a clear Wesleyan mandate to "reform the nation" and to "spread scriptural holiness." Yet we as a denomination, like our mainline Protestant peers, are largely ineffectual in communicating to our membership and to the surrounding culture a compelling vision of the church as a community of moral discourse.

Why should the church be concerned about functioning as a community of moral discourse? Why is it important? I take it as a given that concern for social well-being is firmly grounded in the Bible and in our theological heritage. But the ways in which moral influence can be exerted by religious groups in America are deeply conditioned by the voluntary character of church life. There is no legally defined court of religious moral authority to which church insiders and outsiders can appeal for expert moral judgment. There is no Protestant—and certainly no United Methodist—voting bloc or pressure group to which legislators must attend. For the most part, pastors no longer carry an aura of moral expertise to which laity acquiesce. Laity are well aware that many if not most of our pressing social needs and issues require technical expertise at least as much as theological expertise.

The church is deeply affected also by the pervasive democratization of social life in our nation. As James Gustafson has observed, "American church members do not shed this democratic heritage when they stand in the presence of ministers and the Bible, or of church agencies for social action." American Christians—including United Methodists— feel free to dissent from the ecclesiastical experts and even from the ecclesiastical norms and standards. "They expect to have been brought into a personal conviction of the rightness or truth of the statements being made, the policies being formed, and the actions being counseled."[1]

The tendency of many leaders in the church is to rely upon personal

or institutional authority to carry the day. At the local level this often
means that, rather than rely upon open discourse and run the risks that
accompany it, pastors and other church leaders rely on the persuasive
power of personality to engender support to some moral judgment or
cause. At the level of annual conferences, general conference, the
Council of Bishops, and national agencies, the tendency is sometimes to
"settle" an issue in private or limited discussion and then issue a pro-
nouncement about the matter, which is supposed to win assent if not
enthusiasm. But given the voluntary nature of the church and the persuasive democratization of social life in the United States, neither
appeals to personality nor appeals to institutional authority are likely to
be effective as means of exercising moral influence. Church members
expect to be *convinced,* not merely told. They withhold support until
they are *persuaded.* Particularly when the social needs or issues are complex or controversial, participation in serious dialogue and exploration
is required before assent is given and action is forthcoming.

As I will discuss below, there can and should be considerable variety
in the forms moral discourse may assume. But there is something any
community of moral discourse has in common. The definition offered
by Gustafson is a helpful beginning point:

> By a community of moral discourse I mean a gathering of people with the
> explicit intention to survey and critically discuss their personal and social
> responsibilities in the light of moral convictions about which there is some
> consensus and to which there is some loyalty.[2]

Actions ultimately are motivated and directed by convictions and
intentions about foundational matters. What do we think God's purposes are? How do we appropriate the Bible as a source of moral identity, authority, and direction? What other sources of moral wisdom do
we recognize and claim? What do we think is true and right and good?
What values are most important? What achievement of values is possible and plausible in our time and place? What is expected of us in terms
of social responsibilities? What are the reasons for deciding that one
judgment or course of action is better than another? Questions such as
these are the stuff of which moral discourse is made.

One of the things going on in moral discourse is learning a language.
Moral discourse requires using the language of morals and ethics in the
life of the church. Again, I think Gustafson has a helpful word of caution:

If the language of salvation, self-fulfillment, relief from guilt and anxiety, in short the language of what religion can do for you (i.e., your self-interest) dominates, the purpose of the church is askew. . . . The language of command and obedience, of responsibility, of good and evil, of right and wrong, better and worse, [is] part of this language of morals. . . . Moral discourse requires moral language.[3]

(As we will see, the language of morality includes, but is not restricted to, the sometimes abstract language of ethics.)

The point or purpose of moral discourse is threefold. It is, first of all, the means by which we are most likely to arrive at a conclusion that is a sound response to a particular social need or issue. Second, and equally important, participation in moral discourse is necessary to cultivate the skills of moral discernment and moral decision making. The process of participating in moral discourse is the best means for deepening, broadening, and enlarging our capacity as individuals and groups for making moral judgments. And third, wide participation in moral discourse is necessary to win support for whatever outcome emerges from the process of decision making.[4]

Having proposed that one essential role for the church, at various levels and locations, is to function as a community of moral discourse, let me add two caveats. First, I am by no means suggesting that moral discourse is the only or even the primary function of the church. Religious gatherings can serve all sorts of purposes: worship, Bible study, prayer, budget decision making, fellowship, therapy, and more. Moral discourse is one crucial function of the church, not its total purpose.

Second, even when the scope of church activity focuses on Christian response to a social need or social issue, the need for *explicit* moral discourse may vary. Sometimes a simple warrant is a sufficient "bridge" to move from a problematic situation to some reasonably appropriate response. In the face of a general awareness of housing problems facing the underemployed, for instance, a congregation may more or less spontaneously decide "We as Christians in this community should do something about that," then seize upon volunteer construction of homes under the auspices of Habitat for Humanity as the appropriate response. One could hardly fault such a response to a pressing human need. A will and a way to respond sometimes emerge without a great deal of self-conscious deliberation or exploration. In such cases I would be inclined to say that the church is functioning as a community of *latent* moral discourse. That is, theological and moral values and claims are embedded in the response to human need. They could, if it became necessary or fruitful, be made explicit and discussion about them could take place. But in many cases, self-conscious articulation of support for a moral warrant and detailed analysis of a problematic situation and response are superfluous. The energies of volunteer church members can be invested directly in doing something to help someone.

But in many instances the social need or issue is so complex or so controversial that something more *is* needed: a more robust moral discourse. For some reason the moral warrant (e.g., "We as Christians should do something about that") is not felt as persuasive or compelling. Something more is needed to generate motivation and to provide direction for action.

Robust moral discourse about a social need or social issue involves four major structural elements or moments.[5] The first is an account of the *situation.* As H. Richard Niebuhr has observed, ethical analysis entails the question, What is going on?[6] What is the situation that faces us? What is the problem that attracts our attention and calls for our response? We need a careful, accurate description of the problem—its scope, its causes, and the possibilities for its resolution or alleviation. Collecting and critically assessing the empirical evidence about a problematic situation is a fundamental step.[7]

Description of the problematic situation is, of course, no simple matter. The identification of a problem *as a problem* often is guided by one's basic values. Also, biases of value commitments frequently intrude unannounced into supposedly pure descriptions. Selectivity of description is a consequence, too, of the objects and methods of social scientific analysis.[8] So it is important to listen to more than one voice and to attend to the possible distortions of methods and perspectives.

To describe the situation more or less adequately, moral discourse needs the participation of a variety of people.[9] Persons who suffer most because of a problem, who know firsthand what it feels like to bear the brunt of a problem, deserve to be heard. Sometimes such persons are found within a congregation wrestling with an issue or problem. Sometimes they are not and special pains must be taken to ensure that their voices are heard. But people who are suffering do not always know why they are suffering or the best means to alleviate that suffering. That is why people with factual and technical expertise can be helpful. They can help describe the problem and suggest plausible responses to it. Many of our congregations have such people available, either as members or as guests who would happily participate in a discussion if asked. Finally, the observations and opinions of Christians who are neither experts nor directly affected by a problem can be a valuable resource when assessing a situation. Sometimes the plain common sense of committed Christians can be enormously helpful.

A careful, thorough sifting of empirical evidence is crucial. While no description can be utterly value-neutral, critical control of biases and distortions is crucial. Sorting through conflicting claims and complex evidence can, however, usually lead to a reasonably fair picture of a situation.

Even within this critical stance toward the empirical evidence, a theological or philosophical point of view can drive participants in a moral dialogue to *attend* to particular features of the evidence. The point of the critical stance is that assessment of the evidence should not be so heavily controlled by a theological or philosophical view that the description of the situation has no independent credibility.

Only in the light of a satisfactory account of what is going on can we discern a second element in robust moral discourse: the identification or classification of actions that would be an effective *action response*. Here we are asking with some specificity *what could* be done to remedy a morally problematic situation and *who could* plausibly assume a role in that remedy. Here we are talking about something more specific than a statement of a social or political philosophy informed by religious premises. The action response might be direct services on behalf of individuals or groups in the neighborhood or overseas. Or the action response might be a matter of advocacy for specific institutional change in local government, in federal government, in corporate policy, or in church polity.

In a sense the action response emerges from the description of the problematic situation. That is, the recommended judgment or course of action must fit the problem. It must suggest a direction that we have convincing reasons to believe would improve the situation. The action response is not merely deduced from some abstract value or principle. Rather, it is tailored (in part) to fit the empirical situation.

And yet, the action response cannot simply be derived from the description of what is going on. The movement from the descriptive to the prescriptive, from what *is* the case to what *ought* to be done, requires additional justification. It would be perfectly reasonable to agree with an empirical description and yet deny that one ought to support the corresponding action response—if there is no warrant or inference license to serve as a bridge that will legitimize the move. Put differently, the challenge to a description of a situation and proposals designed to remedy that situation might be, not simply "What have you got to go on?" (which might be a plea for more empirical data), but "How do you get from the data to the conclusion?" (which requires an answer of a different sort from merely factual information). The second kind of question can be answered only by appealing to some moral rule, maxim, warrant, or inference license that justifies or legitimizes the movement. What is needed is a third element in robust moral discourse: a moral *warrant* that makes legitimate the passage from the description of the problem to the recommended response. It is the "bridge" from the *descriptive* account of the situation to the *prescriptive* conclusion in the action response. A moral warrant (1) explains why *some* action is required to remedy the situation and (2) provides a general standard with which any *particular* proposed action must be compatible.[10]

But why should we accept a warrant as authoritative? Why should we respect such-and-such rule or maxim? What support for it can be given? Here we are driven to supply a fourth element in robust moral discourse: *backing* or grounding for the moral warrant.

The appeal to backings is often made in shorthand fashion. That is, we only occasionally give full critical attention to our interpretive, undergirding frameworks. But those frameworks can be made explicit so that we can reclaim, modify, or abandon them. Typically theological backings appeal to some portion of Scripture, some aspect of tradition, or some mixed source of moral wisdom.

I want to suggest that backings can be understood helpfully as offering not only different substantive support or grounding for a moral warrant but also different forms, styles, types, and approaches to the entire task of moral discourse. Each form or type of backing has its own strengths and weaknesses. No single form or type of backing is suited to the full range of legitimate moral concerns before the church. Some problems or issues lend themselves to one approach or type of backing more than another. Some forms of backing work better with some audiences than with others. A particular type of argument may serve a needed purpose in a particular stage of engaging a social need or issue and yet not be so useful or effective at an earlier or later stage. Self-conscious attention to four categories of backing or categories of moral discourse—prophetic, narrative, ethical proper, and policy—can help us make sense of the various efforts at exerting moral influence within and beyond the church and can help us broaden the range and deepen the quality of moral conversation across The United Methodist Church.[11]

Let me describe briefly each of these types of moral discourse that can function as backings for a moral warrant. *Prophetic discourse* typically takes two distinguishable forms. *Indictment* tries to show how far short of the ideal a current situation has fallen. Prophetic discourse typically provides a radical critique of the *roots* of what is perceived to be fundamentally or systemically wrong. Specific problems are often seen as manifestations of a larger evil or injustice. This kind of backing is usually passionate. It uses metaphors and analogies that are meant to stir the listener's emotions. Appeal is frequently made to scriptural texts from the prophets: Hosea, Micah, Amos, Jeremiah, Isaiah, and others.

The second form of prophetic discourse is *utopian.* This version pictures an ideal future state of affairs that functions as a lure, an aspiration, a spur to motivation. Like the language of indictment, utopian language is often dramatic, symbolic, and metaphorical. It is designed to arouse human hopes and motivate listeners to act so as to bring those hopes closer to fulfillment.

Prophetic discourse has considerable strengths. The resonance with selected Old and New Testament texts is obvious. Empowered by an encounter with God, the prophets convey a vision of a community ruled by God and defined in terms of covenantal fidelity, justice, righteousness, holiness, love of God and neighbor, new creation, and the like. Often using the most concrete, vivid language and imagery, the prophets managed paradoxically to convey principles and ideals that transcend particular contexts.

Appealing as it does to moral indignation and moral aspirations, prophetic discourse can have an enormous capacity to motivate people. It can evoke a sense of crisis and urgency. It can arouse awareness of evil and can offer a glimpse of a better future. And the focus on the fundamental values of social life can undercut preoccupation with short-range means and ends.

But prophetic discourse also has its drawbacks. While it can, if internalized by listeners, *motivate* action, it is often not sufficient to *direct* or *guide* action. It may help us reclaim, for instance, the biblical witness to God's preferential concern for the weak and vulnerable. But that in itself does not tell us what to do in particular cases to cooperate with God's purposes.

Another type or form of moral discourse that can function as a backing for a moral warrant is *narrative discourse.* This approach deals with what we should *do* by rehearsing the stories and images that tell us who we *are.* The formative narratives of our community shape identity, character, and moral ethos. Our actions as individuals and as groups ultimately spring from that character and ethos.

Narrative discourse has considerable strengths. Recent literature in theology and ethics has highlighted the importance of narrative as the primary form of Scripture itself and as a fundamental means by which scriptural and theological meanings can be apprehended and integrated into the lives of Christians. Narratives can function to sustain a common memory in a community. Stories (including parables), symbols, and images can illumine moral direction and can carry meanings and emotional freight that no purely rational argument can hear.

Stories from the Bible, especially, and also from the Christian tradition and from our more immediately past heritage can become the measure of our lives. To some degree, the influence of the stories we tell and hear is subliminal. The stories convey pictures of lives lived faithfully, which we gradually absorb. But we can bring formative stories to conscious reflection, seeing in them analogies or precedents for our lives that enable us to grasp simultaneously who we are and what we should be doing.

However, narrative discourse leaves us with some unanswered questions. A specific religious narrative has power only for those who share a conviction of its authority and proper interpretation. Its audience is limited not just to the church but typically to particular segments of the church. What basis, if any, does a narrative ethics backing provide for dialogue and cooperation with those who do not recognize the authority of a story or who disagree sharply about its interpretation? How can we discern *which* stories are appropriately applied to situations before us? And even if there is a shared appreciation for particular stories and symbols of the Christian faith, how do we discern the proper moral stance that follows?[12] Another predicament that narrative ethics does not resolve is that sometimes even people whose attitudes, dispositions, and intentions we would describe as virtuous still do not know what action is good or right or the least objectionable of available evils in particular situations. What then? The problem is usually exacerbated when we move from the level of personal and interpersonal action to the level of policy advocacy.

A third type or form of moral discourse that can function as a backing is *ethical discourse proper*. This is a rubric that gathers in the use of concepts and distinctions formulated over centuries in the disciplines of moral philosophy and moral theology. Among other things, it may entail clarification and evaluation of rights, duties, and obligations or be concerned with identifying principles or values that can help us decide between competing rules or laws. This kind of applied ethical thinking wrestles with moral quandaries, sometimes using the classic procedures of casuistry, the application of principles to cases. And ethical discourse in this narrow sense can sometimes offer precision in descriptions of morally relevant features of the situations facing us.

Much has been written in recent years about the wrong-headedness of trying to construe ethics as a function of autonomous reason. A universal, objective perspective is simply not within our reach, according to the complaint. But it does not follow that we should ignore rational insights into moral behavior that come from secular sources (such as philosophy). The apostle Paul certainly thought it was acceptable—even necessary—for the Christians at Philippi to draw upon their wider knowledge of moral excellence (Phil 4:8). The wisdom literature of the Old Testament provides further testimony of the legitimacy of special insight gained from experience and reflection. Most of the wisdom literature deals with questions of practical wisdom; that is, how to live the good life. Wisdom literature is not, for the most part, rooted in the specific religious tradition. Rather, it distills insights from common human experiences. Authority in the wisdom tradition is grounded in human reason. While reason is a gift from God, it is a gift given to all human beings, regardless of whether they are in the church. The same important insights are available to everyone. So there is solid biblical precedent for openness to sources of moral insight outside of the Christian tradition. Pastors need to know the language and insights of ethics as a discipline alongside biblical studies or pastoral care.

Two limitations of ethical discourse in this narrow sense are apparent. Sophistication in analysis and evaluation does not by itself provide the motivation for action. And it is possible to be so captivated by the language and categories of common, human morality that one forgets to ask, "How is such-and-such principle or value grounded in and transformed by a Christian theological framework?"

The fourth form or type of moral discourse that can also function as backing for a moral warrant is *policy discourse*. The general aim here is to determine and achieve what is *desirable* within the constraints of what is *possible.* What resources are available or could be made available? What legitimate interests compete for those resources? What personnel and institutional arrangements are needed?

Policy discourse becomes important when the action response called for is some type of advocacy for institutional activity or institutional change. The institution may be public (such as a local government agency) or private (such as a church or a business corporation). At the level of action response, policy discourse has to do with specifying what particular action will be taken and by whom. At the level of backing, policy discourse has more to do with clarifying and justifying the church's role in engaging a social need or issue as a matter of policy.

To summarize, let me suggest that robust moral discourse about a social need or issue might be schematized as follows:

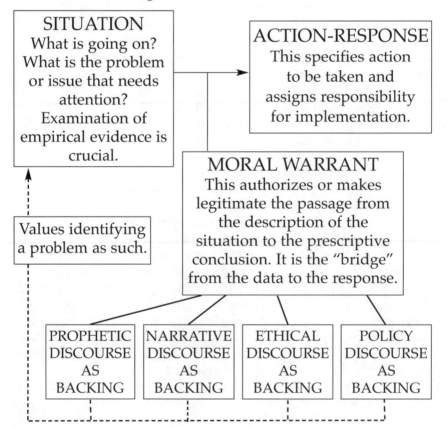

Some latitude is allowable and even desirable in the order in which the elements of moral discourse are represented in any actual case. The thoroughness with which the elements or moments are rehearsed may also vary widely from one circumstance to another. But the four elements—description of the situation, delineation of action response, moral warrant, and appropriate backing(s)—need to be engaged to some degree and in some fashion.

It is important to remember that no single variety of moral discourse, which I have couched in this article as backings for a moral warrant, is wholly adequate for all occasions. Since the moral life is complex it should come as no surprise that no single style is sufficient to capture all that is important. Each style—prophetic, narrative, ethical, and policy—illumines some aspects of moral reality and obscures or overlooks others. And different audiences resonate with different styles. It would be a grievous mistake to insist that only one style will do, that one style must fit all moral conversations or deliberations. We would fare much better if we learned to recognize these several styles of moral discourse as potentially helpful and inherently limited and to develop some facility in each mode of reasoning. Then we could take pains to discern which approach serves us best in a particular instance. Self-conscious attention to these categories of moral discourse would enable us to improve the quality of moral discourse that is going on and could be going on at various levels and locations in The United Methodist Church. Having a clear picture of the elements of and various styles of robust moral discourse can and should enable participants at various levels and locations to *evaluate* the quality of discourse already actually going on and to *improve* the quality of that discourse.

As one example, let us summarize moral discourse during the current quadrennium in The United Methodist Church about the social problem of homelessness and insufficient affordable housing. Comprehensive analysis would be far beyond the knowledge of this researcher and the limitations of space in this article. But we can get a glimpse of the state of the discussion by looking at several kinds of evidence of activity: (1) resolutions adopted at the 1992 General Conference; (2) material published by the General Board of Church and Society in *Christian Social Action;* (3) adult curriculum resources; (4) books on the general topic published by Abingdon Press; and (5) the type of efforts under way in local congregations.

Two resolutions on this topic were adopted at the 1992 General

Conference.[13] The resolution entitled "Homelessness in the United States" describes the problematic *situation* briefly by citing some statistics about the current and projected number of homeless people. Further it identifies some of the factors that contribute to the growing numbers of homeless individuals and families: the deinstitutionalization of persons with chronic mental illness, reduction of public benefits to the elderly and to disabled persons, underemployment and unemployment, breakups of families for various reasons, and the acute shortage of affordable housing for low-income persons.

The moral *warrant* claimed is stated clearly: All persons have a right "to live without deprivation in safe, sanitary, and affordable housing."

The *backing* for the warrant is an illustration of *prophetic discourse.* Matthew 25:31-46 and Isaiah 58:6-7 are cited in support of the conviction that homelessness is a violation of human dignity and an affront to the biblical mandate to do justice.

The *response* recommended is sweeping in scope: what is called for is nothing less than a comprehensive attack on poverty, since poverty and homelessness are inextricably related. *Agencies* of the UMC are charged to: provide educational resources that address the root causes of poverty and that present models for addressing the problem; work with national, regional, and local housing advocacy groups; and affirm local churches that provide ministries of compassion (e.g., soup kitchens, shelters, food pantries, clothes closets, and utility assistance programs). *Local congregations* are urged to get individuals involved in volunteer networks, direct-service programs, and ecumenical coalitions, and influencing government at every level.

A resolution entitled "Available and Affordable Housing" was also adopted in 1992. It is even briefer in its general comments about the *situation* of global need. It includes a moral warrant not dissimilar to the warrant for the resolution mentioned above: "When persons are denied access to, or opportunity for, decent housing, their humanity is diminished." Supporting that are the theological claims that "all persons are equally valuable in God's sight" and that housing can properly be understood as "the means of preserving and protecting the human body which is characterized by the Apostle Paul as the Temple of God."

Churches and individuals are urged to *respond* by becoming advocates for affordable housing, by prophetically denouncing lending institutions that discriminate against certain neighborhoods and communities, and by taking on individual construction and renovation projects.

So both Resolutions touch upon the four structural elements of robust moral discourse, appealing only to prophetic discourse as backing. Their brevity and limited exposure in the *Book of Resolutions* mean that they function primarily as permission to enter into moral discourse elsewhere for those so inclined.

The General Board of Church and Society publishes a monthly magazine called *Christian Social Action* (the successor to *Engage/Social Action*). During the current quadrennium four articles appeared that dealt with some aspect of the inadequate housing–homelessness cluster of issues. Three of the articles told about success stories at the local or metropolitan level. One article described how one United Methodist laywoman in Norman, Oklahoma, working with the director of Neighborhood Services Organization, a UM-related agency in Oklahoma City, created a school to educate the children of homeless families.[14] An inner-city UMC offered space. The Women's Division of the General Board of Global Ministries offered funds for a half-time director. The demand was soon greater than the church facility and volunteer personnel could meet. The Oklahoma City Public Schools joined in, funded by a large grant from the federal government. Eventually the school found a new home at a YWCA facility, and two full-time teachers and a full-time social worker were in place. A second article featured a "building blitz" in Evansville, Indiana, in which twenty-one homes were built under the auspices of Habitat for Humanity in six consecutive days.[15] Three of the twenty-nine congregations involved were United Methodist. The third article rehearsed the impressive record of the Tampa United Methodist Center's success as a nonprofit housing agency.[16] Among other things, TUMC manages a one-hundred-unit apartment complex for the elderly and handicapped and has purchased and renovated a thirty-two-unit apartment complex, built seventeen single-family detached houses for moderate income families, literally moved seventy-one homes out of the path of an expressway to other city sites, developed more than eighty affordable units available in inner-city neighborhoods, provided home ownership counseling, and assisted home owners in getting financing for rehabilitating their homes. The fourth article presents an indictment of practices of mortgage discrimination and insurance discrimination because of race.[17] The article presents anecdotal evidence about the problematic *situation* in various cities and identifies existing laws and pending legislation that could, if given enforcement "teeth," help remedy the problem.

All four of these articles portray what I would call latent moral discourse. A problematic situation is involved, and a corresponding response is highlighted, but the moral warrant involved and any backing(s) are left unarticulated. The articles provide a summary of important social action and witness, but the articles do not help the reader cultivate the skills of robust moral discourse.

One avenue for generating moral discourse about social issues is adult curriculum resources. In fact, volume four in the set of booklets titled *Challenge: Christian Perspectives on Social Issues*[18] does include two relevant chapters. The article on biblical and theological background for concern for "the least of these" provides a rich *backing*. Four theological themes are discussed, the first two of which might be described as *prophetic discourse:* (1) the witness in the Bible to God's concern for the weak and vulnerable is pervasive (e.g., Exod 22:22-23; Deut 10:18-19; 24:21-22; Pss 82:3-4; 103:6; 140:12; 146:7; Jer 22:3; Amos 5:24). (2) Equally clear is that Jesus was concerned with helping the weak, the sick, the powerless (see, e.g., Matt 25:31-46; Luke 4:18-19; 10:29-37; 16:19-31).

The latter two themes might fit better under the rubric of *narrative discourse* as backing: (3) The church is the body of Christ. Therefore, we should be extensions of the Incarnation, carrying on Christ's work of healing and reconciliation. We are members of one another and, as such, should want to respond to human suffering (see, e.g., 1 Cor 12:14-27; 11:17-22; 2 Cor 8:1-15; James 2:1-7, 14-17; 1 John 3:17-18). (4) John Wesley's concern with the physical as well as the spiritual needs of the poor and downtrodden provides United Methodists with a heritage of social concern. Concern about homelessness is a natural extension of that heritage.

Presuming that background lesson allows the writer of the session on "Homelessness in the United States" to focus on description of the *situation* and the recommended *action response*. The situation is described *both* by rehearsing briefly statistics about the magnitude of the problem and the typical reasons persons join the ranks of the homeless *and* by presenting anecdotal, personal vignettes of homeless persons. The latter carry some emotional weight that is not unimportant as a motivating factor. The recommended action response is strong on direct services by individuals and congregations: survey community needs and services, volunteer at a soup kitchen or shelter, provide child care and/or tutoring to homeless children, and collect and distribute basic necessities (food, clothing, personal hygiene items). The greatest strength of the

Challenge resource may be its inviting tone. It is passionate without feeling strident; it is informed without being arrogant.

Abingdon Press has published three books during this quadrennium that contribute to moral discourse on this general topic in one form or another. The most immediately practical is Charles F. Strobel's *Room in the Inn*,[19] which is a manual on how to set up and operate a "room in the inn" program for homeless people. The idea is not to construct more shelters but to enlist congregations of every faith to open their facilities to welcome twelve to fifteen homeless people on cold winter nights. While most of the book deals with answers to nitty-gritty how-to questions, the book does convey in a quiet way what I have called narrative discourse as backing. Christians are the kind of people who want to rewrite Luke's Christmas story by serving as innkeepers who welcome the needy strangers in our midst.

Two scholarly books, published by Abingdon Press in cooperation with The Churches' Center for Theology and Public Policy, deal with an issue broader than housing and homelessness. Warren R. Copeland's *And the Poor Get Welfare: The Ethics of Poverty in the United States*[20] begins with a detailed history of poverty as a public issue in the United States. He then offers a detailed critical review of several quite different, leading contemporary analyses of poverty and welfare in American society. Drawing upon insights from process theology and from the discipline of ethics, he presents a theological view of freedom and community as a backing for the moral warrant calling for reform of the current welfare system.

Pamela D. Couture's *Blessed Are the Poor? Women's Poverty, Family Policy, and Practical Theology*[21] presents a detailed critique of assumptions implicit in prevailing descriptions of the situation regarding women's poverty. Drawing on Luther as a source for an ethic of domesticity, John Wesley as a source of suggestions for an economic ethic, and the American women's tradition as a source of wisdom, Couture explores the values and policies of "shared responsibility."

Both *And the Poor Get Welfare* and *Blessed Are the Poor?* provide rich discussions of all four basic elements in robust moral discourse. Their greatest strength is the high quality of the ethical backing they contribute directly to the discourse about poverty, and indirectly to discourse about homelessness and inadequate housing. Their limitation, of course, is that the arguments are sufficiently complex and demanding to restrict the audience to teachers and students in an academic setting.

While there is no way to know what is going on in thirty-six thousand United Methodist congregations, I think it is safe to say that at the local church level the most frequent response to the problem of homelessness and inadequate affordable housing has been direct service. For example, Habitat for Humanity partnerships with UM congregations are springing up everywhere. And programs providing emergency shelter are likewise popular. Moral discourse about such matters typically remains latent. Only when the action response becomes more complex and controversial (typically when advocacy for institutional change is involved) does more explicit and robust moral discourse become necessary.

Taken together, these five kinds of evidence of moral discourse activity suggest a rich and tolerably balanced conversation in the church. But, of course, all five kinds of evidence *seldom are* taken together. Particular conversations on this or any other topic usually take into account only one or two or at most three resources. So it is important that pastors and church leaders aim for an appropriate level of complexity and balance in moral discourse. The *situation* needs to be examined critically. An *action response* needs to be clarified. Moral *warrants* need to be articulated so they can be claimed or changed. And various forms or types of discourse functioning as *backings* need to be considered and examined. Taking seriously the church as a community of moral discourse means taking seriously the educational task of teaching the skills of robust moral discourse. And the best way to teach those skills is to invite persons to participate in an honest and transparent process of conversation-discussion-deliberation about social needs and issues that matter.

Douglas M. Strong

Douglas Strong's essay helps us understand the complex reality that Methodism in American culture is a mainstream movement that nevertheless includes diverse marginal groups of peoples. That Methodism is characteristic of "middle America" is documented by historians and sociologists. In fact some historians have suggested that, especially in the nineteenth century, the "average" American was a Methodist. Because of this fact, Methodism both shaped and was shaped by middle America. The two are difficult to separate, in fact. At the same time, Methodism formed groups of persons who did not easily fit within that broad middle. There was often tension, and some left the denomination. The marginal movements within Methodism were important to the overall movement, however, and must be explored and understood. Strong does this through a case study.

The reader will want to ponder the way in which individuals or groups become marginal. Why is it that some are uncomfortable with the theology or practice of dominant Methodism? How is it that some break away and some remain—but with a kind of love-hate relationship? How do marginal individuals and groups affect the dominant tradition? Is it fair or accurate to suggest that the dominant middle is bland while the margins are characterized as diverse and exciting? What does such a historical study suggest for the church in our time?

Exploring both the Middle and the Margins: Locating Methodism Within American Religious History

Douglas M. Strong

Theodore Faron, the fictional protagonist of P. D. James's suspense novel, *The Children of Men,* is a historian of the nineteenth century. Faron is interested in studying the Victorian period because the nineteenth century is "like a world seen through a telescope, at once so close and yet infinitely remote—fascinating in its energy, its moral seriousness, its brilliance, and [its] squalor."[1] For historians of American religion, the nineteenth century—often referred to as the "Methodist century"[2]—conveys a similar impression. It is close enough to invite suggestive analysis, yet our understanding of it still seems infinitely remote.

Recently, a number of monographs—led by the important work of Nathan Hatch, but including also the writings of Russell Richey, A. Gregory Schneider, and John Wigger—have begun to recover the essential role that Methodism played in nineteenth-century culture.[3] For these interpreters, Methodism was, in Hatch's words, "the most powerful religious movement in American history," the chronicle of which must be "moved to the foreground" of scholarly interest. Because of Methodism's evangelical emphasis on individual freedom and its superlative ability to organize converts, it became "the most dramatic social movement between the Revolution and the Civil War." Historians both inside and outside of the Wesleyan tradition are in agreement that the renewed interest in the story of American Methodism is long overdue. Moving beyond denominational hagiography or the mere narration of institutional development, these newer monographs assist us in locating Methodism within the broad sweep of American social and cultural history.[4]

One of the themes stressed by Hatch and others in their demonstration of the relevance of the study of American Methodism is the central role played by Methodism in facilitating the social mobility of common people in the early republic. Methodists, it is asserted, appealed "to the petty bourgeoisie, [to] people on the make." Hatch believes that because Methodists participated so uncritically in a "cultural accommodation" to the emerging capitalist society, American historians have taken the Wesleyan movement for granted and have not studied it as seriously as they should. If we ever hope to understand the lives of ordinary Americans in the nineteenth century, according to these scholars, then we must understand the way in which the Methodist Church became thoroughly "domesticated," the way in which it became "the prototype of a religious organization taking on market form."[5] Methodists are important to comprehend not because their message or their methods were unique but because they so accurately represented "the bland, uninspired middle of American society."[6] Interpreted in this way, Methodists became a kind of early role model for Babbitt, Sinclair Lewis's infamous caricature of bourgeois religiosity.[7]

Thanks to the recent writings of these historians, it is now evident that the Methodist church functioned as the classic example of a religious institution in which the social and economic ideology of "middle America" could flourish. The religious development of the broad center of American society was correlated to a great extent with the organizational growth of the Methodist Episcopal Church and its successors.

The large net cast by Methodism resulted in a wide range of expression—theologically, politically, and socially. From the nineteenth century to the present, the church people who populated the Methodist Episcopal-Methodist-United Methodist institutional lineage displayed a spectrum of differences. Yet, although Methodism was internally diverse, each of the sundry groups that made up the denomination was culturally influential in its own respective arena. That is, despite the fact that mainline Methodists have differed among themselves, the major opposing views articulated by groups within the church have usually represented the shaping values of American culture. Conservative Methodists, for instance, have often been some of the leading voices of American conservativism; likewise, liberal Methodists have been leaders of American liberalism. The denomination has provided the religious nurturing for an amazing conglomeration of diverse, yet ultimately middle-American figures; contemporary examples would include such antithetical pairs as George McGovern and George Wallace, Rush Limbaugh and Hillary Rodham Clinton, Donald Wildmon and Hugh Hefner. In what other denomination could the McGoverns, the Clintons, and the Doles all be attendees of the same

Washington congregation (Foundry UMC)?[8] For better or worse, the narrative of Methodist history has reflected the various strands of the dominant culture in the United States.

This interpretation of Methodism—as a faith tradition that accommodated rather uncritically to American culture—is a necessary corrective to the sanitized accounts of the Wesleyan movement typical of older Methodist historiography. It is also a useful challenge to those historians who have tended to view Methodism as the vanguard of liberation for the oppressed.[9] For many United Methodist historians who have interpreted the Wesleyan tradition to their theological colleagues in language appropriate to the politically correct academy in which they operate, such brutal honesty about the movement's blatantly bourgeois past is embarrassingly humbling.

But does this characterization present a full and adequate portrayal of the development of nineteenth- and twentieth-century Methodism? Perhaps not. By now it is an established maxim of American studies that certain well-known aspects of the early national period—political egalitarianism and economic commercialization, for example—were never consistently progressive trends but were, rather, social constructs that operated in constant and dynamic tension. American culture in general, and Methodism more specifically, contained a host of conflicting attitudes regarding the degree of democratization that was appropriate and the values of the emerging market culture. While Methodism did represent the religious interests of a vast and growing "middle" of American society, the ethos of that middle was always in flux, and a large portion of Methodists were never comfortable with the middling status to which others in the movement were aspiring. Perhaps the story of Methodism is most useful in comprehending American church history not because it was the personification of Protestant Babbittry but because it was a stage on which the social and religious conflicts of American society were played out.

Along with the study of the large number of Methodists who advanced into the economic mainstream of American society, it is important to explore how religion functioned among the equally large number of miscellaneous Methodists who, for varied reasons, could not identify with the urbane values of the middle class. In the nineteenth and early twentieth centuries, those unwilling (or unable) to pursue the market culture included such diverse groups of Methodists as African Americans, abolitionists, poor rural southerners, urban Norwegians,

persons of German ancestry, opponents of episcopacy, women preachers, fundamentalists, and advocates of Holiness and Pentecostal beliefs.

Within Methodism today, the rebellion against an imposed mainline
ideological consensus continues among groups as dissimilar as "Good
News" conservatives, the "Confessing movement," charismatics, people of color, gay people, "Re-Imagining" women, and persons on both
sides of the abortion debate. It is interesting that a wide variety of
Methodists—who would characterize their theological beliefs very
divergently (as "liberationist," "feminist," or "evangelical," for example), all use nearly identical language to talk about their alienation from
the values of middle America as represented by the United Methodist
Church. Despite the ability of Methodism to hold diversity together (as
represented by the continuum of mainstream political opinions found at
Foundry church in Washington), the development of the Methodist
movement in its totality was much more complex and multifaceted than
simply an aggregate of the bourgeois middle. The unwillingness on the
part of many Methodists to accept the dominant culture of the religious
majority becomes clear when one moves beyond the relatively subdued
institutional history of the Methodist Episcopal Church in order to
study the dynamics that led to the founding of the African Methodist
Episcopal Church, the African Methodist Episcopal Zion Church, the
Colored (now Christian) Methodist Episcopal Church, the Methodist
Protestant Church, or the Methodist Episcopal Church, South.
Historians interested in studying Methodism as a movement must also
come to terms with the continued and thriving vitality of Methodist off-
shoots such as the Southern Methodist Church, the Bible Protestant
Church, the Wesleyan Methodist Church (now Wesleyan Church), the
Free Methodist Church, the Church of the Nazarene and hundreds of
holiness sects, and the Church of God in Christ and thousands of
Pentecostal sects. Clearly the best way to make sense of all these conflicting views is not to minimize the influence of the differences but to
plumb their depths—by studying the fringes as well as the dominant
components of Methodism. From this wider perspective, Methodism
can indeed be used as a lens from which to view the broad contours of
religious history in the United States, but now the story that will be told
is anything but "bland."

The recurring tensions that have existed within American Methodism
have existed at large within the religious culture of nineteenth- and
twentieth-century society. Some of these tensions within Methodism

have already been (and are being) investigated by scholars—such as the regional tensions between North and South (as articulated by Donald Mathews and others),[10] the racial tensions between European Americans and historically discriminated ethnic groups (as articulated by Will B. Gravely, James S. Thomas, William B. McClain, and others),[11] and the tensions regarding gender relations (as articulated by Catherine Brekus, Diane H. Lobody, Nancy Hardesty, Rosemary Skinner Keller, and others).[12]

One oft-described tension is the theological ambiguity that existed among nineteenth-century Methodists and other American Christians—what one historian has called the "divided conscience" of antebellum Protestantism.[13] On the one hand, Methodist theology in the nineteenth century was basically conservative and "pessimistic about human nature."[14] Most Methodists believed that persons had a native propensity to commit sinful deeds. Individuals had the free will not to sin, but inevitably would do so. Due to the persistence of sin, only a volitional conversion experience could overcome the habitual inclination to disobey God. Since the greatest task at hand was to assist people toward an experiential freewill conversion, social and political activism was considered to be an adjunct to evangelistic efforts. While such activism was important, Methodists usually doubted its ultimate efficacy if not accompanied by a religious revival.

At the same time, and in tension with this relatively "pessimistic" doctrine of the inevitability of sin, nineteenth-century Methodist theology also emphasized natural human ability—thus making it progressive and optimistic. Following conversion, Methodists believed that it was possible to be sanctified from all known sin. Since society was simply a composite of the individuals who made up that society, then a sinless society was theoretically attainable when all persons were converted and sanctified. Indeed, it was incumbent upon Christians to strive toward the "perfect state of society" that will precede the millennium.[15] This postmillennial concept encouraged some Christians to work for human rights and social transformation, such as temperance, antislavery, and women's suffrage, in preparation for the establishment of the reign of God.

In describing the theological tension produced by this doctrinal synthesis within the American Methodist tradition, one nineteenth-century commentator wrote that Methodism held "the middle ground between Calvinism and Universalism."[16] While such doctrinal mediation did, in fact, occur, the theological "middle ground" was an unstable place on which to remain standing.

For instance, it was hard to maintain the "middle ground" when the side of the theological tension dealing with the propensity to make sinful choices was overemphasized. Some Methodists accentuated the importance of personal volitional religious experiences. This trend toward particularly defined experiences was heightened by the Methodists' appropriation of the rather un-Wesleyan, but typically nineteenth-century stress on free will.[17] By promoting individual free will rather than free grace, one's pure motives for social activism became more important than one's actual activism; more emphasis was placed on the intentional choice for holiness and less on the ethical results of holiness. For some Methodists, then, their priority shifted from sanctification as the means of social transformation to sanctification as the goal of personal transformation.[18]

The "middle ground" was also hard to maintain on the "human ability" side of the Methodist theological tension. The uncritical optimism that was characteristic of much of early twentieth-century popular liberalism tended to make the fatal mistake of downplaying the inherence and pervasiveness of personal and corporate sin.[19] Methodism has continued late into the twentieth century to live with the residue of this tension.

There is another tension that conflicted Methodism, as well—but one that is perhaps less obvious. I first became aware of this tension—the tension between structure and anti-structure—while doing research on the maverick Methodist preacher, Lorenzo Dow.[20] Dow was nicknamed "Crazy Lorenzo" because of his odd dress, his long hair, and his bizarre antics. He was a Methodist itinerant who itinerated wherever he wanted, to the consternation of everyone in authority. Dow's image as an idiosyncratic religious democratizer was a perception that he consciously cultivated. He proudly identified himself with a rather unique label: he called himself "the eccentric cosmopolite."[21] On the surface, this term simply describes Dow's practice of wandering around and his self-appointed role as a "fool for Christ." But the image of an eccentric cosmopolite also connotes something deeper. It represents Dow's twofold sense of vocation. He saw himself both as an eccentric—an independent antiestablishmentarian, and as a religious cosmopolitan—a messenger called by God to extend the universal imperative of the gospel. Significantly, the dual aspects of this self-conception were and are also characteristic of much of Methodism. Thus, the image of the eccentric cosmopolite is a useful way to comprehend the tensions inherent in the missional strategy of American Methodism.

The concept of "eccentricity" literally refers to something that is off center, someone who deviates from the established pattern of accepted conduct. An accusation of being "eccentric" was considered a badge of honor among those people in the early republic who saw themselves as challengers of existing structures. Eccentricity was a way of distinguishing oneself from the status quo, and particularly from the undemocratic elites that had exercised power in both church and state.[22] Dow's eccentricity challenged the hierarchical power structures of his day, and especially the institutionalism of Methodism. In this Dow was a model for the general trend toward independence and anti-institutionalism among many Methodists who followed him: Methodist Protestants, certain African American Methodists, the Holiness movement, Pentecostals, and other religious "outsiders."

Dow's use of the term "cosmopolite" is also helpful in understanding the tensions of Methodism. A cosmopolite, or cosmopolitan, was one who believed that truth was to be universally diffused. When this concept was applied to Christian theology, it became evident to Dow and other early American Methodists that the claims of the gospel should be widely disseminated, similar in some ways to Wesley's view of a worldwide parish. Calvinist determinism seemed to represent a narrow view of human accessibility to the truth of the gospel, while Arminianism provided a universal offer of the gospel and hence a larger vision of what God desired for society. As a Wesleyan cosmopolite, Dow was convinced of the need for each person to experience regeneration and sanctification—resulting in a sort of soteriological upward mobility—a chance for every person to know the justifying and perfecting grace of God.

Such "cosmopolitan" views led to two further dilemmas that have had a profound impact on Methodist history. First, some Methodists in the nineteenth century began to ask themselves what seemed (to them) to be an obvious question: If persons were to be upwardly mobile in their relation to God, should they not also be upwardly mobile in their relation to the economy? Those who assumed a positive response to this question were able to correlate the exercise of theological free will quite easily with middle-class advancement. Others, however, answered the question in another way. They assumed that the appropriate response for persons experiencing divine uplift was to work for the economic uplift of the entire society. In later years, such persons often became supporters of the social gospel. Clearly, different groups of Methodists provided differing perspectives on the appropriation of America's capitalist expansion.

A second query that developed from the idea of cosmopolitanism represented yet another dilemma for American Methodists: the tension between the congregation and the connection. If each individual's vocational emphasis was on the universal spread of the gospel and if preachers were committed to this broad vision, would not their loyalty be to the connection that supports that vision rather than to any particular parish or locality? This conflict of interest between localism and cosmopolitanism became manifest within Methodism as a tension between particular churches and the Conference.

Historians such as Russell Richey have helped us to understand the significance of "conference" and connectionalism among American Methodists;[23] now, more work needs to be done on the local manifestations of the Wesleyan movement. How, for example, did the various tensions just described work themselves out in the week-to-week life—the lived experience—of Methodist congregations? An understanding of the broad connectionalism of the denomination is essential information for historians of Methodism, but it is also important for us to know how local units operated. Why were some congregations empowered for significant sociopolitical transformation and evangelism while others were not? Unfortunately, the story that is recorded in many congregational histories is nothing but an antiquarian account of (using Hatch's term) "uninspiring" examples of middle-class cultural accommodation. But a closer look at the local stories of specific Methodist churches may provide us with a more multifaceted picture of American Methodism.

For example, let us take the case of Methodism in Georgetown, a community in the "Federal District" (now known as the District of Columbia). On the surface, the narrative history of the well-established Dumbarton Methodist Episcopal church of Georgetown seems to be a rather simple exercise. The historian could trace the various religious transmutations of middle-class culture in the Washington region by tracing the history of the Dumbarton church: the congregation grew and prospered during the late nineteenth and early twentieth centuries as a professional bourgeoisie was established in the city; the congregation declined precipitously in the 1950s and 1960s as the Washington area suburbanized; and the congregation has had a slight recovery during the most recent period of Georgetown's re-gentrification—the church is now home to a small but committed group of progressive, relatively well-to-do social activists. This, then, is the official account of the Dumbarton church, a story line that follows quite closely the demographic and economic developments of the Georgetown middle class.[24]

But if the scholar relates the historical record in this way, he or she has not portrayed a complete picture of Methodism in Georgetown; the rest of the story must take into account the narratives of other groups of people who seceded from the Dumbarton church. These other groups represented a Methodism very different from the bourgeois religious conservatism of the nineteenth century or the bourgeois religious liberalism of the late twentieth century.

The first offshoot from the Dumbarton church was an 1814 secession of African American members. The resulting Mt. Zion Methodist Episcopal Church was the earliest independent black congregation in the District of Columbia. Not surprisingly, a long history of racial discrimination precipitated that secession. The second congregation to break away from Dumbarton was Congress Street Methodist Protestant Church in 1828. The Methodist Protestants were established specifically to counteract a perceived hierarchicalism within the Methodist Episcopal denomination, and thus demonstrated the strong democratizing trends that persisted within early American Christianity. Over the years, less formalized defections from the Dumbarton church have involved individuals of varied economic status who held nonmainline beliefs—persons who had holiness, charismatic, or conservative evangelical convictions, for instance.[25]

The full story of Methodism in Georgetown is a rather exciting story of conformity and plurality, of structure and antistructure, of the middle and the margins—people who came from several kinds of social locations. Similarly, a study of Methodism as a whole, particularly when the tensions of the movement are viewed through the lens of the local contexts of the denomination, will present not only the "bland, uninspired middle" but also the rich, dynamic diversity of the American religious experience.

David Lowes Watson

David Lowes Watson has devoted considerable effort to reviving small-group life in The United Methodist Church. In this essay he uses his training as a historian to study the Methodist tradition of class leaders and class meetings. His research and insights suggest that class meetings played a large role in the formation of Christian discipleship within Methodism. The care given by lay leaders of classes for both the group and for individuals in the group meant that there was growth in spiritual depth that in turn sustained the larger Christian community. Watson's interest in lay leadership is significant. He finds that lay leadership is vital to serious renewal of faith and practice. Covenant discipleship groups are one example of a way that the contemporary church can reclaim the small-group tradition. Watson sees this as necessary for the well-being of the church into the future.

The reader is invited to think about ways in which the small-group movement can be of help to the local congregations as well as to the larger church. Can this emphasis assist church members with their growth in discipleship in the way Watson envisions? Is this a way that United Methodism can adjust to the realities accompanying the financial costs of ordained leadership? Are the lessons derived from history applicable to the church at the beginning of the twenty-first century, or do the realities facing the church today, including increased demands on church members' time, work against such a vision? Is there sufficient discipline among those who are part of The United Methodist Church to bring about a reinvention of its small-group life?

Class Leaders and Class Meetings: Recovering a Methodist Tradition for a Changing Church

David Lowes Watson

I. The Ecclesial Context

1. A Lack of Christian Formation

In common with many denominations of the North American church, there is a widespread perception among United Methodists that they are in the midst of an acute identity crisis.[1] There is less agreement, however, on the reasons for the crisis. Still less is there agreement on the kind of leadership needed to bring them through it.[2] The result is a general climate of ecclesial misgiving on the part of clergy and laity alike. More important, there is a serious questioning of the nature and purpose of Christian witness in a culture that increasingly co-opts religious beliefs and practices to meet its social and personal needs.

This essay will argue that one of the major factors contributing to the present state of affairs is a failure to develop the most important aspect of leadership in our congregations, and also the most basic: the forming of Christian disciples. Discipleship is a craft, as Stanley Hauerwas has cogently argued.[3] As with any craft, it has to be handed on, person to person, generation to generation. Yet this is not being done in most United Methodist congregations. Within a decade, the last generation of church members who can remember being formed as Christian disciples will have passed on, and if nothing is done we shall have lost the tradition of faithful discipleship that once earned Methodism its very name. More immediately, without seasoned Christian disciples in our congregations, programs and projections will be largely ineffective, however well intentioned or skillfully designed. Resources alone have never been sufficient for Christian living in the world, least of all in the individualistic and hedonistic Western culture of the late twentieth century.[4] What we need are leaders in discipleship.

Yet these are the very leaders we lack, among clergy and laity alike.

Few clergy know how to form Christian disciples in their congregations. Indeed, many are patently uncomfortable with the idea, not least because the formative disciplines of the Christian life have long been disdained in many of our theological schools and seminaries.[5] Programming and administration are thus much more appealing and far less demanding than facing the harsh reality that mature disciples are dwindling in their congregations, and that something must be done about it—soon. By the same token, few laity know how to form Christian disciples, not least because discipleship has largely become a matter of personal preference. Guidelines for Christian living are often regarded as restrictive or even legalistic, and church members are thus left to fulfill their Christian potential as best they can. In such an environment there is little room for Christian wisdom, and small demand for experienced Christian leaders. In a word, each person's discipleship is virtually autonomous.[6]

2. A Wesleyan Compass Heading

Ironically, one of the best compass headings through this crisis can be found in the very heritage of Methodism. Some of the earliest directives John Wesley gave to the Methodists made clear that the gospel does not merely foster faithful discipleship, but requires it. The *General Rules of the United Societies*, first published in 1743, not only provides the guidelines for Christian living in the world, but also stipulates that "works of mercy" and "works of piety" are the practical condition of being a Christian.[7] The point is a fine one, but altogether critical for how one views the Christian life. According to the *General Rules*, the good works in which we engage as disciples of Jesus Christ are not optional, but necessary. If we do not obey his teachings, we weaken and ultimately break our covenant relationship with God. If we do not work out our salvation, we lose it.

The issue has profound theological implications for Christian discipleship, and requires more than a passing reference.[8] Following his experience at Aldersgate Street in May of 1738, Wesley undertook a visit to the Moravian community at Herrnhut. With the freedom of one who has completed a spiritual apprenticeship, he began to question some of the religious perspectives and practices of those who had been so influential in leading him to that critical juncture in his pilgrimage.[9] On his return to England, the entries in his *Journal* repeatedly dwell on the extent to which the assurance of faith was or was not concomitant with justification, culminating on October 29 when he records that, while "doubtful of [his] own state" and wondering whether he should wait in "silence and retirement" for an assurance of the kingdom of God, he came upon the words in his Testament that "by works faith [is] made perfect."[10] Just as significant is his entry for November 12, when he notes that he "began more narrowly to inquire what the doctrine of the Church of England is concerning the much-controverted point of justification by faith."[11]

The question with which Wesley was wrestling was as old as the Reformation; in fact, as old as the church itself. In general terms it can be described as the issue of faith and works: the extent to which good works are integral to our salvation, and the extent to which failure to make them a priority of our discipleship is detrimental to, and even destructive of, Christian faith. The issue was to emerge in varying contexts throughout his leadership of the Methodist movement, but a sampling of his *Journal* and early treatises indicates that Wesley recognized its theological significance at the very outset of his evangelical ministry. We find it, for example, in his account of the dispute over Quietism at the Fetter Lane Society,[12] in his discussion of the objections at Bristol to his preaching on free grace,[13] and in "The Principles of a Methodist," where he addresses it in relation to assurance of faith and Christian perfection.[14] Of particular interest for our present concerns is the way in which it shaped the polity of early Methodism, where it is clear that the regulation of the societies was honed not only by pastoral exigency, but also by sound theology.

3. Methodical Discipleship

Even though Wesley himself resisted the name, the methodical discipleship fostered by the societies quickly became the identifying mark of Methodism.[15] More than any other aspect of the movement, it was the office of class leader and the insistence on attendance at class meetings that gave definitive expression to the tension of faith and works in the lives of the members. Given the pressures of churchly logistics in our own time, it is heartening to note that this office and its attendant weekly gatherings had their genesis in the most practical of considerations: the clearing of a building debt. Wesley's account is well known. At the society in Bristol on February 15, 1742, it was agreed to have weekly collection of monies by designated leaders from subgroupings of the society, known as classes. These weekly visits quickly became pastoral as well as financial, and within a year the system had evolved into weekly class meetings, which then became the normative means of mutual support and accountability for the discipleship of society members.[16]

In the plethora of small groups across the church of today it is sometimes forgotten that the earliest classes in Methodism were formed around the leader, and that this remained Wesley's priority. In the *General Rules*, the duties of the class leader were to see each person in his or her class at least once each week, to receive what they were willing to give toward the relief of the poor, to enquire "how their souls prosper," and to "advise, reprove, comfort or exhort as occasion may require." In turn, the leader was to be accountable to the minister and stewards of the society, reporting "any that are sick" or "walk disorderly and will not be reproved."[17] This makes clear that the intent of the classes was pastoral oversight, whatever the other benefits of the weekly meetings might have been—an important point to which we shall return.

The *Rules* then proceed to the particular requirements of membership; but first there is an important statement of purpose that directly addressed the issue of faith and works:

> There is one only condition previously required, in those who desire admission into these Societies, *a desire to flee from the wrath to come, to be saved from their sins:* But, wherever this is really fix'd in the soul, it will be shewn by its fruits. It is therefore expected of all who continue therein, that they should continue to evidence their desire of salvation, *First,* By doing no harm, by avoiding evil in every kind. . . . *Secondly,* By doing good, by being in every kind merciful after their power. . . . *Thirdly,* by attending upon all the ordinances of God.[18]

The theology of these words is incisive. Neither the immediate assurance of justifying grace nor the incipient sanctification of the new birth is a prerequisite for Methodist membership, but merely a *desire* for salvation. In other words, Wesley makes a distinction between prevenient and justifying grace. The liberation of God's grace is not license, but rather the opportunity to respond to the divine initiative in obedient discipleship. The acceptance of God's grace, in whichever form, brings immediate obligations, a dimension of Christian discipleship that had been seriously weakened by the doctrinal overloading of justification in the theology of the Reformation.[19] This doctrinal and ethical issue had caused the English Reformers grave concern during the sixteenth century, and it was the same concern that impelled Wesley to research the original Anglican Homilies following his Aldersgate Street experience. The question was not whether undue attention to good works would deny the fullness of God's grace in human salvation, but whether lack of attention to good works would cheapen it. Accordingly, the *General Rules* stipulated that there were no *pre*conditions for membership in a Methodist society, but very clear *post*conditions if membership was to be continued.

Put differently, the *Rules* identified the basics for Christian living in the world with whatever "degree of faith" one had been graced, as opposed to identifying a standard Christian experience that then condoned a wide range of "Christian" behavior. This is what caused such tension between Wesley and the Calvinist wing of the Revival, and occasioned the charge of Pelagianism. Today it runs no less counter to the widespread gnosticism that passes for discipleship in so much of North American Christianity.[20]

4. A Matter of Heart and Life

One of the most succinct statements of the issue is a *Journal* entry following Wesley's examination of the classes in the northern town of Gateshead in 1747. "The question is not concerning the heart, but the life. And the general tenor of this I do not say cannot be *known,* but cannot be *hid* without a miracle."[21] Wesley is not presenting heart and life as alternatives. It goes without saying that Christian faith and Christian living are wholly interdependent. But he is most certainly presenting a priority. If the foremost objective of the Christian life is to seek the right kind of faith, then discipleship tends to be viewed primarily as belief in and experience of Jesus Christ, irrespective of obedience to his teachings. Whereas, if the priority is to follow the teachings of Jesus, discipleship can be attempted irrespective of one's strength of belief or depth of experience.

Of the two notions of discipleship, Wesley clearly was at pains to advocate the latter. He affirmed that faith in Christ is a gracious gift from God, given to different persons in differing degrees. Discipleship, on the other hand, consists of learning to follow the teachings of Jesus with whatever faith we have been given. Thus, while faith and good works are wholly interdependent, the priority of discipleship, as the word implies, must be a disciplined commitment to doing what Jesus tells us to do.

Discipleship has to be disciplined quite simply because the teachings of Jesus run counter to so many of our natural inclinations. Learning to be a Christian disciple goes against the grain of human sin—personally, socially, and systemically.

This is why mutual accountability, the "method" of early Methodist discipleship, was so effective. By telling one another what they were actually doing to follow the teachings of Jesus, our forebears made obedience their watchword, and thereby avoided the pitfall of self-deception in the Christian life. By contrast, when faith is made the priority of discipleship, the Christian life becomes fraught with self-deception. Instead of a craft to be learned from seasoned leaders, discipleship is viewed primarily as a credal experience to be shared in the company of like-minded people. And in an individualized culture such as late-twentieth-century North America, where community life is at a very low ebb, such self-centered companies can fill a tremendous social need. This is not to suggest that Christian discipleship should be devoid of experience. On the contrary, a deepening relationship with Christ and with companions in the faith is one of the richest dimensions of the Christian life. But when these relationships become the priority of discipleship, rather than obedience to the teachings of Jesus which he himself stipulated as the measure of our love for him (John 14:21, 23), then we do indeed deceive ourselves.

II. Historiographical Pitfalls

With these theological and pastoral concerns in mind, an attempt was made some twenty years ago to revitalize the early Methodist class meeting for the church of today.[22] From the outset it was clear that such an exercise would be fraught with historiographical pitfalls, not least because of heightened interest in the heritage of Methodism during the 1970s. This was due in particular to the keen anticipation of two significant events: the new edition of *The Works of John Wesley*,[23] and the 1984 Bicentennial Celebration of the founding of the Methodist Episcopal Church at the Christmas Conference in Baltimore. There is always a tendency in the recovery of a tradition, and especially a religious tradition, to draw unwarranted contemporary inferences from selected historical data, and while the new edition of Wesley's *Works* has done much to forestall this, there nonetheless remains the need for careful adaptation rather than hasty replication of the work of our spiritual forebears.

1. Ecclesiola in Ecclesia

The first and most obvious pitfall was to ignore the fact that early Methodism was a movement within the Church of England. Wesley spent a great deal of his time and energy explaining this to the members of the societies. He was at pains to advocate the necessity of retaining their status, pointing to the undesirable aspects of separation evident in English Nonconformity.[24] While he was ultimately thwarted by the separatist tendencies of the movement, fueled as it was by ecclesial, social, political, and economic pressures, and while the American Revolution forced the issue on this side of the Atlantic, the disciplined character of the Methodist societies remained essentially that of an *ecclesiola* in the *ecclesia* of the Church of England.[25] As such, membership in a Methodist society could be, and was, more exacting than merely being part of an Anglican parish. By the same token, Christian interaction in Methodist circles could be, and was, more intimate.

To make the point ecclesiologically, in many ways The United Methodist Church of today is the ecclesial equivalent of the Church of England in Wesley's day. This is not to suggest that The United Methodist Church is identical or even similar to the eighteenth-century Church of England. For one thing, history does not permit such ready comparisons, albeit in the context of Christian tradition. But more immediately, in the voluntaristic context of the American church, members are much more aware of their congregational identity than in the formalized parishes of an established church, then or now. This in turn engenders a degree of participation in churchly life and work, by clergy and laity alike, that would be altogether incongruous in a parish-oriented system, then or now.

The equivalence between the eighteenth-century Church of England and The United Methodist Church of today lies rather in the familiar "church" and "sect" typology of Ernst Troeltsch. While this distinction is increasingly outmoded in the changing patterns of Western culture, it can still provide helpful insights into recent ecclesial history.[26] According to Troeltsch, the church is a type of Christian society that is "a universal institution," adapted to "the whole of secular life" in preparation for "the higher supernatural state." By contrast, the sect derives its ideals "purely from the Gospel and from the Law of Christ," upholding "the ideal of Christian perfection as binding on all Christians alike."[27] To state the issue in more functional terms, the church is an inclusive community of the Christian faith, interacting with its cultural context in a way that makes the gospel accessible to a wide range of persons with a wide range of commitments. On the other hand, the sect serves as a *locus* for those who are called to a deeper commitment—to a disciplined, or methodical discipleship. The tension between the two usually centers on whether such disciplined disciples remain within the larger church, or form separatist ecclesial groupings.

Accordingly, the first pitfall to be avoided in adapting the early class meeting for the church of today was to mismatch the characteristics of an *ecclesiola* with that of an *ecclesia*. Any attempt to apply the dimensions of Wesley's polity, designed as it was for the disciplined life of a religious society, to the wider ecclesial life of inclusive congregations would inevitably have encountered marked resistance. Disciplined accountability would have appealed to the average churchgoer of today no more than it did at the time of Wesley.

2. Small Groups

Another historiographical pitfall was the identification of the early class meeting with the small-group culture of North America. As so often happens when the church lacks motivated leadership, congregations have reflected and embraced this aspect of their cultural context with vigor. Small groups have proliferated in seemingly limitless variety: growth groups, enrichment groups, prayer groups, Bible study groups, sharing groups, outreach groups, action groups, and much more. They have become such an accepted means of pastoring that there are few seminars or workshops held in church settings today that do not assume the familiarity of participants with this particular pedagogical approach.[28]

While many small groups in congregations are focused on the benefits and obligations of the Christian life, many are little more than churchly versions of what seem to be helpful responses to the needs of contemporary culture—small-group programs with no explicitly Christian content that are nonetheless hosted and embraced by local congregations.[29] The converse is also true. Many small-group movements in society at large, especially twelve-step programs, adopt principles and practices that have an honored pedigree in the spiritual renewal movements of the church.[30] Moreover, all of these groups, cultural and ecclesial alike, embody what social anthropologists have long identified: that any small group can be expected to engender cohesiveness of purpose and relationship.[31]

Inasmuch as the early class meeting appeared to exhibit these criteria, the notion of bringing it back into the fabric of Methodism had an immediate appeal. It appeared to provide the mutual support and intimacy of an interaction that the church no longer seemed to foster in its congregational life and work. It likewise appeared to fulfill the scriptural directive to meet together for a range of Christian activities that tend to be neglected when left to individual responsibility, such as prayer, Bible study, and Christian service. Perhaps most important of all, it apparently could help overextended clergy to feel that they were more in touch with their members, if only vicariously through a network of groups or cells serving as an extension of their pastoral leadership.

A modicum of research into the early class meetings, however, quickly dispelled any such cursory connections. While their benefits, as far as we can tell, might have included small-group cohesiveness and organizational efficiency, their purpose was at once more spiritual and ecclesial: pastoral oversight through mutual accountability. They were the most immediate means of ensuring that the conditions of membership in the early Methodist societies were being fulfilled: regular attendance at meetings, following the basic tenets of doing good and avoiding evil, and using the means of grace. The weekly class meetings were supplemented by a quarterly examination of one's discipleship, on the basis of which a new membership ticket was or was not granted for the next three months. Of course, as with any small group, the class meeting generated interpersonal relationships that became warm and supportive.[32] This was not, however, their purpose. The relationships were rather a blessing that emanated from the fulfillment of their purpose. If the class meeting was to provide any direction for the church of today, it could not be just another small-group program.

3. Historical Method

These pitfalls pointed to the need for clarity of historical method. To have begun with what seem to have been the results of the early class meeting, and then to have sought to replicate those results in contemporary American culture, would have been to put the cart before the horse. The question rather to be asked was how the leaders and members of these eighteenth-century groups saw their purpose, and then to emulate them in that purpose, allowing the Holy Spirit to work freely in our time as in theirs. The imposition of retrospective interpretation on these pristine forms of Methodism, whether theological, sociological, or even experiential, would have been a spiritual impediment to the revitalization of class leaders and class meetings. It would also have been a weighty error in Christian traditioning.[33]

Clarity of historical method was no less important in exploring the reasons for the decline of class leaders and meetings in American Methodism. They diminished in importance from the mid nineteenth century onward, and by the turn of the twentieth century they had effectively ceased to play a role in the life and work of the church.[34] Among the reasons for this, two have particular relevance for The United Methodist Church of today. The first is that the disciplined religiousness of class meetings in the early Methodist societies, conditioned as they were by the social structures of eighteenth-century England, was quickly superseded on this side of the Atlantic by the unrestrained democratic spirit of the American Revolution.[35] The mark of American Methodism, especially on the frontier where it most rapidly expanded, was an egalitarianism of religious experience, rendering the class meeting merely one of the "nodal points in a network of friendship and community."[36]

The second reason was the increasingly dominant role of the clergy, not only in congregations, as circuit riding gave way to stationed appointments and a concomitant investment in property for worship, education, and clerical residence, but also in the wider connectional church, as Methodism moved toward an ethos of corporate governance rather than pastoral oversight.[37] Preaching and organization became the primary modes of pastoring, rendering class leaders and class meetings optional and ultimately marginal—as they remain to this day.

III. Traditioning Class Meetings and Class Leaders

1. Covenant Discipleship Groups

The groups that were formed in the late 1970s as an adaptation of the class meeting sought to emulate the spiritual integrity of this early Methodist institution. They were given the name of Covenant Discipleship, and were pioneered on the campus of Perkins School of Theology at Southern Methodist University. Some fifty students each semester met voluntarily once a week to be accountable for their discipleship, and within several years the groups had spread to a number of churches in the South Central Jurisdiction of The United Methodist Church. In 1984 the General Board of Discipleship adopted them as a programmatic emphasis and published their first resource.[38] Grounded in the Wesleyan doctrine of justification, covenant discipleship groups use the objective and dynamic of the class meeting, mutual support and mutual accountability, to provide a weekly compass heading for their members' lives according to the teachings of Jesus.[39] They are open to anyone, with no restrictions regarding age or gender. The only requirement is a willingness to "watch over one another in love" as the surest way of walking with Christ in the world.[40] The groups help their members not to resist God's grace, and thus to avoid self-deception in the Christian life.

As covenant discipleship groups moved from the campus of Perkins School of Theology into the wider United Methodist Church, two questions quickly became clear. First, many of the aspects of the early class meeting could already be found in the ongoing life and work of congregations, albeit to a greater or lesser degree. To prevent duplication of existing pastoral work, it was asked which characteristics of the early class meeting were *not* being addressed in contemporary church life. The answer emerged with some cogency: While many aspects of the class meeting—mutual support, assurance of identity, confessional interaction, spiritual discernment, and more—could be found in a multiplicity of congregational activities, the one aspect that could rarely be found was mutual accountability for Christian living in the world. Accordingly, while covenant discipleship groups would obviously evince many of the characteristics of small groups in general, it was established that their intent would be for the members to hold themselves mutually accountable in their walk with Christ.

The second question followed from the first: How much time would be necessary to accomplish this purpose? The answer likewise quickly emerged: One hour, provided the agenda of the group was focused and intentional; provided also the number in the group did not preclude a meaningful engagement. Thus covenant discipleship groups consist of up to seven persons who agree to meet once a week for one hour in order to hold themselves mutually accountable for their discipleship. They do this by agreeing on a covenant of intent and engaging in a process of catechesis: questions asked by one of the group who serves as leader for that week, and answered by each of the members in turn in light of their covenant. The limit on membership is not rigid, but more than seven has been found to be a strain on the process of mutual accountability. By the same token, fewer than four members pressures the group toward a more intimate process of sharing than the declared intent. The character of the groups is collegial rather than intimate, allowing for a great degree of flexibility in patterns of membership and scheduling. Precisely because the meetings have an agenda and are limited to one hour, they can meet at any time of any day in the week. Groups meet at six in the morning, ten at night, and everything in between. Members honor the starting time and can likewise rely on a prompt conclusion.

Covenant discipleship groups can now be found in many parts of The United Methodist Church, and are currently supported by teaching congregations in thirty-four Annual Conferences. They are increasingly a feature of college campus ministries and United Methodist theological schools and seminaries, and are one of the subjects of a growing dialogue within the Pan-Methodist Community of North America as well as the Methodist family worldwide.[41] The format has been adapted by a number of Conference Cabinets and Councils on Ministry as a dimension of their work together, and a wide range of published resources is available, including versions for children, high school youth, and college students.[42]

2. Class Leaders

As we have noted, the early class meeting was a feature of Methodist societies that were already selective *ecclesiolae in ecclesia*. Accordingly, the disciplined accountability of Covenant Discipleship has never been viewed as a criterion for small-group ministries in the wider pastoral ministry of the church. Accountability, however, is precisely the criterion and the context needed to develop pastoral leadership in congregations. On the premise that the most effective mentors for discipleship are to be found among laity, since clergy rarely experience the brunt of Christian living in the world, the next phase of Covenant Discipleship was to make explicit what was already implicit in the weekly meetings, namely, a lay office that could be revitalized in and through covenant discipleship groups as a means of pastoral support and oversight in the congregation as a whole.

The vanguard for this consisted of legislation passed by the General Conference of 1988, sponsored by the Northern New Jersey Annual Conference and drafted by one of its district superintendents, now Bishop Hae Jong Kim. This was one of those occasions in the life of The United Methodist Church that has quietly slipped into its history, but may well prove to have been momentous, for it restored the office of class leader and the institution of class meetings into the *Book of Discipline* for the first time in fifty years.[43] Responsibility for implementing the legislation was lodged with the General Board of Discipleship, where the Section on Covenant Discipleship and Christian Formation made the resourcing of the office of class leader a major focus of its work. Additional resources were published, and a Commissioning Service for Class Leaders was included in the new *United Methodist Book of Worship.*[44]

One of the most stimulating dimensions of these initiatives was the fresh appreciation they provided for The United Methodist Church of the mission and ministry of its ethnic constituencies. Class leaders are still active in many Korean and African American congregations, providing valuable role models and a significant potential for cross-cultural mission in an increasingly diverse society. It was also a strong reminder that the genius of early Methodism was not the regimentation of society members into manageable subunits, but the recognition and empowerment of indigenous lay leadership in the societies. These leaders were *ipso facto* responsive to their worldly context, and therefore the best possible touchstone for the mission of the church in their culture.[45]

3. Unrealized Pastoral Leadership

The potential for such leadership in the contemporary church is considerable, yet for the most part remains unrealized, given the present patterns of pastoral power. These patterns tend to be parish-oriented, where the priority is the maintenance of pastorates rather than the forming of Christian disciples. In countless congregations energies are expended on the well-being of the church rather than the teachings of Christ. This is especially the case with the small-membership churches that still compose the greater part of United Methodism, where all too often the overriding objective is the raising of money to support a pastor, who in turn is expected to keep the church alive. But it is often the case in larger congregations as well, where pastoral leadership is almost invariably measured by the extent to which pastoral programs render satisfactory service to the greatest number of parishioners. These ecclesiocentrisms are a far cry from the mission of God. The question is, How do we invert them into a christocentric, and thereby centrifugal, form of pastoral leadership?

Clearly the present pastoral pattern needs to be changed. This does not require radically new forms of the church, but rather the revitalization of existing congregations through truly pastoral leadership—clergy and laity whose primary concern is the formation of Christian disciples. With such leadership, we might well become a church freshly empowered by the Holy Spirit to serve the risen Christ in a Western culture, which, as David Bosch, Lesslie Newbigin, and others have made altogether clear, is the newest and most challenging missional frontier.[46]

The answer lies in our roots. The genius of our pastoral heritage was the creative complementarity of itinerant preachers and faithful laity: the vigorous proclamation of the gospel by those who were called and gifted to be evangelists; and the building up of converts in the faith by seasoned Christian disciples who formed the bedrock of the societies and later the congregations of the church. If we can integrate their dynamic methods with our present pastoral structures, we might once again be a church in mission—salt, light, leaven in our culture, and seed of the coming reign of God, on earth as in heaven. To declare publicly that the commandments of Jesus Christ for personal and social behavior are to be taken seriously, and to pattern our lives accordingly, will mean considerable tension with the world in which we live. But it will also bring us the honor of a faithful church: the power and presence of the Holy Spirit in our life and work: grace upon grace upon grace.

IV. Missional and Pastoral Implications

Such a spiritual and pastoral re-traditioning would require a concerted commitment to three connectional initiatives: (1) a new generation of class leaders; (2) a new generation of circuit riders; (3) revitalized lay preaching.

1. A New Generation of Class Leaders

The significance of class leaders in early Methodism was their responsibility for the discipleship of the society members, which meant they had a marked degree of pastoral oversight. Given the present pattern of congregational leadership, it is not surprising that this is the very responsibility many clergy are unwilling to share. Even those who are willing to share it hesitate to do so, for the wholly valid reason that it is a sacred trust. It should not and cannot be delegated, except to those who prove themselves trustworthy—a quality that unfortunately is not sufficiently stressed in many contemporary renewal programs.

With appropriate criteria, however, the office of class leader would allow the pastoral workload in congregations to be shared to the benefit of everyone concerned. Most of the faithful members of our congregations are not being pastored in the truest sense: they are not being helped to live the Christian life in the world. Class leaders, working under the supervision of the clergy, could provide this hands-on pastoral guidance. They would exercise the kind of leadership that always commands respect: leadership by example.

Covenant discipleship groups are a very effective way to establish the criteria for such a lay pastoral office. The basic requirement for Covenant Discipleship membership is quite straightforward: a willingness to be accountable for one's discipleship. Yet this simple condition often proves to be a stumbling block for those who see themselves as pastoral leaders, but in fact are not ready for the task. While a personal relationship with Christ and an eagerness to live out his teachings are both prerequisites for pastoral leadership, they are not always found together in a Christian. Those who are best able to show others the way of discipleship are those who have learned and are still learning what it means to walk with Christ in the world—a pilgrimage that is deeply relational and a relationship that involves us in some very particular actions. It is the essential characteristic of Covenant Discipleship to keep these two dimensions of the Christian life in balance, and class leaders who are members of covenant discipleship groups are thus well placed to help other members of the congregation grow in their discipleship, at whatever stage of the Christian life these members happen to be.

What is needed is the recognition and revitalization of this office throughout the church. Making it just another organizational option will not suffice, nor will it serve the connectional church to have it adopted or adapted on a piecemeal basis, congregation by congregation. Indeed, there are many places where clergy and laity already function very effectively in some such relationship, especially in larger pastorates. The point is that *all* of our congregations need leaders in discipleship—the weak no less than the strong, the small no less than the large. In short, class leaders must be given connectional clout. If they are to assume their proper pastoral role, they must be given church-wide authority to complement the administrative and programmatic leadership roles already assigned to laity in our polity.

The office of class leader would further provide vocational fulfillment for a considerable number of laity in our congregations who have no way of exercising pastoral leadership other than to seek professional employment in the church. Quite apart from the personal disruption this often causes, it deprives many congregations of valuable indigenous leadership. Moreover, many such potential leaders, often out of frustration with the lack of leadership in their own pastoral settings, become involved in the parachurch activities and organizations that thrive in many of our communities, and that sometimes lead to congregational disputes. Yet these laypersons could be doing valuable pastoral work right where they are in their home churches. Allowing them to assume the office of class leader could focus their pastoral energies in building up the body of Christ for ministry and mission in the immediacy of the congregation where they witness and worship.

2. A New Generation of Circuit Riders

Class leaders would also allow the connectional church to revitalize another aspect of early Methodism: the circuit rider. This would require a move toward two tracks for the ordained ministry: pastorates, in which the gifts and graces of stationed clergy could be used to full advantage through long-term and multiple-staff appointments; and circuits, in which teams of itinerant clergy could minister to multiple congregations by delegating much of the local pastoral leadership to class leaders. Both tracks would require intentional logistical support in a number of areas, the most obvious being that each track should receive equal recognition and respect. At a practical level, it would mean paying circuit riders at parity with their colleagues in larger pastorates. This could be done by forming much larger circuits than we presently have, and reducing the number of clergy that serve them. But it would also require a realignment of priorities in terms of appointments and perceived seniority in pastoral service.

For example, a circuit of forty congregations with an aggregate membership of several thousand could function very well with a team of six or eight circuit riders in strategically located offices and parsonages. There are clergy and laity alike who would regard this pattern of pastoring as a liberating challenge, and in many instances are waiting for such an opportunity. Circuits could obviously be formed with fewer congregations or with more, the only proviso being that each one be structured with adequate membership and resources, and that there were class leaders in each congregation. The finances in such circuits would quickly improve, and much missional energy would thereby be released. Another pattern could be a circuit hub, in which a larger congregation would serve as a staffing and resource center along with a number of smaller congregations in a given area. The collegiality between the clergy could be greatly facilitated in this way, and the training and support of class leaders likewise enhanced.

Of course, such concepts are not new. Parish ministries in various forms have been with us for quite some time, and flexibility of pastoral leadership has long been a basic tenet of contemporary congregational studies.[47] However, the revitalized circuit could provide a particularly Methodist way of addressing these leadership issues, drawing not only on the wealth of analytical data now available, but also on the richness of a tradition that is well known for its effective pastoral guidance.

3. Revitalized Lay Preaching

To facilitate this pastoral flexibility there would have to be a third connectional initiative: greater recognition and utilization of lay preachers. The role of lay preaching comes under the category of what John Wesley described as the "extra-ordinary call."[48] He acknowledged such a call in his own ministry, and he affirmed it among his preachers, even though this was initially against his better judgment. Indeed, he came to regard it as self-evident, for women as well as for men.[49] The early Methodist preachers in England were not ordained, nor were the earliest circuit riders in North America. Yet their preaching gifts and skills were authenticated by the large numbers who responded to the gospel they proclaimed, repented of their sins, and were converted to Christ. Ironically, the very effectiveness of the circuit riders led to a diminished role for lay preaching once the pastoral pattern of Methodism became parish-oriented. The call to preach became the call to ordained ministry, the "ordinary" call, and the "extraordinary" call to preach was rendered peripheral to congregational life and work, as was the office of class leader.

Even so, the extraordinary call remains alive in our congregations. There are laity whose gift of preaching the gospel can grace the mission and ministry of the church, but their gift requires fresh recognition as an authentic means of grace. Their leadership in the pulpit must be acknowledged in the church at large, and even more in their own congregations. Our present identification of these persons as "lay speakers" says much about the adjustment we would have to make in reviving this Methodist tradition. But the lay speakers we already have, and the many who would join them if they were given recognition and encouragement, are living proof of the authenticity of their call.

Such preaching is in our blood and in our bones. We need to hear it again, not only because it was powerfully used by God during the formative years of Methodism on both sides of the Atlantic, but also because it is still a vital part of Methodism elsewhere in the world. Lay preaching does not rival or supplant the preaching of ordained clergy. It provides complementary insights and perspectives that help to ground the gospel in the rough and tumble of worldly living. It is an incarnational means of grace that proclaims and embodies an incarnational gospel, and it has a long and honored tradition, beginning with the Hebrew prophets and first disciples of Jesus of Nazareth.

V. Connectional Benefits

1. Centered on Christ

If adopted with full commitment and intentionality, these three connectional initiatives could benefit all of our congregations. Class leaders most especially would prove beneficial. While their contribution in small-membership churches would be immediate and obvious, they would be no less helpful in large pastorates. If truth be told, our larger congregations find the pressures of enculturation most difficult to resist. Precisely because they minister to so many people, they become responsive to a wide range of interests, and in so doing they can easily lose the focus of the gospel in their life and work. Cadres of class leaders committed to the nurturing of discipleship throughout the life and work of congregations would prove invaluable in keeping the diverse ministries of larger membership churches centered on Jesus Christ.

2. Vocational Freedom

Revitalization of this lay office would also provide greater freedom for clergy and laity to pursue their respective vocational gifts. With the assistance of class leaders, clergy would be freed to focus more directly on the ministries of Word, Sacrament, and Order. These are the distinctive privileges of ordination, yet they are the very tasks that our present pastoral pattern prevents so many clergy from fulfilling. The result is overwork on the one hand, and on the other, a widespread professional and vocational disillusionment.

Likewise laity who are presently frustrated in the exercise of their pastoral gifts would find rich vocational fulfillment. Given the opportunity to lead both in pastoring and in preaching, they would provide fresh avenues for ministry and mission. They would also acquire a deeper empathy for pastors as they discovered the burdens of pastoral responsibilities and the workload of preparing regular sermons. Such discoveries would alleviate a great deal of the friction in congregations between pastors and lay leadership, frequently caused by miscommunication and lack of mutual understanding. Class leaders and lay preachers would in due course become the pastor's closest colleagues in a congregation. Just as important, they would also become the pastor's firmest allies, since they would experience the full range of pastoral encounters: the positive and rewarding, but also the negative and demanding.

No less beneficial would be the collegiality extended by class leaders to the clergy. While it remains true that many pastors are uncomfortable with the notion of Christian formation, there are many more who wish to provide their congregations with just such a ministry, but are unable to do so because there are not enough hours in the week. The result, as we have noted, is that very few church members receive the personal guidance and support they need for their daily Christian living in a world where it is not easy to be a Christian. With the help of class leaders, this situation could quickly be remedied. Clergy would find themselves with the best possible support group they could have: pastoral teams of laity who share the burdens as well as the privileges of forming Christian disciples.

3. Missional Identity

Through the consolidation of membership and resources, expanded circuits and circuit hubs would afford countless small congregations a renewed identity. They would be freed from the crippling burden of trying to maintain what in many instances have become outdated pastorates, thereby acquiring new energy in mission and ministry, especially in partnership with peer congregations. Larger churches working in circuit hubs would also be freshly empowered by the missional possibilities in the midst of changing social and community patterns. By contrast, congregations caught up in ecclesiocentric patterns of ministry find these changes difficult if not impossible to understand, and withdraw even further into themselves.

VI. Shared Pastoral Power

All of this depends on a concept that has always been disturbing to the church: the sharing of pastoral power between clergy and laity. The concept becomes even more disturbing in an individualistic culture such as contemporary North America, in which leadership is so mistrusted. Our problem, as the late Orlando Costas astutely observed, is a clergy-dominated church and a laity-dominated clergy.[50] These are patently the wrong power struggles for any church to be fighting. They distract, they enervate, and they discredit the gospel. Clergy and laity alike must acknowledge that the lodging of pastoral power so overwhelmingly with the clergy merely results in most church members not being pastored at all; whereas, if pastoral leadership were to be shared between the clergy and those laypeople who, like their forebears in the faith, are gifted and called to this work, our congregations would learn afresh what it means to truly walk with Christ in the world.

This sharing of pastoral power will not come easily. The idea that some church members can be pastoral leaders because they are more seasoned than others in their discipleship runs counter to the egalitarianism of experience that has marked so much of the history of North American Christianity. But this may need radical reassessment, and we do not have much time. Discipleship in our church is all but detraditioned, and without disciplined disciples in our ranks, we will increasingly be held hostage by our culture. Such a church is unworthy of Jesus Christ, and most assuredly is no match for the forces of the world that oppose the coming reign of God.

Frederick Herzog

One of the most significant changes for the Protestant churches in the course of the twentieth century has been attitudes toward, and policies concerning, Christian missionary efforts in other countries. The missionary movement was a dominant characteristic of the late nineteenth century. The churches were convinced that their obligation was to convert those in other countries who were not Christians. Extensive campaigns were undertaken to raise funds and recruit missionaries and elaborate programs were put into place. Mission boards became known as "sending agencies." As time went on, mission programs expanded to hospitals, orphanages, schools, universities, and seminaries. In the course of the twentieth century attitudes began to change, especially after the Second World War. Newly developing nations were increasingly uncomfortable with the role of missionaries from Northern and Western churches, and a movement for autonomy of indigenous churches began.

Frederick Herzog, who is widely known for his work in liberation theology, developed an interest in the Methodist Church in Peru. Before his death in 1995, he gave many years to building a mutual relationship between United Methodism in North Carolina and Methodism in Peru, especially through the Methodist seminary in Lima. This essay exhibits his mature thinking about the way in which The United Methodist Church, and particularly the United Methodist Board of Global Ministries, has related to the autonomous Methodist Church of Peru. Herzog came to believe that the dominant reality was the great financial wealth of the church in the United States in comparison with the financial poverty of the church in Peru. Thus he interprets the whole enterprise as one in which money is the dominant reality.

This essay is appropriate to a volume on Methodist theology because it occasions reflection on what the theological convictions were that motivated Methodist missionary activity in the first place, and how those convictions have changed by the end of the twentieth century, at least for the official sending agencies of most Protestant churches. Now, when pressed, mission officials seek to interpret mission more as a helping endeavor than a converting endeavor. This is not what bothered Herzog. He was bothered by the control that the helping endeavor involved, especially because that control was exercised by money. What is suggested is that with the gospel of Jesus Christ the Protestant churches of the United States were also exporting

American culture, including a culture *enamored with the U.S. dollar*. For United Methodism, in particular, for reasons explored in our study of United Methodism and American Culture, it was difficult to separate the mission of the church from the culture of America.

It is worthwhile to think about what the theological principles are that motivate mission in The United Methodist Church today. This is *one of the areas where the church is most divided*. The mission agencies are *wealthy, with large endowments supporting a considerable portion of their work*. Yet their theological convictions are confused and confusing to many in the church. The intentions of those who began the mission boards were informed by a clear theology of conversion while the intentions of those who sustain and operate the boards today are informed by a theology more characterized by a concern for helping and supporting persons both at home and abroad. If there is concern for conversion it is a conversion by indirection. Nevertheless, underneath the intentions, even those that are "liberal" and thought to be most "enlightened," Herzog contends, is *a control that is still basically colonial*, because it is fueled by the economic *wealth of the dominant churches.

Is the emphasis on money adequate for understanding what is going on in missions today? What are the theological emphases of United Methodism at the end of the twentieth century that inform missional outreach? Is there a place for traditional mission activity in the new global realities of the beginning of the twenty-first century? How do the considerable financial resources of The United Methodist Church in the United States influence the Church's role with persons in other countries?

Methodism, Missions, and Money

Frederick Herzog

There is a strange tension in our churches between the official respect we pay to mission, and our actual embodiment and study of mission, especially since the moment about a decade ago when someone discovered that United Methodism was losing a thousand members a week. Then the word *mission* was on everyone's lips again. But has mission therefore gained new momentum in the Christian life as well as in research?

This essay will develop the theme of Methodism and Mission in three parts. (1) A Historical Overview, taking into account two recent assessments of Protestantism in Latin America. (2) The Methodist Church of Peru as concrete test case of mission. (3) A possible Methodist contribution to being freed from the monetary captivity of the church.

My presupposition is that the model of mission prevalent in the nineteenth and first half of the twentieth centuries with "sending" churches and people who were "sent" to the heathen in foreign lands, is being changed into a model of a mutual discipleship covenant between "sending churches" and the former mission stations. Yet while the change has been going on for some time, the old pattern continues in the mainline Protestant churches without radical surgery in the basic concept of the missionary effort. The essay will address the issue with the expectation that in mission work critically examined, we see ourselves as churches as in a mirror. The crucial eye-opener is the realization: "'Missions' are dead. Long live God's mission!"

"'Missions' are dead" means that the human effort to expand Christianity in its Western cultural form has run its course. In terms of my hypothesis there was the idea that money could fix almost anything, while we forgot that God is already directing history in a primal mission outreach to every person in conscience and thereby to the *sensus communis* of human groups. Missions often turned out to be a usurpation of God's own mission in which God invites us to participate. What does it mean to share in God's own mission in the world as compared with our clumsy efforts to persuade others that Christianity is a superior bargain on the religious market?

267

Theologians have presented Christian theology in the twentieth century with various hermeneutical foci in mind. There was Rudolf Bultmann with demythologizing, Tillich with deliteralizing, and Dietrich Bonhoeffer with the nonreligious interpretation of the Christian faith. With a number of foci in between, today we hear much of postmodern or poststructuralist interpretation. I did not plan on adding a monetary interpretation. And yet today it seems almost inevitable to see H. Richard Niebuhr's *Christ and Culture* (1951) "formula," that has kept haunting us since midcentury, in terms of "Christ and money."

Much of the present North American endeavor to look for new answers is centered in "Christ and the Church." But keeping strictly to the formula of "*and* the church" in many cases does not get us beyond the Constantinian ambivalence that has haunted us much longer than the formula "Christ and Culture."

As best I can tell, in our time there has not been an attempt to view the "*and* the Church" in terms of mission, as there certainly has not been a query of Christ *and mission* in the specific sense of systematic theology. Thus many of the new interpretative schemes stay within the Constantinian ambience of the church focused merely on itself, however much they might seem to critique some of its drawbacks. An example is Carl E. Braaten, "The Il/legitimacy of Lutheranism in America?" (*Lutheran Forum*, 28:1 [February 1994]).

Beginning with the nineteenth century a "vast outlay" of goodness, commitment, and money in Methodism focused on missions—which affected not just North American culture, but especially other cultures. Is there a lesson to be learned? Scripture tells us: "Do not be over-righteous and do not be overwise. Why make yourself a laughing-stock?" (Eccl 7:16). We might also say: Do not be "over-good." There is Augustine's idea that our greatest virtues are splendid vices. Might there not be attached to missions a vast self-deception of goodness, which made us a laughingstock? Will we examine "United Methodism and Culture" in terms of the beaten track of the "Christ and Culture" formulas, or does United Methodism compel us to elaborate a new model? My research increasingly points in the direction of a "Christ and money" focus.

The challenge is now together with the former missions to understand who the enemy is who distorts our common humanity, and to work together on stopping the perversion of human beings as money-beings.

1. The Modern History and Recent Interpretations

When David Martin's *Tongues of Fire: The Explosion of Protestantism in Latin America* appeared in 1990, it seemed that the '90s were going to bring a new wave of interpreting Methodist missions. Devoted to explaining the vast rise of Protestantism in Latin America, it focused especially on the Pentecostals. There is the figure of more than forty million Latin American Protestants Martin tries to interpret. Several crucial points undergird this major analysis of the growth of Protestantism. Early on, Martin mentions three decisive elements in his analysis: the varied political attitudes attendant to fraternal kinds of religiosity; the relation of given forms of religion, for example, pietism, to the tension between centers and peripheries; and the contribution of religion to mutually supportive networks and to personal advancement.[1]

In his introduction to the volume, Peter Berger finds an interpretive handle for the overall outcome of the analysis historically:

> Martin makes a distinction between three, not two, waves of Protestant cultural revolution—the Puritan, the Methodist, and the Pentecostal. The second did not fully replace the first, and the third continues to co-exist with its two predecessors. All the same, the great wave sweeping across the Third World today is primarily Pentecostal—hence the "tongues of fire" in Martin's title. . . . It is different from the Methodist experience and very different indeed from the Puritan one.[2]

Pentecostalism will bring now to large parts of the world what Puritanism and Methodism brought in one way or other to the North American continent: the emergence of a solid bourgeoisie "with virtues conducive to the development of a democratic capitalism."[3] I do not know of any other interpretation of Methodist missions that sees such a clear coordination between Methodism, Puritanism, and Pentecostalism in order to draw us into those economic structures that, as I will argue, bring suffering to millions of human beings.

So there are Puritan, Methodist, and Pentecostal cultural revolutions subject to a secular dynamics.

> They are, when all is said and done, the components of what Weber called the "Protestant ethic"; what is more, now and then, the ethos of Protestantism shows itself to be remarkably helpful to people in the throes of rapid modernization and of the "take-off" stage of modern economic growth. The same ethos also continues to evolve its time-honoured affinities with the

"spirit of capitalism," with individualism, with a hunger for education and
(last but not least) with a favorable disposition toward democratic politics.[4]

Next in his assessment of these "data," Berger suggests that the affini-
ties are mainly unintended and certainly not the result of interpreted
doctrine. They are unexpected but not surprising results of doctrine as
well as religious experience. Doctrine and religious experience often
function as legitimators of society and culture.

Berger talks about a first, second, and third internationale of world-
transforming Protestantism. The first and second, Puritanism and
Methodism, are predominantly Anglo-Saxon in origin. The third one
will be centered in Pentecostalism in Latin America with satellites in
other parts of the globe: "What one may expect is that the new
Protestant internationale will produce results similar to those of the preceding one—to wit, the emergence of a solid bourgeoisie, with virtues
conducive to the development of democratic capitalism. It hardly needs
emphasizing that this would be an immense event in Latin America as
well as elsewhere in the Third World."[5]

History does not go by what theoreticians suggest might happen. It
has its own mind. And yet there are also self-fulfilling prophecies.
Berger might be operating on such a premise. Protestant religion has
contributed to the growth of capitalism in the nineteenth and early
twentieth centuries, so it might be expected to continue doing this.
Berger might want Protestantism to direct history that way.

Berger emphasizes that he is not quite as cautious as David Martin:

> Martin is a cautious analyst; he refrains from making too many predictions.
> His book is a severe temptation for this reader, at any rate, to be less cautious.
> Be that as it may, this is a book of very great importance. It should be read by
> anyone interested in the condition and the future of the Americas, but also by
> anyone concerned with the relation of religion and social change throughout
> the contemporary world.[6]

Berger wants to see democratic capitalism emerge from Protestant religion. At this point we either choose a different path or submit to fate.

"Fate" here begins with the North European model of Protestantism:
"It is of prime importance because of the varied legacy of Luther and of
Pietism, passed on alike to Methodist and Pentecostal nonconformity.
Thus the Protestant University in Guatemala City immediately con-
fronts you in the doorway with a genealogy going back to Luther and

to Wittenberg."[7] There is a dialectic here: Luther represents a relationship between church and state "which successfully prevented the voluntaristic denominationalism from which Pentecostalism derives, *and* yet nourished the forms of piety on which Pentecostalism ultimately rests."[8]

Martin underscores this as the major source of the Pentecostalist stance toward politics. The basic origins lie in Spener's *collegia pietatis*—the spirituality groups meeting regularly during the week apart from official church services. The Christian "affection" that went along with them was also mediated to Methodism. At the same time, Luther's view of Christian subordination to the powers-that-be was made part of the Pietist traditions with often complete withdrawals from politics. Only at rare occasions did Pietism take on the role that the Protestant internationale would take on today. There have been earlier instances of co-optation by secular powers. The teaming up of missions and capitalism leads of necessity to the power drive of Christianity.

In many ways, the nature of the church as ecclesiological challenge was bracketed very early in Latin American mission efforts. An example is the volumes of the 1916 *Panama Congress* that summarize much of the theological framework of Latin American Protestant missions at that time.

The history behind it is worthwhile knowing. The great mission conference in Edinburgh 1910 is also key for understanding missions in Latin America. In the preparation of the conference German mission folk insisted that Latin American missionaries should not have part in it because Latin America has been a Christian continent since Christopher Columbus set foot on it in 1492. Converting Roman Catholics was unlike converting heathen. So Edinburgh 1910 went ahead without official representatives of Protestant missions in Latin America. Latin American missionaries therefore decided they would have their own meeting in 1916, the so-called *Panama Congress.* Here they decried the perversion of Christianity in the Roman Catholic Church: it had not learned anything from the Reformation. Its clergy was still languishing in the medieval framework of ideas. In other words, Protestants had every right to missionize among the lost sheep of Roman Catholicism.

There also appears a lengthy listing of economic interests in the midst of a mission report of the Panama Congress. For example, in the preceding decade, Latin American trade had increased from $2 billion to $3 billion. It was expected to increase to $5 billion within another ten years. The United States had the largest share in trade, if one considered

Latin America as a whole. If one focused on South America only, Great Britain and Germany were the major trade partners. In any case, with its vast resources, Latin America could some day dominate the world market. Once industrialization would pick up speed, there would be no limits to possibilities of transforming the world.

> During this period of world transformation which is just ahead of us, the old order will give way to the new. The people and their institutions will be plastic; and the men who come to build railways, open mines, set up machinery, establish electric plants, and organize industries will be far more numerous than the missionaries.[9]

The point is: Missions participated in the total mentality of the enterprise from the North. People and institutions becoming "plastic" (then meaning open to change) sounds like a ludicrous prophecy from today's point of view. On first reading one might think that the *Panama Congress* papers might be referring to "natives" to be served by missions. Not so. What the *Panama Congress* missionaries are worrying about are the "young men who for the most part compose the North American colonies found in the large cities of the southern continent" who "have usually had excellent professional training and are of more than average ability." They should have moral equipment equal to their intellectual capacities. For what? To make their transition to an industrial society in Latin America more believable and also more effective.

Now all this happens to be argued in awe of the great corporations who are industrializing South America: "Whether the great corporations which are developing the resources of South America would call for the services of such young men cannot be demonstrated without actual test, but we may reasonably expect that open-eyed businessmen will recognize a good thing when they see it." And then comes the punch line: "Some of the Englishmen and North Americans in control of great concessions are Christian men who would be quick to recognize character as a good business asset."[10]

We do not want to underestimate the value of business and Christians in business. But when we hear of big corporations developing the vast resources of South America as a foil of a missionary endeavor assisting this development, we need to doubt the "Christian" nature of missions. The Peter Berger thrust in the direction of capitalism has formidable historical precedent. We just did not as yet pay attention to it theologically.

2. *Methodist Work in Peru as Case Study*

When we turn our attention to the Methodist mission in Peru, we can observe a great drive toward education; for a long time the focus was almost exclusively on Methodist schools. In terms of the overall North American missionary drive, it was integrated into the efforts of great corporations from the North developing the resources of Latin America. Part of this development was capital formation. So, David Martin matter-of-factly observes that the "arrival of American Methodism was therefore parallel to the arrival of American capital."[11]

That was 1889.

> Methodist work in Peru over the following two generations focused on social transformation. Just as in Mexico, Methodist schools offered a social alternative and embraced quite ambitious ideas of moral and intellectual renovation. . . . The Methodist schools aimed at the newly influential middle classes, but also provided education for workers. What they offered was a business and commercial competence allied to a strong emphasis on punctuality, discipline and truthfulness, as well as access to English. They also offered an advanced pedagogy and a progressive curriculum for women.[12]

One might say that in major respects the very successful movement had spent its creativity within two generations. After that we find consolidation and protection of the astonishing pioneer achievements. Looked at from today, even the consolidation and the protection gradually became questionable: "Methodism is almost everywhere in difficulties, at least in the developed world and in Latin America"[13]—that is, as David Martin sees it.

Why is it so important to ponder this history? There was a time when Methodism in North America was expanding. But it was expanding in the direction of counting membership figures, including, missions and members in foreign lands. It was building the salvation-institution (*Heilsanstalt*). Was it at the same time already losing its character? There is this strange Jesus-word: "You cannot serve God and mammon" (Matt 6:24). It does not mean even in Jesus' own life the elimination of money from the circle of discipleship. Someone in the group of disciples carried the purse for the group. Money retained its practical usefulness as legal tender in selling and buying.

Serving mammon obviously happens in varied ways. In missions in Latin America it apparently meant also making the mission stations almost totally dependent on money from *el Norte*. The issue here is not money as such, but the mind-frame that goes along with money. According to the major treatise of the Methodist mission in Peru, Rosa del Carmen Bruno-Jofré, *Methodist Education in Peru: Social Gospel, Politics, and American Ideological Penetration, 1888–1930* (1988), there is a peculiar mentality that makes for the distinctive pattern of Peruvian Methodism. It fits perfectly into the *Panama Congress* framework of 1916. At the outset of a brief overview of the Methodist mission in Peru, Bruno-Jofré makes a few summary points:

> In principle the Methodist teachings in Peru were addressed to everyone, without regard to social conditions, and within an atmosphere of "brotherhood." But the details of Mission practice show that the idea of "brotherhood" was not free from class distinctions and political choices. During the first thirty years of existence (1890 to 1920), the Mission, in its pursuit of prestige and influence, assiduously cultivated the dominant classes, including semi-feudal landowners.[14]

Entry "into good homes and higher classes"[15] was part of the goal of the Methodist preacher. In the sociopolitical atmosphere of the country in those days, "Methodist missionaries in Peru found an ideological space to enable them to play a bourgeois-democratic role."[16] In summing up the period of the founders, 1890–1920, we are told: "In fact, the democratic role the Mission was able to play was determined by both the uneven and combined character of the Peruvian socio-economic formation and by the missionaries' democratic conceptions, which, in spite of their reformist content, were not in conflict with imperialism."[17]

Throughout this time a very deep religiosity developed that undergirded the Methodist lifestyle. There are two large high schools in Lima that even now show the pervasiveness of this religiosity in the lifestyle of its students and teachers. But as a whole, the general judgment of David Martin also covers the present situation. "Methodism is almost everywhere in difficulties, at least in the developed world and in Latin America."[18]

We need to see as in a mirror what we have done to Latin Americans in missions. In some respects this mirror is the key to the insight into our own dilemma today that brings forth the will to change. There is of course the awesome gap between what we assume or pretend a history to have been and what it actually was. Bruno-Jofré writes her story to a large extent in terms of the PR materials the missionaries put out for all the world to pay attention to, but little in terms of what happened to actual folk who were on the receiving end of the missionaries' ambition. A Lutheran missionary in Lima said to me, as we were discussing this "reality gap": the mission boards at home will put out any propaganda you send them and often will not examine what the actual situation is, just so they have something to print—which in turn will bring in money.

In Peru, Methodism was the pioneering Protestant church. It began in 1889 with the American Bible Society asking Francisco Penzotti to develop an agency there and to expand the work to Ecuador, Bolivia, and Chile. When he arrived in Callao, the harbor of Lima, he organized a small church for Spanish-speaking people. This brought an immediate clash with Roman Catholicism. The chapel, which had been offered Penzotti for use by the British community, was threatened to be blown up by Catholic priests. So an old warehouse was restored, and on August 31, 1889, a first preaching service was held with 170 people attending.

From the beginning it was rough sledding for the small Methodist mission. "In January 1889, when Penzotti went to Arequipa to sell Bibles, the local Bishop accused him of introducing immoral books, and personally ordered that he (along with two Peruvian associates) be arrested. He remained in jail, without a charge being laid, for ninety days."[19] Upon returning to Callao he was again jailed at the behest of the church, staying in prison from July 26, 1890, to March 28, 1891, the date the Supreme Court judged that "private" worship could take place in Peru without fear of arrest. Penzotti returned to Buenos Aires, and an American missionary, Dr. Thomas B. Wood, took his place. He came from Argentina where he had been the founder in 1889 of what today is the Methodist Theological Seminary (ISEDET). With him the creation of Methodist schools in Peru began while the struggle for civil rights continued.

The development of the Methodist mission was relatively slow when it comes to numbers. It spread from Lima and Callao on the coast north and south as well as into the Sierra and even into the eastern jungle. In 1908 there were 499 members; in 1909, 637; in 1921, 797; in 1923, 1,228; and in 1933, 1,368. Just what happened during this time to the people becoming Methodists? There is the story of the simple people who found Christ as their personal Savior, who became active as free agents in the church, assuming responsibilities they had never known laypeople to have. Today the number is 2,300, with all family members 7,000, according to one official record. They are people like human beings everywhere, wonderful, terrifying, loving, and searching. But then there is the management, the people who run things from the top. And unfortunately that is what happened during most of the "official" history. One of the great challenges is to find out just what the people themselves understood to have happened to them when they became Methodist. What shaped their way of life?

According to Bruno-Jofré, from the very beginning the Methodist mission in Peru was dependent on the money-givers from the North. But in the cultural atmosphere of the 1920s, an anti-imperialist trend developed with some insistence on an "autonomous church." Since the missionaries figured that the Methodist church of Peru could not do work on its own,[20] there was never any effort to train indigenous leadership, so that the missionaries at some point could have turned over their work to qualified natives. A major problem was the lack of graduate studies in theology, so that trained pastors and eventually native seminary teachers would be forthcoming.

In 1922 there were fourteen missionaries (not counting wives). As in many mission fields, the missionary salaries were high, while remuneration for services rendered in the church by natives was low. In this way the missionaries were bent on creating "new human beings."[21] It was not altogether clear what that meant. Most leading Peruvian converts seemed to admire American achievements. The worship of progress intensified the sense of backwardness.

In their self-understanding the Methodists thought of themselves after half a century as the leading force among the so-called Evangelicals in Peru as well as the pioneers of Protestantism. Already at that time, however, one of the leading Peruvian thinkers, José Carlos Mariátegui, observed: "Protestantism does not penetrate Latin America as a spiritual and religious power, but through its social services (YMCA, Methodist missions in the Sierra, etc.). This and other signs indicate that it has exhausted its possibilities for normal expansion."[22]

Obviously in those days the wave of Pentecostalism had not spilled over Latin America. A lot of things were still in a state of flux. The complexities of the Social Gospel had not been grasped very clearly. It was a type of "discourse" in mission reports, but hardly a pervasive influence among the people of the pew.

The challenge is to understand from the Peruvian Methodist Missions a basic dilemma of the missionary approach, and to answer a question that can be applied to every Latin American missionary situation: How was it possible that North American Methodism allowed itself to create a dependency syndrome in Latin America—a "colony church"?[23]

The North probably created a "colony church" because it was a colony church itself. There is a certain culture mentality that goes along with being within the U.S.A. in "colonial" dependence on European thought, besides initially having been part of thirteen colonies. I became aware of it fully only when I began to read the reports of the *Panama Congress* of 1916. It is awesome to think that hardly any Latin Americans participated, mainly North American missionaries deciding on Latin American missions "business." But more awesome yet is that North Americans thought they could transplant their mentality to Latin America and thus do the Lord's work.

Rosa del Carmen Bruno-Jofré points out that the Methodist mission in Peru "transplanted not only a formal organization but also a formalized language and pre-established forms of communication for use among the members and with God."[24] But that was only a derivative of what already had happened in North America when the United States still had been colonies: the rite of worship, the ecclesiastical organizational expression, and the discourse were transplants from Europe, where they had been part of a basic pattern of meaning that as such was not transplanted to these shores. People had lived for their king, their queen, some feudal baron, some duke or bishop. In the States increasingly individualistic "money making" took the void left by an absence of this ancient pattern of loyalty.

The notion of making money, and making more and more money, became a kind of openly celebrated subcurrent in the North American denominations. By the time missions began, the principle became transferred to the mentality of missionaries and mission recipients alike, so that the measure of progress in the colony church was found less in the spiritual growth of the congregations, and more in money that could be wrested from the mother church for the annual budget, detailed in educational, medical, or agricultural projects.

3. The Money Virus

As there is a computer virus, there is also a "money virus." The problem is whether missions today are still missions or whether they have widely turned into money management.

A little over a decade ago the unofficial United Methodist magazine

Good News began to question United Methodist mission enterprises. It was also the time when the Mission Society appeared on the horizon. The issue has been with us for a long time. If I understand it rightly, the bone of contention between official and unofficial mission boards is more the way mission money is spent than any notion that there might be too much "obsession" with money.

When the ideology of monetarism infects our culture, it changes us imperceptibly. That is what I mean by the money virus. Money actually changes us to be different people, another type of human being. I was helped in these reflections by Jonathan J. Bonk's work.[25] Recently, in connection with the globalization efforts of the Association of Theological Schools, Bonk quoted John Kenneth Galbraith: "Nothing so gives the illusion of intelligence as personal association with large sums of money."[26] I rephrased that to say: "Nothing so gives the illusion of mission success as personal association with large sums of money." Somehow Bonk wonders whether in the process a change of personality takes place,[27] so that we measure all things and all people in terms of money.

A 1983 *Good News* piece, "Missions Derailed: A Special Report on the United Methodist General Board of Global Ministries," authored by James S. Robb, begins with charging that instead of marching forward to win the world for Christ, the Board is engaged in a retreat from its historic tasks. We have not always been frank about the money angle. The Board's first annual Financial Disclosure report was published in 1981. Since then there was ample opportunity to go after what Robb calls "one of the largest flagships of Protestantism." He tries to show how and why the Board is failing in its assignment and "has become derailed from its mission."[28] During these past ten years the Mission Society took hold of what it understood to be some of the neglected tasks of Methodist mission. We now have Methodist mission "competition" in several areas of the world. The Board is in the tedious process of reorganization and, as I understand it, of making itself much smaller. Be that as it may, my suggestion is that mission is the key to rethinking the history of Methodism and culture at the point where the shoe hurts: our blindness to the function of money in today's culture and how we are absorbed by it as churches.

Expenditures of the Board for 1981 were $63,761,027; income was $70,395,456. The charge against the Board is not that it is spending beyond its means, but that its allocation of the monies is misplaced.

Robb underscores that the monies are to be used for a variety of causes, according to the *Discipline*. But he finds that United Methodism is using more money on the New York home staff than on all missionaries overseas and the United States combined. The basic question for him is: "How well is the Board doing in balancing its vital and traditional role of sending missionaries and evangelizing the world with its more recently acquired duties of dialogue and social transformation?"[29] Robb figured that only 67.4 percent of the total budget went to missionary support and grants whereas in the same category, for example, the Southern Baptists achieved 88 percent. Here he scores the actual promotion of an "enemy" ideology: "Socialism [as] the truly Christian economic system."[30] All of this had been explained in terms of a 1980 mandate of the General Conference that it is important to "engage in building societies where full human potential is liberated."[31] But Robb believes that the Board has adopted a liberation theology that wants to create a new kind of missionary serving "those who are at the levers of economic and social affairs."[32] Robb's conclusion is very direct: "So we've come full circle as a church. No longer do we send missionaries to preach conversion to the lost. Rather, we should send troubleshooters armed with economic redemption."[33]

It has been heart-wrenching for a decade to follow the debate. The issue for me is not too large an overhead of the Board's expenses, but the person of the missionary, whether the Board's kind of missionary, or Robb's kind. Both have been infected by the money virus.

The bottom line here is the issue of Christian *anthropology*. Who is the human being today? The money-being. In industrialized societies we have money-multiplication. In the process a quantity leap becomes a quality leap. Now money is something "inside" us, a power that determines our identity.

Robb warns that in United Methodism we are expected to arm ourselves with economic redemption.[34] The economic, in my view, should not be left behind or forgotten—it *is* the bone of contention—in the sense that the money-being is the economic being, the consumer (Latin, *homo economicus*). We are completely market-directed beings.

Missions and Money. Our neoliberal economic systems, while not having broken down as yet de facto, have already broken down spiritually. Missions are the firing line on which the spiritual breakdown is being tested. Much of this Geiger testing has been done in Jonathan J. Bonk, *Missions and Money.* The general tendency today is to excoriate the colonialism and imperialism the missionaries were party to, including high salaries. Bonk is adamant in suggesting that we had better look at the mission dynamics as a mirror of our own home base:

> Statistically, the West is one of the least encouraging areas of the world, manifesting neither the burgeoning numerical growth of sub-Saharan African Christianity nor the dynamic activity of Latin American Christians. Can it be that our personal affluence is the source of this myopia? . . . What we are told is that the materially blessed members of the Church of Laodicea were blind to their own spiritual destitution, and were unaware that they themselves constituted a mission field in desperate need of Christ.[35]

The right access to the dilemma we are facing with money is to see our affluence as sending church. The priority for "Methodism and Culture" is to do a scholarly job on the function of money in the church.

When Bonk mentions an upsurge of interest in missions among young people in the West, he points to Intervarsity and Campus Crusade in order to say that interest of these young people "will not be enough to reverse the creeping impotence of the Western churches. Unless these young men and women are willing to renounce the privilege and security that have come to be the hallmark of the Western way of doing mission, there can be no reversal."[36] The appeal here is still to the moral hero to perform a giant moral feat in renouncing privilege and security. Scholarship, however, needs to insist on an analysis of societal structures so that we can work on a more just distribution of resources.

What we are up against are not socialist ideologies, but the realities of the global village and the United Nations. *The Human Development Report 1992* for the United Nations Development Program (UNDP) makes a major point:

> For the first time in human history, the world is close to creating a single, unified global system. But an agreed and participatory system of global governance remains a distant dream. This has left an urgent and disturbing question wandering unanswered round the corridors of power: In a period of rapid economic globalization, who will protect the interests of the world's poor?[37]

If we understand that today "mission begins at home" (like "charity begins at home"), then we need to see that "global governance" becomes part of it. But it is a fact that there are "no development institutions managing the new integrated global economy—much less doing so democratically in the interests of the world's people."[38]

We need to bring down the implications of the International Monetary Fund (IMF), the World Bank, and GATT to the local scene. Not one of these institutions is adequately fulfilling its assignment. It is part of God's mission that this be done. Too many people are dying and too much of the environment is destroyed because of gigantic profits on all sides. The financial markets have become transnational and have been deregulated. There is mobile capital around that escapes taxation by leaving the country and turning itself into more capital in some hide-away bank. Ulrich Duchrow suggests that Germany in 1992 lost at least $40 billion that way. Speculations on the financial markets are not subject to taxes.[39] Many of our banks push the interest of debtor nations higher and higher when loans are renegotiated. Obviously there is the vast increasing debt, now for the States as well as countries like Peru. The States as the great creditor nation has become the debtor nation, and in this richest nation on earth, "an estimated 20 percent of all children are defined as living in poverty."[40]

Mutualization. In the "Concept Paper on Structural Proposal" of October 19, 1993 (for the General Board of Global Ministries' restructuring), it is suggested that there be "annual conference dialogue focused on missional concerns, mission education models to connect local church initiatives with the General Board."[41] This already is happening in the North Carolina conference in regard to Peru. The Board document stresses a "shift to a more facilitating style," involving a "move in emphasis from mission management to mission facilitation."[42] This belongs to the heart of the matter. It calls for personal involvement on both sides, the former sending church and the former mission church. It means mutualization. There is nothing more urgent than people from a poor country and people from a rich country to meet and to decide how "available money" needs to be used for the common good. Beginning in 1961 the new Division on World Mission and Evangelism of the World Council of Churches initiated a process for joint action in mission. The point was to find real and effective use of the resources of all parties concerned, poor as well as rich. "This concept of joint action for mission has focused the continuing difficult discussion between rich churches, with their traditional mission boards or societies, and the churches which emerged from their missionary activities. Attempts at promoting the ecumenical sharing of resources have so far produced meagre results. . . . The 'implementation of partnership in obedience' is still hardly a reality."[43] The time has come to make good on partnership in obedience.

This insight of Philip A. Potter, former General Secretary of the World Council of Churches, clinches the core argument about money we are facing in the churches between the South and the North, also in United Methodism. This is exactly where we are between the North Carolina Conference of The United Methodist Church and the Iglesia Metodista del Perú. United Methodists need to understand what it means to have moved from "having missions" to "being in mission," and from *talking* about global church to *being* a global church, as the *Concept Paper* of the Board of Global Ministries suggests. There is a specific goal envisioned: "The reorganization will enable United Methodists and their congregations to personify the global church in thinking and action through more direct involvement with Christian witness and communities of faith around the world."[44]

The Church as Mission. The core of our culture is money; everything else is footnote. Money has taken over many attributes of a religion:

> Like a religion it binds together different parts of the world, providing the means by which people and nations judge each other. Like a religion it demands great faith, a huge priesthood with rituals and incantations that few ordinary people understand. Like missionaries, the bankers and brokers travel the still unconverted parts of the world, bringing the deserts and jungles into the same system of values, seeking to convert still more tribes to their own faith in credit, interest rates, and the sacred bottom line. Today it is bank managers rather than priests who are the guardians of people's secrets and confessionals. . . . The old language of religion is transmuted into the language of money: redemption means the future repayment of government stock; creed means credit; miracle means high economic growth; forgiveness means forgiveness of debt and is transformed from a virtue to a vice.[45]

As the culture is threatened by money, the church is threatened. The sheer multiplication of money turns everything in culture into a commodity, including human beings and God. Profit is the very opposite of the gift character of nature and history. The Sacred Spirit is at work in nature and history to assure the sacredness of all beings. In this sense the ecumenical church for many years has spoken of the *missio Dei*. The story of this renewal has been told in David J. Bosch, *Transforming Mission: Paradigm Shifts in Theology of Mission* (1991). "It is not the church which 'undertakes' mission; it is the *missio Dei,* which constitutes the church."[46] We are drawn into God's own missionizing work of destroying the idols, today especially the idolatry of money. There is already a divine work going on that antecedes our culture query. It gives us the critical leverage to find our way back into the sacred church: "The mission of the church needs constantly to be renewed and re-conceived."[47] We will need to go through the needle's eye of working together with the members of a mission church to get in touch with the *missio Dei.*[48] Since the Lilly Project on Methodism and Culture is carried on under the aegis of theological education at Duke, one of our questions will be: In a period of rapid economic globalization, who protects the interests of theological education? The second question has to put it differently: "In a period of rapid economic globalization, who protects the interests of the poor?"[49]

Contributors

Michael G. Cartwright is chair of the Department of Philosophy and Religion at the University of Indianapolis. He is an ordained elder in the Western Pennsylvania Conference of The United Methodist Church and holds the M.Div. and Ph.D. degrees from Duke University. In addition to his scholarly contributions on the use of Scripture in Christian ethics and the interpretive traditions of the historic black church, Cartwright has written essays on American Methodist ecclesiology and the evolution of American Methodist disciplinary practice in pan-Methodist denominations.

Frederick Herzog was Professor of Systematic Theology at Duke Divinity School from 1960 until his death in 1995. His books include *Understanding God, Liberation Theology, Justice Church,* and *God-Walk: Liberation Shaping Dogmatics.* An ordained minister of the United Church of Christ, Dr. Herzog served on UCC and World Council of Churches commissions working on concrete ecumenical union, doctrinal renewal, and globalization of theological education. He was a member of the Oxford Institute of Methodist Theological Studies.

L. Gregory Jones is Dean of Duke University Divinity School. He is an ordained elder in the Western North Carolina Conference of The United Methodist Church. The author of three books and numerous articles, Dr. Jones is coeditor of *Modern Theology.* His most recent book is *Embodying Forgiveness.* He has contributed editorials, reviews, and other articles to popular publications, among them the "Faith Matters" series in *The Christian Century.*

Jack A. Keller, Jr., is Director of Academic, Bible, Professional, and Reference Resources and Project Director of the twelve-volume *New Interpreter's Bible* at The United Methodist Publishing House in Nashville, Tennessee. A graduate of the University of Puget Sound and Claremont School of Theology, he holds the Ph.D. from Vanderbilt University. Dr. Keller is the author of several articles in academic and professional journals and of numerous church publications.

Randy L. Maddox holds the Paul T. Walls Chair of Wesleyan Theology at Seattle Pacific University. An alumnus of Northwest Nazarene College and of Nazarene Theological Seminary, he earned the Ph.D. from Emory University. Dr. Maddox is an elder in the Dakotas

Conference of The United Methodist Church. He is the author of *Responsible Grace: John Wesley's Practical Theology*, a co-author of *Wesley and the Quadrilateral*, and contributed to and edited *Aldersgate Reconsidered* and *Rethinking Wesley's Theology for Contemporary Methodism*. He is co-chair of the Wesleyan Studies Group of the American Academy of Religion and General Editor of Kingswood Books.

J. Steven O'Malley is J. T. Seamands Professor of Methodist History at Asbury Theological Seminary. A church historian with special interest in German-American religious traditions, he is a graduate of Yale University and holds the Ph.D. from Drew University. Dr. O'Malley has published four books and numerous journal articles in German and English. He coedits the Pietist and Wesleyan Studies Series for Scarecrow/University Press of America, and has been a frequent lecturer and preacher in Europe as well as in the U.S.

Bruce W. Robbins is General Secretary of the General Commission on Christian Unity and Interreligious Affairs of The United Methodist Church, based in New York City. He is an ordained elder in the Troy Conference. Dr. Robbins holds a Ph.D. from Southern Methodist University. He has written extensively on matters pertaining to the church in Latin America and Christian-Jewish relations, and is highly regarded in the field of ecumenical theology.

A. Gregory Schneider is Professor of Behavioral Science at Pacific Union College in the Napa Valley region of California. He is the author of *The Way of the Cross Leads Home: The Domestication of American Methodism* and has written numerous articles on Wesleyan Holiness movements in the United States. He earned his Ph.D. from the University of Chicago Divinity School in the field of Religion and Psychological Studies.

Douglas M. Strong is Professor of the History of Christianity at Wesley Theological Seminary in Washington, D.C. He is a graduate of Houghton College and holds the M.Div. and Ph.D. from Princeton Theological Seminary. An elder in the Baltimore-Washington Conference, Dr. Strong's scholarly interests center on the history of Christianity in America. He is the author of *They Walked in the Spirit: Personal Faith and Social Action in America* and *Perfectionist Politics: Abolitionism and the Religious Tensions of American Democracy*.

Karen B. Westerfield Tucker is Assistant Professor of Liturgics at the Duke University Divinity School. She is a graduate of Emory and Henry

College and Duke University, and holds the Ph.D. from the University of Notre Dame. An elder in the Illinois Great Rivers Conference of The United Methodist Church, Dr. Westerfield Tucker is an assistant editor for the ecumenical and international journal *Studia Liturgica*. She commissioned and compiled *The Sunday Service of the Methodists: Twentieth-Century Worship in Worldwide Methodism* (Abingdon/Kingswood, 1996), and is the author of *American Methodist Worship,* forthcoming from Oxford University Press.

David Lowes Watson is Director of the Office of Pastoral Formation for the Nashville Episcopal Area of The United Methodist Church. He was formerly Professor of Congregational Life and Mission at Wesley Theological Seminary. His six books include *Accountable Discipleship* and *The Early Methodist Class Meeting: Its Origins and Significance.* He has written numerous scholarly articles and contributes regularly to various denominational publications of The United Methodist Church. He is a graduate of Oxford University and Eden Theological Seminary, and holds the Ph.D. from Duke University.

Elliott Wright, an ordained elder in the Tennessee Conference of The United Methodist Church, is currently affiliated with the United Methodist Board of Global Ministries in New York City. He holds M.Div. and D.Min. degrees from Vanderbilt University. Dr. Wright is author or coauthor of seven books, including *The Big Little School* (with Robert W. Lynn), a history of the American Sunday school. He has written extensively on the issue of religion in American public schools under Lilly Endowment grants.

Editors

Dennis M. Campbell is the Headmaster of Woodberry Forest School in Woodberry Forest, Virginia. He was Dean of The Divinity School and Professor of Theology at Duke University, in Durham, North Carolina, from 1982 until 1997. Professor Campbell is the author of *Authority and the Renewal of American Theology, The Yoke of Obedience: The Meaning of Ordination in Methodism,* and *Who Will Go for Us? An Invitation to Ordained Ministry,* as well as other books and articles dealing with theology and ethics. He is President of the University Senate of The United Methodist Church, is past President of the Association of United Methodist Theological Schools, and has been a delegate to three General and Jurisdictional Conferences. Dr. Campbell is widely known for his work in moral education and for his analysis of educational institutions and their work in the formation of character. He is codirector of the United Methodism and American Culture project.

William B. Lawrence is Senior Pastor, Metropolitan Memorial United Methodist Church, Washington, D.C. Previously he was Professor of the Practice of Christian Ministry and Associate Director of the J. M. Ormond Center for Research, Planning, and Development at The Divinity School, Duke University. He has served as the project associate for this study of United Methodism and American Culture. His recent publications include *Sundays in New York: Pulpit Theology at the Crest of the Protestant Mainstream, 1930–1955.* A graduate of Duke, Union Theological Seminary in New York, and Drew, he served as a United Methodist pastor and district superintendent.

Russell E. Richey is Associate Dean of Academic Programs and Professor of Church History at The Divinity School, Duke University, in Durham, North Carolina. Dr. Richey is a member of the Historical Society of The United Methodist Church and the American Society of Church History. He is the author of *The Methodist Conference in America* and coauthor with James Kirby and Kenneth Rowe of *The Methodists.* Dr. Richey is codirector of United Methodism and American Culture.

Notes

1. For a recent study see Richard P. Heitzenrater, *Wesley and the People Called Methodists* (Nashville: Abingdon Press, 1995).

2. For this reason we chose connectionalism as the organizing theme for the first volume of this series. See Russell E. Richey, Dennis M. Campbell, and William B. Lawrence, eds., *Connectionalism: Ecclesiology, Mission, and Identity* (Nashville: Abingdon Press, 1997).

3. See also Randy L. Maddox, *Responsible Grace: John Wesley's Practical Theology* (Nashville: Kingswood Books, 1994).

4. For full scholarly analysis of the controversial ordinations, and my theological explanation of it, see Dennis M. Campbell, *The Yoke of Obedience: The Meaning of Ordination in Methodism* (Nashville: Abingdon Press, 1988).

5. For primary documentation see *The Journal of the Rev. John Wesley, A.M.*, ed. Nehemiah Curnock (London: Epworth Press, 1938), vol. 1, 418; vol. 3, 232; vol. 7, 15-16, 23.

6. *The Letters of the Rev. John Wesley, A.M.*, ed. John Telford (London: Epworth Press, 1931), vol. 7, 21.

7. For a helpful study of Wesley on these matters, see Ted A. Campbell, *John Wesley and Christian Antiquity: Religious Vision and Cultural Change* (Nashville: Kingswood Books, 1991).

8. For a useful study of American Methodism, see Russell E. Richey, Kenneth E. Rowe, and Jean Miller Schmidt, *Perspectives on American Methodism* (Nashville: Kingswood Books, 1993).

9. See Thomas A. Langford, *Practical Divinity: Readings in Wesleyan Theology* (Nashville: Abingdon Press, 1999), vol. 2.

10. Janice Love, "Is United Methodism a World Church?" in Russell E. Richey, William B. Lawrence, and Dennis M. Campbell, eds., *Questions for the Twenty-First-Century Church*, vol. 4, *United Methodism and American Culture* (Nashville: Abingdon Press, 1999), 258-68.

11. *The Works of John Wesley* (Nashville: Abingdon Press, 1984–). The Wesley Works Project, now based at Duke University, is called the Bicentennial Edition, and will ultimately include the entirety of Wesley's sermons, journal, letters, theological writings, and occasional works.

12. For a thoughtful analysis see Robert E. Cushman, "Church Doctrinal Standards Today," *Religion in Life* 44 (Winter 1975): 401-11.

13. Ted A. Campbell, "The 'Wesleyan Quadrilateral': The Story of a Modern Methodist Myth," *Methodist History* 29 (January 1991): 87-95.

14. See, e.g., Jerry L. Walls, *The Problem of Pluralism* (Wilmore, Ky.: Bristol Books, 1986).

15. This whole matter of the 1972 and 1988 Disciplinary statements is analyzed at length in a collection of essays edited by Thomas A. Langford, *Doctrine and Theology in The United Methodist Church* (Nashville: Kingswood Books, 1991).

16. For a recent study of Baptism, see Gayle Carlton Felton, *This Gift of Water: The Practice and Theology of Baptism Among Methodists in America* (Nashville: Abingdon Press, 1992).

17. John B. Cobb, Jr., *Grace and Responsibility: A Wesleyan Theology for Today* (Nashville: Abingdon Press, 1995); Theodore W. Jennings, Jr., *Good News to the Poor: John Wesley's Evangelical Economics* (Nashville: Abingdon Press, 1990).

18. See, e.g., David C. Steinmetz, *Memory and Mission: Theological Reflections on the Christian Past* (Nashville: Abingdon Press, 1988).

19. E.g., William J. Abraham, *Waking from Doctrinal Amnesia: The Healing of Doctrine in The United Methodist Church* (Nashville: Abingdon Press, 1995).

20. A useful discussion of some of these matters is found in Thomas Edward Frank, *Polity, Practice, and the Mission of The United Methodist Church* (Nashville: Abingdon Press, 1997).

NOTES TO AN "UNTAPPED INHERITANCE"

1. See Robert Bellah et al., *Habits of the Heart: Individualism and Commitment in American Life* (New York: Harper, 1985); and Reginald W. Bibby, *Mosaic Madness: The Poverty and Potential of Life in Canada* (Toronto: Stoddart, 1990).

2. Bellah et al. had suggested this possibility in their first book. It is much more central to their sequel: *The Good Society* (New York: Alfred A. Knopf, 1991), esp. 16-17, 217-18. See also Parker Palmer, *The Company of Strangers: Christians and the Renewal of America's Public Life* (New York: Crossroad, 1983).

3. See the analyses of Wade Clark Roof and William McKinney, *American Mainline Religion* (New Brunswick, N.J.: Rutgers University Press, 1987); Robert Wuthnow, *The Restructuring of American Religion* (Princeton, N.J.: Princeton

University Press, 1988); and Philip E. Hammond, *Religion and Personal Autonomy: The Third Disestablishment* (Columbia, S.C.: University of South Carolina, 1992).

4. Cf. Steve Tipton's chapter (dealing with United Methodism), "The Public Church," in Bellah et al., *The Good Society*, 179-219; Reginald W. Bibby, *Fragmented Gods. The Poverty and Potential of Religion in Canada* (Toronto: Irwin Publishing, 1987); and Robert Wuthnow, *Sharing the Journey: Support Groups and America's New Quest for Community* (New York: Free Press, 1994), 340, 360-66.

5. The role of character in human actions has been broadly acknowledged in recent work in ethics; cf. the overview in Terence R. Anderson, *Walking the Way: Christian Ethics as a Guide* (Toronto: United Church Publishing House, 1993). For one Methodist application of this insight to the mission of the church, see Stanley Hauerwas and William Willimon, *Resident Aliens* (Nashville: Abingdon Press, 1989).

6. For some recent complaints about the need for greater theological formation of laity (and clergy!) in United Methodism, see Earl Hunt, *A Bishop Speaks His Mind* (Nashville: Abingdon Press, 1987), 83-101; James W. Holsinger, Jr., and Evelyn Laycock, *Awaken the Giant: 28 Prescriptions for Reviving the United Methodist Church* (Nashville: Abingdon Press, 1989), 122, 142; and William J. Abraham, "The Revitalization of United Methodist Doctrine and the Renewal of Theology," in James Logan, ed., *Theology and Evangelism in the Wesleyan Heritage* (Nashville: Kingswood Books, 1994), 35-50.

7. For a survey of these calls and discussion of the characteristics of such a theology, see Randy L. Maddox, "The Recovery of Theology as a Practical Discipline," *Theological Studies* 51 (1990): 650-72.

8. Randy L. Maddox, "John Wesley—Practical Theologian," *Wesleyan Theological Journal* 23 (1988): 122-47.

9. For more details and documentation of the following summary, see Maddox, "Recovery of Theology."

10. For documentation of this summary of Anglicanism, see Maddox, "John Wesley—Practical Theologian."

11. Demonstrating this is central to Randy L. Maddox, *Responsible Grace: John Wesley's Practical Theology* (Nashville: Kingswood Books, 1994).

12. Letter to Charles Wesley (25 March 1772), in *Letters of the Rev. John Wesley, A.M.*, ed. John Telford (London: Epworth, 1931), 5:314. See also "Large Minutes," Q. 23, *Works* (Jackson), 8:309. These definitions of the role of clergy must be read in light of Wesley's therapeutic understanding of what "salvation" involved; cf. Maddox, *Responsible Grace*, 141ff.

13. See his "Address to the Clergy," *Works* (Jackson), 10:480-500, esp. p. 482.

14. Cf. 1765 *Minutes*, Q. 24 (p. 51); 1781 *Minutes*, Q. 25 (p. 151); 1782 *Minutes*, Q. 34 (p. 158); and 1788 *Minutes*, Q. 22 (p. 224) in *Minutes of the Methodist Conferences, from the First, Held in London, by the Late Rev. John Wesley, A.M., in the Year 1744*, vol. 1 (London: John Mason, 1862).

15. For discussion of the question of how much theological training Fletcher actually received in Geneva, see Patrick Philip Streiff, *Jean Guillaume de la Flêchère* (Frankfurt am Main: Peter Lang, 1984), 44-45.

16. For a more detailed survey of developments in the EA and UBC, see William H. Naumann, "Theology and German-American Evangelicalism: The Role of Theology in the Church of the United Brethren in Christ and the Evangelical Association" (Ph.D. thesis, Yale University, 1966).

17. See respectively, *The Journal and Letters of Francis Asbury*, ed. Elmer T. Clark (Nashville: Abingdon, 1958), 1:263; and *The Doctrines and Discipline of the Methodist Episcopal Church in America. With Explanatory Notes by Thomas Coke and Francis Asbury* (Philadelphia: Henry Tuckniss, 1798; reprint: Rutland, Vt.: Academy Books, 1979), 7.

18. Cf. the 1787 *Discipline* of the MEC, pp. 22, 44 (reprinted in *Methodist Disciplines, 1785–1789* [Nashville: Abingdon Press, 1992]).

19. See in this regard Richard Heitzenrater, *Mirror and Memory* (Nashville: Kingswood Books, 1989), 189-204.

20. See the quote from the 1892 debate in Edwin Voigt, "Worship in American Methodism," *Encyclopedia of World Methodism* (Nashville: United Methodist Publishing House, 1974), 2606-7; and Charles Giffin, "More Liturgy or More Life?" *Methodist Review* 84 (1902): 71-79. Thomas Summers introduced an abridgement of the *Sunday Service* in the MECS in 1867, but it was not widely used. For a detailed study of this period, see William Nash Wade, "A History of Public Worship in the Methodist Episcopal Church and Methodist Episcopal Church, South, from 1784 to 1905" (Ph.D. thesis, University of Notre Dame, 1981).

21. E.g., Daniel Goodsell, "Is It a Good or a Bad Inheritance?" *Methodist Review* 85 (1903): 177-92.

22. Cf. the helpful historical surveys in James F. White, "Methodist Worship," in *Protestant Worship: Traditions in Transition* (Louisville, Ky.: Westminster/John Knox, 1989), 150-70; and White, "A Short History of American Methodist Service Books," *Doxology* 10 (1993): 30-37.

23. Note, e.g., the reflections of Albert Outler on the decision not to develop an integrated creed in the 1968 merger of the MC and EUB, in *Albert Outler: The Churchman*, ed. Bob Parrott (Anderson, Ind.: Bristol House, 1995), 92, 370, 460ff.

24. Cf. J. Steven Harper, "Wesley's Sermons As Spiritual Formation

Documents," *Methodist History* 26 (1988): 131-38; and Heitzenrater, *Mirror and Memory*, 174-88.

25. Cf. *Methodist Review* 2 (1819): 161-62; and the absence of this section starting with volume 10 (1830). Note: I am following the convention of using *Methodist Review* to refer to the theological journal of the MEC (which had a fluctuating name) and *Methodist Quarterly Review* for the journal of the MECS.

26. *The Methodist Preacher; or, Monthly Sermons from Living Ministers,* vols. 1–4 (1830–33). Shipley Wells Willson describes his purpose for launching the series in 1:iv.

27. Abel Stevens, *Essays on the Preaching Required by the Time and the Best Methods of Obtaining It* (New York: Carlton & Phillips, 1855), see 19-24, 59-60.

28. Daniel P. Kidder, *A Treatise on Homiletics,* rev. ed. (New York: Carlton & Lanahan, 1864), esp. 192, 274, 456. Kidder was on the MEC course of study from 1864 to 1892, and the MPC course from 1880 to 1908.

29. Namely, John A. Kern, *The Ministry to the Congregation: Lectures on Homiletics,* 2nd ed. (New York: W.B. Ketchan, 1897). The motto is on the title page; see also 233. Kern replaced Kidder on the MEC course in 1904 and stayed through 1912. He was on the MECS course from 1898 to 1942.

30. C. M. Bishop, "A Modern Statement of the Doctrine of the Holy Spirit," *Methodist Quarterly Review* 54 (1905): 332-39; see esp. 338.

31. Cf. James O'Kelly's challenge against episcopal authority in *The Author's Apology for Protesting Against the Methodist Episcopal Government* (Richmond, Va.: John Dixon, 1798); and the response in Coke and Asbury's notes appended to the 1798 *Discipline* (which was printed in the very first year of the MEC book concern).

32. Cf. Asa Shinn, *An Essay on the Plan of Salvation* (Baltimore, Md.: Neal, Wills & Cole, 1813); Nathan Bangs, *The Errors of Hopkinsianism* (New York: Totten, 1815); Bangs, *The Reformer Reformed* (New York: Totten, 1818); Willbur Fisk, *Calvinistic Controversy* (New York: Mason & Lane, 1837); Francis Hodgson, *An Examination of the System of New Divinity* (New York: Lane, 1840); Shinn, *On the Benevolence and Rectitude of the Supreme Being* (Philadelphia: James Kay, Jr., & Brother, 1840); Albert Bledsoe, *Theodicy: or, Vindication of the Divine Glory* (New York: Carlton & Porter, 1856); Daniel Denison Whedon, "Arminian View of the Fall and Redemption," *Methodist Review* 43 (1861): 647-66; Whedon, "Doctrines of Methodism," *Bibliotheca Sacra* 19 (1862): 241-74; and Whedon, *The Freedom of the Will* (New York: Carlton & Porter, 1864).

33. The following summary draws on two helpful studies that place Wesley in this context: Robin W. Lovin, "The Physics of True Virtue," in *Wesleyan*

Theology Today, ed. Theodore H. Runyon (Nashville: Kingswood Books, 1985), 264-72; and Isabel Rivers, *Reason, Grace, and Sentiment: A Study of the Language of Religion and Ethics in England, 1660–1780* (Cambridge: University Press, 1991).

34. This point has been demonstrated conclusively by Richard B. Steele, *"Gracious Affections" and "True Virtue" According to Jonathan Edwards and John Wesley* (Metuchen, N.J.: Scarecrow, 1994); and Gregory S. Clapper, *John Wesley on Religious Affections: His Views on Experience and Emotion and Their Role in the Christian Life and Theology* (Metuchen, N.J.: Scarecrow, 1989). For further discussion and documentation of the following summary of Wesley's anthropology, see Maddox, *Responsible Grace,* 65ff.

35. Cf. Thomas Reid, *Essays on the Active Powers of Man* (Edinburgh: John Bell, 1788; reprint, New York: Garland, 1977), 59-60, 75-76, 88, 117-19.

36. The best survey of these debates is Allen C. Guelzo, *Edwards on the Will: A Century of American Theological Debate* (Middleton, Conn.: Wesleyan University Press, 1989).

37. See the explicit appeal to Reid in Shinn, *Plan of Salvation,* 109, 334; and Nathan Bangs, *Letters to Young Ministers of the Gospel, on the Importance and Method of Study* (New York: Bangs and Emory, 1826), 84-85. Bangs even reissued Reid's works through MEC channels: *The Works of Thomas Reid,* 3 vols., ed. Dugald Stewart (New York: Bangs & Mason, 1822).

38. The first clear recognition that Wesley identified the will with the affections, while American Methodist theologians do not, is in Thomas Summers, *Systematic Theology* (Nashville, Tenn.: MECS Publishing House, 1888), 2:66.

39. Cf. Letter to Richard Morgan (15 January 1734), *Works,* 25:369; Sermon 91, "On Charity," § III.12, *Works,* 3:306; and Sermon 120, "The Unity of the Divine Being," § 16, *Works,* 4:66.

40. "Plain Account of the People Called Methodists," § I.2, *Works,* 9:254-55.

41. For a detailed discussion of the following summary, see Maddox, "Opinion, Religion, and 'Catholic Spirit': John Wesley on Theological Integrity," *Asbury Theological Journal* 47.1 (1992): 63-87.

42. For a few examples, see Shinn, *Plan of Salvation,* pp. ii, vi; Fisk, *Calvinistic Controversy,* 197-98; Shinn, *Benevolence of Supreme Being,* vi; A. A. Jimeson, *Notes on the Twenty-Five Articles of Religion, as Received and Taught by Methodists in the United States; in Which the Doctrines Are Carefully Considered, and Supported by the Testimony of Holy Scripture* (Cincinnati, Ohio: Applegate & Co., 1855), 394; and (Bishop) E. M. Marvin, *The Doctrinal Integrity of Methodism* (St. Louis, Mo.: Advocate Publishing House, 1878), 56-57, 128. For evidence of the same move in the EA and UBC, see Naumann, "German-American Evangelicalism," 9, 141ff., 181, 222.

43. Cf. Maddox, *Responsible Grace,* 40-42.

44. See esp. *The Works of the Reverend John Fletcher,* 4 vols. (Salem, Ohio: Schmul, 1974), 1:90-91; 1:545-48; and 2:186-92.

45. Fletcher, *Works,* 1:545-46.

46. A perusal of the works cited in n. 32 above will demonstrate that Fletcher is cited or drawn on much more frequently than Wesley. See also the review of the third American edition of Fletcher's *Checks* in *Methodist Review* 11 (1828): 413-20, which begins by saying that the present doctrinal struggles with Calvinism require that more preachers avail themselves of this resource.

47. Texts for each tradition (with years on the course of study) are as follows. **MEC:** Thomas Upham, *Elements of Mental Philosophy,* 2nd ed. (New York: Harper & Brothers, 1840–41) (1864–80); Francis Wayland, *The Elements of Moral Science,* 2nd ed. (Boston, 1837) (1864–80); and Noah Porter, *The Elements of Intellectual Science* (New York: Charles Scribner & Co., 1871) (1880–92). **MECS:** Laurens Hickok, *Empirical Psychology* (Boston: Ginn & Co., 1854) (1878–82); Hickok, *A System of Moral Science* (New York, 1853) (1878–82); Richard Rivers, *Elements of Mental Philosophy* (Nashville, Tenn.: MECS Publishing House, 1862) (1878–86); Rivers, *Elements of Moral Philosophy* (Nashville, Tenn.: MECS Publishing House, 1871) (1878–86); and Porter, *Intellectual Science* (1882–98). **MPC:** James Beattie, *Elements of Moral Science* (Edinburgh: A. Constable, 1817) (1834–58); Upham, *Mental Philosophy* (1880–1920); Wayland, *Elements of Moral Science* (1880–88); Henry Calderwood, *Handbook of Moral Philosophy* (London: Macmillan, 1881) (1888–1920); Hickok, *Empirical Psychology* (1888–1920); Mark Hopkins, *Lectures on Moral Science* (Boston: Gould & Lincoln, 1862) (1888–1920); and Noah Porter, *The Human Intellect* (New York: Scribners, 1877) (1888–1920). **UBC:** Upham, *Mental Philosophy* (1853–65); and Wayland, *Moral Science* (1853–73). There are no lists for the **EA** during this period.

48. E. P. Humphrey, *Our Theology and Its Development* (Philadelphia: Presbyterian Board of Publication, 1857), 68-69.

49. The most significant case is Nathan Bangs, "Scholastic Divinity," *Methodist Review* 14 (1832): 367-88; and Bangs, "Theological Education," *Methodist Review* 17 (1835): 85-105.

50. See John Emory, "Review of Watson's *Theological Institutes,*" *Methodist Review* 12 (1830): 272-307, esp. 273; and the quote attributed to President Stephen Olin of Wesleyan University in B. F. Tefft, *Methodism Successful* (New York: Derby & Jackson, 1860), 168.

51. The first American edition was Watson, *Theological Institutes: or, A View of the Evidences, Doctrines, Morals, and Institutions of Christianity* (New York: Emory & Waugh, 1830). Watson's agenda in producing the *Institutes* is summarized in

Thomas Jackson, *Memoirs of the Life and Work of the Rev. Richard Watson* (London: John Mason, 1857), 274.

52. Watson was on the MEC course of study 1833–92; MPC, 1830–1920; MECS, 1878–1906; UBC, 1841–93; and is reported as used in the EA from 1843 (no official course until much later).

53. See Watson, *Theological Institutes,* 1:278-79, 2:9-11, 2:439-42.

54. Cf. the arguments in William McKendree Bangs, "Observations on Watson's Theological Institutes," *Methodist Review* 19 (1837): 332-46; 20 (1838): 80-89; Benjamin F. Cocker, "The Metaphysics of Watson's Institutes," *Methodist Review* 44 (1862): 181-207; and John Levington, *Watson's Theological Institutes Defended* (New York: Barnes & Burr, 1863).

55. The most significant example is Asbury Lowrey, *Positive Theology: Being a Series of Dissertations on the Fundamental Doctrines of the Bible; the Object of Which Is to Communicate Truth Affirmatively in a Style Direct and Practical* (Cincinnati, Ohio: Methodist Book Concern, 1860); note his disparaging description of "systematic divinity" like that of Watson on pp. 15-16.

56. Bishop of Protestant Episcopal Church, "Review of [Ralston's] Elements of Divinity," *Methodist Quarterly Review* 3 (1849): 533-45.

57. See Amos Binney, *Theological Compend: Containing a System of Divinity or a Brief View of the Evidences, Doctrines, Morals, and Institutions of Christianity, Designed for the Benefit of Families, Bible Classes, and Sunday-Schools,* rev. Daniel Steele (New York: Nelson & Phillips, 1875); and Thomas Neely Ralston, *Elements of Divinity: or a Course of Lectures, Comprising a Clear and Concise View of the System of Theology, as Taught in the Holy Scriptures* (Louisville, Ky.: E. Stevensen, 1854). The only prior work that approached a full survey text by an American Methodist was Ara Williams, *The Inquirer's Guide to Gospel Truth; or Doctrinal Methodism Defended Against the Assaults of Its Enemies, by Scriptural Proofs and Rational Arguments* (Buffalo, N.Y.: Steele & Faxon, 1832); Williams drew heavily on Watson in his attempt to defend those Methodist doctrines currently under attack by Deists, Calvinists, and Universalists.

58. For Humphrey's rejection of Watson see the footnote in *Our Theology,* p. 69. A. A. Jimeson makes specific reference to Humphrey as motivating his production of *Notes on the Twenty-Five Articles of Religion* (see p. viii).

59. Samuel Wakefield, *A Complete System of Christian Theology: Or, A Concise, Comprehensive, and Systematic View of the Evidences, Doctrines, Morals, and Institutions of Christianity* (Pittsburgh, Pa.: J. L. Read and Son, 1862). A later, similar revision of Watson for the MECS was Thomas Summers' *Systematic Theology* (1888).

60. See esp. Wakefield, *Complete System of Theology,* 314-16.

61. The most interesting case is Luther Lee, *Elements of Theology: or, An Exposition of the Divine Origin, Doctrines, Morals, and Institutions of Christianity* (Syracuse, N.Y.: Wesleyan Methodist Publishing House, 1865). Lee stressed (p. iii) that theology is a human enterprise that addresses timely issues of the day, not just timeless truth, and remains fallible in its claims (one is left with the distinct impression that a major reason for this insistence is that Lee was writing from a camp of American Methodism that rejected Wesley's endorsement of an episcopal form of government!). Even so he keeps the same structure as Watson and supplemented his theology text with an apologetic: Lee, *Natural Theology; or, The Existence, Attributes, and Government of God* (Syracuse, N.Y.: Wesleyan Methodist Publishing House, 1886).

62. The best surveys of this matter are Gerald O. McCulloh, *Ministerial Education in the American Methodist Movement* (Nashville: Board of Higher Education and Ministry, 1980); Glenn T. Miller, *Piety and Intellect: The Aims and Purposes of Ante-Bellum Theological Education* (Atlanta, Ga.: Scholars Press, 1990), 393-436; and Russell E. Richey, "The Early Methodist Episcopal Experience," in *Theological Education in the Evangelical Tradition*, ed. D. G. Hart and R. A. Mohler, Jr. (Grand Rapids, Mich.: Baker, 1996), 45-62.

63. On the course of study in Methodism, see Louis Dale Patterson, "The Ministerial Mind of American Methodism: The Courses of Study for the Ministry of the Methodist Episcopal Church, the Methodist Episcopal Church, South and the Methodist Protestant Church" (Ph.D. thesis, Drew University, 1984. For UBC and EA, see Naumann, "German-American Evangelicalism," 31-49, 78ff.; and Paul Eller, *Evangelical Theological Seminary, 1873–1973* (Naperville, Ill.: ETS, 1973), 11-25.

64. Cf. David Meredith Reese, "Brief Strictures on the Rev. Mr. Sunderland's Essay on Theological Education," *Methodist Review* 17 (1835): 105-18; Benjamin Harrison Nadal, "Educational Qualifications for Ministry," *Methodist Review* 49 (1867): 221-36; and Neal Fisher, "Context and Concern," in *Truth and Tradition*, ed. N. F. Fisher (Nashville: Abingdon Press, 1995), 13-36.

65. E.g., Daniel Smith, "On the Importance of a Well-Instructed Ministry," *Methodist Review* 21 (1839): 267-75, esp. 273.

66. Daniel Curry, "Ministerial Education," *Methodist Review* 68 (1886): 586-90. See also the irenic response from a Garrett professor, Charles Bradley, "The Best Training for Our Ministry," *Methodist Review* 68 (1886): 911-16.

67. Cf. Lefferts A. Loetscher, *Facing the Enlightenment and Pietism* (Westport, Conn.: Greenwood, 1983), 150-60.

68. Cf. Paul F. Douglass, *The Story of German Methodism* (Cincinnati, Ohio: Methodist Book Concern, 1939).

69. *Cyclopedia of Biblical, Theological, and Ecclesiastical Literature,* 12 vols., ed. John McClintock and James Strong (New York: Harper, 1867–87).

70. McClintock, *Cyclopedia,* 3:190.

71. John McClintock, *Lectures on Theological Encyclopedia and Methodology,* ed. John T. Short (Cincinnati, Ohio: Hitchcock & Walden, 1873).

72. George Richard Crooks and John F. Hurst, *Theological Encyclopedia and Methodology* (New York: Phillips & Hunt, 1884), based on Karl Rudolf Hagenbach's *Encyklopädie und Methodologie der theologischen Wissenschaft* (Leipzig, 1833). The only earlier American translation of a German theological encyclopedia was the publication of the oral lectures of Friedrich August Gottreu Tholuck by Congregationalist Edward A. Park as "Theological Encyclopedia and Methodology," *Bibliotheca Sacra* 1 (1844): 178-216, 332-67, 552-78, 726-34.

73. Histories of the seminaries are listed in Kenneth E. Rowe, *United Methodist Studies: Basic Bibliographies* (Nashville: Abingdon Press, 1992), 78-80. On the course of study, see Patterson, "Ministerial Mind," 77.

74. See the critique of this curriculum in Edward Farley, *Theologia: The Fragmentation and Unity of Theological Education* (Philadelphia: Fortress, 1983).

75. Cf. William Warren, "Review of C. B. Moll's *Das System der praktischen Theologie,*" *Methodist Review* 46 (1864): 159-61; Daniel Whedon, "Ministerial Education in Our Church," *Methodist Review* 54 (1872): 246-67, esp. 251; McClintock and Strong, *Cyclopedia,* 8:463-64; Crooks and Hurst, *Theological Encyclopedia,* 472ff.; and Jonathan Weaver, ed., *Christian Doctrine: A Comprehensive View of Doctrinal and Practical Theology* (Dayton, Ohio: United Brethren Publishing House, 1890), 7.

76. Compare Mark Michael Pruett-Barnett, "'Be Thou My Vision'—Theology, Pastoral Care, and Culture in the Methodist Episcopal Church 1848–1939" (Ph.D. thesis, Drew University, 1991); the discussion of pastoral theology in *Religion in Life* 28 (1959): 483-525; and the discussion of Practical Theology in *Perkins School of Theology Journal* 35.3 (1982): 1-38.

77. Cf. Russell E. Richey, "The Legacy of Francis Asbury: The Teaching Office in Episcopal Methodism," *Quarterly Review* 15 (1995): 145-74.

78. From 1867 to 1877, Albert Bledsoe's *Southern Review* (Baltimore) was a semiofficial replacement for the *Methodist Quarterly Review,* which had been disrupted by the Civil War.

79. John Dempster was 61 when he started teaching at Garrett (MEC) in 1855. His successor in 1864, Miner Raymond, was 53. Randolph Foster brought thirty years of pastoral ministry to Drew (MEC) in 1868. John Miley was already 60 when called from the pastorate in 1873 to succeed Foster (who had been elected

bishop). Thomas Summers was 63 when made inaugural professor of theology at Vanderbilt (MECS) in 1875. James Ward brought twenty-five years of pastoral experience to his position at the new Westminster Theological Seminary (MPC) in 1884. And Lewis Davis was 57, with extended service as pastor and bishop, when he helped open Union Biblical Seminary (UBC) in 1871.

80. Henry Sheldon spent three years in the pastorate before beginning a forty-six-year teaching career at Boston in 1875. Wilbur Tillett came to Vanderbilt in 1886 after only six years in pastoral ministry, to spend fifty-four years teaching. Olin Curtis also had six years of pastoral experience when he succeeded Miley at Drew in 1896. Charles Forlines's thirty-eight years at Westminster (1905–43) were preceded by only five years in the pastorate. And Augustus W. Drury had only three years of ministry experience when he began a fifty-four-year career at Union in 1880.

81. Cf. Albert Cornelius Knudson, "Henry Clay Sheldon—Theologian," *Methodist Review* 108 (1925): 175-92, esp. 190-91.

82. For the *MEC* this included Miner Raymond, *Systematic Theology*, 3 vols. (New York: Eaton & Mains, 1877–79); John Miley, *Systematic Theology*, 2 vols. (New York: Hunt & Eaton, 1892–94); Henry Clay Sheldon, *System of Christian Doctrine* (Cincinnati, Ohio: Jennings & Pye, 1900); and Olin Alfred Curtis, *The Christian Faith Personally Given in a System of Doctrine* (New York: Eaton & Mains, 1905). In the *MECS* there was Thomas O. Summers, *Systematic Theology: A Complete Body of Wesleyan Arminian Divinity*, 2 vols., ed. J. J. Tigert (Nashville, Tenn.: Publishing House of the MECS, 1888). The *MPC* produced no native publication, but added Raymond and Summers to their course of study in 1888. Pressures to systematize their doctrine led in the *UBC* to the initial attempt in *Christian Doctrine: A Comprehensive View of Doctrinal and Practical Theology*, ed. Jonathan Weaver (Dayton, Ohio: United Brethren Publishing House, 1890). Perceived shortcomings in this attempt were addressed by adding Miley to their course of study in 1897. The *EA* fostered similar attempts at systematization in Anton Hülster, *Die Christliche Glaubenslehre vom Standpunkt des Methodismus* (Cincinnati, Ohio: Cranston & Stowe, 1888); and John Jacob Escher, *Christliche Theologie: Eine Darstellung biblischer Lehre vom Standpunkt der Evangelishen Gemeinschaft*, 3 vols. (Cleveland, Ohio: Thomas & Mattill, 1899). From 1888 to 1909 they also had on their course of study a work by the German Methodist Arnold Sulzberger, *Christliches Glaubenslehre*, 3 vols. (Bremen: H. Neulsen, 1875–78).

83. In addition to *System of Christian Doctrine*, Sheldon published such works as *History of Christian Doctrine*, 2 vols. (New York: Harper & Bros., 1886); *History of the Christian Church*, 5 vols. (New York: T. Y. Crowell, 1894); and *New Testament Theology* (New York: Macmillan, 1911). His commitment to the fourfold curriculum is evident in *Theological Encyclopedia* (Cincinnati, Ohio: Jennings & Graham, 1911).

84. See the protest in Daniel Curry, "Ministerial Education," *Methodist Review* 68 (1886): 586-90. Two major attempts to refocus doctrinal theology as an inductive study of Scripture were published at the turn of the century: Nathanael Burwash (a Canadian Methodist), *Manual of Christian Theology on the Inductive Method*, 2 vols. (London: Horace Marshall & Son, 1900); and Milton S. Terry (professor of theology at Garrett), *Biblical Dogmatics: An Exposition of the Principle Doctrines of the Holy Scriptures* (New York: Eaton & Mains, 1907). Neither of these was ever placed on a course of study.

85. In particular, Curtis, Gamertsfelder, Miley, and Sheldon. Note the specific praise of Miley for excluding apologetics and ethics in John Wesley Etter's review in *United Brethren Review* 3 (1892): 374-78.

86. Two of the more influential early examples were Benjamin F. Cocker, *Lectures on the Truth of the Christian Religion* (Detroit, Mich.: J. M. Arnold & Co., 1873) and Charles Wesley Rishell, *The Foundations of the Christian Faith* (New York: Eaton & Mains, 1899).

87. Cf. the article on ethics in McClintock and Strong, *Cyclopedia*, 3:319-25; and John J. Tigert, "Ethics: The Science of Duty," *Methodist Quarterly Review* 47 (1898): 582-90; 49 (1900): 97-101. These programmatic pieces help explain the abrupt switch from earlier works in the (Anglo-American) discipline of moral philosophy to works on Christian ethics in both the MEC and MECS course of study about 1890. *MEC:* C. F. Paulus, *The Christian Life: A Popular Treatise on Christian Ethics* (Cincinnati, Ohio: Curts & Jennings, 1890) (1892–1900); Newman Smyth, *Christian Ethics* (New York: Scribners, 1892) (1900–1916); James Seth, *A Study in Ethical Principles* (New York: Scribners, 1907) (1908–12); and Thomas Hall, *Social Solutions in the Light of Christian Ethics* (New York: Eaton & Mains, 1910) (1912–16). *MECS:* Mark Hopkins, *Law of Love and Love as Law; or, Christian Ethics* (New York: Scribners, 1886) (1886–1906); Noah K. Davis, *Elements of Ethics* (New York: Burdett, 1900) (1906–30); and David Stowe Adam, *A Handbook of Christian Ethics* (Edinburgh: T. & T. Clark, 1925) (1934–39).

88. Cf. John James Tigert, "Theological Method," *Methodist Quarterly Review* 21 (1884): 444-48; James Strong, "Theology as a Science," *Methodist Review* 71 (1889): 518-23; and Job S. Mills, "The Essence of Christianity," *United Brethren Review* 6 (1895): 35-36.

89. William F. Warren, *Systematische Theologie, einheitliche behandelt*, Erste Lieferung: Allgemeine Einleitung: (Bremen: Verlag der Tractathauses H. Neulsen, 1865); see esp. 140-41. Note the emphasis on a unifying (*einheitlich*) approach in the title.

90. John McClintock immediately published a translated digest of the book: "Warren's Introduction to Systematic Theology," *Methodist Review* 48 (1866): 100-124 (see his praise of the proposal on p. 105). Note the continuing attention

to Warren in Milton Terry, "Scope and Methods of Christian Dogmatics," *Methodist Review* 77 (1895): 190-206.

91. Cf. the contrast between theology and religious literature in Wilbur Fisk Tillett, *Personal Salvation: Studies in Christian Doctrine Pertaining to the Spiritual Life* (Nashville, Tenn.: Cokesbury, 1902), 504, 508-9.

92. Note this contrast in Crooks and Hurst, *Theological Encyclopedia*, 46.

93. Richey, "Legacy of Francis Asbury," 160.

94. See the extended argument to value Wesley as a preacher but not as a model theologian in Tillett, *Personal Salvation*, 510-14. Note also that the only references to Wesley in McClintock's *Theological Encyclopedia* are in the section on practical theology.

95. The best example is Crooks and Hurst, *Theological Encyclopedia*, 47.

96. Note how Anglican theological activity is specifically dismissed in Warren, *Systematische Theologie*, 87 n. 1. Importantly, Warren never directly discusses Wesley in this book!

97. The suggestion of McClintock in "Warren's Introduction," 102-4.

98. Wesley's *Notes* was dropped from the course of study in MEC in 1864; MPC, 1878; and MECS, 1906. The MPC also dropped the *Sermons* in 1878. The MEC initially dropped the *Sermons* in 1916, but protest led to their restoration 1920–36. The MECS brought the *Sermons* into the 1939 merger, at which time the MC opted to list only *Selections of Writings of John Wesley*, ed. Herbert Welch (New York: Eaton and Mains, 1901), and this only as collateral reading.

99. Olin Curtis, "Professor Denney's Irenic Attempt," *Methodist Review* 91 (1909): 694-707; see esp. 703.

100. Demonstrating this point is a special interest of William McCutcheon. Cf. "Praxis: 'America Must Listen,'" *Church History* 32 (1963): 452-72; and "American Methodism and the Theological Challenge of the Twentieth Century," in *Forever Beginning, 1766–1966*, ed. Albea Godbold (Lake Junaluska, N.C.: Methodist Historical Society, 1967), 156-65.

101. An influential early analysis of the negative impacts of the Enlightenment on North American churches was Langdon Gilkey, *How the Church Can Minister to the World Without Losing Itself?* (New York: Harper & Row, 1964). The most vigorous recent analysis is Hauerwas and Willimon, *Resident Aliens*.

102. The quote is from Foster, *Studies in Theology*, vol. 1, *Prolegomena: Philosophic Basis of Theology; or, Rational Principles of Religious Faith* (New York: Hunt & Eaton, 1891), pp. vi-vii. The only passing reference to Wesley I have found is in vol. 6, *Sin* (New York: Hunt & Eaton, 1899), 179-81.

103. Sheldon, *System of Doctrine*, 479. See also the discussion of the move from "sinful man" to "moral man" in Robert Chiles, *Theological Transitions in American Methodism, 1790–1935* (New York: Abingdon, 1965), 115ff.

104. Cf. Randy L. Maddox, "Social Grace: The Eclipse of the Church as a Means of Grace in American Methodism," in *Methodism in Its Cultural Milieu*, ed. Tim Macquiban (Oxford: Applied Theology Press, 1994), 131-60.

105. James Mudge, *The Perfect Life in Experience and Doctrine* (Cincinnati, Ohio: Jennings & Graham, 1911), 6.

106. Daniel Dorchester, *The Problem of Religious Progress* (New York: Phillips & Hunt, 1881), see 41, 115, 124. My emphasis is intended to capture Dorchester's stress on human value and ethical progress. Note as well in this connection Milton S. Terry, *The New Apologetic: Five Lectures on the True and False Methods of Meeting Modern Philosophical and Critical Attacks upon the Christian Religion* (New York: Eaton & Mains, 1897), esp. 157ff.

107. Although Dorchester was not himself an academic theologian, he was a very influential liberal MEC pastor and his book was placed on the MEC course of study from 1896 to 1904. William Warren had forecast this transition in "Impending Revolution in Anglo-Saxon Theology," *Methodist Review* 45 (1863): 455-74, 579-600; see esp. 580.

108. Henry C. Sheldon, *The Essentials of Christianity* (New York: George Doran, 1922), note esp. 24, 283, 297-302.

109. Admittedly, Curtis's *Christian Faith Personally Given in a System of Doctrine* was published in 1905, but the title itself suggests that he was transitional from pure Systematics to a more interpretative approach (cf. pp. ix, 183-84). It should also be noted that Sheldon remained on the MEC course of study until 1932, and the MECS until 1939; with Curtis on the MEC until 1916, MPC until 1936, and MECS until 1939. The production and assignment of systematic theologies would continue longer in the EA and UBC: esp. Samuel J. Gamertsfelder, *Systematic Theology* (Cleveland, Ohio: C. Hauser, 1913); and Augustus Waldo Drury, *Outlines of Doctrinal Theology* (Dayton, Ohio: Otterbein Press, 1914).

110. The major examples through midcentury, most of whom made it on the course of study, would include: L. Harold DeWolf, *A Theology of the Living Church* (New York: Harper & Row, 1953); Georgia Harkness, *Understanding the Christian Faith* (New York/Nashville: Abingdon-Cokesbury, 1947); Albert Cornelius Knudson, *The Doctrine of God* (New York: Abingdon Press, 1930); Knudson, *The Doctrine of Redemption* (New York: Abingdon-Cokesbury, 1933); Knudson, *Basic Issues in Christian Thought* (New York/Nashville: Abingdon-Cokesbury, 1950); Edwin Lewis, *Jesus Christ and the Human Quest* (New York: Abingdon, 1924); Lewis, *A Manual of Christian Beliefs* (New York: Charles Scribner's Sons, 1927); Lewis, *God and Ourselves* (New York: Abingdon, 1931);

Lewis, *The Faith We Declare* (Nashville, Tenn.: Cokesbury, 1939); Franklin Nutting Parker, *What We Believe: Studies in Christian Doctrine* (Nashville, Tenn.: MECS Publishing House, 1923); Harris Franklin Rall, *The Meaning of God* (Nashville, Tenn.: Cokesbury, 1925); Rall, *A Faith for Today* (New York: Abingdon, 1936); Rall, *Christianity: An Inquiry into Its Nature and Truth* (New York: Charles Scribners, 1940); Rall, *Religion as Salvation* (New York/Nashville: Abingdon-Cokesbury, 1953); Gilbert Theodore Rowe, *The Meaning of Methodism: A Study in Christian Religion* (Nashville, Tenn.: Cokesbury, 1926); Gilbert Theodore Rowe, *Reality in Religion* (Nashville, Tenn.: Cokesbury, 1927); and Tillett, *Personal Salvation.*

111. There was even some openness to liberalism in the EA and UBC early in the century, though it was soon quelled by a broader and more sustained reaction than in the mainline Methodist traditions; cf. Naumann, "German-American Evangelicalism," 197ff.

112. Frank Wilbur Collier, *Back to Wesley* (New York: Methodist Book Concern, 1924), 5.

113. A classic example is the response to fundamentalism by (MECS bishop) Edwin D. Mouzon, *Fundamentals of Methodism* (Nashville, Tenn.: MECS Publishing House, 1923), 8. See also Harris Franklin Rall, "Making a Methodist Theology," *Methodist Quarterly Review* 74 (1925): 579-86; and Rall, "Do We Need a Methodist Creed?"

114. See (again a forerunner) Randolph Sinks Foster, *Philosophy of Christian Experience* (New York: Hunt & Eaton, 1891), esp. 2-8; John J. Tigert, "The Theological Situation," *Methodist Quarterly Review* 50 (1901): 906-9; John C. Granbery, "Method in Methodist Theology," *Methodist Quarterly Review* 58 (1909): 230-43; John Wright Buckham "Experiential Theology," *Methodist Quarterly Review* 66 (1917): 279-85; and Clifford G. Thompson, "Prolegomena of Empirical Methodist Theology," *Methodist Quarterly Review* 71 (1922): 230-39.

115. Rall describes his method in "Theology, Empirical and Christian," in *Contemporary American Theology,* ed. Vergilius Ferm (New York: Round Table, 1933), 2:245-73. The major examples of his method are *The Meaning of God, A Faith for Today, Christianity: An Inquiry into Its Nature and Truth,* and *Religion as Salvation.* He won the esteemed Bross Prize for *Christianity!*

116. This is most evident in Rall, *What Can I Believe* (Chicago: Commission on Men's Work, Board of Education, MEC, 1933).

117. Note the specific suggestions of correlations between Schleiermacher and Wesley (with a lament that Methodism has yet to develop these enough) in J. A. Reubelt, "Schleiermacher: His Theology and Influence," *Methodist Review* 51 (1869): 211-28; and Granbery, "Method in Methodist Theology," 235. See also the

argument that Rall was a key initial voice in introducing Ritschl to America in William J. McCutcheon, *Essays in American Theology: The Life and Thought of Harris Franklin Rall* (New York: Philosophical Library, 1973).

118. The most provocative example is Rowe's *Meaning of Methodism,* a running contrast between Methodism's emphasis on experienced salvation and all sacramentalism, institutionalism, and intellectualism.

119. Bowne's major philosophical works include: *Metaphysics* (New York: Harper, 1882), *Philosophy of Theism* (New York: Harper, 1887; rev. as *Theism* [New York: American Book Co., 1902]), and *Personalism* (Boston: Houghton Mifflin, 1908).

120. For an interpretative survey of Bowne and his tradition, see *The Boston Personalist Tradition in Philosophy, Social Ethics, and Theology,* ed. Paul Deats and Carol Robb (Macon, Ga.: Mercer University Press, 1986). The most influential second-generation personalists at Boston were Edgar Sheffield Brightman, Albert C. Knudson, and Francis L. Strickland. Interest in Boston Personalism within the UBC is evident in the various issues of *United Brethren Review* (in print from 1890 to 1908). For an EA appropriation, see George J. Kirn, *Religion: A Rational Demand* (Cleveland, Ohio: Thomas & Mattil, 1900).

121. See Francis Strickland, *The Psychology of Religious Experience* (New York: Abingdon, 1924), 106 and 89, respectively. The individualism and rationalism of Strickland are further evident on pp. 56, 98, 107ff.

122. Cf. Borden Parker Bowne, *The Immanence of God* (Boston: Houghton Mifflin, 1905), 146-47; Bowne, *Studies in Christianity* (Boston: Houghton Mifflin, 1909), esp. vi, 337, 345-46; and Bowne, *The Essence of Religion* (Boston: Houghton Mifflin, 1910), esp. 36-41, 73-74, 216-21.

123. The roots of this change would go back once more to Randolph Foster! In the first volume of his *Studies in Theology,* titled *Prolegomena: Philosophic Basis of Theology; or, Rational Principles of Religious Faith* (1891), Foster distinguished doctrinal theology from a "higher" science of theology that discusses philosophically the preconceptions of revelation (p. 286).

124. Cf. Edgar Sheffield Brightman, *The Finding of God* (New York: Abingdon, 1931), 11; Albert C. Knudson, *Basic Issues in Christian Thought* (New York/Nashville: Abingdon-Cokesbury, 1950), 45; Knudson, *Doctrine of God,* 64; and Francis L. Strickland, *Foundations of Christian Belief: Studies in the Philosophy of Religion* (New York: Abingdon, 1915).

125. See Albert C. Knudson, "A Personalistic Approach to Theology," in *Contemporary American Theology,* ed. Vergilius Ferm (New York: Round Table, 1933) 1:219-41, esp. 228.

126. Note this explicit contrast in Albert C. Knudson, *Principles of Christian Ethics* (New York: Abingdon, 1943), 258.

127. Cf. Bowne, *Studies in Christianity*, v, 378.

128. See esp. Edwin Lewis, *A Christian Manifesto* (New York: Abingdon, 1934), 206-7. Even his earlier works, like *Jesus Christ and the Human Quest* or *God and Ourselves*, give a more prominent role to traditional convictions in their apologetic structure than was typical in Methodist liberalism.

129. Note the entire issue of *Religion in Life* 29.4 (1960), which is devoted to the topic of "Neo-Wesleyanism."

130. The most relevant example is Robert Burtner and Robert Chiles, *John Wesley's Theology* (Nashville, Tenn.: Abingdon, 1954), 7. See also John Alfred Faulkner, "Shall We Leave Wesley for Ritschl?" *Methodist Review* 98 (1916): 447-59.

131. It is very revealing to compare in this regard Edwin Lewis, *The Practice of the Christian Life* (Philadelphia: Westminster, 1942) to Wesley's conception and pattern of the means of grace (best analyzed in Henry Knight III, *The Presence of God in the Christian Life: John Wesley and the Means of Grace* [Metuchen, N.J.: Scarecrow, 1992]).

132. Cf. Albert Outler, "The Current Theological Scene: A View from the Beach at Ebb Tide," in *Proceedings of the Eleventh World Methodist Conference*, ed. Lee Tuttle and Max Woodward (New York: Abingdon, 1967), 157-67.

133. E.g., Schubert Ogden, *The Reality of God* (New York: Harper, 1963); John B. Cobb, Jr., *A Christian Natural Theology, Based on the Thought of Alfred North Whitehead* (Philadelphia: Westminster, 1965); Harvey Potthoff, *God and the Celebration of Life* (Chicago: Rand McNally, 1968); Delwin Brown et al., *Process Philosophy and Christian Thought* (Indianapolis, Ind.: Bobbs-Merrill, 1971); John B. Cobb, Jr., and David Ray Griffin, *Process Theology: An Introductory Exposition* (Philadelphia: Westminster, 1976); and Marjorie Hewitt Suchocki, *God, Christ, Church: A Practical Guide to Process Theology* (New York: Crossroad, 1982).

134. E.g., Schubert Ogden, "Process Theology and the Wesleyan Witness," *Perkins School of Theology Journal* 37.3 (1984): 18-33; Sheila Greeve Davaney, "Feminism, Process Thought, and the Wesleyan Tradition," in *Wesleyan Theology Today*, ed. Theodore Runyon (Nashville: Kingswood Books, 1985), 105-16; Marjorie Hewitt Suchocki, "Coming Home: Wesley, Whitehead, and Women," *Drew Gateway* 57.3 (1987): 31-43; and John B. Cobb, Jr., *Grace and Responsibility: A Wesleyan Theology for Today* (Nashville: Abingdon Press, 1995).

135. See esp. John B. Cobb Jr., *Becoming a Thinking Christian* (Nashville: Abingdon Press, 1993); and Cobb, *Lay Theology* (St. Louis: Chalice Press, 1994).

136. This stream carries on the emphases of Charles Hartshorne's appropriation of Whitehead. For a Methodist representative, see Schubert Ogden, *On*

Theology (San Francisco: Harper & Row, 1986), 1, 69-93, and 94-101 (his definition of the specialty-discipline of Practical Theology).

137. See esp. Stephen Toulmin, *Cosmopolis: The Hidden Agenda of Modernity*
(New York: Free Press, 1990).

138. Note this worry in Robert E. Cushman, "A Case-Study in Ecumenism:
Fifty Years of Theology at Duke," *Duke Divinity School Bulletin* 42.1 (1977): 3-22,
esp. 19-20.

139. Thomas Oden, *Systematic Theology*, 3 vols. (San Francisco: Harper,
1987–92). It should be noted that Oden's is purposefully an ecumenical (or
"generic") Systematics, so Wesley is rarely mentioned, least of all in terms of
method.

140. See Albert C. Outler, "Towards a Re-appraisal of John Wesley as a
Theologian," *Perkins School of Theology Journal* 14 (1961): 5-14.

141. Albert C. Outler, "A New Future for 'Wesley Studies': An Agenda for
'Phase III,'" in *The Future of the Methodist Theological Traditions*, ed. M. Douglas
Meeks (Nashville: Abingdon Press, 1985), 34-52, see esp. 48.

142. E.g., Neal F. Fischer, *Context for Discovery* (Nashville: Abingdon, 1981);
M. Douglas Meeks, "John Wesley's Heritage and the Future of Systematic
Theology," in *Wesleyan Theology Today*, ed. Theodore Runyon (Nashville:
Kingswood Books, 1985), 38-46; D. Stephen Long, *Living the Discipline: United
Methodist Theological Reflections on War, Civilization, and Holiness* (Grand Rapids,
Mich.: Eerdmans, 1992), 11; and Randy L. Maddox, "Wesleyan Resources for a
Theology of the Poor," *Asbury Theological Journal* 49.1 (1994): 35-47.

143. For an account of how these psychologies have undermined Wesley's
specific conception of sanctification as character-formation in later American
Methodism, see Randy L. Maddox, "Holiness of Heart and Life: Lessons from
North American Methodism," *Asbury Theological Journal* 51.1 (1996): 151-72.

144. It is fitting that Stanley Hauerwas, one of the leading advocates of recov-
ering character ethics, is a Methodist. See esp. his *Character and the Christian Life:
A Study in Theological Ethics* (San Antonio: Trinity University Press, 1975); and
Hauerwas and Willimon, *Resident Aliens*. But note as well the criticism that
Hauerwas's character ethic undervalues the role of the emotions (Wesley's
"affections") in Patricia B. Jung, "Sanctification: An Interpretation in Light of
Embodiment," *Journal of Religious Ethics* 11 (1983): 75-95; Paul Lauritzen,
Religious Belief and Emotional Transformation (Lewisburg, Pa.: Bucknell University
Press, 1992), 7; and Paul Lewis, "'The Springs of Motion': Jonathan Edwards on
Emotions, Character, and Agency," *Journal of Religious Ethics* 22 (1944): 275-97,
esp. 287-91.

145. The most promising proposal in this direction of which I am aware is

Joseph C. Hough, Jr., and John B. Cobb, Jr., *Christian Identity and Theological Education* (Chico, Calif.: Scholars Press, 1985), esp. 95ff.

146. This dimension is well discussed in Marjorie Suchocki, "A Learned Ministry?" *Quarterly Review* 13.2 (1993): 3-17.

147. There are some hints in this direction in Donald Messer's chapter "Publish *and* Parish" in *Calling Church and Seminary into the Twenty-first Century* (Nashville: Abingdon Press, 1995), 101-12.

NOTES TO "THE DISTINCTIVE WITNESS OF THE EVANGELICAL UNITED BRETHREN CONFESSION OF FAITH"

1. *The Book of Discipline of the United Methodist Church* (1992) (Nashville: UM Publishing House), 55, 57.

2. It has also been identified as carrying "some of the unique Wesleyan holiness doctrines" into the present *Discipline* (K. James Stein, "Doctrine, Foundation, and Life in the Foundational Documents of the United Methodist Church," *Quarterly Review* 8 [Fall 1988]: 56).

3. E.g., Norman P. Marsden, "The Articles of Religion: Should We Take Them Seriously?" *Circuit Rider* 2 (February 1987).

4. Both come under the provisions of the Restrictive Rules, which forbid either their deletion or alteration. *U.M. Discipline* (1992), paragraph 16. The question has recently been raised whether the Restrictive Rule of 1808 of the former M.E. Church sought to protect only the A.R. (Heitzenrater), or whether it was meant to include Wesley's Sermons and Notes. See R. P. Heitzenrater, "At Full Liberty: Doctrinal Standards in Early American Methodism," *Quarterly Review* 5 (1985): 6-7; and Thomas Oden, "What Are Established Standards of Doctrine? A Response to Richard Heitzenrater," *Quarterly Review* 7 (1987): 41-42.

5. Stein, "Doctrine, Foundation, and Life," 42.

6. These issues are discussed in ibid., 42-62.

7. Ibid., 51.

8. Ibid., 52.

9. Ibid., 56. This point is also recognized by Stein when he notes that the CF is "carrying some of the unique Wesleyan holiness doctrines."

10. See Henry Spayth, *History of the United Brethren in Christ* (Circleville, Ohio: U.B. Publishing House, 1851); cited in A. W. Drury, *History of the Church of the United Brethren in Christ* (Dayton: Otterbein Press, 1924), 158, 282.

11. Otterbein served the Evangelical Reformed congregation in Baltimore from 1774 to 1813, which is today the Old Otterbein U.M.C.

12. Minutes of Studies of a unified CF (EUB), Nov. 30–Dec.1, 1960, unpublished minutes of Board of Bishops, compiled by A. Core. Its teaching has been called infralapsarian, single predestinarian Calvinism, which reflects its minority status in the religious establishment of the Holy Roman Empire, where Lutheranism and Catholicism were the dominant confessions. The CF study commission of the Board of Bishops overlooked this tradition and erroneously stated that the teachers of Otterbein at Herborn were "disciples of the University of Halle."

13. J. S. O'Malley, *Pilgrimage of Faith: The Legacy of the Otterbeins* (Metuchen, N.J.: Scarecrow, 1973), x, 95. His most influential brothers were Johann Heinrich, as instructor at the Herborn Academy; Georg Gottfried, author of several volumes on the *Heidelberg Catechism,* and Johann Daniel, author and pastor at Berleburg.

14. F. A. Lampe, *Milch der Wahrheit* (1718), evaluated in O'Malley, *Pilgrimage of Faith,* 64-78. Lampe listed these steps in the order of salvation *(Heilsordnung)*: the powerful appeal, faith, regeneration, justification, sanctification, sealing, glorification. Otterbein's brother Georg published two large volumes of sermons on the *Catechism* that Philip William Otterbein distributed in America. His brother Johann Daniel Otterbein, in 1790 published a series of counseling sessions that he had conducted with a condemned convict, in which the convict was led through the steps of the *Catechism* to a full conversion to Christ prior to his execution. See J. D. Otterbein, *Jesus und die Kraft seines Blute* (Lancaster, 1790), and O'Malley, *Pilgrimage of Faith,* 153-60.

15. See P. W. Otterbein, "The Salvation-Bringing Incarnation and Glorious Victory of Jesus Christ over the Devil and Death," in Arthur Core, ed., *Philip William Otterbein: Pastor, Ecumenist* (Dayton, 1968), 77-90.

16. See the "Protocol of the United Brotherhood in Christ Jesus" (1800–1812), in Core, 120-27.

17. "To tell the truth, I cannot side with Calvin in this case [predestination]. I believe that God is love and that he desires the welfare of all his creatures" (Letter to Deputies in Holland, Core).

18. Letter concerning the Millennium, by P. W. Otterbein (n.d.); Core, 102-3.

19. Otterbein had shared in the ordination of Asbury at the Methodist "Christmas Conference" of 1784. Other contacts between the two men are mentioned in Asbury's *Journal.*

20. Otterbein, "The Salvation-Bringing Incarnation," 85-86.

21. "Die Lehre der Vereinigten Bruder in Christo," Article 4; in A. W. Drury, Disciplines of the United Brethren in Christ (Dayton: U.B. Publishing House, 1895), Parts 2, 3.

22. G. G. Otterbein, *Predigten über den Heidelbergischen Katechismus* (Duisburg: Helwing, 1800), I, vi-viii.

23. *The Heidelberg Catechism* (1563) (Philadelphia: United Church Press, 1962), Question 2, 11-12.

24. It was from Herborn that Jan Comenius had ventured forth in the seventeenth century on his mission to the Czech brethren, when they were reorganized as the *Unitas Fratrem*.

25. Protocol of the United Brethren in Christ, May 13, 1812, and September 23, 1801, in Core, 121.

26. At their "big meetings," which were forerunners to the later camp meetings, baptism in all three major modes was honored, since the important matter was the inward baptism in the Holy Spirit. See S. S. Hough, ed., *Journal of Christian Newcomer* (Dayton: U.B. Board of Administration, 1941), 22-24.

27. Another *Confession of Faith* had been prepared in 1812 by Christopher Grosh, but, as Drury explained, Grosh "brought together a variety of materials, well enough for a treatise, but unsuitable for a confession" (A. W. Drury, "Our Confession: Its History," *United Brethren Quarterly Review* XVI [1892], 36).

28. A. W. Drury, "Our Confession," 36.

29. See again the discussion concerning the meaning of the First Restrictive Rule of 1808, as to whether it was meant to refer only to the AR (Heitzenrater's position) or to the AR *plus* the *Sermons* and *Notes* (Oden).

30. Drury, "Our Confession," 38; see also Minutes (1815 General Conference), Drury, *History*, 318.

31. Drury, "Our Confession," 39; see also J. C. Wenger, *The Complete Writings of Menno Simons* (Scottdale, Pa.: Herald, 1956), 863.

32. "Wir glauben an den heiligen Geist, . . . welcher uns reiniget von Aller befleckung des fleisches und des geistes" (U.B. Confession of Faith [1814], in Drury, *Disciplines,* Parts 2, 3); see also *Doctrines and Discipline of the Evangelical Association* (Cleveland: Ev. Publishing House, 1909), paragraphs 82-47.

33. U.B. Confession of Faith (1817), in Drury, "Doctrines and Disciplines," 28.

34. See Question 51 of the *Catechism* where it asks, "What benefit do we receive from this glory of Christ, our Head? A: First, that through His Holy Spirit He pours out heavenly gifts upon us his members. Second, that by his power he defends and supports us against all our enemies" (*Heidelberg Catechism,* 52).

35. The preaching of entire sanctification, that had been emphasized in Otterbein's preaching *(supra),* ceases to be prominent among later generations of

United Brethren. This contrasts with the continuing emphasis upon this doctrine in the Evangelical Association.

36. *The Heidelberg Catechism*, Question 54.

37. Drury, "Our Confession," 39.

38. See Core, 28-38.

39. Calvin, *Institutes*, III, 2 and 3.

40. *Discipline* of 1817, in Drury, *Disciplines*, 28.

41. Christian Newcomer, *Journal*, 24.

42. *UB Discipline* (1817), in Drury, *Disciplines*, 28.

43. Drury, "Our Confession," 40.

44. However, this Conference itself made two small changes before enacting this restrictive legislation (Drury, "Our Confession," 40).

45. It was probably for this reason that small alterations in wording in the CF continued to appear, occurring as late as 1857, as noted by Drury ("Our Confession," 40).

46. Drury, "Our Confession," 42.

47. Indeed, this had been the critique made by Francis Asbury against the early United Brethren of Otterbein's day; Asbury wrote on August 2, 1803, "There are now upwards of twenty preachers somehow connected with Mr. Otterbein and Mr. Boehm but they want authority, and the church wants discipline" (Asbury, *Journal* [August 2, 1803], II, 400).

48. Bruce Behney and Paul Eller, *A History of the Evangelical United Brethren Church* (Nashville: Abingdon, 1979), 123-24. UB had adopted an antislavery platform in 1821.

49. "Protocol of the United Brethren in Christ," 1800–1812; cited in Core, 121.

50. In 1855, at the same time these agitations over CF revision began to be heard, the UB launched their first overseas mission project to Sierra Leone, West Africa. In selecting this site, they were motivated by their antislavery commitment, and, once on site, they identified as their major adversary the presence of "secret societies" among the native Africans! They were using American antimasonic expressions in dealing with traditional male and female cults among tribal members. See D. K. Flickinger, Journal (Unpublished handwritten manuscript at the EUB Archives. United Theological Seminary, Dayton, Ohio).

51. See Daryl M. Elliott, Bishop Milton Wright and the Quest for A Christian America (unpublished Ph.D. Diss., Drew University, 1992), 217-28.

52. Ibid., 240.

53. Ibid. Elliott provides a detailed breakdown of the voting results.

54. Milton Wright, "The Influence of Secret Societies on the Churches," *Christian Cynosure* 4 (August 1887), 3; cited by Elliott, 178.

55. Wright, "Millennium's Approach," 5, cited by Elliott, 129.

56. Arthur C. Core, ed., *Philip William Otterbein* (Dayton: EUB Board of Publication, 1968), 102.

57. Drury, "Our Confession," 41. Drury argued here that those leaders who followed Otterbein lacked his education and wisdom.

58. The arguments cited in this paragraph were advanced by the liberal UB historian, A. W. Drury, in "Our Confession," 41-42.

59. In 1849, the question asked of candidates to the order of elder (the only order recognized by UB) was, "Do you believe in the Holy Ghost, as presented in our Confession of Faith?" Second, in 1877, the following question for applicants for quarterly license appeared: "Do you believe in our Confession of Faith, as taught in our *Book of Discipline?*" (cited in Drury, "Our Confession," 42).

60. *Doctrine and Discipline of the United Brethren in Christ* (Hagerstown, Md.: 1816), as cited in Drury, "Our Confession," 42.

61. Drury, "Our Confession," 43.

62. *Origin, Doctrine, Constitution, and Discipline of the United Brethren in Christ* (Circleville, Ohio: 1841), cited in Drury, *Disciplines,* 207.

63. Drury, "Our Confession," 45.

64. Cited by Drury, "Our Confession," 44. In the 1888 episcopal report of the bishops of the M.E. Church, referring to their constitution, said, "We dislike the thought that this section is unalterable, or incapable of modification, by any possible method or process. The provision for amending the restrictive rules ought to be sufficient to amend any part of it."

65. E. W. Curtiss, "Philip William Otterbein," *Quarterly Review of this United Brethren in Christ* 8 (1897): 249-50.

66. The so-called große Versammlungen.

67. Curtiss, "Otterbein," 251.

68. Drury, *Doctrines and Disciplines,* 3.

69. See *The Doctrines and Discipline of the Evangelical United Brethren Church* (Harrisburg and Dayton: EUB Board of Publication, 1947), paragraphs 1-44, for the text of the 1889 CF.

70. *Origin, Doctrine, Constitution, and Discipline of the United Brethren in Christ* (1841), cited in Drury, "Doctrines and Disciplines," 211.

71. "The Confession of Faith of the Church of the United Brethren in Christ," in *The Discipline of the Evangelical United Brethren Church* (Harrisburg and Dayton: 1959), 21-23.

72. H. M. DuBose, *The Symbol of Methodism* (Nashville, Tenn.: M.E. Church South Board of Publication, 1907), 47.

73. Wesley had intended that they should be supplemented by his *Sermons and Notes* on the New Testament, regardless of whether the Restrictive Rule of 1841 recognized that intention.

74. The latter was finally excluded in the 1889 United Brethren CF.

75. Adam Riegel and Isaac Davies, respectively. See Behney and Eller, *History of the Evangelical United Brethren Church,* 69-70.

76. His family church had been the Bergstrasse Lutheran Church, where Jacob learned Luther's *Small Catechism* (Behney and Eller *History of the Evangelical United Brethren Church,* 69).

77. He served as bishop for six months, to his death in 1808, on a *de facto,* not *de jure* basis, since there was as yet no formal ecclesial organization.

78. In fact, his followers briefly used the title "The Newly-Formed Methodist Conference."

79. Behney and Eller, *History of the Evangelical United Brethren Church,* 78.

80. This volume also contained "doctrinal essays taken from the writings of Wesley and Fletcher on Christian Perfection, Predestination, Final Perseverance of the Saints, and a dissertation against 'antinomianism'" (Reuben Yeakel, *History of the Evangelical Association* (Cleveland: Thomas and Mattill, 1894), I, 101.

81. George Miller, *Thäetiges Christenthum* (Neu Berlin, 1814). He also wrote a brief biography of the life of Albright entitled *Kurze Beschreibung der wirkenden Gnade Gottes bey dem Jakob Albrecht* (Reading, 1811), 26 pp.

82. These included the polemical articles directed against works of supererogation (XI), Purgatory (XIV), the five Catholic sacraments rejected by the Reformers (paragraph 2 of XVI), the withholding of the cup in Communion (XIX), and forbidding the marriage of priests (XXI). Articles XVII and XVIII on baptism and the Lord's Supper, Article XXV, "Of a Christian Man's Oath," which is directed against the Anabaptists, is also deleted.

83. See the discussion of this question in Kenneth E. Rowe, "Christian Perfection in the Evangelical Disciplines," *Methodist History* 18 (1979): 66-72.

84. Behney and Eller, *History of the Evangelical United Brethren Church,* 78-80.

85. Yeakel, *History*, I, 101. For an excellent discussion of that literature, see Ernest F. Stoeffler, *German Pietism in the Eighteenth Century* (Leiden: Brill, 1973). Stoeffler has shown here that the two most widely reprinted and read Pietists in Pennsylvania were the Lutheran Johann Arndt (author of *Wahres Christenthum*) and Gerhard Tersteegen (the great Rhineland poet and spiritual leader).

86. "So mußer wirklich tief in Gott gegrundet sein, und in Wahrheit Gott von ganzen Herzen, von ganzer Seele und aus allen Kräften lieben" (*Die Glaubenslehre und Kirchenzuchtordnung der Evangelicschen Gemeinschaft* [Cleveland, 1876], 16).

87. See J. S. O'Malley, "Tersteegen and Wesley" (unpublished paper presented at the 1995 Conference of the Wesleyan Theological Society, Nampa, Idaho). The most popular Pennsylvania-German revival hymn was written by John Walter, Albright's early colleague. It is entitled "Kommt, Bruder, kommt, wir eilen fort" and it is an adaptation of Tersteegen's beloved "Kommt, Kinder, lasst uns gehen." Yeakel (*History*, I, 449) stated that the early Evangelicals "delighted in singing Gerhard Tersteegen's hymn for spiritual pilgrims," and Walter's version as well.

88. "Durch treuen Wandel und Nachfolge des Lammes. . . . durch mächtigen Gnadeneinfluß des göttlichen Geistes in der Seele" (*Die Glaubenslehre*, 18).

89. Evangelicals claimed as their mission the evangelization of the continuing stream of German immigrants to North America, that numbered over six million persons by the end of the nineteenth century.

90. Füßle (d. 1918), as editor of the *Evangelische Botschafter* (1868–1916), frequently printed a Tersteegen hymn on the front page of this periodical, thereby interspersing it with poems of his own creation. Although he was the leading literary figure of European Evangelicals, his work has not yet been examined by Anglo scholars. See J. S. O'Malley and Thomas Lessmann, *Gesungenes Heil* (Christliches Verlagshaus: Stuttgart, 1994).

91. Seybert, their first constitutional bishop, was to Evangelicals what Asbury was for the Methodists and what Christian Newcomer was for the United Brethren. A theological exposition of the themes of his *Journal* is found in J. S. O'Malley, *Touched by Godliness; Bishop John Seybert and the Evangelical Heritage* (Topeka, Kans.: Granite Press, 1986).

92. Philip Schaff called Neitz the leading German orator in America (R. K. Schwab, *History of the Doctrine of Christian Perfection in the Evangelical Association* [Menasha, Wis.: Collegiate Press, 1822], 45).

93. "The View of the Evangelical Association on Sanctification," *Christliche Botschafter* (January 16, 1856).

94. Neitz's views are summarized in Behney and Eller, 203.

95. See Terry Heisey, "Immigration as a Factor in the Division of the Evangelical Association," *Methodist History* 19 (October 1980): 41-57.

96. The senior bishop was Joseph Long and his junior colleague was J. J. Esher. Their service is reviewed in Raymond Albright, *History of the Evangelical Church* (Harrisburg: Evangelical Press, 1942), 275-77, 375.

97. His satire, entitled "Sporadisches" ("Sporadic Verses") was published in *Der Christliche Botschafter.* The editor of the English-language *Evangelical Messenger,* T. G. Clewell, also received episcopal rebuke for opposing the position on sanctification in the *Discipline* (Schwab, 147-49).

98. The majority met in Indianapolis and the minority in Philadelphia.

99. Still, a limited episcopal polity was continued, with greater limits on episcopal authority. Property ownership was vested in the local church, and lay representation in General Conference was recognized (Behney and Eller, *History of the Evangelical United Brethren Church,* 284).

100. Harold P. Scanlin, "The Origin of the Articles of Faith of the United Evangelical Church," *Methodist History* 18 (July 1980): 210-38; see also Milton S. Terry, *Doctrines of American Methodism* (Evanston, Ill.: University Press, 1887), 7 pages.

101. The remaining two articles added were No. 13, "Of Apostasy," and No. 14, "Of Immortality" (U.E. *Discipline* [Harrisburg: U.E. Bd. of Publication, 1894], 13-21).

102. U.E. *Discipline* (1894), 22-30.

103. Heisey notes that the Association's leaders, such as Esher, came from families who had migrated more recently and tended to be more concentrated in the Midwestern sectors of the church. The UE strength was in the East Pennsylvania area, which was Neitz's former base (Heisey, 48-54).

104. J. J. Esher, *Christliche Theology,* 3 vols. (Cleveland: Thomas and Mattill, 1899–1901).

105. Cf. *The Doctrines and Discipline of the Evangelical Association* (1909), paragraphs 23-31; with *The Doctrines and Discipline of the United Evangelical Church* (1894), paragraphs 1-32; and "The Articles of Faith, and the Doctrines of Regeneration, Sanctification, and Christian Perfection of the Evangelical Church," in *The Discipline of the Evangelical United Brethren Church* (1959), paragraphs 14-44.

106. *The Discipline of the Evangelical United Brethren Church* (Dayton and Harrisburg: Board of Publication, 1947), chap. 1, paragraphs 1-44.

107. E.g., paragraphs 542, 553, and 581.

108. "This We Believe; A Unified Creedal Statement of the Confession of Faith; The Evangelical United Brethren Church" (private document, prepared by the authority of the Committee on Catechetical and Doctrinal Instruction and Board of Christian Education, and approved for theological content by the Board of Bishops [1962]), 3.

109. "This We Believe," 3.

110. Declaration of the Joint Commission on Church Federation and Union (1946), cited in "This We Believe," 3.

111. The CF Studies meeting of the Board of Bishops stated in its report on March 2, 1962, that in the CF revision work "there was a conscientious effort to conserve not only the true core of each creedal statement as found in both branches of our church but also to 'make use of words, phrases, and expressions in the existing sets of articles'" (CF study commission minutes, March 2, 1962, 2).

112. "Whereas, this Confession of Faith as adopted is a continuance of and is in fact 'The Confession of Faith of the Church of The United Brethren in Christ' and 'The Articles of Faith and the Doctrines of Regeneration, Sanctification, and Christian Perfection of the Evangelical Church' as stated in the 1947 edition of the *Discipline* on pages 41-55. . . . Resolved, that we do hereby solemnly declare and affirm that the single creedal statement, 'The Confession of Faith of the Evangelical United Brethren Church,' is a continuance of both of the earlier creedal statements of our Church and is in agreement with the doctrines of the Christian religion as contained in the Holy Scriptures and accepted and held by the Evangelical United Brethren Church" (Proceedings of the Evangelical United Brethren General Conference, October 23–November 1, 1962, p. 274).

113. See the seven-step *Heilsordnung* of F. A. Lampe, cited in n. 14 above.

114. The full text of the 1962 E.U.B. CF (abbreviated EUB-CF) is found in the *Book of Discipline* (1996), ¶ 62.

115. The covenantal scheme upon which the Adam-Christ typology is based has a distinguished history in Paul (Romans 5), Irenaeus (*Against Heresies,* trans. J. Unger [New York: Paulist, 1992]), and in the Reformed Pietism of Lampe (*Geheimnis des Gnadenbundes,* 6 vols., 1712–21) and of P. W. Otterbein ("The Salvation-Bringing Incarnation," in Core, *Philip William Otterbein,* 77-90).

116. *The Heidelberg Catechism,* Part III.

117. The UB Article (No. 11) uses the older Reformed Pietist expression "to follow holiness," as the narrow path of the *Heilsordnung.*

118. UB-CF (1889), Article 4, in EUB *Discipline* (1947), paragraph 5.

119. The minutes of the CF study commission reveal considerable disagree-

ment over the status of this article on sanctification: one member, J. Stanley Barnes, suggested that the Article be deleted altogether until it can be "clearly shown" to be "thoroughly grounded" in Scripture; another member, T. A. Kantz, urged that study guides be prepared to teach this doctrine to laity (a suggestion that was apparently never followed) (CF study commission minutes, 73, 12).

120. Professor Harry A. DeWire, a member of the 1962 CF study group, commented on this statement on baptism as follows: "We seem to be taking the position that baptism carries with it more potentiality than immediate reality. . . . It appears to be more of a 'futurity' in which the child is now undergoing, in the presence of the congregation, a ritual which has a defined action"; Professor Arthur Core questions the propriety of the use of the term "confirmed" ("This baptism is confirmed by the child upon his profession of faith"): "While we can probably do no better at this juncture than allow the word 'confirmed' to be used in Article VI, it seems to me such usage is not actually true to our theological heritage from Reformed Pietism" (Note: This is the *sole* reference in the minutes of the CF study commission that refers to the Reformed Pietist heritage of the UB-CF, but, unfortunately, this theme is not developed) (H. A. Dewire, Minutes of CF study commission, 51; and A. C. Core, minutes, 12-13). Core also notes (13) the appearance of the "ritual of dedication without baptism" that first appeared in the U.B. *Discipline* in 1945, which, he noted, the catechisms of the church do not support.

121. The work of this commission was reported in Albert Outler, "Introduction to the Disciplinary Statement," in *Wesleyan Theology: A Sourcebook,* ed. Thomas A. Langford (Durham, N.C.: Labyrinth Press, 1984), 271-78; the critique of this position is found in Robert E. Cushman, "Church Doctrinal Standards Today," also in *Wesleyan Theology,* 279-90.

NOTES TO "WHAT MAKES 'UNITED METHODIST THEOLOGY' METHODIST?"

1. Thomas A. Langford, *Practical Divinity: Theology in the Wesleyan Tradition* (Nashville: Abingdon Press, 1983), 269-70.

2. For a significant diagnosis and critique of the churches' contentment with having "friendly division with permeable borders," reflecting a lack of distinctive marks among those churches, see Michael Root, "The Unity of the Church and the Reality of the Denominations," *Modern Theology* 9 (October 1993): 385-401.

3. See Robert Wuthnow, *Sharing the Journey* (New York: Free Press, 1994).

4. See, e.g., John Cobb's similar diagnosis about "mainline" Protestantism, "Faith Seeking Understanding: The Renewal of Christian Thinking," *The Christian Century* 111-20 (June 29–July 6, 1994): 642-44.

5. These complex heritages include the fact that contemporary United Methodism also comprises the traditions of the Evangelical and United Brethren Churches. A full historical investigation of the ambiguities in our ecclesial heritages would need to include more detailed exploration of the ways in which those heritages bear on contemporary issues within United Methodism. Even so, my focus on the origins of United Methodism in terms of the Wesleyan movement is, I think, justified both in relation to United Methodism's dominant self-understanding and the specifications of doctrine and theology in the *Book of Discipline*. At the same time, however, more detailed reflection on the role of the Evangelical United Brethren "Confession of Faith" would be important in a more comprehensive account of the relations between doctrine and theology in contemporary United Methodism.

6. The story of Methodism's origins, and its gradual transformation from a "movement" to a "church," is well narrated by Richard P. Heitzenrater, *Wesley and the People Called Methodists* (Nashville: Abingdon Press, 1995).

7. See, e.g., the instructive discussion in William B. McClain, *Black People in the Methodist Church* (Nashville: Abingdon Press, 1984).

8. The "Confessing Church Movement" originated in a meeting convened by Thomas Oden, Bishop William Cannon, and Maxie Dunnam in April 1994. The group issued a statement at the conclusion of the meeting, "Invitation to the Church," and asked for signatories to the document. A second meeting was held in April 1995, designed to assess the future of the movement and to work on a "Confessional Statement." The movement has been criticized both for its style and for the content of its theological judgment; the most direct theological responses have come from the Administrative Council of Trinity United Methodist Church in Atlanta, and in a short paper by Professor James Will of Garrett-Evangelical Theological Seminary.

9. *The Book of Discipline of the United Methodist Church 1992* (Nashville: United Methodist Publishing House), para. 68.

10. M. Douglas Meeks, "John Wesley's Heritage and the Future of Systematic Theology," in Theodore Runyon, ed., *Wesleyan Theology Today* (Nashville: Kingswood, 1985), 39.

11. See John B. Cobb Jr., *Grace and Responsibility: A Wesleyan Theology for Today* (Nashville: Abingdon Press, 1995), 9.

12. Cobb, *Grace and Responsibility*, 187 n. 13.

13. An important example is the doctrine of the Trinity. Wesley took this doctrine for granted in much of his writing, though he also clearly understood the Trinity to be central to the "main branches" of Christian doctrine (see particularly his late sermon "On the Trinity"). For a significant account of Wesley's doc-

trinal views on the Trinity, see Geoffrey Wainwright, "Why Wesley Was a Trinitarian," chap. 17 of his *Methodists in Dialog* (Nashville: Kingswood Books, 1995), 261-74. More generally, Wainwright adheres closely to Wesley's own views in his sketch of a constructive proposal for the place of Christian doctrine in relation to "opinion" and a "catholic spirit" in chap. 14, "Doctrine, Opinions, and Christian Unity: A Wesleyan and Methodist Perspective," 231-36. A constructive "Wesleyan" proposal concerning doctrine need not adhere as closely as does Wainwright to Wesley's own views; however, a "Wesleyan" proposal does need to at least present a balanced account of Wesley's own views on, and relation to, Christian doctrine. In my view, Cobb's account (and in this he is not atypical among Methodists) does not do so.

Further, to assert that the doctrine of the Trinity is central in Wesley's thought (and, I would suggest, in Wesleyan and Methodist doctrine) does not mean that it must be interpreted restrictively; indeed, the doctrine then needs to be interpreted through creative and diverse theological proposals about how best to understand the doctrine and to live faithfully in relation to the Triune God. But that is to emphasize the important distinction between doctrine and theology, a distinction often missed in contemporary debates.

14. See Cobb, *Grace and Responsibility*, 135-44. It may be significant that "doctrine" does not even merit an entry in the index. More important, note Cobb's oversimplified description in the preface: "Since the Wesleyan tradition takes Christian life as its essential requirement, it is open to a wide range of theological thinking" (p. 11). There is not one "essential requirement" for theology in the Wesleyan tradition, and surely for Wesley and the people called Methodists (including the current *Discipline*'s description), doctrine is an essential requirement that *enables* rather than precludes a wide range of theological thinking that remains faithful to the Christian gospel.

15. This neglect of the role of doctrine afflicts Cobb's discussion of the Wesleyan "quadrilateral" in his concluding chapter. There Cobb offers an interesting proposal for a contemporary "Wesleyan" understanding of the relations of Scripture, tradition, reason, and experience; but as an interpretation of Wesley's own views it is seriously inadequate, even on Cobb's own terms of "dialogue" with Wesley.

16. Undoubtedly, some will object that my proposal is too tied to my own substantive theological convictions as well as controversial judgments about theological method. This is surely, in some sense, true; however, I have tried to articulate my constructive proposal in ways that are faithful to what I understand to be the vision articulated not only by Wesley *and* the people called Methodists of the eighteenth century, but also by United Methodism today as identified in the *Discipline*. In that sense, I hope that the contours of my proposal can set the framework for conversations and arguments among people who share a com-

mitment to the practices and convictions of the Wesleyan tradition yet who articulate their theological vision and method in ways divergent from my own.

17. The phrase is Outler's, developed more recently by Wainwright. See Albert Outler, "Do Methodists Have a Doctrine of the Church?" and "Methodism and the World Christian Community," in Thomas C. Oden and Leicester R. Longden, eds., *The Wesleyan Theological Heritage: Essays of Albert C. Outler* (Grand Rapids: Zondervan, 1991), 211-26, 241-50; see also Geoffrey Wainwright, "Ecclesial Location and Ecumenical Vocation," in M. Douglas Meeks, ed., *The Future of the Methodist Theological Traditions* (Nashville: Abingdon Press, 1985), 93-129.

18. *The Book of Discipline of The United Methodist Church 1992*, para. 66 (p. 58).

19. This follows Wainwright's suggestion in "Ecclesial Location and Ecumenical Vocation," p. 102, though I add the specification of "scriptural" to holiness.

20. See the suggestion of Meeks, "John Wesley's Heritage and the Future of Systematic Theology," 45; see also the work of the Oxford Institute of Methodist Studies, particularly Theodore Runyon, ed., *Sanctification and Liberation* (Nashville: Abingdon, 1981), and M. Douglas Meeks, ed., *The Portion of the Poor* (Nashville: Kingswood Books, 1995).

21. This would include not only those "hot-button" issues facing the church such as homosexuality, but also matters of family life, ecology, and abortion. I suspect that to explore all of these issues in relation both to Christian doctrine and "scriptural holiness," well understood, would provide some surprising turns in the debates.

22. See my discussion of some of these themes in "For All the Saints: Autobiography in Christian Theology," *The Asbury Theological Journal* 47 (Spring 1992): 27-42.

23. His actual term in the turn of phrase is that "demographic extrapolation" has replaced "eschatological expectation"; however, his larger account involves a critique of sociological explanation being treated as fundamental. Bishop Kenneth L. Carder, "A UMC Prognosis: Naming the Diseases and Finding the Cures," *The Circuit Rider* (September 1993): 7.

24. See Marjorie Hewitt Suchocki, "A Learned Ministry?" *Quarterly Review* 13 (Summer 1993): 3-17.

25. See, for examples, my own reflections in "Toward a Recovery of Theological Discourse in United Methodism," *Quarterly Review* 9 (Summer 1989): 16-34; and the historical investigations of Russell E. Richey, "The Legacy of Francis Asbury: The Teaching Office in Episcopal Methodism," *Quarterly Review* 15 (Summer 1995): 145-74.

26. I am grateful for the comments and criticisms offered to an earlier version of this work, delivered at the 1994 Duke-Lilly Conference on United Methodism and American Culture. I am also indebted to James Buckley, Michael Cartwright, Scott Jones, and Susan Jones for their comments on earlier drafts of the formal essay.

NOTES TO "DISCIPLINE IN BLACK AND WHITE"

1. "Letter of Lovick Pierce, D.D." in *Journal of the General Conference of the Methodist Episcopal Church,* held in Baltimore, Md., May 1-31, 1876, ed. George W. Woodruff, D.D. (New York: Nelson and Phillips, 1876), 419.

2. Ibid., 420.

3. The record of the name of the fraternal delegate who gave this address to the 1876 General Conference of the M.E. Church (North) is confused due to an editorial mistake. See the "Letter of W. F. Dickinson," in *Journal of the General Conference of the Methodist Episcopal Church,* 492-94. Apparently the editor of the *Journal* misstated the name of this delegate. The correct name is W. F. Dickerson. At the time he served as fraternal delegate to the 1876 General Conference, the Reverend Mr. William Fisher Dickerson had just been appointed as pastor of the Bethel A.M.E. Church in New Haven, Connecticut. I am indebted to Dennis Dickerson, the official historiographer of the A.M.E. Church, for clarifying this matter. For the relevant details about the life and ministry of this man, see Dennis Dickerson, "William Fisher Dickerson: Northern Preacher/Southern Prelate" in *Methodist History* 23/3 (April 1985): 135-52.

4. Ibid., 493. The *double-voiced* character of Dickerson's remarks, with the "signifying" play(s) on the story of the Prodigal Son were no doubt quite provocative, and one wonders what kind of response Dickerson's witty admonition evoked from those in attendance at the 1876 General Conference. I am indebted to C. Jarrett Gray Jr. of Duke University for calling this incident to my attention.

5. In keeping with the focus of the Lilly Project on United Methodism in American Culture, this essay will examine the implications of nineteenth-century Methodist disciplinary practice for contemporary United Methodism in American culture. Obviously, one could analyze the relationships of the four denominations in question from other angles of vision as well.

6. See for example Mechal Sobel's study, *The World They Made Together: Black and White Values in Eighteenth Century Virginia* (Princeton: Princeton University Press, 1987), which explores the similarities and differences in religious and cosmic worldviews within the framework of a regional study. Gary Nash's study of *Forging Freedom: The Formation of Philadelphia's Black Community 1720–1840* (Cambridge, Mass.: Harvard University Press, 1988) provides an example of the way a cultural historian analyzes the role of religious affiliations and biracial

religious congregations in the context of the political movements of an emerging urban center in the midst of the transition from being a British colony to the early republic. Finally, Randy Sparks's study, *On Jordan's Stormy Banks: Evangelicalism in Mississippi, 1773–1876* (Atlanta: University of Georgia Press, 1994), provides a good example of a regional interdenominational-interracial study.

7. Milton C. Sernett, *Black Religion and American Evangelicalism: White Protestants, Plantation Missions, and the Flowering of Negro Christianity, 1787–1865* (Metuchen, N.J.: Scarecrow, 1975), 17-18.

8. Ibid., 18.

9. It is interesting to observe that most contemporary observers and veteran ecumenists have come to think that the division between "faith and order" and "life and work," while useful for some concerns, is not as straightforward as it once would have been thought to be. Many of the issues that are being raised in ecumenical circles today do not fit neatly in these two divisions.

10. Moreover, I think it is important that we take seriously that part of what makes assessment of these convergences difficult is the fact that our own twentieth-century conceptions of "discipline" (as a negative or "Puritanical" set of practices) easily cloud assessments of the groups in question. For this reason, I have tried in this study to take into account the fact that there are several different levels of disciplinary practice in each of the four denominations that must be assessed, which in turn suggests the possibility of strong conflicts at one level in the midst of shared practices at another level.

11. David W. Lotz, "A Changing Historiography: From Church History to Religious History" in *Altered Landscapes,* ed. David W. Lotz with Donald W. Shriver Jr. and John F. Wilson (Grand Rapids: Eerdmans, 1989), 333-36. Lotz's historiographical reflections have, in part, inspired the alternative approach that I have attempted in this study. Lotz characterizes the new historiography or "religious history" in this way:

> Here the focal concern—while still oriented to communal self-understanding—shifts from church to nation, from people of God to American people, from sacred to profane America, from Christ to culture. The resultant history-as-written is biography (a religious history of the American people), couched in a rhetoric of description. Likewise, the new historiography's shift from the *church* to the *churches* involves a parallel shift from autobiography to biography and from the language **of** faith to the language **about** faith.
> (333)

Lotz goes on to argue for the need to a return to "old-style" church history for this reason.

> Yet if catholic Christian self-identity and self-knowledge are to be preserved
> and promoted in a religiously pluralistic culture, there remains a pressing
> need, it seems for church histories expressly written **for** *ecumenical* Christians
> **by** *ecumenical* Christians **out of** *ecumenical* Christian commitments and
> unabashedly written in a *confessing* style. Ironically, the rise and rule of reli-
> gious history has made a revival of old-style church history a genuine, even
> urgent desideratum. (334, boldface emphasis mine)

While I share Lotz's concern for an unabashedly ecumenical approach to church
history, as this essay demonstrates, I think it is important to pursue this quest by
taking on precisely those conflicts of interpretation and practice that have
played such a crucial role in the shaping of American Christian identity.

12. "Explanatory Notes" to the 1798 edition of *The Doctrines and Discipline of
the Methodist Episcopal Church in America*, 135, as reprinted in *The Methodist
Discipline of 1798* (facsimile edition), ed. Frederick A. Norwood (Rutland:
Academy Books, 1979).

13. As late as 1885, Bishop Henry McNeal Turner described the General Rules
as "one of the most unique and complete systems of moral ethics found any-
where upon the face of the globe" (*The Genius and Theory of Methodist Polity, Or
the Machinery of Methodism. Practically Illustrated Through a Series of Questions and
Answers*, approved by the General Conference of the A.M.E. Church, 1885, 1888;
reprinted by the AMEC Sunday School Union, 1986, 135). Whether Turner was
drawing on the "Explanatory Notes" of Coke and Asbury in this work is not
clear.

14. At the same time, those members of the Methodist societies who were *not*
accountable for their discipleship were admonished, disciplined, and—if necessary—expelled from the "society" of Methodists. Practices ranging from the distinction between "probationary" and full membership to the use of "communion tickets" marked the link between the moral and spiritual dimensions of
disciplinary practices.

As the American Methodist movement became a church—however provi-
sionally—the context(s) of application of American Methodist church discipline
also began to change, and thereby the roles of laity and clergy also changed.

15. See Section III, Restrictive Rules, Para. 19, Article V. of the Constitution of
The United Methodist Church as found in *The Book of Discipline of the United
Methodist Church 1992* (Nashville: United Methodist Publishing House), 27. See
also the discussion in Frederick Norwood, *The Story of American Methodism*, 126.
In the original formulation of the Restrictive Rules, this would have been the
fourth restrictive rule.

16. Here, I am indebted to Sarah Brooks Blair's unpublished paper "The
Reformed Methodists: Anti-War, Anti-Episcopacy, Anti-Slavery, 1814–1843"

given at the Annual Meeting of the Historical Society for United Methodists, Madison, New Jersey, on August 14, 1994. Brooks notes that the *second* edition of *The Reformer's Discipline* (Bennington, Vt.: Darius Clark, 1815) makes clear which of Wesley's General Rules were accepted and which were discarded. According to Brooks Blair, most of these changes were made to reflect the Reformed Methodists' stance against episcopacy, against slavery, and against war. I hope that the forthcoming dissertation by Sarah Brooks Blair (Drew University) will provide more clarification about the ways the Reformed Methodist Church diverged from the disciplinary practice of the Methodist Episcopal Church in particular, and, more generally, from the pattern of disciplinary practice shared by African American Methodists and Euro-American Methodists.

17. See *The Constitution and Discipline of the Methodist Protestant Church* (Baltimore: John J. Harrod, Book Agent of the Methodist Protestant Church, 1831), 14. The eleven elementary principles of the Constitution of the Methodist Protestant Church included a statement that (4) "Every man has an inalienable right to private judgment in matters of religion, and an equal right to express his opinion in any way which will not violate the laws of God, or the rights of his fellow man." While this principle was clearly envisioned to stand in tension with the other ten principles—including (9) "It is the duty of all ministers and members of the church to maintain godliness, and to oppose all moral evil"—it also posed a significant challenge to the context of application of the General Rules, not only because it challenged episcopal authority, and clergy privilege, but also because it suggested a different context for disciplinary practice, and a more limited set of conditions for excommunication than had been the case in the M.E.C. Thus, it would be correct to surmise that the relationship of the "rhetoric of separation" and the "rhetoric of unity" in the Methodist Protestant Church was quite different from that in the Methodist Episcopal Church.

18. See, e.g., *The Doctrines and Discipline of the African Methodist Episcopal Church* (first edition) 1817, Preface, 2-9.

19. See, e.g., *The Doctrines and Discipline of the Colored Methodist Episcopal Church in America,* rev. ed. (Jackson, Tenn.: Publishing House, C.M.E. Church, 1902), Preface, 3-5. See also F. M. Hamilton, *A Plain Account of the Colored Methodist Episcopal Church in America* (1887), 15-29, 53.

20. Early on, Nathan Bangs expressed concern that the General Conference of the Methodist Episcopal Church had diverged from Mr. Wesley in its interpretation of the General Rule dealing with the buying and selling of spirituous liquors.

21. Space does not permit discussion of the many examples that could be presented, but historical records of the way disputes with the leaders of the

Reformed Methodists, the Methodist Protestants, the movement to gain laity participation in the conferences, and the struggle for women's participation (and ordination), all exhibit these kinds of claims and counterclaims.

In this respect, the story presented in the "Historical Sketch of the Origins of the Methodist Protestant Church" in *The Constitution and Discipline* of *the Methodist Protestant Church 1904* is exemplary. As copies of a pamphlet on "Mutual rights of ministers and laity" were distributed in the late 1820s, and "union societies" began forming in various conferences of the Methodist Episcopal Church, leaders in this movement were threatened with expulsion (typically by their pastors) if they did not stop distributing the tract and forming the societies.

> When they were brought to trial and insisted on being informed what law of the Church or the Bible they had violated, they were referred to a clause of one of the "General Rules" of John and Charles Wesley, which forbids speaking of magistrates or of Ministers—yet it should have been well known that by ministers Mr. Wesley meant Ministers of State, and not clergymen. (Historical Sketch, xii)

22. Russell Richey, "The Role of History in the Discipline," *Quarterly Review* (Winter 1989): 15. The focus of Richey's article is the way in which history functions in the 1988 *Book of Discipline of the United Methodist Church,* particularly Paragraph 66, beginning with "Our Distinctive Heritage as United Methodists," which Richey also identifies as a jeremiadic narrative.

23. For an interesting example of this debate, see Franklin H. Littell's *jeremiad,* "Toward the Recovery of Discipline in Methodism," *The Christian Century* (26 June 1963): 826-28, and the "Readers' Response" by Harold Bosley in the column entitled "Returning Franklin Littell's Fire" (17 July 1963): 911-13. Bosley's own historical narration and assessment is noteworthy for its implicit confidence that changes in church discipline have not affected the course of American Methodism negatively.

24. A. Gregory Schneider, *The Way of the Cross Leads Home: the Domestication of American Methodism* (Indianapolis: University of Indiana Press, 1991), 78-91.

25. Coke and Asbury, "Explanatory Notes" to the 1798 *Discipline,* p. 80, in elaborating on reason #7 for further directions given "to him who has the charge of a circuit."

The bishops' commentary continues with these words: "On this account all our conferences throughout the world mutually require, that every member of our society who changes his place of abode, shall previously obtain a certificate from the preacher who has the charge of his circuit, who is most likely to be acquainted with his character, his relations excepted; and that without such certificate he shall not be received into any other society. . . . How much more then is it our duty to use every precaution to preserve the purity of our church, in these days when persecution has ceased, and it is the interest of many to be united to a religious party."

26. Ibid., 91.

27. Ibid., 107.

28. Ibid., 108.

29. Ibid.

30. On the one hand, there is no evidence that leaders of the Methodist Episcopal Church consciously chose to exempt themselves from the mandate for maintaining spiritual unity. Thus, it is not the case that all such language was expunged from the book of discipline of the M.E.C., South. On the other hand, the deletion of this one section at the particular time that it was taken out of the book of discipline surely can be taken as significant.

31. Here, however, it is important to observe that the "means of grace" section, which typically contained sections on the "class meetings" and later "Sunday schools" focused almost entirely on laypeople. From very early on, then, the discussions of "Conference" *did not* take place within the framework of "Christian conference" as a means of grace (however much this notion may or may not have been present for leaders as diverse as Jesse Lee and Nathan Bangs). Sections on "Conference" in the books of discipline of the Methodist Episcopal Church and M.E. Church, South, would remain largely "organizational" in scope, and largely unrelated to the material in the "means of grace" section. Still later, "means of grace" becomes a kind of "catchall" for the latest set of concerns. At different times in the nineteenth century, "Sunday school" and "temperance" are placed under this rubric.

But however significant this reconstructed rhetoric of inclusion may have been, there is no question that over the course of the nineteenth century, the practice in question comes to be channeled less and less in public ways, and with it also the context in which disciplinary admonition can take place as a positive expression of *the unity* of the people called Methodists in American culture.

32. See, e.g., L. H. Holsey's "Introduction" to F. M. Hamilton's *A Plain Account of the Colored Methodist Episcopal Church in America, Being an Account of Her History and Polity; Also, Her Prospective Work* (Nashville: Southern Methodist Publishing House, 1887), 10.

33. Mary Sawyer, *Black Ecumenism: Implementing the Demands of Justice* (Trinity International Press, 1994).

34. *The Doctrines and Discipline of the African Methodist Episcopal Church* (Philadelphia, 1817), Section V "Of Slavery," as found in the facsimile Reprint Edition of the First Edition of the Discipline of the African Methodist Episcopal

Church with Historical Preface and Notes by C. M. Tanner (Atlanta, Ga., 1916), 105.

35. Gayraud Wilmore, *Black Religion and Black Radicalism*, 2nd rev. ed. (Maryknoll, N.Y.: Orbis Books, 1984), 86.

36. Ibid., 87.

37. Emphasis mine.

38. Daniel Alexander Payne, *A History of the African Methodist Episcopal Church* (Nashville: A.M.E. Sunday School Union, 1891), 22.

39. See for example the prefatory letter by Richard Allen, Daniel Coker, and James Champion, [addressed] "To the Members of the African Methodist Episcopal Church in the United States of America" in *The Doctrines and Discipline of the African Methodist Episcopal Church* (1817), 2-9; see also 11-14 in Tanner's reprint ed. of 1916.

40. Henry McNeal Turner, *The Genius and Theory of Methodist Polity*, 142 (619 Q).

41. The office of stewardess appears to have originated in Savannah, Georgia, while Henry McNeal Turner was pastor (1872–80). Stephen Ward Angell reports that Turner "advocated an expanded role for women in church affairs, appointing nine women in St. Philip's Church to the new office of stewardess and giving them broad powers on matters of discipline." Angell, *Bishop Henry McNeal Turner and African-American Religion in the South* (Knoxville: University of Tennessee Press, 1992), 111-12.
Although stewardesses were clearly not to operate outside the authority of the preacher in charge, it is striking that they were also charged with maintaining the discipline of the congregation including offering admonition and reproval, roles that typically had been reserved for the class leader in the Euro-American Methodist congregations. For an extensive commentary on the responsibilities of stewardesses, and the link with the office of deaconess created by the 1888 General Conference of the A.M.E. Church, see Turner, *Methodist Polity*, 142-45.

42. For example, it is fascinating to consider the ad hoc ways in which the *Discipline* was implemented (and ignored) before, during, and after Reconstruction by such figures as Bishop Matthew Simpson of the M.E. Church and (later to be) Bishop Henry McNeal Turner of the A.M.E. Church. Biographers of both of these leaders have noted the ways in which they bent the *Discipline* of their denominations to their own sense of missional need in the course of taking advantage of the "opportunity" presented by Northern occupation of the South during Reconstruction.

43. In the fourth edition (1881) of *The Cyclopedia of Methodism* (242-43) Matthew Simpson had described the Colored Methodist Episcopal Church in ways that Hamilton and other C.M.E. ministers found offensive. In his *Plain Account* (1887), Hamilton reproduces Simpson's account (39-41), and goes to great lengths to "correct" Simpson's discussion of five specific points in question, each of which has a bearing on the legitimacy of the "mutual agreement" between black and white Methodists in the M.E.C., South, to form the Colored Methodist Episcopal Church.

44. The first chapter of Hamilton's *Plain Account* is filled with examples of familiar language in which the C.M.E. Church is regarded as "daughter."

45. Ibid., 22-23.

46. Ibid., 25-26.

47. Ibid., 26. In particular, Hamilton quotes Abraham's words to Lot, "Let there be no strife between me and thee," as exemplifying the spirit of separation that characterized the decision of the Methodist Episcopal Church, South, and the Colored Methodist Episcopal Church to separate. More dubious still is Hamilton's interpretation of the significance of the split between Paul and Barnabas. Hamilton's comment, "This separation resulted in general good to both Jew and Gentile" (26), glosses over the struggles at Jerusalem and Antioch discussed in Acts 15ff.

48. Ibid., 47-48.

49. Here is another case in which it appears that Gregory Schneider's discussion of the "domestication" of American Methodism could be *extended* for the purpose of analyzing the "political" and polemical uses of familial metaphors to challenge or redirect Pan-Methodist denominational conflicts in the nineteenth and twentieth centuries.

50. Lucius H. Holsey, "Introduction" to *A Plain Account of History of the Colored Methodist Episcopal Church in America,* 9-10.

51. Charles Spencer Smith, *A History of the African Methodist Episcopal Church Being a Volume Supplemental to a History of the African Methodist Episcopal Church, by Daniel Alexander Payne* (Philadelphia: Book Concern of the A.M.E. Church, 1922), 84. The delegation in question was commissioned by the General Conference of the M.E. Church, South, meeting in New Orleans in 1866.

52. Ibid., 84.

53. Ibid.

54. Ibid., Appendix, 520. The full text of the Report can be found appended to "The Minutes of the Third Session of the South Carolina Annual Conference of

the African M.E. Church," in the Appendix to Smith, 520-21. The report in question was signed by J. M. Brown, R. H. Cain, H. M. Turner, G. W. Brodie, C. L. Bradwell, Robert Meacham, and Wm. H. Brown.

55. Ibid.

56. From the Quadrennial Address to the Bishops, *Journal of the 20th, Quadrennial Session of the General Conference of the A.M.E. Church,* held in St. Stephens A.M.E. Church, Wilmington, N.C., May 4-22, 1896, p. 98. Also cited in Peter Paris, *The Social Teaching of the Black Churches* (Philadelphia: Fortress, 1984), 13.

57. For example, writing in 1922, Charles Spencer Smith, the official historian of the A.M.E. Church, still felt the need to defend the A.M.E. Church against the "mistaken" belief that it was "a political church."

58. It must be noted, however, that while this self-perception of itself as having "spiritual" ecumenical vocation has remained a prominent feature of the C.M.E. Church in the twentieth century, denominational leadership arguably can be said to have become much more critical of racist practices in church and society. See, e.g., Joseph H. Johnson's book, *Christian Methodist Beliefs* (1978).

59. C. H. Phillips, *The History of the Colored Methodist Church in America; Comprising Its Organization, Subsequent Development, and Present Status* (Jackson, Tenn.: Publishing House, C.M.E. Church, 1898), 247.

60. See, e.g., the statement on "Human Rights" in the "Social Creed" of the C.M.E. Church as found in the 1990 edition of the *Book of Discipline of the Christian Methodist Episcopal Church* (Memphis: C.M.E. Publishing House, 1990), Para. 130.3 (f), p. 23. Arguably, however, this statement bears more similarity to more statements of The United Methodist Church's "Social Principles" than of the A.M.E. Church.

61. In his commentary on the General Rules, Bishop Joseph A. Johnson Jr. calls attention to the 1789 addition, which prohibited the buying and selling of slaves. Johnson provides a fairly extensive commentary on this article, in the course of which he distinguishes between "physical slavery," which technically was ended by the Emancipation Proclamation, and other types of slavery that continue to constrict the lives of human beings because of the continuing effects of racism.

> Physical slavery is condemned by the judgment of God and the teachings of Jesus Christ.
> Physical slavery is still a fact of life in many sections of our world today. Far more damaging than physical slavery are the psychological, sociological, economic, and political types of slavery which are experienced by men the world over. Black Americans, though freed physically by the Emancipation

Proclamation are still caught in the constricting net of racism, which is a form of slavery and they are victims of every conceivable form of repression. Black Americans['] quest for human dignity, identity, liberation and power represents revolts against the subtle forms of slavery which are still prevalent in our world today. There, the fight against slavery in all of its subtle and vicious forms must be continued by Methodists until all men enjoy the freedom and liberty, which are made available to them through Jesus Christ, our Lord.

See Bishop Johnson's *Basic Christian Methodist Beliefs* (Shreveport: Fourth Episcopal District [C.M.E.] Press, 1978), 107.

62. *Journal of the General Conference of the Methodist Episcopal Church* held in Chicago, Illinois, May 2-29, 1900, ed. David S. Monroe (New York: Eaton & Mains, 1900), 59-60, emphasis mine.

While the bishops were not willing to jump to conclusions about the questions they articulated, it may also be significant that they did not answer these questions the way that American Methodists did in the mid nineteenth century. See, for example, the answer given to a similar set of questions about the class meeting as a "humble but essential means of grace" in G. Coles's "Introduction" to *Heroines of Methodism* (1857), 21, citing *Jobson's Portrait of His Mother* (1857). I am indebted to Dr. Stephen Long for calling these documents to my attention.

63. To some extent, it could be argued that this statement encapsulates what Russell Richey has identified as the four "languages" or rhetorics of early American Methodism: terms derived from the "religious vernacular" of the Second Great Awakening are mixed easily with the arcane "Wesleyan" terminology of early British Methodism, and the rhetoric of "republicanism" appears in the voice of "episcopal" authority. See Richey's study *Early American Methodism* (Bloomington: Indiana University Press, 1991), xvi-xix.

This observation in itself indicates a kind of rhetorical *separation* between American Methodism and its British analogue where attempts were made (in vain) to encapsulate all of Methodist experience within the language of "Wesleyanism." The result, "Buntingism," revealed the fallacy of pretending that change does not occur and that power held by the few cannot corrupt. For a discussion of Jacob Bunting and his rise to power in British Methodism, see Robert Currie, *Methodism Divided: A Study in the Sociology of Ecumenicalism* (Longon: Faber and Faber, 1968), 31-43.

64. Stephen Long, *Living the Discipline: United Methodist Theological Reflections on War, Civilization, and Holiness* (Grand Rapids: Eerdmans, 1992), 8-9.

65. See the "Historical Statement" in *The Doctrines and Discipline of the Methodist Episcopal Church* (New York: Methodist Book Concern, 1904), 10. These

(last) two paragraphs were printed in boldface from the 1904 edition to the 1920 edition of the *Discipline*.

66. This statement, which appeared in every book of discipline from 1940 to 1964 under the heading "Episcopal Greetings," appears to have come into the *Book of Discipline* without having been discussed in a public venue. It was not included in the "Prospectus of the Discipline of The Methodist Church," and therefore was not discussed at the 1939 Uniting Conference held at Kansas City, Missouri. By contrast, there were discussion and debate about the "Historical Statement" (which immediately follows the "Episcopal Greetings" in the 1940 *Book of Discipline*). See the *Journal of the Uniting Conference of the Methodist Episcopal Church, Methodist Episcopal Church, South, Methodist Protestant Church* (1 May 1939), 226-29.

Appended to the end of the statement was a note (which appears to have originated in the "Bishops' Recommendation and Greeting" of the M.E.C., South), which stated:

We wish to see this little publication in the house of every Methodist; and the more so, as it contains the Articles of Religion maintained more or less, in part or in whole, by every reformed Church in the world.

67. Given the cumulative force of the rhetorical shifts that occurs in this preface to the 1939 *Discipline,* one might claim that it is an unprecedented statement. However, there is plenty of evidence available from the three denominations which were united in 1939 that the rhetorical glosses that I have mentioned were already so well established in each of the thre e branches of American Methodism that this statement offered by Bishops A. Frank Smith, Ernest G. Richardson, and G. Bromley Oxnam simply gave authoritative standing to what was, de facto, the collective practice of the three largest branches over Euro-American Methodism.

68. Norwood, *Church Membership in the Methodist Tradition* (Nashville: Methodist Publishing House, 1958), 10, emphasis mine.

69. Herman C. Riley, *A Manual of the Discipline of the Christian Methodist Episcopal Church (Revised) Including Decisions of the College of Bishops and Rules of Order Applicable to Ecclesiastical Courts and Conferences* (by L. H. Holsey), revised and ed. Herman C. Riley (privately published and distributed, 1984); see "Appeal of the Rev. Bleland Ash, Jr.," 98-107.

As Riley reports, the specific charges made against the minister in this case were "making loans without the probability of paying, and intemperate and [using] abusive language when asked by his creditors to pay." (See the last item listed under "First, By Doing No Harm" in the General Rules.) He was also charged with having "damaged the good name of Faith Chapel C.M.E. Church and the Christian Methodist Episcopal Church generally..." (101). The presiding elder's suspension of the minister was upheld.

The significance of this case is rendered all the more complex by virtue of the fact that the presiding elder of the Oakland District who brought charges against Rev. Ash was none other than Herman C. Riley, the editor of the revised edition of Holsey's *Manual!*

70. See "Creation of Plan of Union Proposed for Four Methodist Denominations" in *The United Methodist Newscope* (23) no. 18 (5 May 1995): 1. News reports of the meeting at which this proposal was initially discussed explained that United Methodist Bishop James K. Mathews (retired) opened the meeting of Sixth Consultation of Methodist Bishops with a "history of the road toward unity." Mathews suggested a plan based upon the model of "'federal union' where states formed a 'more perfect union' by fashioning a strong center, with considerable latitude to the constituent parts." Christian Methodist Episcopal Bishop Charles L. Helton of Charlotte, North Carolina, warned against the implications of this Americanist proposal with its suggestion of "union imposed from the top." Helton reminded the body that "we must grow together at the local level instead of forcing union at the upper levels." Others in the gathering expressed pessimism about the idea of organic union because of "extreme racism" in contemporary American culture.

71. Because of the unusual scope of this comparative project, I had to deal with several different libraries and archives in order to have access to the materials needed for this study. As usual, Margaret Moser and her staff at the Pelletier Library at Allegheny College have been very helpful in dealing with all my research requests related to my analysis of the Methodist Episcopal Church. I am grateful to Minnie H. Clayton and Wilson Flemister, the Archives and Special Collections section staff of the Robert Woodruff Library, for their assistance in locating materials on the A.M.E. Church and C.M.E. Church found in the collections of the Interdenominational Theological Center housed at the Atlanta University Center in Atlanta, Georgia. I am also grateful to Ken Rowe and the staff at the United Methodist Archives at Drew University, Madison, New Jersey, for their assistance in completing my research file of materials on the A.M.E. Church, the M.E. Church (North), and the M.E. Church, South.

Finally, I would like to thank the following persons for comments and criticisms that they offered in response to two previous oral presentations of this essay: L. Gregory Jones of Duke University; Doug Strong of Wesley Theological Seminary in Washington, D.C.; A. Gregory Schneider of Pacific Union College; and Dr. Russell Richey of Duke University. Greg Jones provided a very timely and helpful critical response to the penultimate draft of this essay. C. Jarrett Gray Jr. of Duke University called several technical errors to my attention for which I am very grateful.

NOTES TO "CONNECTIONALISM VERSUS HOLINESS"

1. Phineas F. Bresee, "A Serious Question," *The Nazarene* (28 June 1900), 4.

2. Leon H. Vincent, *John Heyl Vincent: A Biographical Sketch* (New York: Macmillan, 1925), 283-84.

3. Bresee, "The Denver Revival," *The Nazarene* (5 April 1900), 4.

4. Three standard studies of the Holiness movement and its conflicts with mainstream Methodist denominations are Charles Edwin Jones, *Perfectionist Persuasion: The Holiness Movement and American Methodist, 1867–1936* (Metuchen, N.J.: Scarecrow, 1974); Melvin Easterday Dieter, *The Holiness Revival of the Nineteenth Century* (Metuchen, N.J.: Scarecrow Press, 1980); and Timothy L. Smith, *Called Unto Holiness: The Story of the Nazarenes: The Formative Years* (Kansas City, Mo.: Nazarene Publishing House, 1962).

5. These paragraphs characterizing the early Methodist community and the norms of the world it opposed are based on the author's book *The Way of the Cross Leads Home: The Domestication of American Methodism* (Bloomington: Indiana University Press, 1993).

6. For the importance of refinement as a measure of character and a tool of ranking in American culture, see Richard L. Bushman, *The Refinement of America: Persons, Houses, Cities* (New York: Vintage Books, 1993 [1992]). On the significance of liberal education for the identity of the gentleman, see Samuel Haber, *The Quest for Authority and Honor in the American Professions, 1750–1900* (Chicago: University of Chicago Press, 1991), ix-x, 3-8.

7. For an interpretation of the significance of this action in relation to the life and work of one of the principal figures in the present study, see Harold W. Mann, *Atticus Greene Haygood: Methodist Bishop, Editor, and Educator* (Athens: University of Georgia Press, 1965), 57-60.

8. William McGuire King, "Denominational Modernization and Religious Identity: the Case of the Methodist Episcopal Church," *Methodist History* 20 (January 1982): 75-89.

9. *The Incorporation of America: Culture and Society in the Gilded Age* (New York: Hill and Wang, 1982).

10. In addition to Trachtenberg's work, these generalizations are based upon Robert H. Wiebe, *The Search for Order, 1877–1920* (New York: Hill and Wang, 1967); Burton J. Bledstein, *The Culture of Professionalism: The Middle Class and the Development of Higher Education in America* (New York: W. W. Norton, 1976); Peter Dobkin Hall, *The Organization of American Culture, 1700–1900: Private Institutions, Elites, and the Origins of American Nationality* (New York: New York University Press, 1982); and Haber, *Quest for Authority*. On the role of church voluntary associations in these trends, see Russell E. Richey, "Institutional

Forms of Religion" in *Encyclopedia of the American Religious Experience: Studies of Traditions and Movement*, vol. 1, ed. Charles H. Lippy and Peter W. Williams (New York: Charles Scribner's Sons, 1988), 38-41; William McGuire King, "The Role of Auxiliary Ministries in Late Nineteenth-Century Methodism," in *Rethinking Methodist History: A Bicentennial Historical Consultation*, ed. Russell E. Richey and Kenneth E. Rowe (Nashville: Kingswood Books, 1985), 167-72; Ben Primer, *Protestants and American Business Methods* (n.p.: UMI Research Press, 1979); Gregory Singleton, "Protestant Voluntary Organizations and the Shaping of Victorian America," *American Quarterly* 27 (December 1975): 549-60.

11. A. Gregory Schneider, "Objective Selves Versus Empowered Selves: The Conflict Over Holiness in the Post-Civil War Methodist Episcopal Church," *Methodist History* 32 (July 1994): 237-49.

12. For evidence of the extensive influence of these eighteenth-century English exemplars, see John Allen Wood, *Autobiography of J. A. Wood* (Chicago: Christian Witness Company, 1904), 12; Harold E. Raser, *Phoebe Palmer: Her Life and Thought* (Lewiston, N.Y.: Edwin Mellen, 1987), 43-47; A. F. N., "Holiness Misrepresented. No. III" (Philadelphia) *Methodist Home Journal* (5 April 1873), 105; and "Victory Through Testimony," *The Nazarene* (15 March 1900), 3.

13. The Wesleyan holiness autobiographers, both early and late, were examples of what William C. Spengemann calls "historical autobiographers," those who, like Augustine, Dante, and John Bunyan before them, attempted "to say more than human things with a human voice." See Spengemann, *The Forms of Autobiography: Episodes in the History of a Literary Genre* (New Haven: Yale University Press, 1980), 34-61, 166-69.

14. Wood, *Autobiography*, esp. pp. 8-10, 46-54; Milton L. Haney, *Pentecostal Possibilities, or, The Story of My Life* (Chicago: Christian Witness Co., 1906), esp. pp. 32-36, 68-74.

15. See Delbert R. Rose, *Vital Holiness: A Theology of Christian Experience* (Minneapolis: Bethany Fellowship, 1975), 79-136.

16. E. A. Girvin, *Phineas F. Bresee: A Prince in Israel* (1916; reprint, New York: Garland Publishing, 1984).

17. Daniel Curry, "A Discord Harmonized," *Christian Advocate* (30 April 1874), 140; Charles Fowler, "Abuses of Experience," *Christian Advocate* (27 December 1877), 828-29.

18. "The Autobiography of Bishop Vincent," was serialized in the *Northwestern Christian Advocate* beginning April 6, 1910, pp. 432-33. The twenty-fifth and last installment was published November 2, 1910, pp. 1392, 1407. Leon H. Vincent, the bishop's nephew and biographer, comments on the autobiography in conjunction with several other of Vincent's publications in *John Heyl Vincent*, 184-97.

19. Mann, *Atticus Greene Haygood*, vii.

20. Milton L. Haney, *Pentecostal Possibilities, or, Story of My Life: An Autobiography* (Chicago: Christian Witness Co., 1906), 32-36. For the account of Haney's experience of sanctification, see pp. 68-74. For accounts of the formative experiences for the other holiness leaders, see John Allen Wood, *Perfect Love; or, Plain Things for Those Who Need Them, Concerning the Doctrine, Experience, Profession, and Practice of Christian Holiness*, revised and enlarged (Chicago: Christian Witness Co., 1915 [1880]), 316, 322-23; Girvin, *Prince in Israel*, 27-29, 42-44, 49-52; Smith, "His Grace…Not in Vain," (Cincinnati) *God's Revivalist and Bible Advocate* (3 December 1925), 2-4; and (10 December 1925), 2-4; "My Sixty-Third Anniversary," *God's Revivalist and Bible Advocate* (15 April 1937), 5.

21. The idea of a "deconversion" and the following characterizations of Haygood's more naturalistic faith draw on Mann's analysis in *Atticus Greene Haygood*, 198-201. Two major sermons in Haygood's that evince his more naturalistic outlook are "A Thanksgiving sermon" (Macon, Ga.), *Wesleyan Christian Advocate*, 25 December 1880, p. 2; and "Growth in Grace: A Sermon by Atticus G. Haygood, D.D., LL.D., preached before the District Conference of the Oxford District, North Georgia Conference, M. E. Church, South, held at Covington, Ga., July 18, 1885, and published by formal request of the conference" (Macon, Ga.: J. W. Burke and Co., 1885).

22. Vincent's criticisms of the traditional revivalist religion of his childhood are scattered throughout his autobiography. See, for instance, "Autobiography," *Northwestern Christian Advocate* (8 June 1910): 715; and (6 July 1910): 846-47. His comprehensive critique of revivalism is found in J. H. Vincent, *The Revival After the Revival* (New York: Phillips and Hunt; Cincinnati: Cranston and Stowe, 1882).

23. For a description and analysis of this ritual form, see A. Gregory Schneider, "The Ritual of Happy Dying Among Early American Methodists," *Church History* 56 (September 1987): 348-63.

24. J. H. Vincent, "Autobiography," *Northwestern Christian Advocate* (22 June 1910): 782-83; (29 June 1910): 815.

25. John H. Vincent, "Autobiography," *Northwestern Christian Advocate* (29 June 1910): 814-15, 836. For John Vincent's mature reflections on the spirituality Henry Hurd introduced him to, see John H. Vincent, *The Inner Life: A Study in Christian Experience* (Boston: United Society of Christian Endeavor, 1900). Leon Vincent describes the book as "in part an exposition of transcendentalism," in *John Heyl Vincent*, 195.

26. J. H. Vincent, "Autobiography" (18 May 1910): 626, 644; (1 June 1910): 683, 707.

27. Vincent mentions explicitly that his mother read an extensive literature of spiritual autobiography promoted by that fountain of holiness thought and practice, Phoebe Palmer. See J. H. Vincent, "Autobiography," *Northwestern Christian Advocate* (29 June 1910): 815.

28. John S. Inskip, "A Felt Want," *Advocate of Christian Holiness* 8 (July 1877): 157.

29. Joseph H. Smith, "His Grace . . . Not in Vain," *God's Revivalist and Bible Advocate* (10 December 1925): 3.

30. "Searching for the Cause," *The Nazarene,* 24 (May 1900): 1.

31. J. A. Wood, *Autobiography,* 37-38.

32. Girvin, *Prince in Israel,* 50.

33. "The First Nazarene Church Building," *The Nazarene* (3 July 1899): 2. For further evidence of holiness advocates' concern for issues of wealth, poverty, and what analysts today would call social class, see W. A. Powers, "Israel, Past and Present," *The Nazarene* (28 August 1899): 3; T. B. Welch, M.D., "Christian Aristocracy in Earnest: An Improvement upon Pewed Churches" (Philadelphia), *Advocate of Christian Holiness* 7 (January 1873): 17; Matilda C. Edwards, "The Church Walking with the World," *Advocate of Christian Holiness* 8 (September 1877): 198-99; T. L. Smith, *Called Unto Holiness,* 47-53, on holiness social work.

34. Paul Merritt Bassett, "Culture and Concupiscence: The Changing Definition of Sanctity in the Wesleyan/Holiness Movement, 1867–1920," *Wesleyan Theological Journal* 28 (Spring-Fall 1993): 59-127.

35. Articus G. Haygood, *The Monk and the Prince* (Nashville: Publishing House of the MEC, South, 1895), 54-55.

36. J. H. Vincent, "Autobiography" (20 April 1910): 496-97; (4 May 1910): 562, 580.

37. J. H. Vincent, "Autobiography" (4 May 1910): 562, 580; (1 June 1910): 683, 707; (20 April 1920): 496-97.

38. Haygood, "Our Methodist Parents" (Macon, Ga.) *Wesleyan Christian Advocate* (11 January 1993): 5; *Monk and Prince,* 48-49.

39. J. H. Vincent, "Autobiography" (2 November 1910): 1392, 1407.

40. M. L. Haney, *Pentecostal Possibilities,* 73-74.

41. See, e.g., "Victory Through Testimony," *The Nazarene* (15 March 1990): 3; "Dialogue," *Guide to Holiness* 8 (February 1850): 55-58.

42. T. L. Smith, *Called Unto Holiness,* 118-20; "The Culmination" (Los Angeles), *Nazarene Messenger* (4 Jan. 1912): 1.

43. J. A. Wood, *Autobiography*, 52-54; George D. Watson, A *Holiness Manual* (London: Smyth and Yerworth, 1883), 126-28.

44. Walter J. Ong, *Orality and Literacy: The Technologizing of the Word* (London: Methuen, 1982).

45. The following discussion of orality is adapted from A. Gregory Schneider, "From Democratization to Domestication: The Transitional Orality of the American Methodist Circuit Rider," in *Communication and Change in American Religious History*, ed. Leonard I. Sweet (Grand Rapids: Eerdmans, 1993), 141-64.

46. L. H. Vincent, *John Heyl Vincent*, 283-85.

47. J. H. Vincent, *The Inner Life: A Study in Christian Experience* (Boston and Chicago: United Society of Christian Endeavor, 1900), 23-24; see also *Revival After the Revival*, 57-59.

48. Haygood, *Monk and Prince*, 110-11.

49. J. H. Vincent, *Inner Life*, 16-17, 27-28, 30-31.

50. Haygood, *Growth in Grace*, 15-16, 19-20.

51. J. H. Vincent, "Autobiography," *Northwestern Christian Advocate* (6 July 1910): 846-47; (2 November 1910): 1392; *Revival After the Revival*, 42-48, 60-62, 70-74. For Haygood's reaction to revivalistic fluctuations of feeling, see Mann, *Atticus Greene Haygood*, 164-65.

52. J. H. Vincent, *The Revival After the Revival*, 74-75.

53. J. H. Vincent, "Autobiography," *Northwestern Christian Advocate* (5 October 1910): 1264-65.

54. Ibid.

55. Ong, *Orality and Literacy*, 81-83, 101-8.

56. Of course, it is over-simple to claim that the orality of holiness revivalism was a polar opposite to the textuality of Vincent and Haygood. Wesleyan-holiness practice was shaped by textual forms as much as by oral forms and constituted a transition between the two. For a consideration of the textual elements in such practices, see Schneider, "Democratization to Domestication," 152-59.

57. For Bresee's move from the pastorate to his city mission to the poor at Peniel hall, see Girvin, *Prince in Israel*, 98-103. For the moves of Haney, Smith, and Wood to the role of evangelist, see, respectively, Haney, *Pentecostal Possibilities*, 222-28; Smith, "His Grace...Not in Vain," *God's Revivalist* (10 December 1925): 3-4; Wood, *Autobiography*, 77-81.

58. Haney, *Pentecostal Possibilities*, 222-28.

59. On Haygood's educational endeavors, see Mann, *Atticus Greene Haygood,* chaps. 5, 6, 10, 11; Haygood, *Our Children* (New York: Nelson and Phillips, 1876); *Pleas for Progress* (Nashville: Publishing House of the M. E. Church, South, 1889).

60. On Vincent's educational efforts, see Leon Vincent, *John Heyl Vincent,* chaps. 8, 10, 13; J. H. Vincent, *The Chautauqua Movement* (1885; reprint Freeport, N.Y.: Books for Libraries Press, 1971); *A Study in Pedagogy for People Who Are Not Professional Teachers* (New York: Wilbur K. Ketcham, 1890); Jesse Lyman Hurlbut, *The Story of Chautauqua* (New York: G. P. Putnam's Sons, 1921).

61. Hurlbut, *Story of Chautauqua,* vii-xix.

62. Vincent's biographer wrote that the Palestine class was an unconscious groping toward Chautauqua. "One might almost say that the first meeting at Fair Point on Chautauqua Lake in 1874, was no other than a gigantic Palestine Class" (Leon Vincent, *John Heyl Vincent,* 90-91).

63. J. H. Vincent, "Autobiography," *Northwestern Christian Advocate* (29 June 1910): 814-15.

64. J. H. Vincent, "Autobiography," *Northwestern Christian Advocate* (6 July 1910): 847.

65. See Bledstein, *Culture of Professionalism;* and King, "Role of Auxiliary Ministries," 169. On the connection to the old culture of honor, see Haber, *Quest for Honor.*

66. At least, I am not a theologian in any professionally recognizable sense, but I have been influenced by a few of them. To satisfy any curiosity the reader has about the perspectives from which these judgments come, they include the Anabaptist and quasi-Anabaptist outlooks supplied by John Howard Yoder, Donald Kraybill, and Stanley Hauerwas, the hard-to-classify, but magisterial treatment of "the Powers" by Walter Wink, and the continuing commentary and testimony given by the Sojourner's community in Washington, D.C.

NOTES TO "FAMILY AND MIDWEEK WORSHIP"

1. John Wesley, Sermon 2, "The Almost Christian," I.8, in *The Works of John Wesley* (Oxford: Clarendon, 1975–83; Nashville: Abingdon Press, 1984– ; hereafter cited as *Works*) 1 (ed. Albert C. Outler, 1984), 134.

2. See Diane Karay Tripp, "Daily Prayer in the Reformed Tradition: An Initial Survey," *Studia Liturgica* 21 (1991): 76-107, 190-219.

3. *Works,* 9:77-79 (ed. Rupert E. Davies, 1989).

4. *Works,* 9:73. The original 1743 General Rules did not include mention of "family prayer"; this stipulation was added to the Rules in 1744 (see *Works,* 9:73 n. 30, and stemma, p. 550).

5. Sermon 107, "On God's Vineyard," III.2, *Works* 3 (ed. Albert C. Outler, 1986), 512.

6. "The Character of a Methodist," §8, *Works,* 9:37.

7. Of the personal diaries and journals of American Methodists that I have examined, not one has recorded a single reference to any of Wesley's prayer collections.

8. Jesse Lee, *A Short History of the Methodists, in the United States of America; Beginning in 1766, and Continued till 1809* (Baltimore: Magill and Clime, 1810), 107.

9. Journal, November 16, 1766, *Works* 22 (ed. W. Reginald Ward and Richard P. Heitzenrater, 1993), 68. In his Journal reference for November 30 of that same year, Wesley notes that he preached on "the *Education of Children,* wherein we are so shamefully wanting" (ibid.).

10. The *Large Minutes,* Questions 13 and 33, in *The Works of the Rev. John Wesley, M.A.,* ed. Thomas Jackson, 3rd ed. (London: Wesleyan Methodist Book Room, 1872; reprint, Grand Rapids: Baker Book House, 1979), 8:301-7, 315-16. The requirement that the traveling preacher visit from house to house as a means of maintaining family religion was kept before the Methodist people by including a reference to it in the Methodist Episcopal Church *Discipline,* until 1892 in the section "Of Visiting from House to House," and after that time under the heading "Pastoral Fidelity." With the creation of the Methodist Church in 1939, the stated expectation that family religion was to be encouraged was dropped from this section; pastors are still charged with visiting from house to house, but in order to give "pastoral guidance and oversight" (1939 *Discipline,* ¶ 223.2).

11. Manuscript journal of Ezekiel Cooper, vol. 3, ms. p. 20, 25 July 1787, Library, Garrett-Evangelical Theological Seminary, Evanston, Ill.

12. Manuscript journal of Ezekiel Cooper, vol. 7, no ms. page no., 28 December 1790, Library, Garrett-Evangelical Theological Seminary, Evanston, Ill. Punctuation and spelling changes are mine.

13. For a thorough study of the liturgical life of the Quarterly Meeting, see Lester Ruth, "A Little Heaven Below: Quarterly Meetings as Seasons of Grace in Early American Methodism" (Ph.D. diss., University of Notre Dame, 1996).

14. See David Lowes Watson, *The Early Methodist Class Meeting: Its Origins and Significance* (Nashville: Discipleship Resources, 1985), 109-16.

15. In spite of the decline in the use of the class meeting, a section on the class meeting remained in the Methodist Episcopal *Discipline* until the 1939 merger; no such heading is found in the subsequent Methodist *Discipline,* and the term

"class," when used, seems to refer to something other than the traditional Wesleyan class meeting. It is interesting, however, that in 1872 a new paragraph (¶ 74) in the section "Classes and Class-Meetings" appeared in the Methodist Episcopal *Discipline* in an apparent attempt to reinforce, revitalize, and broaden its usage. Therein was stated that the purpose of a class meeting was "to establish and keep up a meeting for social and religious worship, for instruction, encouragement, and admonition, that shall be a profitable means of grace to our people." In 1920, this paragraph (now included under the heading "Classes and Class Meetings and Units for Prayer and Service" as ¶ 60 § 2) was emended, reflecting the increasing institutionalization of the denomination: "To encourage and support such meetings for social and religious worship and for instruction in Church plans and activities as shall be a profitable means of grace to the Church, and a means of developing intelligent loyalty to all Church enterprises." For comments on the revival of the class meeting during this period, see James Albert Beebe, *The Pastoral Office: An Introduction to the Work of a Pastor* (New York: Methodist Book Concern, 1923), 99-101.

16. Watson, *The Early Methodist Class Meeting,* 145-47.

17. As an apparent attempt to curb the decline of the class meeting, the 1872 Methodist Episcopal *Discipline* added a warning under the heading "Classes and Class-Meetings" (¶ 82): "Let care be observed that they do not fall into formality through the use of a uniform method. Let speaking be voluntary or the exercises conversational, the Leader taking such measures as may best assist in making the services fresh, spiritual, and of permanent religious profit." This paragraph was omitted in 1920.

18. See Robert E. Chiles, *Theological Transition in American Methodism: 1790–1935* (New York and Nashville: Abingdon Press, 1965).

19. William Walter Dean has done an intensive study of the decline of the class meeting in British Methodism, and claims that these conceptual changes are at the heart of the decline. Many of the same principles are applicable to the episcopal Methodist churches. See "Disciplined Fellowship: The Rise and Decline of Cell Groups in British Methodism" (Ph.D. diss., University of Iowa, 1985), 297-376.

20. Two studies, in particular, are helpful on the matter of domestic worship in this period: Colleen McDannell, *The Christian Home in Victorian America, 1840–1900* (Bloomington and Indianapolis: Indiana University Press, 1986); and A. Gregory Schneider, *The Way of the Cross Leads Home: The Domestication of American Methodism* (Bloomington and Indianapolis: Indiana University Press, 1993), esp. pp. 136-43.

21. See, e.g., "Parental Duty and Responsibility," *Methodist Magazine* 5 (February 1822): 62-67; Jacob Moore, "An Essay on the Obligation of Family

Worship," *Methodist Magazine* 9 (July 1826): 254-57 and 9 (August 1826): 294-98; Rufus William Bailey, *The Family Preacher* (New York: John S. Taylor, 1837); and John H. Power, *Discourse on Domestic Piety and Family Government* (Cincinnati: L. Swormstedt & A. Poe, 1852).

22. Charles F. Deems, the editor of *The Southern Methodist Pulpit,* debunks these and other excuses in *The Home-Altar: An Appeal on Behalf of Family Worship* (New York: M. W. Dodd, 1854), 46-100.

23. "On Family Religion," *Methodist Magazine* 4 (December 1821): 473.

24. "Family Worship," *Methodist Magazine and Quarterly Review* 18 (July 1836): 356-60.

25. James W. Alexander, *Thoughts on Family-Worship* (Philadelphia: Presbyterian Board of Publication, 1847), 223-24.

26. The instituted and prudential means of grace identified in the Methodist Episcopal *Discipline* were those laid out in the *Large Minutes,* Question 48 (*The Works of the Rev. John Wesley,* M.A., 8:322-24).

27. Part I, chap. 4, §11.2.10. In 1892, this statement, slightly modified, was moved to the section dealing with pastors (Part III, chap. 8, ¶189 §6) where it remained (again modified) after the 1939 merger.

28. Part III, chap. 1, §5.2.

29. For example, Charles Deems, in *The Home-Altar,* provides a two-year daily lectionary, extra Scripture readings for Sunday mornings throughout the month, two courses of prayers for morning and evening of every day in the week (one course borrowed or adapted from the *Book of Common Prayer* of the Church of England), and selected hymns and doxologies. He also suggests patterns for prayer on Sunday mornings and evenings. For Sunday morning: selected readings from the Old and New Testaments; the Decalogue; a hymn; the prayer for the day; the Lord's Prayer; and the Apostolic Benediction. Sunday evening has a similar structure, though a psalm may be added to the Sunday evening lesson stipulated in the lectionary.

30. Thomas A. Morris, *Miscellany* (Cincinnati: L. Swormstedt & J. H. Power, 1852), 37.

31. See, e.g., the section "The Training of Children in Christian Homes" in *The Methodist Armor; or A Popular Exposition of the Doctrines, Peculiar Usages, and Ecclesiastical Machinery of the Methodist Episcopal Church, South,* first written by Hilary T. Hudson in 1882 and revised and reprinted in several editions.

32. L. D. Palmer's *Aid and Guide to Family Worship,* first published by the Publishing House of the Methodist Episcopal Church, South, in 1886 and reprinted in the first decades of the twentieth century, attests to the continuing

interest in family prayer. Palmer, a layman, stresses this concern in the first sentence of the book: "No religious duty is more emphatically urged by evangelical Churches upon their members, and perhaps no one is more generally neglected, than family worship." See also the editorial "The Church in the Home," *Quarterly Review of the United Brethren in Christ* 10 (1899): 280-82.

33. See also *Journal of the Twenty-eighth Delegated General Conference of the Methodist Episcopal Church* (New York and Cincinnati: Methodist Book Concern, 1920), 677-78; cf. 1920 *Discipline*, ¶446 §2.

34. For J. George Haller, the prayer meeting is to be encouraged precisely because "secret and family prayer are falling into disuse" (*The Redemption of the Prayer-Meeting* [Cincinnati: Jennings and Graham, 1911; New York: Eaton and Mains, 1911; and Nashville: Smith and Lamar, 1911], 24).

35. Edmund E. Prescott, *The New Midweek Service* (Nashville: Cokesbury, 1929), 14-16.

36. W. W. King, "The Redemption of the Prayer Meeting," *Methodist Review* 92 (November 1910): 964-65; cf. P. O. Bonebrake, "Why, As a Rule, So Poor an Attendance at the Midweek Prayer-Meeting?" *Quarterly Review of the United Brethren in Christ* 12 (1901): 350-51.

37. See Chiles, *Theological Transition in American Methodism,* 186-87; John Leland Peters, *Christian Perfection and American Methodism* (New York and Nashville: Abingdon Press, 1956); and E. Brooks Holifield, A *History of Pastoral Care in America: From Salvation to Self-Realization* (Nashville: Abingdon Press, 1983), 84-85, 140-43, 208, 250, 352-53.

38. For a brief overview of change in understanding the nature of conversion found among Americans, see V. Bailey Gillespie, *The Dynamics of Religious Conversion* (Birmingham: Religious Education Press, 1991), 30-40.

39. According to some authors of the period, the spoken word as the chief form of testimony has been replaced by the notion of "life" or one's living as sufficient testimony. See, e.g., Norman E. Richardson, ed., *Present-Day Prayer-Meeting Helps: For Laymen and Minister* (New York: Eaton & Mains, 1910; Cincinnati: Jennings & Graham, 1910), 7.

40. Washington Gladden, *The Christian Pastor and the Working Church* (New York: Charles Scribner's Sons, 1924), 241-42. Gladden, who devotes an entire chapter to midweek worship, gives no substantial attention to family prayer.

41. Beebe, *The Pastoral Office,* 95.

42. Haller, *The Redemption of the Prayer-Meeting,* 46-49.

43. William T. Ward, *Variety in the Prayer Meeting: A Manual for Leaders* (New York and Cincinnati: Methodist Book Concern, 1915), 7.

44. Holifield, *A History of Pastoral Care,* 120; and Robert S. Michaelsen, "The Protestant Ministry in America: 1850 to the Present," in *The Ministry in Historical Perspectives,* ed. H. Richard Niebuhr and Daniel D. Williams (New York: Harper & Brothers, 1956), 272.

45. See, e.g., Haller, *The Redemption of the Prayer-Meeting,* 127-222; Ward, *Variety in the Prayer Meeting,* 139-60; Halford E. Luccock and Warren F. Cook, *The Mid-Week Service* (New York and Cincinnati: Methodist Book Concern, 1916), 53-109; Robert Elmer Smith, *Midweek Messages* (New York and Cincinnati: Abingdon, 1925), 15-192; and Prescott, *The New Midweek Service,* 25-99. Methodists undoubtedly borrowed also from nondenominational and other-denominational resources produced during this period.

46. Beebe, *The Pastoral Office,* 88-90; cf. Gladden, *The Christian Pastor,* 121-22, 250.

47. David Nasaw, *Going Out: The Rise and Fall of Public Amusements* (New York: Basic Books, 1993), 2-4.

48. On the matter of recreation as Christian duty for Methodists, see Glenn Uminowicz, "Recreation in Christian America: Ocean Grove and Asbury Park, New Jersey, 1869–1914," in *Hard at Play: Leisure in America, 1840–1940,* ed. Kathryn Grover (Amherst: University of Massachusetts Press, 1992; and Rochester, N.Y.: Strong Museum, 1992), esp. p. 23.

49. Mary P. Ryan, *Womanhood in America from the Colonial Times to the Present,* 2nd ed. (New York: New Viewpoints, 1979), 79, 185; and Barbara Kuhn Campbell, *The "Liberated" Woman of 1914: Prominent Women in the Progressive Era,* Studies in American History and Culture, no. 6 (n.p.: UMI Research Press, 1979), 25-71.

50. See, e.g., Ann Douglas, *The Feminization of American Culture* (New York: Alfred A. Knopf, 1977), 74-79; Ryan, *Womanhood in America,* 75-80; Maxine Van de Wetering, "The Popular Concept of 'Home' in Nineteenth-Century America," *Journal of American Studies* 18 (1984): 13-28; and Schneider, *The Way of the Cross Leads Home,* esp. pp. 169-78.

51. Texts following a structure of verse, lesson, prayer (from a wide variety of Christian sources) are provided in Wade Crawford Barclay, ed., *A Book of Worship for Use at Table on Every Day of the Year* (New York and Cincinnati: Abingdon, 1923). A similar format was (and is) reproduced by the devotional guide *The Upper Room,* which has been published continuously since 1935.

52. Beginning with the *Discipline* of 1980, ¶74D was included, which indicated, among other matters, that The United Methodist Church affirmed that the state could not require prayer or worship in the public schools, and that students should be left "free to practice their own religious convictions." This state-

ment is particularly ironic since the *Discipline* does not identify those devotional means or settings by which the religious convictions of youth may be formed.

53. While Saliers's study concentrated on thirteen congregations, he also surveyed 135 United Methodist congregations distributed across the United States. The final results of the study are not yet published.

54. This information was obtained through informal conversations that I have had with United Methodist pastors in Illinois and North Carolina, and with other persons (lay and clergy) throughout the United States.

55. Services for praise and prayer in the morning, midday, evening, and night are included in this section. See *The United Methodist Book of Worship* (Nashville: United Methodist Publishing House, 1992), 569-79.

56. Ibid., 579-84.

57. Unfortunately, some United Methodist churches have opted for the design of the Willow Creek Association whereby the evangelistic service is held on Saturday evening or Sunday morning, and the worship of the faithful is held midweek.

58. See, e.g., the book produced by two staff members of the United Methodist General Board of Discipleship, Daniel T. Benedict and Craig Kennet Miller, *Contemporary Worship for the Twenty-first Century: Worship or Evangelism* (Nashville: Discipleship Resources, 1994).

59. See Robert Wuthnow, *Sharing the Journey: Support Groups and America's New Quest for Community* (New York: Free Press, 1994); and Robert Wuthnow, ed., *"I Come Away Stronger": How Small Groups Are Shaping American Religion* (Grand Rapids: Eerdmans, 1994).

NOTES TO "AMERICAN METHODISM AND PUBLIC EDUCATION: 1784 TO 1900"

1. Georgia Harkness, *The Methodist Church in Social Thought and Action,* ed. the Board of Social and Economic Relations of The Methodist Church (Nashville/New York: Abingdon Press, 1964), 80.

2. A notable exception involved Indian schools. The Methodist Episcopal Church was among the denominations that ran government schools on Indian reservations in the nineteenth century. See Wade Crawford Barclay, *History of Methodist Missions. Part Two: The Methodist Episcopal Church 1845–1939. Vol. III, Widening Horizons, 1845–1939* (New York: Board of Missions of The Methodist Church, 1957), 326ff. Harkness, ibid., stated that "state funds and subsidies are sometimes accepted by Methodist institutions both at home and abroad, and there is no consistent policy at this point." The receipt of state money by United Methodist institutions, including colleges and social agencies, often under con-

tract for general services, has grown over the past thirty years in the United States and has become de facto policy in many cases.

3. Ray Allen Billington, *The Protestant Crusade 1800–1860,* reprint (Chicago: Quadrangle Books, 1964), 176-77, 251; Francis X. Curran, *The Churches and the Schools: American Protestantism and Popular Elementary Education* (Chicago: Loyola University Press, 1954), 78-98; Thomas C. Hunt, "Methodism, Moral Education and Public Schools: A Look into the Past," *Methodist History* XIX (January 1981): 94-98.

4. Terrell E. Johnson, "A History of Methodist Education and Its Influence on American Public Education" (Diss., Southern Illinois University at Carbondale, 1988), 77ff.

5. *Journal of the General Conference of the Methodist Episcopal Church 1872,* 441.

6. Thomas Jefferson, "A Bill for the More General Diffusion of Knowledge," 1779. Reprinted in Frederick M. Binder, *Education in the History of Western Civilization* (New York: Macmillan, 1970), 279-89.

7. Robert L. Church, *Education in the United States* (New York: Free Press, 1976), 9.

8. Lawrence Cremin, *The American Common School: An Historical Conception* (New York: Teachers College of Columbia University, 1951), 120. For conditions in the Southwest Territory around 1800 see William C. Davis, *A Way Through the Wilderness: The Natchez Trace and the Civilization of the Southern Frontier* (New York: HarperCollins, 1995), 160ff.; on the Midwest, Elizabeth K. Nottingham, *Methodism and the Frontier: Indiana Proving Ground* (New York: Columbia University Press, 1941), 19, 21.

9. R. Freeman Butts, *The American Tradition in Religion and Education* (Boston: Beacon, 1950), 115; see also Lawrence A. Cremin, *American Education: The National Experience 1793–1876* (New York: Harper & Row, 1980), 19-49.

10. Johnson, "A History of Methodist Education," 127-40; A. Emerson Palmer, *The New York Public School: Being History of Free Education in the City of New York* (New York: Macmillan, 1905), 80ff.

11. Church, *Education,* 183.

12. *The Journal and Letters of Francis Asbury* (Nashville/New York: Abingdon Press, 1958), vol. 1, 639, 716; vol. 2, 81.

13. Raymond Martin Bell, *Methodism Comes to Uniontown* (Washington, Pa.: Mimeographed, 1964), 5, citing *Sketches in the Life and Labor of James Quinn* (1851).

14. Newton Edwards and Herman G. Richey, *The School in the American Social*

Order: The Dynamics of American Education (Boston: Houghton Mifflin Co., 1947), 376.

15. William Ralph Ward, *Faith in Action: A History of Methodism in the Empire State 1784–1948* (Rutland: Academy Books, 1986), 22.

16. *Journal of the General Conference of the Methodist Episcopal Church 1820,* 209.

17. *Journal of the General Conference of the Methodist Episcopal Church 1824,* 295.

18. Robert W. Lynn and Elliott Wright, *The Big Little School: Two Hundred Years of the Sunday School* (Birmingham: Religious Education Press, 1980, 2nd ed.), 41.

19. A. W. Cummings, *The Early Schools of Methodism* (New York: Phillips and Hunt, 1886), 426-27.

20. John O. Gross, "The Field of Education 1865–1939," *The History of American Methodism,* vol. III, Emory Bucke, ed. (Nashville/New York: Abingdon Press, 1964), 213.

21. Johnson, "A History of Methodist Education," 142ff.

22. Ruth Robinson Matthews, *A Light on the Cumberland Plateau: The Story of Baxter Seminary* (Nashville: Commission on Archives and History, Tennessee Annual Conference, United Methodist Church, 1975).

23. Johnson, "A History of Methodist Education," 152ff.

24. *The Autobiography of Brantley York* (Durham: Seeman Printery, 1910), 46.

25. E. C. Brooke, "Introductory Sketch," ibid., xiii.

26. Johnson, "A History of Methodist Education," 77ff.

27. Edmund S. Janes, "Address on Education," *Methodist Magazine and Quarterly Review* XXII (1840): 408.

28. Johnson, "A History of Methodist Education," 171.

29. *Journal of the General Conference of the Methodist Episcopal Church 1924,* 295.

30. "Address of the Bishops," *The Journal of the General Conference of the Methodist Episcopal Church 1844,* 169 (emphasis added).

31. Raymond Benjamin Culver, *Horace Mann and Religion in the Massachusetts Public Schools* (New Haven: Yale University Press, 1929); B. A. Hinsdale, *Horace Mann and the Common School Revival in the United States* (New York: Charles Scribner's Sons, 1937), 181ff.

32. Culver, *Horace Mann,* 7-8, citing figures compiled by Joseph S. Clark, *A Historical Sketch of the Congregational Church in Massachusetts 1620–1858* (1858), 7-10.

33. Johnson, "A History of Methodist Education," 139.

34. *Christian Advocate and Journal,* October 8, 1830.

35. Ibid.

36. February 21, 1834.

37. May 1, 1835.

38. Ibid.

39. Martin E. Marty, *Righteous Empire: The Protestant Experience in America* (New York: Dial, 1970).

40. Butts, *The American Tradition,* 115.

41. Ibid.

42. David Tyack and Elisabeth Hansot, *Managers of Virtue: Public School Leaders in America, 1820–1980* (New York: Basic Books, 1982), 318; see also Lynn and Wright, *The Big Little School,* 28ff.

43. Prayer often accompanied Bible reading but was not as widely practiced. The author has surveyed the prayer issue in American public education for a paper, "Protestant-Catholic-Jews and Public School Prayer: Past and Present," presented to Church-State Study Group, American Academy of Religion, Philadelphia, November 18, 1995. Unpublished. Almost all of the local and state-level conflict over devotional exercises in public school classrooms before 1962 concerned Bible reading, not prayer.

44. Ruth Miller Elson, *Guardians of Tradition: American Schoolbooks of the Nineteenth Century* (Lincoln: University of Nebraska Press, 1972), 42.

45. *Journal of the General Conference of the Methodist Episcopal Church 1872,* 441.

46. *Congressional Record* (44th Congress) 175 (1875).

47. Leo Pfeffer, *Church, State, and Freedom* (Boston: Beacon, 1953), 131.

48. M. C. Klinkhamer, "Blaine Amendment," *New Catholic Encyclopedia,* vol. 2 (Washington, D.C.: Catholic University of America, 1967), 598-600.

49. *The Journal of the General Conference of the Methodist Episcopal Church 1872,* 441.

50. *Journal of the General Conference of the Methodist Protestant Church 1875,* 116; membership statistics, 115.

51. Johnson, "A History of Methodist Education," 139ff. contains a thorough discussion of the New York episode focused on the Methodist role. A general Protestant-Catholic conflict in Philadelphia over the Bible in schools led to riots

and the loss of lives and property. See Michael Feldberg, *The Philadelphia Riots of 1844: A Study of Ethnic Conflict* (Westport, Conn.: Greenwood, 1975).

52. *The Christian Advocate and Journal,* February 21, 1934; February 16, 1842.

53. *Board of Education v. Minor* 23 Ohio (1972). For discussion see Robert G. McCloskey, "Introduction," *The Bible in the Public School: Arguments Before the Superior Court of Cincinnati in the case of Minor v. Board of Education of Cincinnati (1870) with the opinions of the Court and the opinion on appeal of the Supreme Court of Ohio* (New York: Da Capo, reprint of 1870 edition), vii-xvii.

54. *Catholic Citizen* (20 February 1886): 4. See Hunt, "Methodism," 97.

55. *The Journal of the General Conference of the Methodist Episcopal Church 1888,* 457.

56. Ibid.

57. "The Board of Temperance of The Methodist Church," *Handbook of the General Conference of The Methodist Church* (New York: Methodist Publishing House, n.d. [1940]), 436.

58. Ibid., 440.

59. Church, *Education,* 118ff.

60. *Journal of the General Conference of the Methodist Episcopal Church, South, 1854,* 306-7.

61. *Journal of the General Conference of the Methodist Episcopal Church, South, 1966,* 131-37.

62. Hunter Dickinson Farish, *The Circuit Rider Dismounts: A Social History of Southern Methodism, 1865–1900* (New York: Da Capo, 1969; reprint of 1938 edition), 242.

63. *Journal of the General Conference of the Methodist Episcopal Church, South, 1874,* 385-86; *Journal of the General Conference 1878,* 36-37.

64. Luther L. Gobbel, *Church-State Relationship in Education in North Carolina Since 1776* (Durham: Duke University Press, 1938), 195.

65. From an address given at Pacific Methodist College in 1872. See Farish, *The Circuit Rider Dismounts,* 246 n. 1.

66. (Nashville) *Christian Advocate,* November 30, 1872.

67. *Journal of the General Conference of the Methodist Episcopal Church, South, 1888,* 121.

68. Ibid.

69. For a discussion of the impact of reconstruction on schools, see Church, *Education,* 136ff.

70. *Wesleyan Christian Advocate,* March 6, 1889.

71. Church, *Education,* 127.

72. *Journal of the General Conference of the Methodist Episcopal Church, 1884,* 365.

73. Farish, *The Circuit Rider Dismounts,* 250.

74. Ibid., 254.

75. The U.S. Supreme Court in the late 1940s disallowed "released time" classes on school property but allowed them off-site.

76. Sadie Bell in her monumental work *The Church, The State, and Education in Virginia* (Philadelphia: Science Press Printing Co., 1930) details the involvement of Methodists in an unsuccessful attempt in the 1920s to persuade the Virginia legislature to require Bible reading.

77. Grover C. Babgy, *School Prayer,* Hearings Before the Subcommittee on Constitutional Amendments of the Committee on the Judiciary, Senate, Eighty-ninth Congress, 2nd Sess., 1966, 37.

78. "A Statement Concerning Church-Government Relations and Education," *The Book of Resolutions of The United Methodist Church 1968* (Nashville: United Methodist Publishing House, 1969), 32-33.

79. First appeared in the "Social Principles" in 1976.

80. *Education: The Gift of Hope* (Nashville: General Board of Higher Education and Ministry, 1996), 60.

NOTES TO "CONNECTION AND *KOINONIA*"

1. Sermon 74, *Works of John Wesley,* written September 1785, no. 1.

2. Ibid., nos. 14, 15.

3. Richard P. Heitzenrater, *Wesley and the People Called Methodists* (Nashville: Abingdon Press, 1995), 171.

4. Quoted in John C. Bowmer, *Pastor and People* (London: Epworth Press, 1975), 190.

5. Nolan B. Harmon, ed., *The Encyclopedia of World Methodism,* vol. 1 (Nashville: United Methodist Publishing House, 1974), 570.

6. Thomas Edward Frank, *The Polity, Practice, and the Mission of The United Methodist Church* (Nashville: Abingdon Press, 1997), 153.

7. Bowmer, 192. He notes that Alfred Barrett devotes an entire chapter to the "connexional principle" in *The Ministry and Polity of the Christian Church*. Unfortunately, I was unable to use that book in the development of this essay.

8. John Lawson, *History of the Methodist Church in Great Britain,* vol. 1, 206.

9. In *The Character of a Methodist* (1742) by John Wesley, he satirically refers to his own group as a "SECT," always written in uppercase letters and placed in quotation marks.

10. Rupert E. Davies, *The Works of John Wesley,* vol. 9: *The Methodist Societies: History, Nature, and Design* (Nashville: Abingdon Press, 1989), 3.

11. This history and transition are extensively detailed in Richard P. Heitzenrater's *Wesley and the People Called Methodists* (Nashville: Abingdon Press, 1995). See esp. chap. 4, "Consolidation of a Movement."

12. As reported in Harmon's *Encyclopedia of World Methodism,* 570.

13. A special group within the General Council on Ministries had developed this section and submitted it to the Conference.

14. The United Methodist Church was involved in a debate about the so-called Wesleyan Quadrilateral. Disciplinary changes emphasized the primacy of Scripture in relation to tradition, reason, and experience. The phrase "theological pluralism" was eliminated from the *Book of Discipline* in response to these pressures for more definitive doctrinal standards.

15. It is not surprising that "interactive relationships" has replaced "interdependent relationships" in the definition of what holds together the "connectional people." A Connectional Issues Task Force had worked hard during the quadrennium under the guidance of the General Council on Ministries. Within that Task Force, much attention was given to language of "interactivity," which has been popular in recent theories of organizational behavior, particularly in the corporate world.

16. Quotations are taken from the Advance Edition of the *Daily Christian Advocate* for the 1996 General Conference.

17. Unfortunately, there are numerous illustrations of Methodists from one country going to another country with Methodist churches and opening up new churches.

18. In 1991, when the first report of the Global Nature Task Force was presented to the bishops at their fall meeting (Jackson, Mississippi), the number of the regions of the world listed in the report demonstrated the hope that Latin American Methodism would be part of the plan.

19. It is interesting to note the rising criticism of autonomous churches for theological reasons. Recently, Bishop Ruediger Minor suggested to me that, theo-

logically, the concept of an autonomous church is problematic. Churches should be "theonomic." He suggested that the national church structure is a construct of European history and should not be assumed as the only model for international church structure. Today, the World Council of Churches uses a national model even when considering The United Methodist Church. In the selection of assembly delegates, certain numbers are given for Methodists in the different regions of the world. A similar pattern is true in the membership counting within the World Methodist Council.

20. Unpublished manuscript.

21. Thomas F. Best and Günther Gassmann, *On the Way to Fuller Koinonia: Official Report of the Fifth World Conference on Faith and Order* (Geneva: WCC Publications, 1994), 231 (sec. I, ¶ 8).

22. *Works of John Wesley*, vol. 9, 35.

23. Ibid., 42. This is also stated in 1750 in the famous sermon, *Catholic Spirit*.

NOTES TO "THE CHURCH AS A COMMUNITY OF MORAL DISCOURSE"

1. James M. Gustafson, *The Church as Moral Decision-Maker* (Philadelphia, Boston: Pilgrim, 1970), 129.

2. Ibid., 84.

3. Ibid., 89.

4. An analogy attributed to the late Christian ethicist Paul Ramsey is instructive: too often arguments that presume to represent a Christian perspective on social-ethical issues remain largely hidden and, in that respect, are like a submarine trip. The submarine floats on the surface at the beginning of the argument (where one premise of the argument is apparent), then dives underwater, traveling unseen (through various intervening stages of the argument) until surfacing again at some final destination (the conclusion of the argument). The problem, of course, is that such a hidden argument persuades no one.

5. I have adapted Stephen Toulmin's analysis of the structure of practical arguments. Most practical arguments, Toulmin observes, follow not syllogistic logic but a logic analogous to arguments in a court of law. In a court of law, movement from a complete variety of evidence to a judicial ruling is usually not simple or direct. The linkage of fact, theory, and interpretation in legal arguments cannot be tight (strictly deductive), but it is still possible to make a reasonably convincing case. See Toulmin, *The Uses of Argument* (Cambridge University Press, 1958), 94-145.

6. H. Richard Niebuhr, *The Responsible Self: An Essay in Christian Moral Philosophy* (New York: Harper & Row, 1963), 63.

7. See also June O'Connor, "On Doing Religious Ethics," *Journal of Religious Ethics* 7:1 (Spring 1979): 83-84; and Joseph C. Hough Jr.'s account of the training in nontheological disciplines necessary to practice Christian social ethics in "Christian Social Ethics as Advocacy," *Journal of Religious Ethics* 5:1 (Spring 1977): 124-30.

8. See Gibson Winter's groundbreaking analysis of the biases inherent in various social-scientific modes of description in his *Elements for a Social Ethic: Scientific and Ethical Perspectives on Social Process* (New York: Macmillan, 1966). See also the judicious comments on the place of empirical evidence and scientific concepts in ethics by Roger L. Shinn in "Christian Social Ethics in North America," *The Ecumenical Review* 40:2 (April 1988): 230.

9. See J. Philip Wogaman, *Making Moral Decisions* (Nashville: Abingdon Press, 1990), esp. chap. 3, "Human Resources for the Church's Dialogue."

10. In simple, noncontroversial cases, as I noted above, the warrant may remain unspoken and still function effectively.

11. These four categories of moral discourse are drawn from two articles by James M. Gustafson: "An Analysis of Church and Society Social Ethical Writings," *The Ecumenical Review* 40:2 (April 1988): 267-78; and "Moral Discourse About Medicine: A Variety of Forms," *Journal of Medicine and Philosophy* 15:2 (1990): 125-42. My treatment of these categories as both forms of moral discourse and types of backings for a moral warrant goes beyond Gustafson's description.

12. Paul Lauritzen has argued persuasively that one cannot assume that if members of the Christian community share a common story, then they will share common—or even compatible—recommendations for practical action. Lauritzen points out that both Johann B. Metz and Stanley Hauerwas (1) appeal to the biblical narrative about Jesus as the basis of their ethical stance and (2) claim that the truthfulness of the Christian story is to be judged by its practical consequences. Yet Metz and Hauerwas diverge sharply in their moral recommendations. For Metz, fidelity to the biblical story of Jesus requires a life committed to near-revolutionary social action. For Hauerwas, fidelity to the biblical story of Jesus leads to a sectarian, pacifistic witness (Paul Lauritzen, "Is 'Narrative' Really a Panacea? The Use of 'Narrative' in the Work of Metz and Hauerwas," *Journal of Religion* 67 [July 1987]: 322-39).

13. Another resolution, entitled simply "Housing," was adopted at the 1988 General Conference and still appears in *The Book of Resolutions of The United Methodist Church*, 1992.

14. Boyce A. Bowden, "The Kids Should Be in School," *Christian Social Action* (January 1992), 25-27.

15. Ann M. Ennis, "Evansville's Building Blitz," *Christian Social Action* (November 1992), 25-30.

16. Lee Ranck, "Housing: 'Such a Fit for TUMC,'" *Christian Social Action* (October 1993), 4-9.

17. Maude Hurd, "Crushing the Homeownership Dream," *Christian Social Action* (October 1993), 25-29.

18. *Christian Perspectives on Social Issues. Volume 4: The Least of These* (Nashville: Cokesbury, 1993).

19. Charles F. Strobel, *Room in the Inn* (Nashville: Abingdon Press, 1992). See also the earlier volume by Michael J. Christensen, *City Streets, City People* (Nashville: Abingdon Press, 1988).

20. Warren T. Copeland, *And the Poor Get Welfare: The Ethics of Poverty in the United States* (Nashville: Abingdon Press, 1994).

21. Pamela D. Couture, *Blessed Are the Poor? Women's Poverty, Family Policy, and Practical Theology* (Nashville: Abingdon Press, 1992). See also the earlier volume by Theodore W. Jennings, Jr., *Good News to the Poor: John Wesley's Evangelical Economics* (Nashville: Abingdon Press, 1990).

Notes to "Exploring both the Middle and the Margins"

1. P. D. James, *The Children of Men* (New York: Warner, 1992), 33.

2. C. C. Goen, "The 'Methodist Age' in American Church History," *Religion in Life* 34 (1965): 562-72; Winthrop S. Hudson, "The Methodist Age in America," *Methodist History* 12 (April 1974): 3-15.

3. Nathan O. Hatch, "The Puzzle of American Methodism" *Church History* 63:2 (June 1994): 175-89; Russell E. Richey, *Early American Methodism* (Bloomington: Indiana University Press, 1991); A. Gregory Schneider, *The Way of the Cross Leads Home: The Domestication of American Methodism* (Bloomington: Indiana University Press, 1993); *Taking Heaven by Storm: Methodism and the Rise of Popular Christianity in America* (New York: Oxford University Press, 1998).

4. Hatch, "The Puzzle of American Methodism," 177-79, 181.

5. Hatch, "The Puzzle of American Methodism," 180, 186, 188; Schneider, xxii-xxiii.

6. Hatch, "The Puzzle of American Methodism," 186.

7. Sinclair Lewis, *Babbitt* (1922).

8. See the comments of Pastor J. Philip Wogaman regarding the broad political climate at Foundry United Methodist Church (*United Methodist Review* [18

November 1994]: 9). The Dole and the Clinton families attended Foundry during the same period of time from late 1992 until early 1995 (when the Doles left Foundry for a more conservative church). Both the Doles and the McGoverns had attended Foundry for a number of years.

9. Theodore Runyon, ed., *Sanctification and Liberation: Liberation Theologians in the Light of the Wesleyan Tradition* (Nashville: Abingdon, 1981); Theodore Jennings, *Good News to the Poor: John Wesley's Evangelical Economics* (Nashville: Abingdon Press, 1990).

10. Donald G. Mathews, *Religion in the Old South* (Chicago: University of Chicago Press, 1977).

11. Will B. Gravely, "African Methodisms and the Rise of Black Denominationalism," in *Rethinking Methodist History,* ed. Russell E. Richey and Kenneth E. Rowe (Nashville: Kingswood Books, 1985); James S. Thomas, *Methodism's Racial Dilemma: The Story of the Central Jurisdiction* (Nashville: Abingdon Press, 1992); William B. McClain, *Black People in the Methodist Church* (Nashville: Abingdon Press, 1984).

12. Catherine Brekus, *Strangers and Pilgrims: Female Preaching in America, 1740–1845* (Durham: University of North Carolina Press, 1998); Diane H. Lobody, "'That Language Might Be Given Me': Women's Experience in Early Methodism," in *Perspectives on American Methodism: Interpretive Essays,* ed. Russell E. Richey et al. (Nashville: Kingswood Books, 1993); Nancy Hardesty, *Women Called to Witness: Evangelical Feminism in the Nineteenth Century* (Nashville: Abingdon Press, 1984); Rosemary Skinner Keller, *Spirituality and Social Responsibility: Vocational Vision of Women in the United Methodist Tradition* (Nashville: Abingdon Press, 1993).

13. James H. Moorhead, "Social Reform and the Divided Conscience of Antebellum Protestantism," *Church History* 48 (December 1979): 416-30.

14. Leonard I. Sweet, "The View of Man Inherent in New Measures Revivalism," *Church History* 45 (June 1976): 206-21.

15. Jonathan Blanchard, *A Perfect State of Society* (Oberlin: James Steele, 1839).

16. D. A. Goodsell, "Methodism—A Flash or a Flame?" *Christian Advocate* 48 (2 October 1873): 313, cited in Paul A. Carter, *The Spiritual Crisis of the Gilded Age* (DeKalb: Northern Illinois University Press, 1971), 193.

17. This transition within American Methodism from Wesley's original stress on "free grace" to the nineteenth-century stress on "free will" is narrated in Robert E. Chiles, *Theological Transition in American Methodism* (Nashville/New York: Abingdon Press, 1965).

18. See Moorhead, "Social Reform," 429; and Donald W. Dayton, *Theological Roots of Pentecostalism* (Peabody, Mass.: Hendrickson Publishing, 1987), 68-69.

19. Chiles, *Theological Transition*, 115-43; Thomas A. Langford, *Practical Divinity: Theology in the Wesleyan Tradition* (Nashville: Abingdon Press, 1983), 170-96.

20. Douglas M. Strong, "The Eccentric Cosmopolite: Lorenzo Dow and Wesleyan/Holiness Missions," paper presented at Wesleyan/Holiness Study Conference, September 1993.

21. Lorenzo Dow, *History of Cosmopolite: or the Writings of Rev. Lorenzo Dow: Containing His Experiences and Travels, in Europe and America, up to near His Fiftieth Year. Also, His Polemic Writings. To Which is Added, The "Journey of Life," by Peggy Dow.* Revised and Corrected with Notes, 6th ed. (Philadelphia: H. M. Rulison, 1855), 304, 314.

22. See, e.g., George Peck, *Early Methodism Within the Bounds of the Old Genesee Conference from 1788 to 1828; or, The First Forty Years of Wesleyan Evangelism in Northern Pennsylvania, Central and Western New York, and Canada* (New York: Carlton & Porter, 1860), 180, 185, 265, 276, 279, 394, 420, 443, 462; William Henry Foote, *Sketches of Virginia, Historical and Biographical, Second Series* (Philadelphia: J. B. Lippincott and Co., 1855), 223-40; [Matthew St. Clair Clarke], *Sketches and Eccentricities of Col. David Crockett, of West Tennessee* (New York: J. & J. Harper, 1833).

23. Richey, *Early American Methodism*, 65-81.

24. Joseph W. Kirkley, *Centennial Sketch of Methodism in Georgetown, D.C.* (Georgetown: Rufus H. Darley, 1884); Dumbarton Avenue Methodist Church, *A Brief History of the Founding of Methodism in Georgetown* (Georgetown: Dumbarton Avenue Methodist Church, 1941).

25. A chronicle of the Dumbarton church that takes into account the full diversity of the congregation's history has only recently been written. Jane Donovan, ed., *Many Witnesses: A History of Dumbarton United Methodist Church* (Interlaken, N.Y.: Heart of the Lakes Pub., 1998).

NOTES TO "CLASS LEADERS AND CLASS MEETINGS"

1. Thus the impact of volumes such as Richard B. Wilke, *And Are We Yet Alive? The Future of The United Methodist Church* (Nashville: Abingdon Press, 1986), and Stanley Hauerwas and William Willimon, *Resident Aliens: Life in the Christian Colony* (Nashville: Abingdon Press, 1989).

2. See William B. Lawrence, "Clergy Leaders: Who Will They Be? How Will They Emerge? To What Will They Lead Us?" in *Leadership Letters: from The Duke Divinity School Project on United Methodism and American Culture*, vol. 1, no. 3 (March 15, 1995).

3. Stanley Hauerwas, "Discipleship as a Craft: Church as a Disciplined Community," *The Christian Century*, vol. 108, no. 27 (October 2, 1991), 881-84.

4. Brought into focus by studies such as Christopher Lasch, *The Culture of Narcissism* (New York: W. W. Norton, 1979), and Robert N. Bellah et al., *Habits of the Heart: Individualism and Commitment in American Life* (San Francisco: Harper & Row, 1986), these aspects of North American culture are now receiving detailed treatment in the wider context of Western postmodernity. See John Milbank, *Theology and Social Theory: Beyond Secular Reason* (Oxford: Basil Blackwell, 1990), and Stephen L. Carter, *The Culture of Disbelief: How American Law and Politics Trivialize Religious Devotion* (New York: HarperCollins, Basic Books, 1993).

5. A situation in which there is now a welcome change. See, e.g., Susanne Johnson, *Christian Spiritual Formation in the Church and Classroom* (Nashville: Abingdon Press, 1989).

6. For some consequences of this in the North American church, see Ronald J. Sider, *One-Sided Christianity?* (Grand Rapids: Zondervan, HarperSanFrancisco, 1993).

7. *The Works of John Wesley*, vol. 9: *The Methodist Societies: History, Nature, and Design*, ed. Rupert E. Davies (Nashville: Abingdon Press, 1989), 67ff.

8. Ibid., 47-66. I have given these issues detailed treatment in "Aldersgate Street and the *General Rules:* The Form and the Power of Methodist Discipleship," in *Aldersgate Reconsidered*, ed. Randy L. Maddox (Nashville: Kingswood Books, 1990), 33-47.

9. *The Works of John Wesley*, vol. 18: *Journals and Diaries* I (1735–1738), ed. W. Reginald Ward and Richard P. Heitzenrater (Nashville: Abingdon Press, 1988), 266-97; vol. 19, *Journals and Diaries II (1738–1743)*, ed. W. Reginald Ward and Richard P. Heitzenrater (Nashville: Abingdon Press, 1990), 215-24; vol. 26, *Letters II: 1740–1755*, ed. Frank Baker (Oxford: Clarendon Press, 1982), 24-31.

10. *Works*, vol. 19: *Journal and Diaries II*, 20.

11. Ibid., 21. Shortly thereafter he published an extract from the *Homilies* of the Church of England, titled *The Doctrine of Salvation, Faith and Good Works*, a pamphlet that went through twelve editions in his lifetime. The following year he published an edited version of two treatises by the early English Lutheran scholar, Robert Barnes, on justification by faith and on free will. Cf. *The Works of John Wesley*, vol. 2: *Sermons II: 34-70*, ed. Albert C. Outler (Nashville: Abingdon Press, 1985), 187.

12. *Works*, vol. 19: *Journal and Diaries II*, 151ff.

13. *The Works of John Wesley*, vol. 25: *Letters I 1721–1739*, ed. Frank Baker (Oxford: Clarendon Press, 1980), 639-40.

14. *Works*, vol. 9: *The Methodist Societies*, 47-66.

15. The word did not appear on the title page of the *General Rules* until after his death.

16. See *Works*, vol. 9: *The Methodist Societies*, 69-70, 260-61. See also *Works*, vol. 19, *Journal and Diaries II*, 251, 343.

17. *Works*, vol. 9: *The Methodist Societies*, 70.

18. Ibid., 70-73.

19. See Robert E. Cushman, *Faith Seeking Understanding: Essays Theological and Critical* (Durham, N.C.: Duke University Press, 1981), 74.

20. See Philip J. Lee, *Against the Protestant Gnostics* (New York: Oxford University Press, 1987, 1994).

21. *Works*, vol. 20: *Journals and Diaries III*, 163.

22. This in no way implies that class leaders and class meetings had been ignored by The United Methodist Church and its predecessor denominations. See, e.g., Samuel Emerick, ed., *Spiritual Renewal for Methodism: A Discussion of the Early Methodist Class Meeting and the Values Inherent in Personal Groups Today* (Nashville: Methodist Evangelistic Materials, 1958). See also Thomas C. Oden, *The Intensive Group Experience: The New Pietism* (Philadelphia: Westminster, 1972). Even so, until the General Board of Discipleship formed a Section on Covenant Discipleship and Christian Formation in 1986, there had been no concerted effort by The United Methodist Church to revitalize either the office or the institution. By contrast, African American and Korean Methodists have consistently given prominence to class leaders and class meetings in their congregational life and work.

23. Initially published by Oxford University Press and then by Abingdon Press, the first of the 34 volumes appeared in 1975: *Volume 11: The Appeals to Men of Reason and Religion and Certain Related Open Letters,* ed. Gerald R. Cragg.

24. See, e.g., his sermon "On Schism," in *The Works of John Wesley: Volume 3: Sermon III: 71-114,* ed. Albert C. Outler (Nashville: Abingdon Press, 1986), 58-69.

25. The steps taken by the Christmas Conference at Baltimore in 1784 make the Methodist Episcopal Church and its successors the mother church of Methodism. That this is rarely acknowledged on either side of the Atlantic is another instance of historiographical slippage.

26. See, e.g., David O. Moberg, *The Church as a Social Institution: The Sociology of American Religion* (Grand Rapids, Mich.: Baker Book House, 1984), 73ff. Cf. Robert Wuthnow, *The Restructuring of American Religion* (Princeton, N.J.: Princeton University Press, 1988), 176ff.

27. Ernst Troeltsch, *The Social Teaching of the Christian Churches,* 2 vols., reprint ed. (Chicago: University of Chicago Press, 1976), 2:461-62.

28. For an early history of the culture of small groups, see Kurt W. Back, *Beyond Words: The Story of Sensitivity Training and the Encounter Movement*, 2d ed. (New Brunswick, N.J.: Transaction Books, 1987). For an attempt to link them with early Methodism and other forms of Pietism, see Oden, *Intensive Group Experience*. For a detailed analysis of the growing role they play in North American culture, see Robert Wuthnow, *Sharing the Journey: Support Groups and America's New Quest for Community* (New York: Free Press, Macmillan, 1994).

29. Wuthnow, *Sharing the Journey*, 89-122.

30. Ibid., 219ff., 257ff.

31. This cohesiveness has been attributed to the dynamic whereby individual members of a small group are under pressure to conform with the norms of the group as a whole. See Leon Festinger, *A Theory of Cognitive Dissonance* (Evanston, Ill.: Row, Peterson & Co., 1957). For an application of this theory to the spiritual development of John Wesley, see Thorvald Källstad, *John Wesley and the Bible: A Psychological Study* (Stockholm: Nya Bokförlags Aktiebolaget, 1974).

32. *Works*, vol. 9: *The Methodist Societies*, 262.

33. This is common in any Christian tradition, but in Methodism there are two such errors that seem to be particularly well established: the misconstruing of John Wesley's Aldersgate Street experience; and the disregard of the compromise made by the Methodist Episcopal Church on slavery. On Aldersgate, see Richard P. Heitzenrater, "Great Expectations: Aldersgate and the Evidences of Genuine Christianity," in *Aldersgate Reconsidered*, ed. Maddox, pp. 49ff. On slavery, see *Minutes of Several Conversations Between The Rev. Thomas Coke and The Rev. Francis Asbury and Others, at a Conference begun in Baltimore, in the State of Maryland, on Monday, the 27th of December, in the Year 1784* (Philadelphia, 1785); repr. The Library of Methodist Classics (Nashville: United Methodist Publishing House, 1992), 15ff. See also Donald G. Mathews, *Slavery and Methodism: A Chapter in American Morality, 1780–1845* (Princeton, N.J.: Princeton University Press, 1965), 68ff., 296ff.

One of the clearest expositions of these historiographical issues in the wider context of the church remains William A. Clebsch, *Christianity in European History* (New York: Oxford University Press, 1979), esp. 26ff.

34. This was not without pressing appeals from some notable church leaders. E.g., John Miley, *A Treatise on Class Meetings* (Cincinnati: Methodist Book Concern, 1851); Leonidas Rosser, *Class Meetings: Embracing their Origin, Nature, Obligation, and Benefits* (Richmond: published by the author, 1855). The exhortatory tone of these and other publications indicate that class meetings were already well in decline in both of the Methodist Episcopal Churches.

35. Bernard Semmel, *The Methodist Revolution* (New York: Basic Books, 1973),

113ff. See also Nathan O. Hatch, *The Democratization of American Christianity* (New Haven: Yale University Press, 1989), 9ff., 40ff.

36. A. Gregory Schneider, *The Way of the Cross Leads Home: The Domestication of American Methodism* (Bloomington and Indianapolis: Indiana University Press, 1993), 94.

37. See Russell E. Richey, *Early American Methodism* (Bloomington and Indianapolis: Indiana University Press, 1991), 82ff. See also Schneider, *Way of the Cross*, 196ff.

38. David Lowes Watson, *Accountable Discipleship: Handbook for Covenant Discipleship Groups in the Congregation* (Nashville: Discipleship Resources, 1984). An experimental Covenant Discipleship Group functioned at Holly Springs United Methodist Church, North Carolina, from 1975 to 1978.

39. See Randy L. Maddox, *Responsible Grace: John Wesley's Practical Theology* (Nashville: Kingswood Books, 1994), 166ff.

40. This was one of the "prudential" means of grace advocated by Wesley. See *Works*, vol. 9: *The Methodist Societies*, 262, and "The Large Minutes" in *The Works of John Wesley* (Jackson ed.), vol. 8, 323-24. See also Cushman, *Faith Seeking Understanding*, 68ff.

41. See, e.g., Bettye J. Allen, *The Church Class Leaders System: A Guide for Monthly Class Meeting-Council Sessions, 1994–1995* (Nashville: AMEC Sunday School Union/Legacy Publishing, 1994). Seminars on Covenant Discipleship have been held in Australia, Chile, Fiji, Germany, Malaysia, Mexico, Norway, Peru, Puerto Rico, Singapore, and South Africa. Translations of the first resource, *Accountable Discipleship*, have appeared in German and Spanish.

42. The following are all published by Discipleship Resources (Nashville, Tenn.): Paul Wesley Chilcote, *Wesley Speaks on Christian Vocation* (1986). Lisa Grant, *Branch Groups: Covenant Discipleship for Youth* (1987). Kim Hauenstein-Mallet and Kenda Creasy Dean, *Covenants on Campus: Covenant Discipleship Groups for College and University Students* (1989). David Lowes Watson, *Covenant Discipleship: Christian Formation Through Mutual Accountability* (1991). Marigene Chamberlain, ed., *Journal for Covenant Discipleship: A Weekly Record for Covenant Discipleship Groups* (1991). Edie Genung Harris and Shirley L. Ramsey, *Sprouts: Nurturing Children Through Covenant Discipleship* (1995). There are also two videos produced by Discipleship Resources: *We Are the Branches* (1990), *Fancy Footwork: Discipleship Wesleyan Style* (1995); and a newsletter, the *Covenant Discipleship Quarterly*.

43. The *Discipline* of the Methodist Church, following the reunion of the Methodist Episcopal Church, the Methodist Episcopal Church, South, and the Methodist Protestant Church in 1939, had rendered class leaders and class meet-

ings a matter of history rather than polity. While this new legislation was not mandatory, it opened the door for congregations to revitalize both the office and the institution. Incorporated into the 1988 *Book of Discipline* as ¶ 268, it was revised and expanded in the 1992 *Book of Discipline* as ¶ 269.

44. David Lowes Watson, *Class Leaders: Recovering a Tradition,* and *Forming Christian Disciples: The Role of Covenant Discipleship and Class Leaders in the Congregation* (Nashville: Discipleship Resources, 1991). Phyllis Tyler-Wayman, *Guidelines for Leading Your Church, 1993–1996: Class Leader* (Nashville: Abingdon Press, 1992). See also *The United Methodist Book of Worship* (Nashville: United Methodist Publishing House, 1992), 602-4.

45. See, e.g., F. Herbert Skeete, "The Methodist Class Meeting as a Relevant Model for Urban Ministry" (Madison, N.J.: Drew University Doctor of Ministry Project, 1975).

46. David J. Bosch, *Transforming Mission: Paradigm Shifts in Theology of Mission* (Maryknoll, N.Y.: Orbis Books, 1991); Lesslie Newbigin, *The Gospel in a Pluralist Society* (Grand Rapids, Mich.: Eerdmans, 1989), and *A Word in Season: Perspectives on Christian World Missions* (Grand Rapids, Mich.: Eerdmans; Edinburgh: Saint Andrew Press, 1994); Wilbert R. Shenk, ed., *The Transfiguration of Mission: Biblical, Theological, and Historical Foundations* (Scottdale, Pa.: Herald Press, 1993).

47. E.g., Loren B. Mead, *The Once and Future Church: Reinventing the Congregation for a New Mission Frontier* (Washington, D.C.: Alban Institute, 1991); Carl S. Dudley, Jackson W. Carroll, and James P. Wind, eds., *Carriers of Faith: Lessons from Congregational Studies* (Louisville: Westminster/John Knox Press, 1991).

48. *Works,* vol. 25: *Letters I,* 660-61; *Works,* vol. 9: *The Methodist Societies,* 221. See also Frank Baker, *John Wesley and the Church of England* (Nashville: Abingdon Press, 1970), 62ff.

49. *The Letters of The Rev. John Wesley, A.M.,* ed. John Telford, 8 vols. (London: Epworth Press, 1931), 5:257.

50. Orlando E. Costas, *Christ Outside the Gate: Mission Beyond Christendom* (Maryknoll, N.Y.: Orbis Books, 1982), 79.

NOTES TO "METHODISM, MISSIONS, AND MONEY"

1. David Martin, *Tongues of Fire: The Explosion of Protestantism in Latin America* (Oxford, England: Oxford, 1990), 15.

2. Ibid., viii.

3. Ibid., ix.

4. Ibid.

5. Ibid.

6. Ibid.

7. Ibid., 15.

8. Ibid.

9. *Christian Work in Latin America, Being the Reports of Commission I and II presented to the Congress on Christian Work in Latin America, Panama, February 1916, with a General Introduction and Full Records of the Presentation and Discussion of Each Report* (New York, 1917), vol. 1, 291.

10. Ibid., 290.

11. Martin, *Tongues of Fire,* 86.

12. Ibid.

13. Ibid., 42.

14. Rosa del Carmen Bruno-Jofré, *Methodist Education in Peru: Social Gospel, Politics, and American Ideological Penetration, 1888–1930* (Waterloo, 1988), 102.

15. Ibid.

16. Ibid., 107.

17. Ibid.

18. Martin, *Tongues of Fire,* 42.

19. del Carmen Bruno-Jofré, *Methodist Education in Peru,* 30.

20. Ibid., 69.

21. Ibid., 70.

22. Ibid., 74.

23. Ibid., 68.

24. Ibid.

25. Jonathan J. Bonk, *Missions and Money: Affluence as a Western Missionary Problem* (Maryknoll, N.Y.: Orbis Books, 1991).

26. Jonathan J. Bonk, "Globalization and Mission Education," in *Theological Education,* 33:1 (Autumn 1993): 51.

27. Ibid.

28. James S. Robb, "Missions Derailed: A Special Report on the UM General Board of Global Ministries," in *Good News*, 16:6 (May-June 1983): 7.

29. Ibid., 9.

30. Ibid., 19.

31. Ibid., 27.

32. Ibid., 28.

33. Ibid., 29.

34. Ibid.

35. Jonathan J. Bonk, *Missions and Money: Affluence as a Western Missionary Problem* (Maryknoll, N.Y.: Orbis Books, 1991).

36. Ibid., 76.

37. *Human Development Report 1992* (Published for the United Nations Development Programme, New York/Oxford, 1992), 74.

38. Ibid., 78.

39. Ulrich Duchrow, *Alternativen zur kapitalistischen Weltwirtschaft* (Gütersloh: Gütersloher Verlagshaus, 1994).

40. *The State of the World's Children* (New York: Oxford for UNICEF, 1996), 67.

41. Unpublished "Concept Paper on Structure Proposal" (General Board of Global Ministries, October 18, 1993), 2.

42. Ibid., 4.

43. Nicolas Lossky et al., eds., *Dictionary of the Ecumenical Movement* (Grand Rapids, Mich.: Eerdmans, 1991), 694. There are numerous new assessments of the encounter between the "old" Euro-American churches and the "new" mission churches where the issue of money does not even enter the discussion. An example is Lamin Sanneh, *Encountering the West: Christianity and the Global Cultural Process: The African Dimension* (Maryknoll, N.Y.: Orbis Books, 1993), 72, 74, 134, 146, 165. Without claiming that money is the only concern, I do not see how we can go on dialoguing about Methodism and culture without raising the question of money as core of our North American culture.

44. Unpublished "Concept Paper on Structure Proposal," 4.

45. Anthony Sampson, *The Midas Touch: Understanding the Dynamic New Money Societies Around Us* (New York: Datton, 1991), 2.

46. David J. Bosch, *Transforming Mission: Paradigm Shifts in Transforming*

Mission (Maryknoll, New York: Orbis Books, 1991), 519. Here, too, I miss focus on the money issue, in spite of the great admiration of the analysis of the book as a whole.

47. Ibid.

48. I found up to this point European discussions already more explicit on the problem. See, e.g., besides the Duchrow book mentioned in n. 37 Gerard Minnard, "Das Anti-Mannon Programm," *Reformierte Kirchenzeitung*, 3/1994, pp. 75-76; Jörg Baumgarten et al., *Die Kirche und ihr Geld: Vom Geld begeistert-vom Geist bewegt?* (Siegburg, 1993).

49. The paper could not have been written without the mutualization report on the Duke Divinity School/Comunidad Biblico-Teológica (Lima, Peru) relationship and the North Carolina Conference (UMC)/Iglesia Metodista del Peru covenant (1989–1994) I submitted early in 1993 to the Duke Divinity School faculty and later published in the Working Paper Series of the Duke-UNC Program in Latin American Studies, *Tradición Común Shaping Christian Theology: Mutualization in Theological Education* (Working Paper #12, April 1994). The idea of *mutualization* grew out of our common walk since 1989.